AMSCO®

ADVANCED PLACEMENT

Microeconomics

MW00656892

PERFECTION LEARNING®

Senior Consultants

Nick Anello teaches AP® Economics at Homewood-Flossmoor Community High School in Flossmoor, Illinois. He holds a Bachelor of Arts degree from Loras College in Dubuque, Iowa, and a Master of Arts degree in General Administration and Curriculum and Instruction from Governors State University in University Park, Illinois. He has led professional development programs at local, state, and national conferences on the teaching of economics. In 2017, he received the 3M and Econ Illinois Outstanding Economics Educator award. He was a member of the AP® Instructional Design Team.

Woody Hughes taught economics at Converse College in Spartanburg, South Carolina, for 33 years, where he often served as department chair or President of the Faculty Senate. He was awarded the Katherine Amelia Brown Excellence in Teaching Award. He holds a Bachelor of Arts degree from Furman University, a Master of Arts degree from Clemson University, and a Ph.D. in economics from the University of South Carolina. Since 2004, he has regularly served as a reader, table leader, or question leader for the AP® Microeconomics exam.

Reviewers

David Burgin, contributor to the AP® Microeconomics Course and Exam Description
Science Hill High School | Johnson City, Tennessee

Bruce Damasio, AP® Economics Exam Reader
Liberty High School | Eldersburg, Maryland

Matt Pedlow, AP® Economics Exam Table Leader,
Chelsea High School | Chelsea, Michigan

Liz Plautz, AP® Macroeconomics Exam Table Leader
Hun School of Princeton | Princeton, New Jersey

Sue Weaver, AP® Microeconomics Exam Reader
Kings Academy, Madaba, Jordan (retired) | Ramona, California

Contents

Introduction

Studying Advanced Placement® Microeconomics

Welcome to the study of microeconomics. In this course, you will learn about the principles of economics that shape how individuals and businesses make economic choices. It will help you understand the interactions between the people who want to buy goods and services and the people who want to sell them. While the course focuses on buyers and the sellers who are individuals or businesses, it also describes government's role in these transactions. Government sets the ground rules for economic activities, promotes greater efficiency, and addresses issues such as equity. (A different branch of economics, called macroeconomics, focuses on economic decisions made on a national, international, or global scale.) Throughout the course, you will use graphs, charts, and data to help you investigate how people make economic decisions.

What follows is a quick look at how AP® course in general can benefit you, followed by the benefits of the microeconomics course in particular.

Why Take AP® Courses?

Each Advanced Placement® course is the equivalent of a one-semester course at a college or university. Therefore, an AP® course is more challenging than a typical high school course. It demands more of you in terms of recalling material, understanding sophisticated concepts, and analyzing and synthesizing data. Why, then, do students take these courses?

These are some of the reasons students give for enrolling in AP® courses:

- Evidence that the student has the ability to succeed as an undergraduate
- Increased eligibility for scholarships
- Evidence that taking AP® courses strengthens a college application
- Opportunity to save on college expenses by earning college credit
- Opportunity to test out of introductory college courses
- Evidence that AP® students have better college graduation rates
- Enrichment of the AP® student's high school experience

Because microeconomics is often taught as part of more general social studies courses rather than as a discrete subject, you might feel you have not had much specific instruction in it. And if AP® Microeconomics is your first course at the advanced placement level, it can appear very challenging. This introduction will help you understand the structure of the exam and the content of the course. Knowing what you are about to learn can help you focus your mind and get ready to take in new information.

The Structure and Scoring of AP® Exams

The AP® Microeconomics Exam is two hours and ten minutes long and contains these sections.

Section	Question Type	How Many Questions?	How Much Are They Worth?	How Much Time Will I Have?
I	Multiple choice	60	67%	70 minutes
II	Free response	Including one long question and two short questions	33%	60 minutes, including a 10-minute reading period

What Scores Can I Get on the AP® Exam?

If you have taken an Advanced Placement® exam before, you know that you will receive a number grade rather than a letter grade or a percentage of 100. AP® examinations, including the Microeconomics exam, score student performance on a five-point scale. Here is how the College Board will describe your performance on the exam:

5 = Extremely well qualified

4 = Well qualified

3 = Qualified

2 = Possibly qualified

1 = No recommendation

Another way to think about exam scores is to compare them to the performance of a college student:

- A score of 5 indicates the equivalent of earning a grade of A in a college microeconomics course.
- A score of 4 is equivalent to a grade of A-, B+, or B.
- A score of 3 is equivalent to a grade of B-, C+, or C.

Many colleges and universities consider an AP® score of 3 or higher to be evidence that a student has demonstrated proficiency with the material covered in an introductory college course in microeconomics. But policies in this area vary depending on the school.

How Does the AP® Exam Compare to Classroom Tests?

The College Board prepares AP® exams differently from the way a typical classroom teacher prepares a test. Teachers select questions to assess whether you have learned the materials that they have taught you. A teacher knows what you read, heard, practiced, and experienced in your course of study and creates a test that addresses those things specifically. Although you may not always know the answer on a test in your classroom, you most likely realized that it was something that you and the rest of the class had covered in the reading or classroom activities.

The AP® test is different. A team of college professors and high school teachers from across the country prepare it. Because one single exam cannot assess every aspect of microeconomics, the team decides what material the test will address and how the test will present it. Based on the knowledge you acquire and the skills you gain by reading this book and participating in your AP® Microeconomics course, you should be able to understand and answer questions on the exam even if you did not encounter the specific details of the questions in this book or in class.

Are AP® Exams Difficult?

The AP® exam is designed to be more difficult than the typical tests you might take in classrooms. A teacher is pleased to see all students demonstrate understanding by performing well on a test. In contrast, the AP® test is designed so that it can distinguish students who are better prepared from those who are still attempting to master the material.

You should not be surprised if you find that many of the questions seem more difficult than you expected. Do not be overly concerned, though. Many other well-prepared students will be experiencing the same feeling.

Finally, the AP® exam is scored differently from a classroom test. The cutoffs for the different scores vary a little each year. Why? The scores depend on how well a control group of college students did. These students are enrolled in introductory microeconomics courses, and they also took the test. You may feel that you performed poorly on the exam and still receive a score of 4 or 5. Much depends on how your performance on the exam compares to that of others who also take it.

How This Book Is Organized

The makers of this book want to help you succeed on the AP® exam. Therefore, the book is organized so you can find the information you need quickly, gain a thorough understanding of the concepts and examples, and then test yourself to be sure you have understood and retained what you read.

The book is divided into 42 topics contained in 6 units. Each unit contains the following elements:

- *Unit Introduction:* Each of the six units in the book begins with a brief explanation of the topic you are about to master. There is also a list of the topics in the unit. This section is designed to get you ready to learn.

- *Long Free-Response Question:* When you have taken other courses, have you ever worried that you learned information only briefly and then forgot it? Answering the Long Free-Response Question at the end of the unit helps you synthesize what you have learned so it stays in your memory. It is also excellent practice for the Long Free-Response Question that is part of the AP® Microeconomics exam.

Each topic of this book contains the following elements:

- *Topic Narrative:* The 42 topics are organized in a logical sequence as identified by the College Board. Each topic starts with an Essential Question that the entire topic is organized around—a question that you should be able to answer by the time you finish the topic. Within each topic, you will find the basic vocabulary terms and concepts you need to understand and discuss it. Also, you will find real-world examples that illustrate key topics. All of the topics include visuals, such as graphs, tables, or photographs.

- *Answer the Topic Essential Question:* Remember that Essential Question at the beginning of the topic? Now is your chance to answer it in one to three paragraphs. If you have trouble answering the Essential Question, then it makes sense to review the topic until you feel comfortable with it.

- *Key Terms.* At the end of each topic is a list of the vocabulary terms from the topic narrative. Understanding these terms will be an important part of your success on the AP® Microeconomics exam.

- *Multiple-Choice Questions:* How can you be sure you understood what you read? Each topic has three multiple-choice items that give you a chance to apply what you have learned using the question format that will appear on the exam. Some of these questions may include graphs or tables.

- *Short Free-Response Questions:* Each topic has a free-response question that you can use to check your understanding and practice your writing skills. This question may include graphs, tables, or brief quotations, and it may ask you to draw a graph.

- *Think as an Economist Features:* The AP® exam asks you to do more than memorize information and repeat it back at test time. Instead, you will need to develop specific skills that economists have and practice those skills by writing, graphing, or calculating. Each Think as an Economist feature focuses on a specific skill that real economists use, such as creating accurate graphs or describing economic concepts.

To help you even more, this book also contains the following elements:

- *Practice Examination:* Following the final unit is a complete practice examination modeled on the AP® exam.

- *Index:* What if you are trying to recall the definition of an important term, but you cannot remember where in the book you learned it? The index helps you find coverage of key terms and topics for review.

A separate Teacher Resource is also available for teachers and other authorized users of the book. It contains an answer key as well as activities focused on issues of race and justice. The Teacher Resource is available through the publisher's website.

The Study of AP® Microeconomics

Economists, like historians, sociologists, geographers, and others, study human behavior and relationships. What makes economists distinct from these other groups is that they study how people and organizations use money, goods, and resources. By studying microeconomics, you will learn to notice trends, create models, and predict outcomes. This course can be broken down into "big ideas" and a variety of key skills.

Big Ideas

The four big ideas are basis for the content in this book. The chart below states how they are described by the College Board.

THE BIG IDEAS OF MICROECONOMICS	
Idea	**Description**
1. Scarcity and Markets (MKT)	Limited resources and unlimited wants result in the need to make choices. In a market economy, the choices of buyers and sellers determine market prices and the allocation of scarce resources.
2. Costs, Benefits, and Marginal Analysis (CBA):	There are trade-offs associated with any decision. Making optimal decisions requires evaluating the additional costs and benefits of possible actions.
3. Production Choices and Behavior (PRD):	Firms seek to minimize costs and maximize profits, which influences their production decisions in the short run and long run
4. Market Efficiency and Public Policy (POL):	Private markets can fail to allocate resources efficiently, and well-designed public policy can endeavor to promote greater efficiency and equity in the economy.

Source: *AP® Microeconomics Course and Exam Description.* Effective Fall 2019 (College Board).

Skills

The economic skills are the ways you use the content as you develop your understanding of microeconomics. The chart below states how they are described by the College Board.

THE SKILLS OF MICROECONOMICS	
Skill Category	**Description**
1. Principles and Models	**Define economic principles and models.**
	• 1.A: Describe economic concepts, principles, or models.
	• 1.B: Identify an economic concept, principle, or model illustrated by an example.
	• 1.C: Identify an economic concept, principle, or model using quantitative data or calculations.
	• 1.D: Describe the similarities, differences, and limitations of economic concepts, principles, or models.
2. Interpretation	**Explain given economic outcomes.**
	• 2.A: Using economic concepts, principles, or models, explain how a specific economic outcome occurs or what action should be taken in order to achieve a specific economic outcome.
	• 2.B: Using economic concepts, principles, or models, explain how a specific economic outcome occurs when there are multiple contributing variables or what multiple actions should be taken in order to achieve a specific economic outcome.
	• 2.C: Interpret a specific economic outcome using quantitative data or calculations.
3. Manipulation	**Determine outcomes of specific economic situations.**
	• 3.A: Determine the outcome of an economic situation using economic concepts, principles, or models.
	• 3.B: Determine the effect(s) of one or more changes on other economic markets.
	• 3.C: Determine the effect(s) of a change in an economic situation using quantitative data or calculations.
4. Graphing and Visuals	**Model economic situations using graphs or visual representations.**
	• 4.A: Draw an accurately labeled graph or visual to represent an economic model or market.
	• 4.B: Demonstrate your understanding of a specific economic situation on an accurately labeled graph or visual.
	• 4.C: Demonstrate the effect of a change in an economic situation on an accurately labeled graph or visual.

Source: *AP® Microeconomics Course and Exam Description.* Effective Fall 2019 (College Board).

Course Content

When you begin this book, you may have only the slightest understanding of what microeconomics is. By the time you finish, you will understand how economists, government officials, business leaders, and everyday people react to economic opportunities and pressures. Each unit in this book helps you understand another facet of how microeconomics works.

Unit 1: Basic Economic Concepts

- How do people make the most of the resources they have?
- How do specialization and trade help people respond to scarcity?
- How does evaluating marginal costs and marginal benefits lead to rational economic decisions?

Big ideas covered: Scarcity and Markets; Costs, Benefits, and Marginal Analysis

Unit 2: Supply and Demand

- How do individuals and firms respond to economic incentives and face constraints or limits on what they do?
- Why do prices change in response to changes in what consumers demand and what firms supply?
- How do government policies affect how individuals and firms behave?
- How trade influence economic choices and opportunities?

Big idea covered: Scarcity and Markets; Market Inefficiency and Public Policy

Unit 3: Production, Cost, and the Perfect Competition Model

- How do constraints on firms shape their decisions in the short run and the long run?
- How do firms compare marginal benefits and marginal costs to determine the best level of production for making a profit?
- How do firms decide whether to enter or exit the market for a good or service?
- How would firms operate if perfect competition existed?

Big ideas covered: Costs, Benefits, and Marginal Analysis; Production Choices and Behavior

Unit 4: Imperfect Competition

- How do the number and size of firms in a market influence prices and efficiency?
- Why does a firm sell an identical product to various customers at different prices?

Big ideas covered: Production Choices and Behavior

Unit 5: Factor Markets

- How do the markets work for firms to purchase resources they need to make products?
- How do supply and demand affect the markets for labor?
- How do firms try to maximize their profit as they hire labor and purchase natural resources?
- What happens when one firm is the only one hiring people in a market?

Big ideas covered: Production Choices and Behavior

Unit 6: Market Failure and the Role of Government

- How can government make markets work more efficiently?
- What government policies attempt to allocate the costs of producing goods, such as pollution, to the firms that make them
- How are some issues that are important to society not reflected in the price of goods?
- How can government respond to income inequality?

Big ideas covered: Market Inefficiency and Public Policy

AP® Microeconomics Exam Questions

The Course and Exam Description published by the College Board describes both the content of AP® Microeconomics and the basic skills you need to develop. You can practice these skills throughout the school year.

Weighting of Exam Questions

Some units are addressed more frequently on the exam are worth more than others. Look at how the College Board has weighted the different subject areas.

EXAM WEIGHTING			
Unit	Unit Title	How Much of the Exam Will Cover This Unit?	Typical Number of Class Periods Spent in a One-Semester Course
1	Basic Economic Concepts	12–15%	About 7–8
2	Supply and Demand	20–25%	About 11–14
3	Production, Cost, and the Perfection Competition Model	22–25%	About 12–14
4	Imperfect Competition	15–22%	About 9–12
5	Factor Markets	10–13%	About 6–7
6	Market Failure and the Role of Government	8–13%	About 5–7

Source: *AP® Microeconomics Course and Exam Description.* Effective Fall 2019 (College Board).

Since you know that ideas and concepts from Units 2 and 3 will appear most often on the exam, it makes sense to spend a bit more time studying those units. That said, however, everything you learn acts as a foundation for the concepts that follow. Having a thorough understanding of basic economic concepts will make the rest of the book much easier to understand.

Answering the Multiple-Choice Questions

The AP® Microeconomics exam includes 60 multiple-choice questions, which you will have 70 minutes to answer. This portion of the exam accounts for 67 percent (two-thirds) of your score. Each question will consist of a stem that can be either a question or statement and five possible choices. One choice is correct and the others are distractors. Distractors are incorrect, but they may seem believable.

Analyzing the Graphic Some of the multiple-choice questions will refer you to a graphic information source, such as a graph or table. Take a moment to read the question, refer to the graphic, and then reread the question. Be careful to look at elements of the graphic that may be important:

- *Graphs:* Check each axis of any graph. Notice where each begins and ends. For example, does the axis go from 0 to 2,000, or did it begin at 1,200 and then end at 2,000? If an axis denotes a time period using years, notice the time period it covers. How big are the intervals or increments between elements on the axes?

- *Tables and Charts:* As with other types of graphics, note carefully titles and any words on the chart. See if you can sum up the meaning of the table or chart in your own words.

Only some multiple-choice questions will have a graphic. Read them carefully. What if, as you are reading the stem, your eyes glance at the choices and you see what you believe is the correct answer? Finish reading the question before you select it. Information at the end of the stem may show you that the correct answer is not what you thought it was.

Tips on Making a Choice You will often know the right answer to a question quickly and with confidence, but sometimes you will not. Here are a few suggestions to help you when you are uncertain about an answer.

HOW TO ANSWER CHALLENGING QUESTIONS	
Advice	**Rationale**
Answer every question.	Your score will be based on how many correct answers you give. Unlike some standardized tests, the AP® Microeconomics exam does not penalize people for guessing a wrong answer. That means an attempt at an answer is better than a blank space where an answer should be.
Apply what you know.	What if a question asks about a specific place or situation that you have not studied? In that case, focus on the general concept that the question addresses. Use what you know to determine the most reasonable answer.
Move forward.	Since you have 70 minutes to answer 60 questions, you can spend an average of just over 60 seconds on each question. If you find a question difficult, guess the answer, note the question's number, and return to it if you have time at the end.

Recommended Activities Answering multiple-choice questions is a powerful way to review content and practice skills. Each topic in this book presents multiple-choice items to help you check your understanding of important concepts in AP® Microeconomics. Often, the questions include a graph, table, or other source that you need to analyze in order to determine the best answer to the question.

Answering the Free-Response Questions (FRQ)

There are three free-response questions on Section II of the AP® Microeconomics exam. Each FRQ will typically include several parts, lettered (a), (b), (c), and so on. There is one long free-response question and two short ones. The long item is worth 10 points, and each of the shorter items is worth 5 points.

You are expected to answer all three in 60 minutes. That means you have an average of 20 minutes per answer. However, you can divide this block of time in any way you would like. Since the long question will have more parts, you may want to spend 30 minutes on the long free-response question and 15 minutes each on the short free-response questions.

You will be scored based solely on the quality of the content of your response. Try to use correct grammar so that you make your ideas clear, but you will not be penalized for grammatical errors.

Composing Your Response The free-response questions used on the AP® Microeconomics exam are sometimes called constructed response items. This type of question consists of a statement or short introduction followed by a series of related questions or response prompts labeled (a), (b), (c), and so on. Each topic in this book ends with a short free-response question, and each unit ends with a long free-response question.

Your response will often be written as a full sentence, a paragraph, or paragraphs, but be aware that a single word or a phrase will sometimes suffice, depending on the question. The construction of your response should reflect that of the question.

An effective method for answering the questions is to label each part of the question. That is, when you are answering part (a) of the question, label it "A" in your test book. Then label "B," and so on. Within each labeled portion of your response, you may still want to use paragraphing to provide clarity to your writing.

Analyzing the Question The stem of the free-response question is the part that comes before (a), (b), (c), and so on. You can use the stem to help you figure out how to structure your response. You do not need to restate, rephrase, or incorporate the stem in your answer. You do need to pay attention to any limitations it places on you.

Make sure to answer each question fully and completely. Some questions may require you to consider specific concepts, such as "supply and/or demand." In that case, you would look at each part of the question and decide whether to describe effects on supply, demand, or both. Your response should clearly relate to the concepts indicated in the question. Try your best not to stray off topic, as your time is limited.

Task Verbs The key words in the question's prompts that indicate what you are to do are called task verbs. Here are the ones that you will see most often on the exam.

RESPONDING TO VERBS IN FREE-RESPONSE QUESTIONS		
Task Verb	**Definition**	**Expectation**
Identify	To state a clear, concise, specific answer	Often, a single, well-written sentence is enough, but you can add clarifying details. However, do not contradict or add confusion to your original answer.
Explain	To provide information about why a relationship, pattern, position, situation, or outcome occurs	Offer reasons or evidence to make an idea plainly understood, or state how a process occurs. Graphs or symbols may be part of the explanation.
Calculate	To perform mathematical steps to arrive at a final answer	You will need to show your work so the graders can see how you arrived at your answer. When using a formula, write out the formula, plug in the appropriate numbers, and solve the equation.
Draw a correctly labeled ...	To create a graph or visual representation that illustrates or explains relationships or phenomena	You will need to provide accurate labels for your drawing.
Show, label, plot, or indicate	To point out an economic scenario on a graph or visual representation that you create	You will need to clearly label all axes and curves. Show directional changes where relevant. Draw large graphs of 1/4 to 1/3 of a page for clarity.

If a prompt asks you to identify something or someone, you may need to write only a sentence or two for that part of the question. If a prompt asks you to explain, you will probably need to write anywhere from a sentence to a paragraph for each part of the question. If a prompt asks you to calculate, it will remind you to show your work. For answers involving calculations, drawings, or plots, you may not need to write any sentences for that part of the question.

Questions Requiring Examples Many of the free-response questions on the AP® Microeconomics exam ask you to supply more than one example or reason to illustrate or explain a concept. For example, the question might require "two factors that can affect the equilibrium price of a product" or "three factors besides price that can affect the supply of a product." To answer these questions, you might want to begin by brainstorming a list of several ideas and selecting the best ones to include in your answer. Provide exactly the number of examples called for in the prompt. You will not get full credit if you provide too few examples. You will be wasting your time if you provide extra examples.

Questions That Test More Than One Skill or Big Idea Some questions require you to demonstrate your knowledge of multiple skills or big ideas. For example, a free-response question might ask you to create a graph, label its parts, and then make predictions or recommendations based on it. Doing all this can seem overwhelming, but do not panic. Instead, take it step by step. Check your work as you go, and keep in mind that even if you do not answer every part of the question perfectly, you can get partial credit on free-response items.

General Writing Advice The principles of good writing that you have learned in school will help you write a good answer to a free-response question:

- *Plan your time.* Take time to plan your answer before you begin writing. It makes sense to take a few minutes to brainstorm your ideas, select good examples, and organize your response.

- *Consider whether to include introductions and conclusions.* You do not need to restate the prompt or write an introduction to your answer. Conclusions are also not necessary. Answer the questions simply and directly.

- *Make changes.* If you think of something you would like to add to part A (or B, or whichever) of your response but you have already moved on to another part, simply add it and indicate which part of your response it belongs in. If you write something that you decide you do not want included in your response, draw a line through it and it will not be scored.

- *Do not let grammar, spelling, and handwriting limit you.* Your answer to a free-response question will not be graded on grammar, spelling, or handwriting. So, think of it as a rough draft. Try to use correct grammar, spell words as best you can, and write legibly so that readers understand what you are saying. But focus on the content, not on these other concerns.

Evaluation of Your Answer You can find scoring guides from previous AP® exams online at apcentral.collegeboard.org. The most important thing to know about how graders evaluate free-response questions is that you can get partial credit for an answer. In other words, the free-response questions are not all-or-nothing endeavors. Depending on how completely and accurately you answer the question, you may receive the maximum number of points, a partial score, or no points.

MAXIMUM NUMBER OF POINTS AVAILABLE FOR FREE-RESPONSE QUESTIONS	
Question 1: Long	10 points
Question 2: Short	5 points
Question 3: Short	5 points

What does this mean to you? If, for instance, you manage your time poorly on Section II of the exam, you could end up with only a couple of minutes to answer question 3. If this happens, do not skip the question. Even if you do not have time to write as full an answer as you would like to, you could still earn a few points by answering part of the question.

Recommended Activities As with the multiple-choice questions, you should practice writing answers to free-response items. Each topic in this book contains a short free-response question that is clearly related to the material contained within the topic. Each unit concludes with a long free-response question that draws on content from that entire unit. The Think as an Economist activities will also help you practice your skills.

Free-response questions from previous AP® exams are available online at apcentral.collegeboard.org. If you choose to practice with these, be aware that many of them are meant to cut across the topics and skill categories in the course. Therefore, you may see parts of questions that you have not studied yet. Using the accompanying online scoring guides as a study and review tool is also very helpful.

Effective Review Strategies

Use every possible way to make the material your own—read it, take notes on it, talk about it, create visualizations of it, and relate the ideas in this book to your prior experience and learning. In other words, think about how it connects to ideas in your other courses and to your personal life experiences.

Strategies for the Entire Course

Start preparing for the exam on the first day of class using these approaches:

- Form a weekly study group. Use the Essential Question from each topic as the starting point for your discussion, focusing on how the material you learned during the week helps to answer that question. Ask questions about anything you do not understand. The weekly meetings ensure that you will prepare on a regular basis, and they also give you a chance to speak about and listen to the concepts you are learning in addition to reading and writing about them.

- Work collaboratively in other ways, such as discussing items in the news that demonstrate the concepts you are studying.

- Use the techniques of the cognitive scientists (cognitive psychologists) at learningscientists.org. They offer free and more detailed information on the six strategies outlined in the chart below, which have been proven in research to help people learn.

RESEARCH-BASED LEARNING STRATEGIES	
Strategy	**Details**
Distributed Practice	**Spread out** your studying over the entire course in manageable amounts.
Retrieval	After every class, or on another regular schedule, close your book and try to recall the important points, using a practice called **retrieval**. You can use the Reflect on the Essential Question feature at the end of each topic as a framework. Write whatever you can't retrieve from memory alone by going back into the book for the missing pieces. Whether you use sample multiple-choice questions, flash cards, or an online program such as Quizlet, take the time to test yourself with a friend or on your own.
Elaboration	When studying, **ask yourself questions** about what you are reading. How does this material connect to other material in the unit or in other units? As you learn material, elaborate on it by connecting it to how you make economic decisions in your daily life.
Interleaving	When you study, occasionally **interleave** the material by switching up the order of your review. Instead of reviewing units and topics in the order presented in the book, review them in another order.
Concrete Examples	Write down all **concrete examples** your teacher uses in class. Note the examples given in this book. Use these examples to understand the application of the abstract concepts and ideas you are studying.
Dual Coding	Use **dual coding**, different ways of representing the information. Take notes or write reflections on a segment of text. Then create a visual representation of the same knowledge using graphic organizers, concept maps, or other graphics.

What to Do as the Exam Approaches

Set up a review schedule as you prepare for the exam in the weeks before the test date. Studying with a group of fellow students can be helpful. Below is a sample of a 30-day (six-week) review schedule, including information on the topics in this book that cover the content to review. Because AP® tests are given during the first two full weeks of May, this review schedule assumes you begin your review sometime in March.

PROPOSED REVIEW SCHEDULE	
Days	**Content**
5	Introduction and Unit 1: Basic Economic Concepts
7	Unit 2: Supply and Demand
7	Unit 3: Production, Cost, and the Perfect Competition Model
5	Unit 4: Imperfect Competition
3	Unit 5: Factor Markets
3	Unit 6: Market Failure and the Role of Government

The information in the introduction about answering multiple-choice questions and free-response items will help you prepare for the exam.

UNIT 1

Basic Economic Concepts

Many people think of economics as the study of money, wealth, and finance. Those topics are part of economics. But more fundamentally, it is the study of how people choose to use resources to obtain the goods and services they want.

Almost every resources is limited. Because of this, people constantly make choices about what to produce. Similarly, most consumers have only so much money to spend, so they make choices about what to purchase. You might have enough money to go to a movie or to eat at a restaurant, but not enough money to do both.

When people make rational choices, they take into account the additional costs and benefits of their decisions. All decisions have costs and often they involve trade-offs. The cost of something is what you give up in order to get it. It may be money, it may be time, or it may be something else that you want.

Because resources are limited, economics focuses on three basic questions: What goods and services should a society produce? How will it produce them? Who will consume them? Individuals, businesses, and governments make choices to address these questions.

In this unit, you will learn about the basic economic concepts you will use throughout this course.

" DR. KITTLE IS NOW TAKING BIDS FOR HIS TEN
O' CLOCK APPOINTMENT ON TUESDAY. "

Topic Titles and Essential Knowledge

Topic 1.1 Scarcity

- A Economic trade-offs arise from the lack of sufficient resources (scarcity) to meet society's wants and needs.
- Most factors of production (such as land, labor, and capital) are scarce, but some factors of production (such as established knowledge) may not be scarce due to their non-rival nature.

Topic 1.2 Resource Allocation and Economic Systems

- Resource allocation involves answering three basic questions: What goods and services to produce? How to produce those goods and services? And who consumes those goods and services?
- Resource allocation is significantly influenced by the economic system adopted by society, such as command economy, market economy, or mixed economy. Each system involves a particular set of institutional arrangements and a coordinating mechanism for allocating scarce resources and distributing output.

Topic 1.3 Production Possibilities Curve

- The PPC is a model used to show the trade-offs associated with allocating resources.
- The PPC can be used to illustrate the concepts of scarcity, opportunity cost, efficiency, underutilized resources, and economic growth or contraction.
- The shape of the PPC depends on whether opportunity costs are constant, increasing, or decreasing.
- The PPC can shift due to changes in factors of production as well as changes in productivity/technology.
- Economic growth results in an outward shift of the PPC.

Topic 1.4 Comparative Advantage and Trade

- Absolute advantage describes a situation in which an individual, business, or country can produce more of a good or service than any other producer with the same quantity of resources.
- Comparative advantage describes a situation in which an individual, business, or country can produce a good or service at a lower opportunity cost than another producer.
- Production specialization according to comparative advantage, not absolute advantage, results in exchange opportunities that lead to consumption possibilities beyond the PPC.
- Comparative advantage and opportunity costs determine the terms of trade for exchange under which mutually beneficial trade can occur.

Topic 1.5 Cost-Benefit Analysis

- Rational agents consider opportunity costs, whether implicit or explicit, when calculating the total economic costs of any decision.
- Total benefits form the metric "utility" for consumers and total revenue for firms.
- Total net benefits, the difference between total benefits and total costs, are maximized at the optimal choice.
- Some decisions permit rational agents to look at only marginal benefit and marginal cost. Other decisions cannot be broken down into increments in this way and must be evaluated by looking at total benefits and total costs.

Topic 1.6 Marginal Analysis and Consumer Choice

- Consumers face constraints and have to make optimal decisions accounting for these constraints.
- In a model of rational consumer choice, consumers are assumed to make choices so as to maximize their total utility.
- Consumers experience diminishing marginal utility in the consumption of goods and services.
- Consumers allocate their limited income to purchase the combination of goods that maximizes their utility by equating/comparing the marginal utility of the last dollar spent on each good.
- Marginal analysis involves comparing the additional benefit of increasing a given activity with the additional cost. Comparing marginal benefit (MB) with marginal cost (MC) helps individuals (firms) decide whether to increase, decrease, or maintain their consumption (production) levels.
- The optimal quantity at any point in time does not depend on fixed costs (sunk costs) or fixed benefits that have already been determined by past choices.
- The optimal quantity is achieved when marginal benefit is equal to marginal cost or where total benefit is maximized.

Topic 1.1

Scarcity

"There are no solutions; there are only trade-offs."

—Economist Thomas Sowell, 1987

Essential Question: How do individuals and economies confront the problem of scarce resources?

In a perfect world, people would receive everything they wanted or needed at all times. But in the real world, most people have to make choices. Spending money on one thing means having less money to spend on something else. Going out to dinner one night might mean having to skip a movie another night, for instance. That "dinner out tonight or movie later" choice is a **trade-off**. To get something, you need to give up the possibility of getting something else.

You have already made thousands of trade-offs, and you will make hundreds of thousands more. Individuals, groups, organizations, businesses, and governments are constantly making choices about the best uses of their money, time, and attention.

Economics: The Study of Scarcity and Choice

The field of **economics** is the study of how and why people and organizations make the decisions they do to address the gap between limited resources and nearly unlimited desires or wants. The name of that gap is **scarcity**. The concept of scarcity is an essential part of life in general and economics in particular. Because almost everything valuable is limited or scarce, people and groups make choices about what will best satisfy their wants. Here are some examples of how you can see economics at work:

- The price for the new phone and accessories that you want to buy is $495, but you have only $190 available to spend. You can choose between keeping your current phone until you have saved enough money to buy the phone you want and buying a less expensive phone.

- A business that makes a profit can decide whether to use that money to expand production or to increase wages.

- The national government can decide whether use tax revenue to build a new military base or to combat water pollution.

Each of these examples provides two options to choose between. Selecting one means giving up the opportunity to use the other—a trade-off.

Even when choices are plentiful, scarcity still plays a crucial role. A consumer looking for a new phone may be presented with a wide variety of options, but scarcity of funds may eliminate many of them. At that point, consumers may start weighing trade-offs in order to make certain options possibilities again.

Economic Trade-Offs and Constraints Of course, most situations aren't always either-or. For instance, the national government could spend some money on the military and some on fighting pollution—or it could invest in medical research, cut taxes, or do something else. But money is limited, so eventually there has to be a trade-off. Another word for this type of trade-off is a **constraint**. A person, business, or government is constrained from doing something because it lacks funds or time. When an individual or an organization makes a choice, it has an **opportunity cost**, or a loss of the benefit that would have been gained from choosing the alternative. You will learn more about opportunity costs in later topics.

Who Are Economists? Professionals who study economics are called economists. They use models and data to explain why people, businesses, and governments make the choices they do. Economists do this in specific ways:

1. *Tracking Trends* Is the average person spending more these days? Are hardware stores selling more tools? Economists notice and collect information on these changes in behavior.

2. *Making Forecasts* Economists use models, data, and trend information to make forecasts, which are predictions of what will happen to people and markets. Businesses, governments, and media outlets pay economists to tell them what is likely to happen.

3. *Providing Guidance in Decision-Making* Economists use their own forecasts and those of other economists to help firms and governments in numerous ways. They help businesses decide crucial questions surrounding how many workers to hire, how much to pay their workers, and how much to produce. They also help businesses and governments decide how to best use their resources. For example, a forecast pointing to an upcoming downturn in the economy might lead an economist to advise a manufacturer against constructing and equipping a new, state-of-the-art facility. Or, a forecast of increasing tax revenues might lead an economist to suggest a city undertake its plan to upgrade its water-filtration plant.

As economists carry out these tasks, they sometimes make mistakes. What has happened in the past can reveal what may happen in the future. However, past performance is no guarantee of future results. That's why economists' predictions don't always come true—and why people sometimes joke that economists have predicted nine of the last five economic downturns. In other words, economists may forecast that difficult times are ahead, but those difficult times may not arrive. Further, economists often disagree with one another about the best ways to improve the economy.

What Are the Branches of Economics?

Economics has two main branches, but each branch affects the other. For that reason, separating them completely is impossible.

Microeconomics The focus of this book is **microeconomics**—the examination of how economic forces affect individual parts of the economy. (*Micro-* is a prefix meaning "small.") Microeconomics focuses on economic decisions by you, your family, workers in your community, governments, and businesses in your neighborhood. You will also learn about similar decisions elsewhere in the world. A business owner wondering, "What will happen to our sales if we raise our prices?" is an example of a microeconomic challenge.

Macroeconomics In contrast, **macroeconomics** is the study of how changes affect the economy as a whole instead of its individual parts. (*Macro-* is a prefix meaning "large.") The president of a country wondering, "What effect will an increase in taxes have on consumer spending?" is an example of a macroeconomic challenge.

Goods, Services, and Other Terms Economists Use

Using the same terms economists do will help you describe difficult concepts precisely. Here are a few basic terms to understand.

Goods and Services Items that you can see or touch and that have value are **goods**. Clothes, cars, computers, and books are all examples of goods. **Services** are things that have value even though you can't see or touch them. If you get a haircut, see a doctor, or take a college course, you are receiving a service.

Consumers and Consumption Anyone who buys goods and services for his or her personal use is a **consumer**. You may be many things—a human being, a student, an athlete, or a fan of ukulele music. Economics, though, views you primarily as a consumer or a producer. Buying goods and services is called **consumption**.

How do these terms fit in with the issues of trade-offs and scarcity? The vast array of products and services available for sale in a modern economy may give the impression that there is no scarcity of goods and services, but resources are actually always limited. You and other consumers need to decide which services and goods you need and which you can live without. In other words, you face constraints and trade-offs that inform your decision making.

On a larger scale, economic trade-offs arise when a society doesn't have enough resources to meet all of its wants and needs. Imagine a country whose citizens highly value national security and a strong military. A majority of the citizens also support generous social welfare benefits, such as free child care, significant jobless benefits, long-term leave for new parents, and other similar social programs. If the country decides that it cannot maintain both its considerable military budget and its generous social welfare program, citizens and policy makers have a choice to make.

- They can maintain current tax rates and choose to reduce defense spending and/or spending on social programs.
- They can maintain current tax rates and choose to cut funding to other areas of government, such as infrastructure or business development.
- They can increase taxes to allow full funding of both national priorities.

The trade-offs inherent in each of these options are clear. The scarcity of tax revenue means that one or more programs will suffer. And even if taxes are raised and each is "fully funded," there will always be some citizens who want more funding for each: A new missile system or higher pay for soldiers; expanded job training, free healthcare for seniors, or other social programs. Scarcity and trade-offs are unavoidable.

Economic Resources: Factors of Production

The ingredients that go into the making of goods and services are called **economic resources**, which are also known as **factors of production**. Economists identify three types: land, labor, and capital. These resources are the building blocks of the economy, and producers put them together to produce goods and services.

Land All natural resources that the earth provides and that humans use to make goods are referred to as **land**. It includes not just the soil, but the water that flows on it, the minerals underneath it, and the right to use the air above it. Every physical good that is produced uses some type of natural resource. Even though some people and countries have huge supplies of a particular resource, no person or country has an unlimited supply.

Oil is a nonrenewable natural resource. These nodding donkey rigs are pulling crude oil out of the ground.

Labor The people who create goods and services are referred to as **labor**. Other terms for labor are "human resources," "human capital," and "the workforce." Both the number of workers and their degree of productivity are key factors in making choices. A community, state, or country with too few people of working age will be unable to use its other resources effectively.

For example, in 2015, Italy reached a population of almost 61 million. But because its birth rate was so low compared to its death rate, the population began to decrease, and its percentage of retired elderly increased. To increase the size of its working population, the government considered steps to encourage people to have more children and to immigrate into the country. A company can increase its production by hiring more employees.

The productivity of those workers depends on their level of skill, the quantity and quality of tools available to them, and the technology available to them. For example, the European country of Luxembourg is tiny and has a small population, but according to the Organization for Economic Cooperation and Development, it had the most productive workers in the world in 2015. Economists determine a community's or country's productivity by adding up the value of all the goods and services a country produced in a year and dividing it by the number of hours that all employees worked in that year. A company can increase its productivity by investing in training its employees or updating its technology.

Capital The tools, machines, buildings, and factories that are used in the creation of goods or services are known as **capital**. These ingredients are sometimes referred to as capital resources or physical capital. A manufacturing plant where people produce cars is an example of capital. So is a school because it is the site of a service industry (education). At times, people use the term "capital" to mean money used for investment, but economists usually use the term in this broader sense.

One trait that all capital has in common is that it eventually wears out or is used up. For instance, machines and tools break down, and buildings age so much that they have to be repaired or abandoned. The owners of capital must consider how to make the best, most profitable use of the capital that is available to them. If the owner doesn't replace capital that has been used up, then the amount of goods produced will decline.

For example, a bicycle factory is an example of capital. If the factory owners don't repair or replace machinery that breaks down, then the factory will produce fewer bicycles than before and will most likely bring in less money. This reduction in capital can have ripple effects, such as lost jobs and fewer tax revenues to pay for government services.

In addition to physical capital of the kind already discussed, economists often talk about the human capital that labor offers to any organization—a business, a nonprofit organization, or a government. **Human capital** refers to the knowledge, skills, abilities, experiences, and creativity, and that help people maintain and increase their productivity.

Skilled workers with high-quality tools and training are more productive than workers without those tools and training. This welder has the training as well as the angle grinder and safety equipment she needs to complete complex tasks.

Entrepreneurship Putting together the three factors of production (land, labor, and capital) is called **entrepreneurship**. The person who organizes a business is an entrepreneur, and he or she takes on risks and sometimes reaps rewards. If you start a delivery business, develop an app and offer it for sale on the Internet, or make crafts, then you are an entrepreneur.

Entrepreneurs develop new products, figure out more efficient means of production, and pioneer new ways of running the business. By putting in time, money, and effort in a business, the entrepreneur hopes to receive a profit. Entrepreneurship is risky. According to the Small Business Administration, 30 percent of U.S. businesses fail within the first two years of operation, and 50 percent fail within the first five years. However, many entrepreneurs relish hard work and risks. They often agree with the author and business leader John A. Shedd (1850–1926), who noted, "A ship in harbor is safe, but that is not what ships are built for."

Rival and Non-Rival Factors of Production

Scarcity, constraints, and trade-offs apply to products that are in limited supply. Most products have a **rival nature**, only one person can consume them at a time. Even if you and your friends share a plate of nachos, only one of you can consume a single bite of a nacho at a time. Even if you and other family members share a car, only one of you at a time can drive it. Nachos, cars, and most other goods and services have a rival nature because one person's consumption affects the consumption of others.

Non-Rival Factors of Production In 2017, *The Economist* magazine declared that the most valuable resource in the world was no longer oil—it was data. Companies including Facebook, Apple, Microsoft, and Google's parent company Alphabet grew into enormous companies by harvesting user data and selling it to others.

Data has a **non-rival nature** because more than one person or business at a time can use such information without depleting the supply for others. For example, unless you opt out of location tracking on your phone, your service provider sells information about your location to third parties. These third parties then send you advertisements based in part on your location. Many companies can use the same data about your location at the same time without using it up.

Your browsing history and your medical history are two other examples of non-rival data. Companies can use and reuse this data. This situation has caused concern among many people and some governments about individuals' privacy rights.

Non-Rival Does Not Mean Freely Available Just because data is non-rival doesn't mean pieces of such information are free and available to all. Companies spend huge sums on consumer data, so they don't want to share them with the public in general or rivals in particular. Some companies hoard nearly all the customer data they collect, even if universities, hospitals, or government agencies might benefit from using them. The resource isn't scarce, but its owners treat it as if it were. Data hoarding can also lead to disorganized storage and weak security measures—which means that hackers might steal credit card numbers, medical data, or other personal information.

Caption: Seats in a stadium to watch a soccer match are a rival good, but watching on televsion is a nonrival good.

Established Knowledge Data that companies gather aren't always the same thing as established knowledge. Established knowledge is publicly available, has been evaluated and verified by a knowledgeable person or group, and is generally accepted as true. Following are some sources of established knowledge:

- Governments publish medical, scientific, and census data.
- The United Nations provides data about population, health, and trade.
- Some nonprofits share their research results freely with the public.
- Software developers share code snippets for others to use and modify.

As increasing amounts of established knowledge become freely available, people and organizations are able to use it to make medical breakthroughs, develop new inventions, and figure out new ways to provide goods and services more efficiently. However, even when established knowledge makes scarcity less of a problem, humans' time, effort, and attention are limited resources and may get used up.

The Big Questions of Economics

The study of economics comes down to this: in most places and most cases, there is not enough of everything to go around. As a consumer, you think about what resources are available to you and plan carefully to spend them wisely. Families, communities, and societies do this too. Society allocates, or distributes, more resources to people or things that it values more highly than others. Every economic system must answer some basic economic questions:

- *What* goods and services will be produced?
- *How* will those goods and services be produced?
- *Who* will consume the goods and services?

ANSWER THE TOPIC ESSENTIAL QUESTION

1. In one paragraph, explain how individuals and economies confront the problem of scarce resources.

KEY TERMS

trade-off	consumption
scarcity	economic resource
economics	factors of production
constraint	land
opportunity cost	labor
microeconomics	capital
macroeconomics	human capital
goods	entrepreneurship
service	rival nature
consumer	non-rival nature

MULTIPLE-CHOICE QUESTIONS

1. People and groups allocate the factors of production because
   - (A) land, labor, and capital are evenly divided among the members of a society in most economies today
   - (B) some goods and services are of a rival nature, even though most modern goods and services are non-rival
   - (C) regardless of technology, there are never enough resources to satisfy humans' almost unlimited desires
   - (D) capital eventually becomes exhausted and must be replenished, even though land and labor are unlimited resources
   - (E) societies depend on entrepreneurship to combine the three factors of production as efficiently as possible

2. Which of these issues would a microeconomist most likely study?
   - (A) Whether the federal government is managing national parks wisely
   - (B) What impact the opening of two new factories has had on a city
   - (C) How a country can increase its productivity through technology
   - (D) What impact entrepreneurs have on natural resources globally
   - (E) The impact of federal subsidies on international trade agreements

3. Which of these is an example of capital as economists define it?
   - (A) A consumer
   - (B) The oil beneath publicly owned land
   - (C) A forest of pine trees
   - (D) Money used to buy a movie ticket
   - (E) A factory

FREE-RESPONSE QUESTION

1. Third Coast Lumber (TCL) has purchased 100 acres of forestland and intends to harvest the trees for lumber. The company has purchased equipment to log the trees and transport them. It has hired a manager to supervise the project and ten loggers to operate the equipment.
   - (a) Identify the land resource used by Third Coast Lumber.
   - (b) Identify the capital used by TCL.
   - (c) Identify the labor used by TCL.
   - (d) Identify the entrepreneur, and explain his or her role.
   - (e) Is the resulting lumber of a rival or non-rival nature? Why?

THINK AS AN ECONOMIST: *DESCRIBE ECONOMIC CONCEPTS*

Like other social sciences, the field of economics has a unique set of concepts that provides the foundation for its theories. Being able to accurately describe the key concepts is an essential part of understanding these theories. To describe a concept, answer these questions about it.

- What is the definition?
- How does it relate to other concepts?
- What are examples of the concept?
- Why is it important in the field of economics?

For example, consider the concept of scarcity. As you read in this topic, scarcity is defined as the gap between resources, which are limited, and wants or desires, which are practically unlimited. Scarcity is such a fundamental concept that it relates to almost all other economic concepts. In fact, scarcity is the fundamental driver of economic decision-making. A consumer, for example, has a limited budget. Because of that limited budget, she has to make decisions, such as whether to have a mechanic fix the problems in her car or to buy a new car.

Apply the Skill

Practice describing economic concepts by answering the following questions about the concept of economic resources.

1. What is the definition of economic resources?
2. How do resources relate to the concept of scarcity?
3. What are three examples of economic resources?
4. Why is the concept of economic resources important in the field of economics?

Consumers want choices. Further, when asked, they usually say they want more, rather than fewer, versions of an item to select from. But can the number of choices be too many?

The Traditional View The traditional view of choice says that consumers weigh the costs and benefits to make the best choices for themselves. They base their decisions on their personal preferences and long-term goals. This model assumes people are rational, have perfect self-control, and never waver between two opposing wishes. It ignores that habit, emotion, or some other factor can overrule reason.

Behavioral Models In reality, human beings often act unpredictably. For example, they often do not have all the information they need to make rational decisions. They sometimes lack self-control. And they may make decisions based on immediate gratification without taking into account the long-term effects.

Rather than taking a "one size fits all" approach to choice, behavioral economists look at the way the human brain actually works. Choices are the result of many different mental processes, including perception, thinking (which includes reasoning and imagination), memory, and emotion. People may make irrational choices because anxiety produced by stress suppresses those parts of the brain that aid in rational decision making.

The Paradox of Choice According to psychologist Barry Schwartz, people want choices, but not too many of them. Choice overload occurs when consumers are confronted with too many choices. This may be the result of several factors, including the sheer number of options (such as style and color), time constraints, or consumers' preferences. The result of choice overload can lead to unhappiness, stress, just going with the easiest option, or not buying a product.

Consumers can counter choice overload in several ways. They can simply limit the number of available options. They might decide to buy breakfast cereal made by only one company. They can use social networks to "follow the crowd." Rather than collect and evaluate information themselves, they can ask for advice from a friend or a consumer-oriented publication.

Support for Making Positive Decisions Economist Richard H. Thaler and legal scholar Cass R. Sunstein argue that the way government and businesses structure people's available choices makes some choices more likely than others. Hence, people can be "nudged" into making choices that are in their best long-run interest. For example, displaying healthy foods at eye level in a grocery store or at the beginning of the line in a cafeteria can lead more people to eat food that is good for them.

Topic 1.2

Resource Allocation and Economic Systems

"Choosing where to live, what to do, even which clothes to put on in the morning is tough enough for those of us accustomed to making choices; it can be utterly paralyzing for people who've had decisions made for them by the state their entire lives."

—Barbara Demick, *Nothing to Envy: Ordinary Lives in North Korea* (2009)

> **Essential Question:** How do different economic systems allocate resources?

How would you run the economy of your household, your community, or your country if you could? Would you divide up all resources equally, so everyone gets the same? Maybe you would give more resources to people who needed more, people who worked harder, or people who did something to please you.

An **economic system** is defined by the way a society answers three questions:

- *What* goods and services will be produced?
- *How* will those goods and services be produced?
- *Who* will consume the goods and services?

The economic system where you live helps to shape your entire life. In one type of system, you might know from an early age that you would do the same type of work your parents and grandparents had done. In another type of system, the government might assign you a career based on how well you did in school or what economic planners thought the economy needed to prosper. In still another, you might be able to choose your own career— if others valued your goods or services enough to pay you a wage that you found acceptable.

In each system, someone or something different also controls the **means of production**. This term refers to everything used to supply goods and services, such as farmland, copper mines, factories, office buildings, robots, and supercomputers. The owners of the means of production control much of a society's economy.

Types of Economic Systems

To economists, another question that helps define the different types of economic systems is: *Who or what answers the three questions?* There are a few different types of economic systems, and in each, someone or something different answers this question and the three questions above.

Traditional Economy In a **traditional economy**, what has happened in the past answers the three questions. Traditional economies are almost exclusively tied to communities of subsistence farmers and herders. Cultural traditions linked to family and/or tribal units determine what crops are grown or what animals are raised, what farming or herding methods are employed, and how the resources produced are utilized and shared. In this type of economy, the means of production are controlled by the community. Traditional economies are increasingly rare in the modern world.

Command Economy In a **command economy**, a central authority answers the questions. Command economies, also known as planned economies, are often an outgrowth of a socialist or communist government. In these systems, the central government devises and implements a plan for what goods and services will be produced, how they will be produced, and who will consume the goods and services. In a command economy, the means of production are controlled by the state rather than individuals or private companies. As a result, entrepreneurship is rare. Advocates for command economies argue that they can provide more equitable distribution of goods and services and greater efficiency in using resources. As with traditional economies, pure command economies have become increasingly rare.

Market Economy In a **market economy** (also called a capitalist economy), neither tradition nor the state control most economic decisions. Individuals and firms answer the three questions. Far from being discouraged or rare, private property and entrepreneurship are the backbone of a market economy. Individuals and firms have great freedom to produce whatever they like and in whatever manner they see fit. Consumers are free to purchase a wide range of goods and services they want and are able to. Producers try to maximize their profit, and consumers try to acquire the things they want at the best possible price. The market system is broadly considered to be the most efficient economic system.

Mixed Economy Today, every country in the world engages in what is known as a **mixed economy**. Most countries are mainly capitalist, allowing individuals and businesses to act in their own interests, for the most part. However, state involvement also plays a key role through actions such as safety regulations, minimum wage mandates, environmental laws, business development incentives, and many others.

The following chart sums up some of the differences between the various economic systems.

TYPES OF ECONOMIC SYSTEMS				
Key Questions	Traditional Economy	Command Economy	Market Economy (Capitalism)	Mixed Economy
What is it?	A system in which long-standing cultural customs and societal structures determine the economy	A system in which government planners decide what will be produced and who will receive it	A system in which buyers and sellers decide what a society's economic priorities will be	A system with features of both a market economy and a command economy
Who owns the means of production?	The community	The government	Businesses and individuals	Mostly businesses and individuals, but with differing levels of government regulation
What are some examples as of 2020?	The reindeer-herding Sami people of Scandinavia engage in a traditional economy. But no countries have an exclusively traditional economy.	North Korea, Cuba, and Belarus were mostly command economies.	The United States, the United Kingdom, Singapore, and Botswana were mostly market economies.	All countries are mixed economies, but each has its own mixture, where different systems are represented to a greater or lesser degree.

Resource Allocation in Different Economic Systems

A society's economic system strongly influences resource allocation. Every society that has ever existed has had scarce resources, and decisions about who controls the resources and how people use them are usually controversial. What follows is a more in-depth look at the functioning of command, market, and mixed economic systems at work in the modern world.

Resource Allocation in Command Economies For much of the 20th century, large-scale command economies existed in the former Soviet Union, China, and elsewhere. During World War II, the United States became more of a command economy as the government regulated economic activity in order to support the military. Since the late 20th century, many economies have become more market-oriented. Market economies and command economies were once considered to be opposites, but today most command economies include some degree of market-based planning, and vice-versa.

- *What goods and services do people produce?* People produce the goods and services that the government believes are necessary to produce. They do so not to make a profit, but to best serve the country's needs as articulated by the government and its leaders. The government often tightly regulates who can start a business.

- *How do people produce those goods and services?* Central planners who work for the government set economic goals for the country as a whole. They decide where factories and other workplaces will be located, who will do what work, and how much people will be paid.

- *Who consumes those goods and services?* The government decides how much people will earn and what material goods they will be able to buy. Governments might claim to treat all citizens equally. However, in large-scale command economies such as the old Soviet Union, a small group of government leaders, scientists, and top athletes received better housing and far more luxuries than the average person had access to.

Resource Allocation in Market Economies Market economies have existed since the 1600s, as the feudal system (in which most people worked for a local lord or other large landowner) began declining. Today most people live in market economies, but all have some degree of government regulation.

- *What goods and services do people produce?* Market economies provide a vast and sometimes bewildering array of goods and services. Individuals and businesses develop, test, and produce what they believe consumers will demand—whether that is a self-driving car or a phone app that lets the user pretend to pop bubble wrap. If the market rejects a good or service, then its creator loses money.

  How much people and organizations charge for goods and services depends on their competitors—others who sell identical or similar products. If you are an entrepreneur who produces a desired good or service and you have no competitors, then you can charge a high price. However, if you make high profits, other businesses or individuals will enter the market and put downward pressure on the prices you charge.

- *How do people produce those goods and services?* If you live in a market economy, innovation and technology are likely to be all around you. The career that you succeed in may not have existed in your parents' time. In fact, it may not even have been invented yet. Market economies are much larger than traditional economies, and their large populations of consumers often generate huge amounts of trash and pollution. Balancing environmental needs with consumers' desire for innovation is one of the challenges of a market economy, as individuals, businesses, and governments consider constraints and trade-offs.

- *Who consumes those goods and services?* What people consume reflects what they can afford to purchase. Individuals with more resources can consume more, while individuals with fewer resources consume less.

Resource Allocation in Mixed Economies All economies are mixed economies. In other words, no society is driven 100 percent by traditions, markets, or the government. However, mixed economies tend to favor either a command or a market economic system, and the way they answer the *what, how*, and *who* questions depends on the dominant system.

- *What goods and services do people produce?* In a mixed market economy, in addition to individual producers, the central, state, or local governments may provide services that are otherwise not available. In the United States during the 1960s, for example, railroad companies struggled to make a profit by providing passenger service, and several companies went bankrupt. To fill the resulting gap, the federal government in 1971 created Amtrak to provide railroad service between cities. Amtrak receives federal and state subsidies, or public funds, to support its operations.

   In a mixed command economy, the government may permit entrepreneurs to create their own businesses on a limited basis as a way to increase worker motivation or help the economy grow.

- *How do people produce those goods and services?* In a mixed market economy, individuals and businesses have wide latitude on deciding how to provide the goods and services they create. But if the government concludes that production harms the public, it might step in with regulations. For example, the U.S. Congress regulates how food is processed so that it is safe to consume, drugs so that they are safe to consume, emissions from factories and cars to keep the air clean, and employment of children to prevent exploitation of children.

   In a mixed command economy, some businesses can make production decisions based on market forces. However, the government may restrict the use of resources if a business seems to be drawing too many resources away from other endeavors.

- *Who consumes those goods and services?* In a mixed market economy, most decisions about consumption are based on the wealth of a consumer. For example, in 2018, the wealthiest fifth of American households spent $13,348 on food. The poorest fifth spent $4,109.

   However, most wealthy countries provide a social safety net—a set of programs to support the most vulnerable members of society to obtain food, shelter, and usually health care. For example, throughout much of U.S. history, many older Americans lived with or near their children, and many people died within a few years of retiring. However, as people lived longer, families grew smaller, and young people moved to cities in search of jobs, more and more elderly lived in poverty after they retired. In response, the U.S. government created the Social Security system in 1935 to provide retired people with some income. Social Security operates as a required insurance program for which employers and employees provide the funds. As people have lived longer, Social Security has grown into the largest social safety net program in the United States.

Source: DuKai/Getty Images

China was overwhelmingly a command economy in the 1950s through the 1980s. In the 1990s, China began adding free-market elements to its economy, following the advice of its leader Deng Xiaoping to "let some people get rich first." As a result, cities such as Shanghai (shown above) quickly became very wealthy, while rural areas were slower to escape poverty.

Control of Scarce Resources in Economic Systems

Every economic system involves constraints and trade-offs as people and institutions struggle for control of resources. Furthermore, each system makes decisions about the allocation of scarce resources through key institutions, or well-established organizations. Key institutions in a market economy are private businesses, including both large corporations and small enterprises run by individuals or families. In addition, local, state, and national governments are important in organizing and regulating the activities of private businesses.

Each system has coordinating mechanisms, or organizations and technologies through which natural resources reach companies and goods and services reach customers. For example, suppose you are a manager of a company that manufactures bicycles. Think of all the pieces and parts that go into making bikes: pedals, tires, gears, handlebars, and so forth. Your company could make each part, but you are likely to be more efficient if you buy pieces from various specialized manufacturers. Your company coordinates the process of getting all the parts together, assembling the bicycles, and shipping them to stores. All these activities are known as coordinating mechanisms. Resources are treated differently under different economic systems.

Human Resources People who create goods and services (also called human resources or labor) receive different treatment depending on the economic system they are in.

- Traditional economies value workers who can carry on the skills and crafts of their ancestors. Family and community are the key institutions.

- Command economies might support research and innovation sponsored by the government, but they often criticize individual entrepreneurs for being more focused on making money for themselves than on serving the public.

- Market economies value entrepreneurship—being able to combine human resources, natural resources, and capital resources in a way that succeeds in the marketplace.

Natural Resources Materials that the planet provides and that humans use (also called land) are essential to every economic system. In every system, individuals and companies must employ coordinating mechanisms to gather natural resources and supply them to the people who use them to create products.

- Traditional economies use individuals and communities to gain access to natural resources. They place the least burden on natural resources because these societies are small and do not innovate as often as other economies do.

- Many command economies, such as China's, are also industrialized. But in a command economy, government is the controlling institution, making decisions about the kinds of products and services that the country will produce.

- Many market economies are highly industrialized. That is, they use technological processes to turn raw materials into finished products. Market economies use natural resources heavily as producers and consumers continually seek lower-cost, newer, and more desirable products.

Sometimes poor use of natural resources causes the same problems in market economies and command economies. For instance, ill-advised farming methods caused massive dust storms in the United States in the 1930s and in China in the 2010s.

Capital Resources Tools and machines are part of every economic system, and factories and offices are part of most economic systems. Again here, in different systems these resources are treated differently.

- People in traditional economies value the tools and machines their ancestors used, such as fishing nets and sleds.

- In command economies, the government owns capital resources.

- In market economies, individuals and private groups own most capital resources.

ANSWER THE TOPIC ESSENTIAL QUESTION

1. In one to three paragraphs, explain the three main economic systems and how they allocate resources.

MULTIPLE-CHOICE QUESTIONS

1. People in traditional economies, market economies, and command economies allocate resources differently because

   (A) traditional and demand economies value entrepreneurship more highly than market economies

   (B) traditional and command economies do not face the problem of scarcity while market economies do face scarcity

   (C) command economies are smaller than traditional or market economies and therefore have fewer options

   (D) market economies are smaller than traditional or demand economies and therefore have fewer options

   (E) they have different opinions about what is most important, necessary, and worthwhile in a society

2. Which of these are you most likely to find in a command economy?

   (A) A conference on entrepreneurship and starting new businesses

   (B) A multiyear centralized economic plan that lists production quotas

   (C) Baskets woven in the same way they were 300 years ago

   (D) Minimal government policies regulating economic activity

   (E) A wide and varied selection of newly developed consumer goods

3. Which type of economic system would the United States be considered as knowing that government creates regulations, price control mechanisms, and helps to allocate resources while businesses and entrepreneurs still have a chance to be vital decision makers in the productive economy?

   (A) Pure traditional economy

   (B) Mixed traditional economy

   (C) Pure command economy

   (D) Pure market economy

   (E) Mixed market economy

FREE-RESPONSE QUESTIONS

1. An economist studies two countries to determine how efficiently each uses its resources. The economist gathers this data on the two countries.

Country	Percentage of Factories Owned by the Government	Goods and Services Produced Annually	Estimated Number of New Products and Services Introduced Annually	Estimated Failure Rate of New Businesses
Country J	95 percent	$2.0 billion	380	Not applicable
Country L	13 percent	$3.1 billion	4,200	88 percent

(a) Based on the data in this table, is Country J a traditional economy, a market economy, or a command economy? Explain.

(b) Based on the data in this table, is Country L a traditional economy, a market economy, or a command economy? Explain.

(c) Based on what you have read in this topic, why do you think the residents of Country J have access to fewer new products and services each year?

(d) Based on what you have read in this topic, why do you think Country L's estimated failure rate of new businesses is so high?

(e) Based on what you have read in this topic, why is the estimated failure rate of new businesses in Country J listed as "not applicable"?

THINK AS AN ECONOMIST: *DESCRIBE LIMITATIONS OF ECONOMIC MODELS*

The traditional, market, command, and mixed systems are economic models, constructs of how the world works rather than examples of actual economies. Because of its structure and mode of operation, each economic system puts certain constraints on its economic actors. Those constraints impose limitations on economic performance.

To describe the limitations of an economic system, focus on the three basic economic questions:

- What are the limitations on what is produced?
- What are the limitations on how goods and services are produced?
- What are the limitations on who consumes those goods and services?

Consider traditional economies. Because they rely on traditional production methods, these economies have little variety in goods and services being produced. Traditional economies are low on innovation, which hampers variety in two ways. Lack of innovation dampens the inventiveness that leads members of the society to imagine both new goods and services and new methods of production. Traditional economies tend to rely on readily available natural resources and to be low in capital. The resulting limited technology restricts the quantity of goods produced and further constrains variety in goods and services. Finally, traditional societies tend to favor those with the most resources. This can result in some unequal allocation of productive output.

Apply the Skill

Using your knowledge of your own life experiences and the information in this topic, analyze the mixed market economic system of the United States. Write a paragraph that identifies the limitations on what is produced, how it is produced, and who has access to production.

Production Possibilities Curve

"I was missing out on a lot of things that my friends were doing, but in another way, they were missing things I was doing. It was kind of a trade-off I had to make."

—Professional tennis player Victoria Azarenka, 2012

Essential Question: How does the production possibilities curve illustrate constraints and trade-offs?

Which is more important: spending time with friends or training to become a winning athlete? Of course, different people will answer that question in different ways. People make these kinds of decisions every day, because a person's time is a scarce resource. Families, communities, and companies make these decisions as well, not just about scarce time, but also about other scarce resources.

Each of these choices involves a **trade-off**, a sacrifice of one desired thing in exchange for something more highly desired. In other words, to gain something such as athletic training, people must trade off something else for it, such as relaxed time with friends. The "price" that is paid for a trade-off such as this is called an **opportunity cost**.

Economists can use tables and graphs to show trade-offs associated with allocating scarce resources. An economic model called the production possibilities curve uses graphs to demonstrate various production decisions. This model shows how different choices in *what* to produce and *how many* to produce will affect one another.

The Production Possibilities Curve

A basic economic model that illustrates scarcity and opportunity costs is the **production possibilities curve (PPC)**. Like other models, the PPC is theoretical and based on simplified factors (see Topic 1.2). It explains the production possibilities of an enterprise that makes only two different goods when there are limited supplies of a resource that both goods need in order to be produced. No enterprise or economy is that simple, but the simplicity and limitations of the model help make the concepts clear.

To see how the production possibilities curve illustrates scarcity and trade-offs, consider the example of a family-owned business called Poweshiek Forest Furniture, which has six employees. This company produces only two products: tables and chairs, both made of hardwood from the walnut tree. The owners of

Poweshiek Forest Furniture wonder how many tables and how many chairs they can make in a month with the resources they have.

The production possibilities can be represented in a table.

POWESHIEK FOREST'S PRODUCTION TRADE-OFFS	
Production of Tables	Production of Chairs
50	0
45	10
25	35
10	60
0	75

Poweshiek Forest Furniture can look at this table and see that if they make 25 tables, they have enough resources left to make 35 chairs; if they make only 10 tables, they would have the resources to make 60 chairs.

The production possibilities curve (sometimes referred to as the *production possibilities frontier*, or *PPF*, because in some instances, the "curve" appearing in a graph may actually be a straight line) provides a way to visualize the economic relationships in their output.

PRODUCTION POSSIBILITIES CURVE

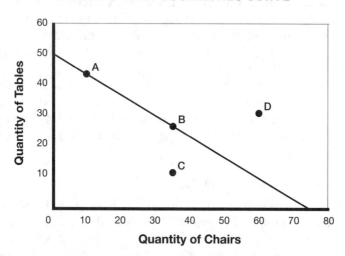

According to the PPC, if Poweshiek Forest uses all its wood and all of its workers' time to produce only tables (50 on the *y*-axis), it would have none left for chairs (0 on the *x*-axis). If it used all its wood and all of its workers' time to produce only chairs (75 on the *x*-axis), it would have none left for tables (0 on the *y*-axis).

Points anywhere *on* the production possibilities curve or *inside* it, however, would show the company how much of each product it could make if the decision-makers want to allocate scarce resources so they can make both. For example, if they want to make 45 tables, they would have enough resources left to make 10 chairs. (See point A on the Production Possibilities Curve graph.) If they want to make 25 tables, they would have enough resources left to make 35 chairs. (See point B.)

Feasibility and Efficiency

The points on the PPC show what the feasibility, or possibility, is of producing certain amounts of two products. That is, Poweshiek Forest Furniture has enough wood and enough workers to make any combination of tables and chairs along the PPC. Those points also show the **efficiency** of those combinations. Production is efficient if it uses all available resources with no missed opportunities.

Points inside the PPC are also feasible, but they are not efficient. If Poweshiek Forest Furniture can make 25 tables and 35 chairs (a point on the PPC), it could also make 10 tables and 35 chairs (point C), but it would be inefficient to do so because it would not be using all its possible resources. In other words, its resources would be **underutilized**. A situation like this represents a **contraction**, a decline in output, which could have many causes. Maybe orders for new tables dropped and the company cut back on hours for workers, or maybe some of Poweshiek Forest's employees took vacation time. Any factor that would put Poweshiek Forest in the position of not being able to use all its resources would create inefficiency.

Now suppose Poweshiek Forest received a big order for 60 chairs and 30 tables (point D) on the graph. Would they have the resources to fulfill that order in a month? No. Anything that lies outside the PPC is not possible to produce with the given resources.

Opportunity Costs

Poweshiek Forest, like any other business, individual, family, or community, faces problems of scarcity and has to make choices. If it decides to make 25 tables in order to make 35 chairs as well (point B), the company has lost the opportunity to use its resources to make another 25 tables, though it has gained 35 chairs in the trade-off. That lost opportunity is called an **opportunity cost**—the loss of a benefit you would have gained (25 more tables) because you chose an alternative (35 chairs).

Calculating Opportunity Costs To calculate opportunity costs using data in a table, compare the numbers in the same row in each column. For example, look back at Poweshiek Forest's Production Trade-Offs above. The second row shows that to produce 10 chairs, Poweshiek Forest can produce only 45 tables. Opportunity costs are calculated based on what is sacrificed in the first column. So the opportunity cost for producing the first 10 chairs is 5 tables.

Calculating opportunity costs from a graph follows the same basic principle, but the graph allows you to see a large range of points at which different combinations are possible. To calculate the same situation as above—the opportunity cost of making 10 chairs—you find the point where 10 chairs (y-axis) intersects with tables (x-axis) on the PPC. That is point A on graph. If you look to the *y*-axis where the quantity of tables is represented, you can see that point A represents 5 tables lost, so that is the opportunity cost. Opportunity costs are calculated based on changes on the *y*-axis.

Constant Opportunity Costs In the production possibilities curve in the graph, every chair is worth 2/3 of a table (50 tables/75 chairs=0.66 or 2/3). For every chair Poweshiek Forest makes, it "pays" an opportunity cost of 2/3 of a table. If it makes three chairs, it gives up the chance to make two tables. If it makes 12 chairs, the opportunity cost is eight tables. The opportunity cost of a chair is always 2/3 of a table. In this scenario, the opportunity cost does not change no matter what combination of chairs and tables Poweshiek Forest makes. This constant cost of 0.66 of a table for each chair made results in a production possibilities curve that is a straight line, since the change in the *y*-axis is always in the same relationship to the change in the *x*-axis.

Increasing Opportunity Costs Suppose, though, that the opportunity cost for each additional chair increases. The first 24 chairs Poweshiek Forest makes (point B) have an opportunity cost of 16 tables (point C), but the next 24 chairs require giving up 30 tables because the chairs take more of the workers' time, which was used more efficiently to make tables. A PPC showing increasing opportunity costs is a curved line bowed outward instead of a straight line.

The increasing opportunity costs reflect the reality that most resources are not as efficiently used for one task as for another. Consider the skills of a lawyer. A firm could ask lawyers who specialize in criminal defense to help out the tax law department. So, instead of working rapidly in a field they are experts in, they would work more slowly in a new field they were gaining experience in.

INCREASING OPPORTUNITY COST PPC

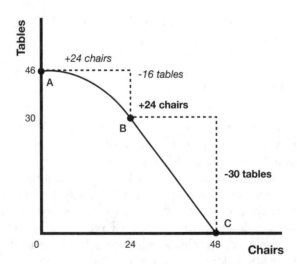

Decreasing Opportunity Costs Up until now, all six workers made both tables and chairs. Suppose, however, the owner trained three of the workers to make only chairs. They took a course in woodworking that increased their skill and speed at making chairs. Before their training, for every 12 chairs Poweshiek Forest produced, they sacrificed 8 tables. After the training in making chairs, though, Poweshiek Forest could make 30 chairs and sacrifice only 6 tables. They kept improving their skills and could soon make 40 chairs for 4 tables. The PPC for a situation in which opportunity costs decrease is a curved line bowed inward instead of a straight line.

DECREASING OPPORTUNITY COST PPC

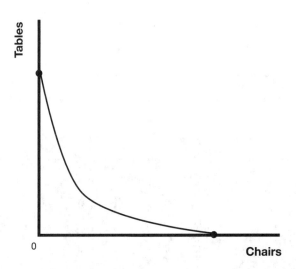

The Production Possibilities Curve and Growth

Most people, businesses, and societies are interested in **growth,** or increasing production. The production possibilities curve can represent growth resulting from possible additional resources, such as hiring more workers, using better management techniques, or improving technology. Any or all of these resources could potentially allow goods to be produced more efficiently. In other words, economic growth occurs through an increase in the quantity or quality of resources. In these cases, the resulting differences can be represented graphically.

The pair of graph on the following page shows two types of shifts that occur when economic growth occurs. In each graph, the original PPC is labeled *PPC1* and the PPC that results from the shift is labeled *PPC2*. In the first graph, increases in production of both tables and chairs are equal, indicating that additional resources are available, and that they are being shared equally by both products. The figure illustrates economic growth—an increase in the output of tables and chairs. (If the direction of the arrow were reversed and the labels were switched, the figure would illustrate economic contraction—a decline in output.)

The second graph illustrates a shift that might be attributed to changes in the factors of production for just one good, just chairs, for example. Some of these changes might be access to additional hardwood, more workers, or the adoption of new technology in the production of chairs.

THE EFFECTS OF ECONOMIC GROWTH ON THE PPC

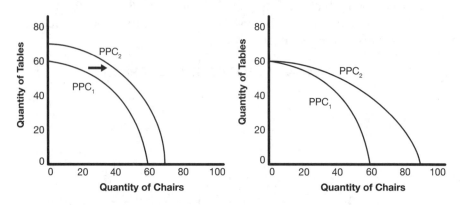

More workers in the shop might translate to the kind of shift seen in the right-hand graph.

ANSWER THE TOPIC ESSENTIAL QUESTION

1. In one paragraph, explain what a production possibilities curve is and how it can be used to show trade-offs.

KEY TERMS

trade-off	contraction
production possibilities curve (PPC)	underutilized
efficiency	opportunity cost
growth	

MULTIPLE-CHOICE QUESTIONS

1. The best definition of a PPC is that it is a model
   - (A) of whether a company's business is likely to decrease
   - (B) of how much competition exists in a market
   - (C) that helps economists determine the one combination of production outputs that will use resources most efficiently
   - (D) that shows the maximum amounts of products that can be produced given current levels of resources and technology
   - (E) that demonstrates how businesses can avoid making trade-offs

2. Which factor would move a company's production possibilities curve to the right?
   - (A) The company's oil suppliers are charging more for oil.
   - (B) The personal computer becomes widely used.
   - (C) The number of engineers on its staff declines.
   - (D) The union has negotiated a wage increase for workers.
   - (E) The country increased taxes on products being imported.

3. If Bryana's Tree Corp has a constant opportunity cost production possibility curve in the production of lumber and furniture. If the company was efficiently producing 10 units of lumber and 5 units of furniture and wanted to produce more of both goods, what would be necessary to produce more of both goods?
   - (A) Increasing wages for workers
   - (B) Decreasing wages for workers
   - (C) Increasing the prices for both lumber and furniture
   - (D) Building a new factory
   - (E) Producing goods more efficiently

1. Jaylan's Jewelry makes both necklaces and earrings at 3 factories around the country. Jaylan's Jewelry's production possibilities can be found in the diagram below. Use the information from the production possibilities curve and your knowledge of economics to answer the questions that follow.

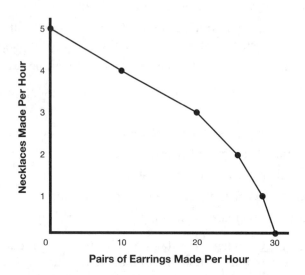

(a) Based on the data in this PPC, identify the production level of 2 necklaces and 20 pairs of earrings as efficient, inefficient, or unattainable. Explain.

(b) Based on the data in this PPC, identify the production level of 4 necklaces and 20 pairs of earrings as efficient, inefficient, or unattainable. Explain.

(c) Based on the data in this PPC, identify the production level of 4 necklaces and 10 pairs of earrings as efficient, inefficient, or unattainable. Explain.

(d) Assume that the company decides to demolish two factories leaving just one factory open. Explain what the change would be to the production possibilities curve.

(e) Assume instead that Jaylan's Jewelry wanted to increase production possibilities to produce 5 necklaces and 25 pairs of earrings. Identify one change that could attain this level of production.

THINK AS AN ECONOMIST: *DRAW AN ACCURATELY LABELED GRAPH*

A production possibilities curve plots the output of any two goods or services by a producer. Producers use it to study and identify opportunity costs inherent in the production process. The curve helps them decide how best to use their resource inputs of land, labor, and capital.

Apply the Skill

Practice creating and accurately labeling graphs by completing the following task using the scenario of Acme Enterprises.

The management team of Acme Enterprises faces a decision. Production for the summer selling season must begin soon. They have to choose how best to use their factories, workers, and budget for materials.

Use the data in the table to create a production possibilities curve the management team can use. Label the graph accurately by including descriptions of the x-axis and y-axis. Give the graph a title as well.

Output of Beach Umbrellas	Output of Beach Chairs
350,000	0
340,000	5,000
310,000	12,000
260,000	19,000
180,000	27,000
110,000	33,000
0	39,000

Comparative Advantage and Trade

"Under a system of perfectly free commerce, each country naturally devotes its capital and labor to such employments as are most beneficial to each."

David Ricardo, *On the Principles of Political Economy and Taxation* (1817)

Essential Question: How does engaging in trade increase overall production and consumption?

Two hundred years ago, the English economist David Ricardo suggested that, instead of trying to produce everything that its citizens needed and wanted, each country should specialize in those goods that it could produce more efficiently than other countries. Each country would then trade for other goods with the countries that specialized in producing them. England had become the world's leading producer of textiles as a result of the Industrial Revolution. But the English climate was not conducive to growing grapes on a large scale. Portugal, on the other hand, was a major grape-growing country, but its textile industry had not yet been mechanized. Thus, it made sense for England to manufacture textiles and not grow grapes and for Portugal to grow grapes rather than producing textiles. The two countries could then trade with one another to satisfy their wants.

Absolute Advantage and Comparative Advantage

A person, business, or country has an **absolute advantage** when it can produce more of a good or service than another producer that has the same quantity of resources. In the late 18th century, industrialization allowed England to produce textiles more cheaply than other European countries, giving it an absolute advantage over them. Today, the United States, with its skilled workforce, plentiful natural resources, and cutting-edge technology, has an absolute advantage over many countries in producing many goods and services, but not in all. Indonesia, because of its climate and the skills of its workforce, has an absolute advantage in the production of spices. Thus, the United States buys spices from Indonesia and sells Indonesia soybeans, a crop in which the United States has an absolute advantage. Australia has an absolute advantage in aluminum production, since it is the leading producer of bauxite, the main aluminum ore. The United States buys aluminum from Australia and sells Australia transportation equipment.

Comparative Advantage In some cases, however, it is advantageous for a country to import goods and services from another country even though they could be produced more cheaply at home. (To import goods is to purchase them from outside a country; to export goods is to sell them to another country.) The principle of comparative advantage helps explain why this is so. **Comparative advantage** is the ability to produce a good or service at a lower opportunity cost than another producer.

In addition to discussing absolute advantage in his 1817 book, Ricardo formulated the law of comparative advantage, which takes into account the opportunity cost of producing two goods or services. If two countries have different opportunity costs in the production of two goods or services, both countries would benefit from specializing in the goods it can produce in which its opportunity costs are lower—meaning they give up less to produce the good. The production of the other item would then be left to the other country. The two countries could then trade with each other.

A hypothetical case might use Ropistan and Wirania as the two countries and rope and wire as the two commodities. Ropistan might take 100 hours to produce a quantity of rope that could be produced in Wirania with 90 hours of labor. And for wire, Ropistan might take 120 hours to produce the same quantity as Wirania could produce with 80 hours of labor.

RICARDO'S COMPARATIVE ADVANTAGE		
Commodity	**Hours of Work Needed to Produce 1 Unit**	
	Ropistan	**Wirania**
Rope	100	90
Wire	120	80

In this scenario, Ropistan needs more labor to produce both goods. Thus, Wirania has an absolute advantage in production of both rope and wire. To determine which country has the comparative advantage, however, look at the opportunity costs. As you can see from the figures in the table above, it takes Ropistan about 10 percent more labor to produce the same amount of rope as Wirania, it takes 50 percent more labor for Ropistan to produce as much wire as Wirania:

- Ropistan is better off concentrating on the production of rope, since it requires 20 fewer hours of labor than wire production.

- Wirania is better off concentrating on wire production, which requires 10 fewer hours of labor than producing rope would.

To determine the opportunity cost to each country of producing rope, divide the number of hours it takes to produce rope by the number of hours to produce wire:

Rope/Wire = Opportunity cost of rope

To determine the opportunity cost to each country of producing wire, divide the number of hours it takes to produce wire by the number of hours to produce rope:

$$Wire/Rope = Opportunity\ cost\ of\ wire$$

The table "Opportunity Costs" shows the opportunity costs of producing rope and wire for both Ropistan and Wirania.

OPPORTUNITY COSTS		
	Ropistan	Wirania
Opportunity cost to produce 1 unit of rope	100/120 = 0.833 units of wire	90/80 = 1.125 units of wire
Opportunity cost to produce 1 unit of wire	120/100 = 1.20 units of rope	80/90 = 0.89 units of rope

The country with the lower opportunity cost in producing a commodity has the comparative advantage. The opportunity cost of producing a unit of rope in Ropistan is 0.833 compared to 1.125 in Wirania, so Ropistan has the comparative advantage. The opportunity cost of producing a unit of wire in Ropistan is 1.20 compared to 0.89 in Wirania, so Wirania has the comparative advantage.

While it has the absolute advantage in production of both commodities, Wirania can exchange the wire for more rope than it could produce by diverting labor from wire production to the production of rope. Therefore, the opportunity cost of trading wire for rope is lower than the opportunity cost of producing the rope. Similarly, Ropistan has a comparative advantage in production of rope because the opportunity cost is lower than that of producing wire.

The example of Ropistan and Wirania is referred to as an input problem. This type of problem uses the amount of resources, usually hours of labor, that go into the production of a particular quantity of goods to assess comparative advantage. However, comparative advantage can also be assessed by comparing how much can be produced (output) when both countries employ an equal level of resources (input). This is known as an output problem.

Drawbacks The law of comparative advantage is a very simplistic two-good/two-country model. It makes many assumptions that, while being true, do not specifically reflect reality. The real world is much more complex, and most countries import and export a wide variety of goods and services. Also, comparative advantage does not take into account factors such as the value of one country's currency versus that of another (See Topic 6.2) and relative prices.

In addition, comparative advantage may change over time. The same factors that can result in changes in opportunity costs can also affect a country's comparative advantage. Such factors as improved technology or the depletion of nonrenewable resources have a positive or negative effect on opportunity costs, which in turn may change the comparative advantage one country has over another.

Specialization and Trade

In his book *The Wealth of Nations* (1776), British economist Adam Smith argued that **specialization** (focusing production on select goods to increase efficiency) and its accompanying **division of labor** (assigning different, specific tasks to workers) were the basis of economic progress. Smith believed that it made more sense for people to work at whatever they do most profitably and to use their earnings to buy the things they want. The same advice applies just as well to regions and countries, a fact that David Ricardo recognized in the passage that opens this topic.

One hundred years ago, there was a great deal of regional specialization in the United States. Cars made in Michigan were sold in Kansas, while baked goods consumed in Michigan might have been made from Kansas wheat. Because of its location on the Great Lakes, availability of steel, capital, and growing workforce, Detroit became the center of the automobile industry. Kansas, on the other hand, had the right soil, climate, capital, and labor to produce wheat. For similar reasons, West Virginia became a major producer of coal, Florida of citrus fruits, and California of semiconductors. These days, however, production is much less regionalized. Automobiles, for example, are made in plants in many states.

As with states, countries tend to specialize in the production of certain goods and services. For example, Brazil is the world's largest producer of coffee beans, while Ecuador leads in the export of bananas. China is the leading exporter of electronics, while the United States produces much of the world's computer software. The United States is the world's largest exporter of services, including financial services, express delivery, energy services, information technology, and telecommunications.

Mutually Beneficial Trade Countries specialize in the production of certain goods and services for many reasons. These include availability of resources (including labor) in addition to absolute and comparative advantage. Specialization according to comparative advantage results in opportunities beyond those on the production possibilities curve (PPC). Trade between two countries allows for higher total output and consumption than would be possible domestically. **Gains from trade** result when two countries specialize in commodities in which they have a comparative advantage and exchange with one another, allowing each to benefit from increased consumption of goods they would not have without trade.

Returning to the examples of Ropistan and Wirania, if each country specializes in the commodity in which it has a comparative advantage and trades the surplus, both countries benefit. This is because the arrangement allows both countries to consume beyond their production possibilities. If Ropistan devotes 220 hours of labor to manufacturing rope, it can produce 2.2 units and trade the 1.2 surplus units for wire, and if Wirania devotes 170 hours to making wire, it can produce 2.125 units and trade the 1.25 surplus units for rope. Each country benefits by being able to consume more of the commodity that it imports from the other than it was able to before trade took place.

GAINS FROM TRADE

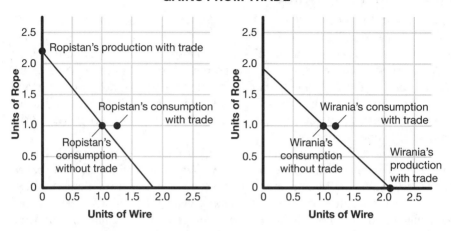

Keep in mind, though, that trade-offs occur as a result of this specialization. For example, workers in some industries lose their jobs when a country no longer specializes in a certain industry. Also, increases in manufacturing can have negative environmental effects.

While comparative advantage and opportunity costs play a part in determining the terms of trade, other factors also come into play. For example, the United States must be able to import manufactured goods from China at lower cost than those items can be produced domestically. The terms of trade are the ratio between the prices of a country's exports, or goods it sells abroad, and its imports, or goods it buys from other countries. The terms of trade are calculated using this formula:

Price of exports/Price of imports x 100 = Terms of trade

As you can see, if from one year to the next, the price of a country's exports goes up (or imports goes down), the country's terms of trade improve. In either situation, the country stands to improve its standard of living as a result.

When two countries such as the United States and China have a rate of exchange that is profitable for both, **mutually beneficial trade** can take place. As a result, both countries are able to enjoy gains from trade.

ANSWER THE TOPIC ESSENTIAL QUESTION

1. In one to three paragraphs, explain how engaging in trade increases production and consumption.

KEY TERMS

---

absolute advantage

comparative advantage

specialization

division of labor

mutually beneficial trade

gains from trade

1. In what term is the opportunity cost of a commodity expressed?

   (A) Resources

   (B) Hours of labor

   (C) Another commodity

   (D) Gains from trade

   (E) Money

2. If a country possesses a skilled workforce and cutting-edge technology, this means that it would

   (A) have an absolute advantage over many other countries in the production of a variety of goods

   (B) have a comparative advantage over many other countries in the production of a variety of goods

   (C) not be subject to the types of trade-offs that other countries must face when engaging in trade

   (D) be virtually guaranteed a trade surplus each year

   (E) have difficulty finding trading partners with whom it can engage in mutually beneficial trade

3. Which of the following is a basic economic concept that makes mutually beneficial trade possible?

   (A) Absolute advantage

   (B) Specialization

   (C) Trade-offs

   (D) Scarcity

   (E) Opportunity cost

FREE-RESPONSE QUESTIONS

1. Suppose that countries A and B produce only two goods: cheese and fish. The table below summarizes the average hourly worker productivity for each country and commodity.

NUMBER OF KILOGRAMS PRODUCED PER HOUR		
Country	Fish	Cheese
A	80	40
B	100	20

(a) Which country has an absolute advantage in the production of fish?

(b) Draw a production possibilities curve that includes both countries. Place *Fish* on the vertical axis and *Cheese* on the horizontal axis, and label each country on the graph.

(c) Calculate the opportunity cost of Country A to produce 1 unit (kilogram) of cheese.

(d) Calculate the opportunity cost of Country B to produce 1 unit (kilogram) of cheese.

(e) Which country has the comparative advantage in producing cheese? Explain.

THINK AS AN ECONOMIST: *IDENTIFY AN ECONOMIC CONCEPT USING CALCULATIONS*

Economists use calculations to explain and identify economic concepts. In this lesson, you learned how to determine the comparative advantage of two countries when considered as an input problem. In an input problem, the amount of inputs (labor, in the text example) varies but the output (the quantity produced) is fixed. Economists calculate the opportunity cost of inputs by dividing the labor required to produce one unit of a good by the labor needed to produce one unit of a second good. The country with a comparative advantage in producing a good is the one with the lowest opportunity cost. In the text example given in this topic, Ropistan had a comparative advantage in producing rope, and Wirania had a comparative advantage in producing wire.

Apply the Skill

Economists also consider the comparative advantage in terms of outputs—the quantity of two goods that can be produced with a fixed set of inputs. The calculation is similar. You compare the output of two goods in two countries based on a specific level of inputs. The country with the comparative advantage for producing a good has the lowest opportunity cost for making that good. Study the table, which shows the output of pounds of chocolate or individual step counters that two countries can produce with 10 units of labor. Calculate the comparative advantage of each country in terms of output. Which good should each country specialize in?

OUTPUT PER 10 UNITS OF LABOR		
	Sweetonia	**Sweatistan**
Chocolate (pounds)	45	20
Step counters (units)	15	4

Cost-Benefit Analysis

*"To me, benefit-cost analysis is analytical common sense.
The idea is that we don't have the resources to do everything.
So we have to choose carefully."*

—Paul R. Portney, economist, 1981

Essential Question: How can you evaluate costs and benefits to make rational economic decisions?

As you know, economics (and life in general) involves trade-offs. Economists refer to these trade-offs as **opportunity costs**. In other words, if you want something, then you'll have to give up something else. Is there a way you can figure out which decisions you should make so that you will get as much use, enjoyment, and satisfaction as possible out of the resources you have? Thinking through such decisions can be complicated, so economists have developed a helpful tool called the **cost-benefit analysis**. This method helps individuals and organizations determine which expenses or sacrifices—as well as which benefits and gains—are most likely to arise from a decision.

Cost-benefit analyses are useful in your everyday life, and they help consumers, workers, businesses, local governments, and national governments make decisions. For example, in addition to obvious costs such as the money paid for goods, a decision usually has hidden or hard-to-see costs, such as changes in how people think or feel.

In addition, economists usually assume that people make decisions based on logic, but emotion and values often shapes how people think. For example, many decisions people make, such as where to work, could easily be assumed to have only monetary motivations. However, many people take jobs that offer comparatively smaller salaries to work for charitable organizations or companies that sell a product or service they believe in—a record store or an outdoor tour provider. People choose these paths because they derive a psychic benefit that is powerful, but difficult to quantify.

Opportunity Costs and Choices

Thinking of all the possible benefits and drawbacks of a course of action can be challenging and calculating the opportunity costs associated with choices can be bewildering. Consider some general examples and then some specifics.

Examples of Cost-Benefit Analyses "These types of analyses are not difficult, no matter what economists think," you might say. "All people have to do is examine what the costs and benefits are and then take whichever course of action gives people the greatest benefit (or the least pain)." However, real-life cost-benefit analyses are rarely that easy. To get a better idea of the concept, look at the following table. Cover up everything but the first column and try to think of what the costs and benefits might be and what you might do in each scenario.

EXAMPLES OF COST-BENEFIT ANALYSES			
Scenario	Possible Costs	Possible Benefits	Decision
A student considers whether to start designing T-shirts to sell.	The student will have less time to study for upcoming exams.	A chance to make a profit and, therefore, have more money and independence; a chance to be creative	The student starts on a small scale, with the possibility of increasing output if the new business does not hurt her grades.
A sandwich shop decides to offer a new line of calzones.	The shop will not be able to devote time and resources to expanding its line of sandwiches.	A greater variety of products that might pull in new customers	The owner decides to stick to his core business and expand the variety of sandwiches, rather than branch out into calzones.
A community decides whether to repair sidewalks in the downtown shopping area.	The community will not have the money needed to invest in a new fire truck.	Fewer injuries on cracked or broken sidewalks (and perhaps fewer lawsuits); a more attractive downtown; more visitors spending more money at local businesses	The community decides to make the repairs, since the benefits are many and the existing fire trucks can do the job for another few years.

Economic decisions are often complex and can result in waves of decisions radiating outward, involving other people and groups and leading to unexpected consequences. Also, people don't always make decisions that are predictable or even sensible to others.

Rational Agents Someone who is rational uses logic to make decisions that are often very predictable. Economists used to assume that people were always **rational agents** when it came to the economic sphere. In other words, people would make decisions based on common sense and a desire to maximize available resources.

Often, people do make rational decisions. For instance, your family would probably decide to spend the monthly food budget on groceries that will feed the family adequately for the whole month rather than spend that sum on one spectacular restaurant meal that would leave little for food the rest of the month. Grocery store owners, restaurateurs, and product marketers all assume that you will act rationally most of the time instead of routinely making foolish and harmful decisions.

But people do not always make rational choices. Economist Daniel McFadden describes an example of irrational decisions. "You go to your car dealer seeking a model that has a sound system you want. He says it will take 3 days to get that exact model, but you can drive away right now with one that has a better sound system and costs $300 more. Most buyers will choose to pay a little more and take their new car now. However, if the dealer said that no car is available right now, and he can get the model you want in 33 days, but a model costing $300 more with a better sound system in 30 days, most buyers will choose to wait the 33 days and get the exact model they want. This is hyperbolic discounting at work. Rational consumers with consistent intertemporal evaluation should treat the trade '$300 for an attractive but unneeded accessory versus 3 days' the same whether it is executed right now or executed in 30 days."

No matter what your interests are, your economic decisions will be more complex than "X costs more than Y, so I'll buy Y." Manufacturers, retailers, economists, and others are all interested in how you analyze costs and benefits and why you make the decisions you do. Your decisions require you to think about opportunity costs—what you will be giving up to get something.

Explicit and Implicit Opportunity Costs Not all opportunity costs are obvious. **Explicit opportunity costs** are ones that require you to spend money. For instance, if you want to spend a summer at basketball camp, you might have to pay $3,000 for room, board, instruction, and equipment. That explicit opportunity cost is easy to calculate and understand.

An **implicit opportunity cost**, though, is one that an individual or a business gives up in order to use a resource that it already has or is using. Consider the example of basketball camp. What are you giving up if you don't go? You might be able to get a summer job that has full-time hours and that pays $13 per hour. Calculate the opportunity cost associated with that choice.

$13 per hour × 40 hours per week = $520
$520 per week × 8 weeks of summer = $4,160

No matter which decision you make, you have an opportunity cost. To go to basketball camp and improve your athletic skills, you not only must pay the tuition but also must give up the chance to earn money and gain experience in business. Calculate the total economic costs of this decision.

CALCULATING TOTAL OPPORTUNITY COST OF ATTENDING BASKETBALL CAMP			
Explicit Opportunity Costs		**Implicit Opportunity Costs**	
Court time and instruction	$1,200	Salary from full-time summer job	$4,160
Room and board	1,500	Room and board with your family	0
New basketball shoes	300	New shoes	Not needed
Total explicit cost	**$3,000**	**Total implicit cost**	**$4,160**
Total explicit costs + Total implicit costs = $7,160 = TOTAL OPPORTUNITY COST			

Defining and calculating opportunity costs in this way helps you make a rational economic decision. Rational agents consider opportunity costs, both explicit and implicit, when calculating the total economic costs of any decision.

Measuring Utility Economists talk about **utility**, the total enjoyment or satisfaction consumers receive from the goods and services they consume. Utility is difficult to measure accurately. After all, who can say that two people get the same satisfaction from eating an orange? One might love oranges and one might not. And do you get the same satisfaction from the last bite of the orange that you got from the first bite?

Even though utility is challenging to measure, economists and businesses do their best to track it by analyzing consumers' choices. For instance, if a film studio makes a movie about giant space pandas, and that movie makes very little money, then it's unlikely that anyone will make another movie on that topic for quite some time. The movie has a low degree of utility for society.

Total Benefits Utility plays a vital part in calculating benefits to a person or group. For consumers, **total benefits** are the amount of satisfaction people receive from all the goods and services they use. For businesses, total benefits are the revenues (incomes) they earn from the goods and services they provide. Because utility is so subjective and hard to measure, economists use total benefits as a metric, or measurement, of how well a person is doing. For companies, economists use total revenue to determine utility.

In cost-benefit analysis, costs represent the other part of the equation. For individuals, **total costs** are the time, effort, and expense they spend to obtain the goods and services. For businesses, total costs are the time, effort, and expense spent on hiring and training people, buying raw materials, buying or renting space to work in, and many other costs.

Maximizing Total Net Benefits

In doing a cost-benefit analysis, then, how do people and groups find the "sweet spot," where they are getting the most possible satisfaction or profit out of the resources they have available? Many times, they guess about what will work best, or they take the action that someone else recommends. But often it's possible to calculate the **total net benefits**, which are the difference between total benefits and total costs.

Comparing Total Benefits and Total Costs It's not enough to consider all the benefits you might gain by taking a particular course of action. You must also consider all the costs you may have to absorb by taking that same action.

For example, suppose you are thinking of starting a business that makes cardboard boxes. The raw materials are not expensive, and your family and friends agree to work for you part time for a relatively low wage because assembling boxes does not require a high degree of skills. As the business takes off, you calculate how much revenue you are making and how much it costs to generate that revenue.

COMPARING TOTAL BENEFITS AND TOTAL COSTS	
Total Benefits (Dollar Amount from Selling Different Quantities of Boxes)	Total Costs (Dollar Amount from Selling Different Quantities of Boxes)
$0	$400
$98	$401
$450	$425
$800	$500
$1,050	$625
$1,122	$689
$1,200	$800

You might think that the more boxes you produce, the more you benefit. After all, producing more boxes means receiving more money, at least to a point. However, the more boxes you produce, the more labor you have to pay to make them and your costs rise, as well. You will want to produce at the level of **optimal choice**, the level at which you receive the greatest benefit for the least cost.

Calculating Total Net Benefits To find that optimal choice, you determine the total net benefit for various quantities. The total net benefit for each row is found by subtracting your total costs from your total benefits. What patterns do you notice in the table below?

CALCULATING TOTAL NET BENEFITS			
Total Number of Boxes Sold	Total Benefits (Dollar Amount from Selling Different Quantities of Boxes	Total Costs (Dollar Amount from Selling Different Quantities of Boxes)	Total Net Benefit (Total Benefits Minus Total Costs)
0	$0	$400	–$400
1	$98	$401	–$303
5	$450	$425	$25
10	$800	$500	$300
15	$1,050	$625	$425
17	$1,122	$689	$433
20	$1,200	$800	$400

In this example, if you keep your total output too small, your net benefits are quite small. It is even possible that you will actually lose money; that is, you will have negative net benefits. This is something you would prefer to avoid. As the table shows, if you sell zero boxes, you get zero total benefits but you have $400 worth of total costs for a net benefit of negative $400. One might think of this $400 cost as your opportunity cost of not producing the boxes.

At first, as you produce more boxes, your cost per box decreases. Since your total benefits are increasing, your total net benefit increases, as well. But if you make too many boxes—in this case, 20 boxes—then your total net benefit decreases. Maybe that's because you are supervising too many workers, or you are all working too many hours and making mistakes.

Notice the $433 amount in the Total Net Benefit column. This is the point at which your total net benefit is greatest. When total net benefits are maximized, you've found the sweet spot—the optimal choice for a rational agent. In this example, producing 17 boxes is your optimal choice.

Marginal Benefits and Marginal Costs Economists often talk about decisions being made at the margin. In economics, margin has a special meaning; marginal means the change in, the additional amount, the incremental amount. Economists attempt to see if behaviors will change if something changes. or example, if a businesses increases buys just one more advertisement on television, how much will it increase sales? The additional sales are the marginal sales.

The same idea can be used to study all types of behavior, including ones that do not involve buying and selling goods. If a band holds one extra rehersal before a concernt, the improvement in how it performs is the marginal benefit it receives from the extra rehersal.

In the example above, you can calculate how much more your benefits would be if you produced more boxes. This amount is called the **marginal benefit**—the additional benefit you gain from producing each additional unit. This marginal benefit is found or calculated as follows:

Marginal Benefit = Change in total benefits / Change in output

Likewise, you can calculate how much more you would have to spend to produce those additional boxes; economists call this the **marginal cost**. The marginal cost formula is:

Marginal Cost = Change in total cost / Change in output

In many scenarios, you can break down the decision into increments and decide which increment would provide maximum benefit. An increment is the amount by which the quantity of something increases. For example, if you owned the box factory, you could figure the marginal benefits and marginal costs for increments of five boxes or ten boxes. In the chart that follows the increment is one box.

	CALCULATING MARGINAL BENEFITS AND COSTS					
	Number of Boxes Sold	Total Benefits (Sales)	Total Costs	Net Benefit	Marginal Benefit	Marginal Cost
A	15	$1,050	$625	$425	$42	$29
B	16	$1,088	$656	$432	$38	$31
C	17	$1,122	$689	$433	$34	$33
D	18	$1,152	$724	$428	$30	$35
E	19	$1,178	$761	$417	$26	$37
F	20	$1,200	$800	$400	$22	$39
G	21	$1,218	$841	$377	$18	$41

To calculate the marginal benefit for each level of output, look at the difference in total benefits between one quantity and the next. For example, the difference in benefits between producing 15 boxes (row A) and 16 boxes (row B) is $38. This is also the marginal benefit because the change in the quantity between row A and row B is only 1. Using math, the marginal benefits for row B is

Marginal Benefit = (1088 – 1050) / (16 – 15) = 38 / 1 = 38

The difference between the total benefits of producing 16 boxes (row B) and 17 boxes (row C) is $34. The difference between producing 17 boxes (row C) and 18 boxes (row D) is $32. Since the difference in quantity is one for each row, the change in total benefits is equal to the marginal benefits. Check to see the amount of change for the quantity; it might not always be one.

Just calculating marginal benefits, however, does not show you what you pay in exchange for those benefits. To calculate marginal costs, look at the difference in total costs between producing one quantity and the next. Then divide this by the change in the quantity, as shown in this example:

- The difference between the cost of producing 15 boxes (row A) and 16 boxes (row B) is $31 (656 – 625).

- The difference between the total costs of producing 16 (row B) and 17 boxes (row C) is $33 (689 – 656).

- The cost difference between producing 17 boxes (row C) and 18 boxes (row D) is $35 (724 – 689).

When marginal benefits are greater than marginal costs, it would make sense to produce the higher level of output. In other words, it makes sense to increase output. It makes sense because you would be adding more to your benefits than you are adding to your costs, so your total net benefits would be increasing. This is what is happening in rows A, B, and C, or up to and including 17 boxes being produced.

If the marginal costs are more than the marginal benefits, as in rows D and beyond, the rational choice would be to not make those quantities. This would make sense because producing the 18th box means you are adding more to your costs than you are adding to your benefits. Thus, the rational choice would be to stop production just before getting to row D. Thus, the benefit maximizing rule is to continue to produce output as long as the marginal benefits are greater than or equal to the marginal costs. In a formula format:

$$MB > MC \quad \textit{increase output}$$
$$MB = MC \quad \textit{optimal level of output}$$
$$MB < MC \quad \textit{reduce output}$$

ANSWER THE TOPIC ESSENTIAL QUESTION

1. In one to three paragraphs, explain how people and groups (such as companies or governments) evaluate costs and benefits to make rational economic decisions.

KEY TERMS

opportunity cost	total benefit
cost-benefit analysis	total cost
rational agent	total net benefit
explicit opportunity cost	marginal benefit
implicit opportunity cost	marginal cost
utility	

MULTIPLE-CHOICE QUESTIONS

1. Which of these is an example of a cost-benefit analysis?

   (A) A town fixes more potholes this fiscal year than in previous fiscal years.

   (B) Three friends make plans to start a business together.

   (C) A company evaluates how hiring new workers will affect profits.

   (D) A city decides to create a public park and plant many types of trees.

   (E) A family wants to move to a larger apartment soon.

2. Your mother agrees to pay you $20 to clean out and organize her closet. If you hadn't struck this bargain, you would have spent the time watching a movie on a streaming service that your mother pays for. The time spent watching the movie is an example of a(n)

   (A) explicit opportunity cost

   (B) implicit opportunity cost

   (C) total benefit

   (D) total cost

   (E) net benefit

3. Your neighbor offers you $12 to rake the leaves in her yard, a task that will take an hour. To take this job, you'll need to give up the chance to deliver groceries to a different neighbor, a job that would have paid you $10 for that same hour. What is the implicit opportunity cost of raking leaves?

(A) $22

(B) $12

(C) $10

(D) $2

(E) A deficit of $2

FREE-RESPONSE QUESTION

1. Your uncle hires you to babysit your cousins. You're happy with the hourly wage he's providing, but it costs you $3.75 each way to take the bus to their house. Your uncle works a split shift, so on days when you babysit for a longer period, he expects you to make two round trips on the bus, taking care of your cousins for a couple of hours in the morning and a couple of hours in the evening.

CALCULATING NET BENEFITS FOR BABYSITTING WORK			
Hours Spent Babysitting	Benefits	Costs	Net Benefit
1.0	$10.00	$7.50	$2.50
2.5	$25.00	$7.50	$17.50
4.0	$40.00	$7.50	$32.50
4.5	$45.00	$15.00	$30.00

(a) Based on the information in this table, which of these four options is optimum for a rational agent? Specify the number of hours of babysitting, and explain your answer.

(b) Use the information in this table to suggest how to negotiate a higher hourly rate from your uncle for the one-hour babysitting jobs. In your explanation, use the words *cost* and *benefit*.

(c) What opportunity cost is missing from this table?

(d) Is the missing opportunity cost explicit or implicit? Why is the missing opportunity cost important to calculate total net benefits? Explain.

(e) Why is it important to calculate total net benefits when deciding how to spend your time?

Economists use calculations to explain and identify economic concepts. In doing so, they present the data, make the calculations, and explain how those calculations demonstrate the concept.

In making production decisions, producers compare total costs and total benefits to find the production point that maximizes their benefits. Suppose a company is considering how large a garage to build in the downtown area of a city. Examine the projections of costs and revenues that the planners develop, as shown in the table.

Number of Parking Spaces	Projected Costs	Projected Revenues
100	$1.2 million	$1.070 million
150	$1.4 million	$1.440 million
200	$1.6 million	$1.850 million
250	$2.0 million	$2.135 million
300	$2.5 million	$2.470 million

Apply the Skill

Calculate the total net benefits for each projected size for the garage. Then determine the size that the company should choose and explain why.

Marginal Analysis and Consumer Choice

"Everything is worth what its purchaser will pay for it."

—Publilius Syrus (1st Century BC), Latin Writer

Essential Question: How do rational consumers make choices?

Just as producers makes choices about costs, benefits, and trade-offs, consumer also make choices based on the constraints they face. For example, suppose you're hungry, and you know you want to spend some of your money on lunch at a Midle Eastern restaurant known for its falafels. But how many falafels should you order to give yourself the maximum satisfaction for the money you're spending? You might think the answer is "As many as possible," but that's often incorrect.

In this topic, you'll find out how consumers make rational choices by considering each purchase unit by unit. Businesses, marketers, and government agencies study these economic patterns to help them figure out how to use their resources wisely and even to anticipate what consumers will do. And understanding this behavior can help you use your resources wisely as well.

Rational Consumer Choice Theory

Suppose you live in a neighborhood that includes factories. Who decides what and how much those factories will produce? If you live in a predominantly command economy (discussed in Topic 1.2), then a central planning committee makes those decisions. However, if you live in a predominantly market economy—as most people do today—consumers decide what and how much gets produced. They do this indirectly, by "voting" with their money.

For instance, if consumers decide that purple-sequined throw pillows are essential for every home, then factory owners will make sufficient numbers of pillows to meet demand and maximize their profits, even if those same factory owners think purple sequins are hideous. When consumers move on to something else and stop buying the pillows, then manufacturers will choose to decrease production of that item if they want to stay in business. They'll start looking for new items that will capture consumers' attention and their money.

Whoever can figure out why consumers act the way they do will be rich and influential, right? That's why economists have created what they call consumer choice theory. It's a series of principles that tries to explain why people buy some goods and services, refuse to buy other goods and services, or stop buying the goods and services that they used to. Consumer choice theory has three aspects.

1. Consumers are Rational. Economists assume that most people base their purchases on a calculation about what will make them happiest. You learned about utility in Topic 1.5, and an essential part of consumer choice theory is that consumers try to maximize the utility they get from goods and services. As a rational consumer, you make the optimal choice possible given the constraints you face.

However, "rational" doesn't always mean "wise." For example, Reed Hastings, the CEO of the streaming service Netflix, boasted, "We're competing with sleep" for consumers' attention. Your family members, teachers, or boss might wish you got more sleep. But you might make the calculation that watching the last episode of your favorite show will bring you more satisfaction than an extra hour of sleep would.

2. Consumers Are Never 100 Percent Satisfied. Go back to the example of the falafel restaurant that was introduced earlier in this topic. You might be hungry and decide that eating falafels will make you happy. And you might even have enough money to eat your fill of falafels—so many that you may not want any more. But you probably will still want to consume something else.

3. Consumer Satisfaction Decreases with Each Unit of Consumption Continuing with the falafel example, your first falafel will be the most satisfying to you because you are most hungry. You might eagerly buy and eat another, but it won't satisfy quite as much as the first. The third won't satisfy as much as the second, and so on, until you run out of money, time, or stomach space.

Diminishing Marginal Utility

The third aspect of consumer choice theory is the concept of **diminishing marginal utility**. To understand this term, break it down into its parts.

- *Diminishing* means "getting smaller."
- *Marginal* means "one additional unit."
- *Utility* means "usefulness or satisfaction."

So, diminishing marginal utility means that each additional unit of consumption provides less usefulness to a consumer than the previous unit. Consumers experience diminishing marginal utility as they consume goods and services.

Calculating Diminishing Marginal Utility Diminishing marginal utility combines all three parts of consumer choice theory. You can use a graph such as the following to calculate diminishing marginal utility.

MARGINAL ANALYSIS OF FELAFEL CONSUMER

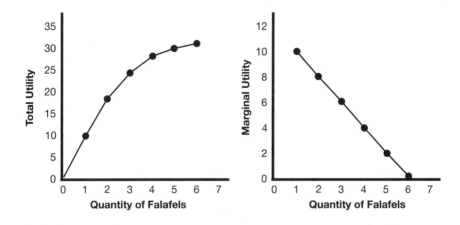

Notice that your first falafel purchase generates tremendous utility—the highest this scale can measure. You're a rational consumer, so you've consumed something that gives you pleasure. And just as you'd expect, that utility decreases with each additional unit of consumption. By the time you reach the seventh and eighth falafels, you experience no utility. Therefore, it makes no sense for you to order them at any price.

How could a restaurant owner persuade you to order more falafels? He or she could lower the price you pay for them.

Marginal Utility Versus Marginal Benefit **Marginal utility** refers to the additional amount of usefulness that someone gets from one extra unit of a good or service. The graph above shows satisfaction levels, which are difficult to calculate accurately.

However, dollars and cents are easy to calculate to the last fraction of a penny. That's why economists use the term **marginal benefit**, which is the amount of additional satisfaction or fulfillment that the consumer receives from consuming one more unit of that good.

One way to place a value on the amount of additional benefit is the price a consumer is willing and able to pay for the extra unit of the good consumed. For example, suppose one falafel at your favorite restaurant costs a dollar. You might eagerly pay that for the first falafel and the next few. But after you've eaten a few, you might decide that you wouldn't get a dollar's worth of enjoyment from another one. In that case, your marginal benefit would be too low to justify the marginal cost to you.

Understanding Marginal Analysis Economists use **marginal analysis** to figure out the balance between marginal benefits and marginal costs. You read about these terms in Topic 1.5, but now, look at these terms from a consumer's point of view, not a producer's. A rational consumer's decision making involves weighing the cost of each unit against the benefit each unit provides.

Understanding Marginal Costs and Marginal Benefits Suppose the falafel restaurant you visit has a pricing structure that rewards larger purchases:

- If you order just one falafel, the price is one dollar.
- If you order a plate of four, the total price is $3.50 total, or about $0.88 each.
- If you buy a party platter of ten, you'll pay $8, or $0.80 each.

The graph shows that you derive no satisfaction by the time you eat the seventh falafel. So why would you buy ten? You might want to save some for later or share them with friends. You compare the decrease in the **marginal cost** (the amount you spend per unit) with the marginal benefit (the satisfaction or usefulness per unit) and make a rational decision based on those factors.

The marginal benefit depends on how much you want another falafel. You might decide that 80 cents per falafel is well worth the money. Alternatively, you might spend that money on something else, or you might save your money for another time. Business owners notice how much you and other consumers spend, and they use that information to help set prices.

Distinguishing Between Marginal and Total You should now know that marginal, to an economist, means additional or change in. Recall that marginal benefit (cost) is defined as the additional benefit received (cost incurred) when one more unit of a good is consumed. The formulas, where Δ means "change in," for these would be:

$$Marginal\ Benefit = \Delta\ benefits\ /\ \Delta\ units\ consumed$$
$$Marginal\ Cost = \Delta\ costs\ /\ \Delta\ units\ consumed$$

However, consumers generally do not think of buying a third unit. They are more likely to think of and talk about buying three units. Consumers are more interested in the total number of units consumed. So, now the problem is how to get from marginal to total, but this can be achieved quite simply. To calculate the total benefits of consuming a good, simply add the marginal benefits of consuming the number of units of the good consumed. In the formulas, Σ means "summation":

$$Total\ Benefit = \Sigma\ marginal\ benefit$$
$$Total\ Cost = \Sigma\ marginal\ cost$$

In summary, using the marginal analysis of marginal benefits and marginal costs shows how many units should be consumed, but the total benefits shows how much the consumer values those benefits.

Calculating Marginal Costs and Marginal Benefits Returning to the falafel example, the table below shows the number of falafels a consumer would purchase and the amount of benefits she would receive.

MARGINAL ANALYSIS OF FALAFEL CONSUMER		
Quantity of Falafels Consumed	Total Utility	Marginal Utility
1	10	10
2	18	8
3	24	6
4	28	4
5	30	2
6	31	1

The consumer earns 10 units of utility when she purchases the first falafel. Since she received zero utility from falafels when she did not purchase any falafels, her marginal utility of the first falafel consumed is 10. Adding 10 to the zero utility when she did not purchase a falafel yields a total utility of 10. For this first unit of the good purchased, the total utility and marginal utility are the same. When the consumer purchases the second falafel, total utility goes up to 18, so the additional, or marginal utility, is 8.

As you go down the table, notice that as the number of falafels purchased increases, the total utility is also increasing—even though the marginal utility is declining. This will always be the case as long as marginal utility is positive.

One way to value the benefits of consuming a good by considering how much the consumer is willing to pay in order to get the benefits received from consuming the good. In this case, the consumer would be willing to pay as much as $10 to buy the first falafel because she gets 10 units of utility from the first unit of the good purchased. She would be willing to pay an additional $8 to get the second falafel, since the marginal utility of the second falafel is 8. The final row of the table illustrates that the consumer would be willing to pay up to $1 to purchase the sixth falafel.

To determine the marginal costs of the falafels, assume that each falafel costs $2. Thus, the marginal cost of each falafel is 2. Knowing this, how many falafels would the consumer purchase? At a price of $2 per falafel, the consumer would purchase five falafels. Why? Would it be to the consumer's advantage to purchase the first one? Most definitely, because she would be gaining $10 worth of benefits and have to pay only $2. Getting $10 worth of additional benefits is greater than the $2 marginal cost of the falafel. What a deal!

Would the consumer purchase a second falafel? Yes. The $8 of additional benefits from the second falafel is greater than the $2 marginal cost of the second falafel.

How many falafels would the consumer buy at $2 each? As long as the marginal benefits of purchasing the next falafel is greater than its marginal cost of $2, it makes sense to buy the falafel. The consumer will continue to purchase falafels until MB equals MC. Since the marginal utility of the fifth falafel is $2, in the example here, the consumer buys five falafels, where MB = MC. This is the **optimal quantity**. At this point the consumer gets a large amount of total utility (30). Since the sixth falafel generates only $1 worth of marginal benefits, the consumer would not buy the sixth unit. Why spend $2 to get only $1 worth of benefits?

In summary, the consumer achieves the optimal quantity by purchasing the amount of output where marginal benefits equal marginal costs.

- As long as marginal benefit is greater than marginal costs, it makes sense for the consumer to buy the next unit of the good.
- When the marginal benefit is less than the marginal cost, the consumer should not purchase the next unit of the good.

Why Economists Calculate on the Margins Economists say that people make choices at the margins. In other words, whenever possible, they consider the cost of one more unit of a good or service rather than the entire cost of the service. They don't think about the **sunk costs,** which means what they have spent in the past on that good or service. In everyday speech, people sometimes use the word *marginal* to mean "unlikely to succeed," but to an economist, on the margin is exactly where informed consumers are.

For example, imagine you have watched all but the last ten minutes of a movie when you have to leave for work. When you get off work, should you watch the last ten minutes? If you are a rational consumer, you will consider the part of the movie you have seen as a sunk cost. Whether you have invested two minutes or two hours of your time in watching the first part is not relevant. Whether you enjoyed it or not is not relevant. Previous time and enjoyment will not affect your decision about whether to spend another ten minutes on the movie. You will focus on the marginal costs and benefits of the decisions, not on what you have already spent.

The Utility Maximization Rule

Most of this topic has considered how much of one good or service that a consumer would want to purchase. Most people want to consume lots of goods and services most of the time. Also, most people are rational consumers who have a good idea of how much utility they would get out of each unit of each purchase.

How can economists quantify consumers' behavior in choosing varying amounts of different products and trying to get the most they can out of the limited money they have to spend? Economists do this with the **utility maximization rule**. In other words, they weigh the marginal utility per dollar spent of each unit of each product for each consumer.

Applying the Rule The utility maximization rule is easier to understand if you consider it as a formula.

$$MUx / Px = MUy / Py$$

In the formula, MUx means "the marginal utility of product X," and Px means "the price of product X." The same goes for product Y. When the two sides of this formula are equal, then you've reached the best possible combination. In most cases, more resources mean more utility. So if you have more money to spend, then you're likely to receive more benefits and be more satisfied with your purchases.

Revisiting the falafel example again, the falafel buyer would like to have something to drink, too. So, with sparkling water added to the menu, how can one determine how much of each product she would purchase? The answer to this question depends on how much money the consumer has to spend on the two goods. Economists refer to this as a **budget constraint,** which means that the consumer has only so many dollars to spend. In the example, assume that the consumer spends all available income, and spends it only two goods.

Below is a table showing the same information as above, but with some additional columns and information. A second product, sparkling water, has been added, and its total and marginal utilities are shown. The price in this example is $1 for each unit of sparkling water. There is also a column for MU/P for each good; this is where the utility maximization rule comes into play.

MARGINAL ANALYSIS OF FALAFEL/SPARKLING WATER							
Quantity – Number of Falafels Consumed	Total Utility of Falafel	Marginal Utility of Falafel	MU of Falafel Divided by Price ($2)	Quantity – Number of Units of Sparkling Waters Consumed	Total Utility of Sparkling Water	Marginal Utility of Sparkling Water	MU of Sparkling Water Divided by Price ($1)
1	10	10	5	1	6	6	6
2	18	8	4	2	11	5	5
3	24	6	3	3	15	4	4
4	28	4	2	4	18	3	3
5	30	2	1	5	20	2	2
6	31	1	0.5	6	21	1	1

So how does the consumer spend all of her income on falafels and sparkling water in order to get the most utility she can? Applying the utility maximization rule answers this question. Recall this rule states that

$$MU_x / P_x = MU_y / P_y$$

Note that the ratios of MU to Price is the key information, not just the MU nor just the price. Also note that in several places these two ratios are equal, so it is necessary to find the one where all the income, in this case $10, is spent.

Where would this consumer get the most utility? The best place to spend the first dollar is where the MU/P is highest. This is where $MU_w/P_w = 6$. This says the first purchase should be the first unit of sparkling water which will cost $1. What is the next purchase made with the remaining $9? The next highest MU/P ratio is 5, which is for each good. So she would buy another unit of sparkling water for $1 and also the first falafel which costs $2. Now she has spent a total of $4 and purchased 2 units of sparking water and 1 falafel.

She still has $6 left to spend so what should she purchase next? The next highest value for MU/P is four for each good. With the remaining $6, she can purchase one more of each good. This gives her 3 units of sparkling water and 2 falafels, and she has spent $7.

Following the same procedure as above, she could buy one more of each product, giving her 4 units of sparkling water and 3 falafels purchased. This exhausts her income of $10. Notice that this also results in a combination of falafels and sparkling water where the $MP_f / P_f = 6/2 = 3$ and $MP_w / P_w = 3/1 = 3$. With this combination of 4 units of sparkling water and 3 falafels, the total utility is 42, as shown below:

18 (total utility of 4 sparkling waters) + 24 (total utility of 3 falafels) = 42

Other Options Could the combination of falafels and sparkling water be changed so that a total utility value greater than 42 is achieved? Suppose the customer bought more falafels. Because of the fixed income of $10, buying more falafels means buying fewer units of sparkling water. If she buys one more falafel at $2, she could only buy 2 units of sparkling water. Buying 4 falafels instead of 3 increases utility by 4, but since she bought fewer units of sparkling water, she loses 9 units of utility (4 + 5). This is a net loss of 4 units of utility. Adding the total utility of 4 falafels and 2 units of sparkling water (28 + 11) yields the customer 39 units of utility, which is exactly 3 less than the 42 units of utility found earlier.

If she purchased more sparkling water and less falafel, she would buy 6 units ofwaters but only 2 falafels, and her total utility would be 39 (18 + 21), which is less than the 42 achieved earlier. This is how the utility maximizing rule works.

ANSWER THE TOPIC ESSENTIAL QUESTION

1. In one to three paragraphs, explain how rational consumers make choices.

KEY TERMS		
consumer choice theory	marginal benefit	optimal quantity
diminishing marginal utility	marginal analysis	utility maximization rule
marginal utility	marginal cost	

1. Your little brother is building a thriving business by buying gum at a discount and then selling individual pieces at a substantial markup to his classmates during recess. What can you predict about his clients' satisfaction rates as they consume more gum?

   (A) They will increase over time.

   (B) They will increase, then decrease, then stabilize.

   (C) They will remain stable over time.

   (D) They will decrease over time.

   (E) They will stabilize but eventually increase.

2. Alana buys and eats one burrito from the Burrito Shack and derives 10 units of utility from the consumption of the burrito. After finishing, she finds that she is still pretty hungry. We would expect that if Alana buys and consumes a second burrito that most likely her total utility would _____ and her marginal utility would be _____ .

   (A) increase; negative

   (B) increase; positive

   (C) decrease; negative

   (D) decrease; positive

   (E) not change; zero

3. For a consumer to get the optimal quantity of a good or service, they should keep consuming until

   (A) total cost < marginal cost

   (B) total cost = marginal cost

   (C) marginal benefit < marginal cost

   (D) marginal benefit = marginal cost

   (E) marginal benefit > marginal cost

FREE-RESPONSE QUESTION

1. You're spending the day at a winter carnival. You've always wanted to learn to ice skate, so you want to take at least a couple of skating lessons. But it's cold out, so you also want to order hot chocolate to warm yourself up. This table shows the marginal utility of each of the products you could buy. Your total budget for the day is $81 from your wages made from a part-time job. Assume that the price of each unit of skating lessons is $25 and each hot chocolate has a price of $3.

MARGINAL UTILITY AND PRICE OF TWO PRODUCTS		
Number of Units	Marginal Utility of Skating Lessons	Marginal Utility of Hot Chocolate
1	100	15
2	75	6
3	50	3
4	25	2

(a) Which item would you consume first, a skating lesson or a hot chocolate? Explain.

(b) How much of each would you buy if you had a budget of $81 to maximize your utility?

(c) Based on the table above, why might you choose to buy more than one skating lesson even though the price is much higher than the hot chocolate?

(d) Notice that as you buy more skating lessons and more hot chocolate, you gain less satisfaction with each purchase. What term would an economist use to describe this?

(e) Assume you are asked to advise the manager of the snack bar at the skating rink. What would you, a student studying economics, advise the manager to do to increase the number of hot chocolates they sell?

THINK AS AN ECONOMIST: *INTERPRET AN ECONOMIC OUTCOME USING CALCULATIONS*

Economists constantly think "on the margin." This means that rational economic agents are constantly weighing the next best option, weighing if consuming one more item is worth it, or deciding how to use the next 15-minute block of time. Many people do not actively think this way but that process is occurring nonetheless. You may think that, "I am going to spend 2 hours tonight studying for my test." However, every so often, you may consider, "should I keep studying?" This thought process is more marginal than the first thought. While you planned to study for 2 hours, you might decide after 30 minutes that spending the next 15 minutes might not be as beneficial as you originally planned due to being tired, needing food, or the feeling you have already mastered the material. While your plan was to spend 2 hours, rational cost-benefit analysis about your *marginal* time is a better way to make decisions.

Apply the Skill

Consumers are constantly considering how to maximize the utility of their scarce budget or time. So, if you are considering how many carrots and celery stalks to buy at the store to make a healthy snack. If we assume that you like both carrots and celery and have a limited budget of $3 set aside to buy both carrots and celery, use the table below to help figure out what combination of carrots and celery would maximize the utility of your budget. Assume that the price of each carrot is $.50 and the price of each celery stalk is $0.75. Also, explain how marginal thinking plays a role in your decisions.

Number of Carrots	Marginal Utility of Carrots	Number of Celery Stalks	Marginal Utility of Celery Stalks
1	10	1	12
2	8	2	9
3	6	3	6
4	4	4	5
5	2	5	3
6	1	6	1

1. Assume Alyssa owns a factory that makes toys for kids. The factory makes both small toys and big toys. Below is a table showing the production possibilities for her factory.

Small Toys	Large Toys
100	0
80	1
60	2
40	3
20	4
0	5

(a) Draw a correctly labeled diagram of Alyssa's factory with large toys on the x-axis and small toys on the y-axis.

(b) Define opportunity cost.

(c) Alyssa's factory is currently producing 1 large toy and 80 small toys. If the factory wants to produce 2 large toys instead, what is the opportunity cost of this decision? Show your work.

(d) What type of opportunity cost does this production possibilities curve represent? Explain using numbers.

(e) Describe the production level of 1 large toy and 40 small toys.

(f) Describe the production level of 3 large toys and 40 small toys.

(g) A trade agreement is reached between the home country of Alyssa's factory and a neighboring country that makes trade easier. Will the trade agreement increase, decrease, or not change Alyssa's production possibilities? Explain.

(h) Assume that Alyssa decides to build a second factory that, based on consumer demand, only make only large toys. Show on your graph in part (a) the effect of this second factory has on the production possibilities curve.

UNIT 2

Supply and Demand

During the 2020 COVID-19 pandemic, the demand for disinfectant sprays and wipes spiked. Even when plants were operating at full capacity, they struggled to keep up with the increased demand. And when products reappeared on the shelves, supplies were limited and, as a result, prices were higher than before the pandemic.

Supply and demand are the two words that you will see most often as you study economics. They provide the means for understanding how markets work, determining the quantity of goods produced, and the prices at which they will sell. In competitive markets, consumers and producers interact to allocate scarce resources and determine market prices.

Events such as natural disasters, pandemics, and wars all affect supply and demand. So do government policies. The COVID-19 pandemic revealed flaws in the supply chain. At the outbreak, most personal protective equipment (PPE), such as masks, gloves, and gowns, was imported from China and other Asian nations. The virus kept many factory workers from their jobs, and the demand at home meant there was less PPE available for export at the same time that global demand surged.

The pandemic brought home to many world leaders the need to reduce reliance on foreign sources, not only of PPE, but also of other essential supplies such as vaccines, prescription drugs, and diagnostics. In April 2020, President Trump invoked the Defense Production Act to make up for shortages of PPE and ventilators. Under this act, the Department of Homeland Security uses its authority to see that companies producing essential equipment get the supplies they need to meet the demand.

"Just the one, thanks."

Topic Titles and Essential Knowledge

Topic 2.1 Demand

- A well-defined system of property rights is necessary for the market system to function well.
- Economic agents respond to incentives.
- Individuals often respond to incentives, such as those presented by prices, but also face constraints, such as income, time, and legal and regulatory frameworks.
- The law of demand suggests that a change in the own-price causes a change in quantity demanded in the opposite direction and a movement along a demand (marginal benefit) curve.
- The conceptual relationship between price and quantity stated by the law of demand leads to downward-sloping demand curves explained by the income effect and substitution effect and/or by diminishing marginal utility.
- The market demand curve (schedule) is derived from the summation of individual demand curves (schedules).
- Changes in the determinants of consumer demand can cause the demand curve to shift.

Topic 2.2 Supply

- A change in own-price causes a change in quantity supplied in the same direction and a movement along a supply curve.
- The market supply curve (schedule) is derived from the summation of individual supply curves (schedules). The market supply curve is upward-sloping.
- Changes in the determinants of supply can cause the supply curve to shift.

Topic 2.3 Price Elasticity of Demand

- Economists use the concept of elasticity to measure the magnitude of percentage changes in quantity owing to any given changes in the own-price, income, and prices of related goods.
- Price elasticity of demand is measured by the percentage change in quantity demanded divided by the percentage change in price or the responsiveness of the quantity demanded to changes in price. Elasticity varies along a linear demand curve, meaning slope is not elasticity.
- Ranges of values of elasticity of demand are described as elastic or inelastic with the separating benchmark being a magnitude of 1, where the change in the price and the change in the quantity demanded are proportional.

  a. When the magnitude of the value of elasticity is greater than 1, the demand is described as being elastic with respect to that price in the range of the given change.

  b. When the magnitude of the value of elasticity is less than 1, the demand is described as being inelastic with respect to that price in the range of the given change.

  c. When the magnitude of the value of elasticity is equal to 1, the demand is described as being unit elastic with respect to that price in the range of the given change.

- The price elasticity of demand depends on certain factors such as the availability of substitutes.
- The impact of a given price change on total revenue or total expenditure will depend on whether demand is elastic, inelastic, or unit elastic.

Topic 2.4 Price Elasticity of Supply

- Price elasticity of supply is measured by the percentage change in quantity supplied divided by the percentage change in price, or the responsiveness of the quantity supplied to changes in price.
- Ranges of values of elasticity of supply are described as elastic or inelastic with the separating benchmark being a magnitude of 1, where the change in the price and the change in the quantity supplied are proportional.
  a. When the magnitude of the value of elasticity is greater than 1, the supply is described as being elastic with respect to that price in the range of the given change.
  b. When the magnitude of the value of elasticity is less than 1, the supply is described as being inelastic with respect to that price in the range of the given change.
  c. When the magnitude of the value of elasticity is equal to 1, the supply is described as being unit elastic with respect to that price in the range of the given change.
- The price elasticity of supply depends on certain factors such as the price of alternative inputs.

Topic 2.5 Other Elasticities

- Elasticity can be measured for any determinant of demand or supply, not just the price.
- Income elasticity of demand is measured by the percentage change in the quantity demanded divided by the percentage change in consumers' income. Economists use the income elasticity of demand to determine whether a good is normal or inferior.
- Cross-price elasticity of demand is measured by the percentage change in the quantity demanded of one good divided by the percentage change in the price of another good. Economists use the cross-price elasticity of demand to determine whether goods are substitutes, complements, or not related.

Topic 2.6 Market Equilibrium and Consumer and Producer Surplus

- The supply-demand model is a tool for understanding what factors influence prices and quantities and why prices and quantities might differ across markets or change over time.
- In a perfectly competitive market, equilibrium is achieved (and markets clear with no shortages or surpluses) when the price of a good or service brings the quantity supplied and quantity demanded into balance, in the sense that buyers wish to purchase the same quantity that sellers wish to provide.
- Equilibrium price provides information to economic decision-makers to guide resource allocation.

- Economists use consumer surplus and producer surplus to measure the benefits markets create to buyers and sellers and understand market efficiency.
- Market equilibrium maximizes total economic surplus in the absence of market failures, meaning that perfectly competitive markets are efficient.

Topic 2.7 Market Disequilibrium and Changes in Equilibrium

- Whenever markets experience imbalances— creating disequilibrium prices and quantities, surpluses, and shortages—market forces drive price and quantity toward equilibrium.
- Factors that shift the market demand and market supply curves cause price, quantity, consumer surplus, producer surplus, and total economic surplus (within that market) to change. The impact of the change depends on the price elasticities of demand and supply

Topic 2.8 The Effects of Government Intervention in Markets

- Some government policies, such as price floors, price ceilings, and other forms of price and quantity regulation, affect incentives and outcomes in all market structures.
- Governments use taxes and subsidies to change incentives in ways that influence consumer and producer behavior, shifting the supply and demand curves accordingly.
- Taxes and subsidies affect government revenues or costs.
- Government intervention in a market producing the efficient quantity through taxes, subsidies, price controls, or quantity controls can only decrease allocative efficiency.
- Deadweight loss represents the losses to buyers and sellers as a result of government intervention in an efficient market.
- The incidence of taxes and subsidies imposed on goods traded in perfectly competitive markets depends on the elasticity of supply and demand.

Topic 2.9 International Trade and Public Policy

- Equilibria in competitive markets may be altered by the decision to open an economy to trade with other countries; equilibrium price can be higher or lower than under autarky, and the gap between domestic supply and demand is filled by trade. Opening an economy to trade with other countries affects consumer surplus, producer surplus, and total economic surplus.
- Tariffs, which governments sometimes use to influence international trade, affect domestic price, quantity, government revenue, and consumer surplus and total economic surplus.
- Quotas can be used to alter quantities produced and therefore affect price, consumer surplus, and total economic surplus.

Source: *AP® Microeconomics Course and Exam Description.* Effective Fall 2020 (College Board).

Topic 2.1

Demand

"The real bosses are the consumers. They, by their abstention from buying . . . determine what should be produced and in what quantity and quality."

Austrian economist Ludwig von Mises (1881–1973)

Essential Question: How are consumer decisions affected by the law of demand and by incentives and constraints?

It's Black Friday, the day after Thanksgiving, which marks the beginning of the holiday shopping season. You're in a store and have been standing in line since the early morning hours, hoping to be among the first to buy a brand-new gaming console, something you pined for all year but couldn't afford. Now that Black Friday is here, you feel that the sale price is simply too good to pass up.

Retailers have been planning their Black Friday sales for months. They know that markdowns are a good economic incentive to draw customers into their store. An **economic incentive** is what motivates people to participate in economic activities, such as buying or selling a product. However, even if you hope to take advantage of the sale, you still face **economic constraints**, or limits. You still might not have enough money. Other economic constraints include laws and regulations. While anyone can buy a gaming console, the sale of some products is restricted to people over a certain age.

Market Systems and Property Rights

Buyers and sellers are part of a **market system**, which is a system for distributing goods and services according to what consumers choose to purchase and producers choose to supply. Within a market system, **economic agents** are people, organizations, and companies that affect the economy by producing, buying, or selling goods or services.

To function well, a market system needs clearly defined **property rights**. The owner of a store, for example, has a contract with a shopping mall to ensure that she can continue to rent space in the mall. Similarly, the owner of a car has a title that shows ownership. Copyright laws make sure that writers and other creative people have clear ownership of their works. Most of the time, people respect these rights because they understand their value and people agree with how to apply them. However, when people ignore them or disagree over how they apply, the government intervenes. Government enforcement of property rights enables people to make economic decisions with confidence that their actions will be protected.

Demand for all sorts of products increases during the holiday season as people flock to stores to find gifts for family and friends.

The Law of Demand

The shoppers standing in line are acting on the basis of their demand. **Demand** is the desire to buy a particular good or service at a specified price and time, accompanied by the ability and willingness to pay.

A want or desire is not the same as a demand for a good or service. Although you may desire a product, for it to become a demand, you have to have the money and willingness to purchase the product at a specific price. Suppose, for example, that a retailer is selling athletic shoes for $100. You say to yourself, "I'd like to own those shoes, but I don't have the money to buy them." You have just expressed a wish or desire. But if you have the money and are willing to spend it on the shoes, you have a demand. **Consumer decision-making** occurs when consumers look at a product or service and decide whether they want it and have the means to purchase it.

A key factor influencing consumers' decisions is the **law of demand**. According to the law, a consumer will purchase more of a product at a lower price and less at a higher price. Economists sometimes refer to the price of the product as the **own-price**. (You will learn more about own-price in Topic 2.3.) Suppose, for example, a merchant is selling paper towels for $2.00 a roll. During a sale, the price of a roll is reduced to $1.50. The law of demand holds that you are more likely to buy more rolls of paper towels at the lower price. The **quantity demanded** is the amount of a product that a person is ready and willing to buy. In general, as the price goes down, the quantity demanded goes up. As the price rises, the quantity demanded goes down.

Lower prices lead to a greater quantity demanded for several reasons:

- more people have the means to purchase the product
- people buy more of the product
- people substitute the product for other products that are more expensive

The reverse happens as prices go up. Fewer people can afford the product, they buy lower quantities, and they buy less expensive substitute products.

Demand Schedules and Demand Curves

The law of demand predicts the behavior of individual consumers, but it also predicts the behavior of an entire market. **Market demand** is the total amount of a product or service that all consumers are willing and able to buy at specific prices in the marketplace. To understand the market demand for a particular good or service, economists create visual tools called demand schedules and demand curves.

Demand Schedules The total amount of a good or service that consumers demand at various price levels can be shown in a chart, which is called a **demand schedule**. Retailers can create demand schedules to figure out how many units of a particular product shoppers will want based on the price of that product. Businesses can also use demand schedules to maximize sales.

A change in the number of goods sold because of their price is known as a **change in quantity demanded**. In the following demand schedule, you can see that as the price of a bottle of fruit juice increases, consumers demand fewer bottles per day. The quantity demanded at $0.50 per bottle is 500 bottles a day. If the price rises to $2.00, the quantity demanded falls to 240 bottles a day. A change in quantity demanded has occurred.

MARKET DEMAND SCHEDULE	
Price of a Bottle of Fruit Juice	Number of Bottles Demanded per Day
$0.25	890
$0.50	500
$0.75	480
$1.00	470
$1.25	410
$1.50	350
$1.75	280
$2.00	240
$2.25	200
$2.50	150
$2.75	100

Demand Curves Another way to illustrate how price and quantity are related is to create a **demand curve**, which is a line graph that shows the quantity of a product demanded at each price. The vertical axis shows the price per unit, and the horizontal axis shows the quantity, or the number of units, demanded.

MARKET DEMAND CURVE

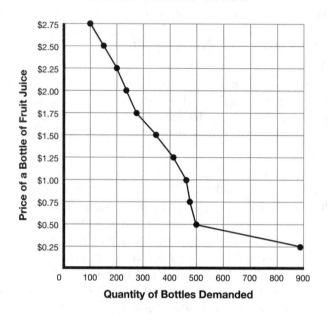

The downward sloping curve represents changes in quantity demanded. As the price of each bottle of fruit juice becomes less expensive, the quantity demanded increases. The more expensive the fruit juice, the lower the quantity demanded. You can see these changes in quantity demanded by tracing your finger along the demand curve. As the price increases, the demand curve slopes downward, showing the gradual decrease in the quantity demanded.

Merchants use the law of demand to make decisions about their businesses. When they want to clear out their inventory to make room for new goods, for example, they will lower prices. The owner of a discount clothing store knows there's no profit in selling a pair of designer jeans for $100 if you and your friends refuse to pay such a high price. But if the store owner drops the amount to $40, the quantity demanded for the jeans increases.

Price and Quantity Demanded

As you can see from the demand schedule above, price is the factor that explains the quantity demanded for a product or service. Price impacts quantity demanded for three reasons: diminishing marginal utility, the substitution effect, and the income effect.

Diminishing Marginal Utility The amount of satisfaction or usefulness (or utility) a consumer gets from buying each additional (or marginal) product or service is the good's **marginal utility**. This concept explains how many economic decisions are made. Is the marginal utility greater than the cost?

Suppose that eating one hamburger satisfies your lunchtime craving. If you eat a second burger, it's not as satisfying as the first one. If you eat a third hamburger, satisfaction is even less—it might even be dissatisfaction.

In economic terms, each additional hamburger provides less satisfaction, or utility, than the preceding one. Economists call this phenomenon **diminishing marginal utility**, the decline of quantity demanded as people consume more of a product or service.

You can apply the concept of diminishing marginal utility to nearly any good or service. One backpack might be very useful, and two might be desirable (maybe one large one and one small one). But would you buy three, four, or five backpacks, especially since you're using money that you could use to buy other products or services? Yes, you might decide to buy a third one—but only at a much lower price. You, the consumer, are making choices, and the law of diminishing marginal utility helps you understand those choices.

Substitution Effect As the price of a product increases, people will often substitute other, less expensive goods in its place. This phenomenon is known as the **substitution effect**. If the price of orange juice increases, for example, people might purchase less of it and more cranberry juice. If the price of your favorite brand of iced tea goes up, so does the quantity demanded for a less expensive substitute.

Income Effect A change in the price of a product that a consumer demands can have a major effect on that consumer's purchasing power. The resulting change in the quantity demanded of the product in question is known as the **income effect**.

For example, think about a family's gas consumption. One family member drives a considerable distance to work every day, and another family member drives 100 miles to visit a relative in another state once every two weeks. If the price of gas increases, the family will, in effect, experience a decline in income. In other words, the family's income will purchase less gas than before. This may cause a change in quantity demanded of gasoline. Maybe the person who drives to work every day will begin to take public transportation, carpool with fellow employees, or request to work from home two days a week. Or maybe the family member who drives to visit a relative will reduce the visits to once a month. In the end, the change in quantity demanded of gasoline results from the change in the family's overall purchasing power brought about by the increased price of gasoline.

Sometimes income effect and substitution effect bump up against each other. On most days, an office worker buys the same sandwich for lunch, a $4.50 tuna melt. Occasionally, though, she splurges on a $10.25 steak sandwich. If the restaurant's owner increases the price of the tuna melt relative to the steak sandwich, however, the worker may no longer feel that she can afford to treat herself to a steak sandwich as often. That's because the higher price of the tuna melt sandwich decreases her real income. Because the consumer has less income, she is more likely to buy the cheaper sandwich—the tuna melt. In this situation, the income effect actually increases the quantity demanded for the tuna melt and reduces the quantity demanded for the steak sandwich. Here, the income effect is more important than the substitution effect.

Changes in Demand

In some situations, the overall market demand for a product or service increases or decreases at *every price*. If consumers are willing to purchase more of a product or service at both low and high prices, demand increases. If they are unwilling to purchase more of a product or service at both low and high prices, demand decreases. In both cases, a **change in demand** has occurred.

Do not confuse change in demand and change in quantity demanded. Although they sound similar, they are two different concepts. With a change in quantity demanded, price is the only variable that changes. When the price goes down, you buy more. When the price goes up, you buy less. When the price changes, there is a movement along an existing demand curve, as you saw in the Market Demand Curve.

A change in demand, though, is different. With a change in demand, the overall demand for a product or service changes because of factors besides the price of the product or service. The demand can change because of factors like fashion, income, the price of substitute goods, the price of complementary goods, just to name a few factors. The demand for personal protective equipment (PPE) exploded when the COVID-19 pandemic began because individuals wanted to reduce their chances of contracting the disease.

With sunblock, for example, the demand changes because of weather. In most of the country, the demand for sunblock changes with the season.

- In the spring, it is relatively low because people are not going to beaches and pools.
- In summer, though, it increases because people do go to beaches and want to protect their skin from the sun.
- As summer turns into fall, the demand decreases because the weather is too cool to go to the beach anymore.

The changing weather, then, is the major factor that causes a change in demand for sunblock. The demand schedule for the change in demand for sunblock from spring to summer looks like this:

DEMAND SCHEDULE FOR SUNBLOCK (PER DAY)		
Price of a Tube of Sunblock	Number of Tubes People Will Buy on April 15	Number of Tubes People Will Buy on July 15
$10.00	2	4
$8.00	4	6
$6.00	6	8
$4.00	8	10
$2.00	10	12

In summer, the demand for sunblock skyrockets. In winter, the demand plummets.

Shift in the Demand Curve You can plot the demand schedule as a demand curve. D_1 represents the demand on April 15, while D_2 represents the demand on July 15.

SHIFT IN THE DEMAND CURVE

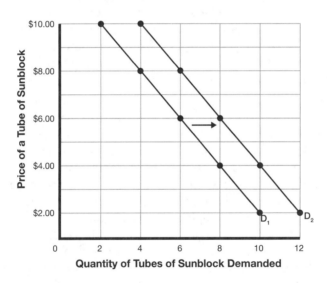

In the graph, the demand curve shifts to the right as demand increases for sunblock from spring to summer. So, in the spring, the demand decreases, and the demand curve shifts to the left. This change is known as a **shift in the demand curve**.

Again, be aware of the difference between a change in quantity demanded and a change in demand. When a change in quantity demanded occurs, there is movement along an existing demand curve. When a change in demand occurs, the entire demand curve shifts to the right when demand increases or to the left when demand decreases.

Determinants of Demand

Besides changes in weather and other seasonable considerations, economists typically identify seven **determinants of demand** (also known as demand shifters) that help increase or decrease demand for a good or a service:

1. *The Price of Substitute Goods* Substitute goods are products that can be used in place of each other. When a related good comes onto the market, it can affect the market for another good or service. Take, for example, the emergence of ride-sharing services. In many cities, their emergence reduced the overall demand for taxicabs. Ride-sharing services offered the same service, but people were able to use their cell phones to order the service, which was more convenient. This convenience decreased the demand for taxis.

2. *The Price of Complementary Goods* Products that are used together, like flashlights and batteries, are **complementary goods**. Gasoline is complementary with cars, SUVs, and trucks. Unless you have an electric vehicle, you need gasoline for the vehicle. Sales trends very clearly show that if the price of gasoline falls, the demand for large SUVs and pickup trucks increases. These vehicles use more gasoline, but consumers don't care so much because the price of gas is low. Conversely, if gas rises in price, the demand for gas-saving small cars increases.

3. *Increase in Most People's Incomes* During a period of economic growth, many people experience an increase in their incomes. During an economic recession, which is a time when a country's economy is shrinking, people often experience a decrease in income. These increases and decreases affect people's demand for products and services. During an economic expansion, the demand for luxury cars rises; during economic downturns, the demand for luxury cars declines. Luxury cars are one example of a **normal good**—a good whose demand changes in the same direction as incomes. If incomes rise, demand for normal goods rises. If income falls, the demand for normal goods falls. Steak, for example, is a normal good because people buy more of it as they make more money. When money is tight, they'll buy less steak and grill more burgers. The burgers are **inferior goods**, which are products a person buys more of when income decreases.

4. *Preferences among Consumers* The more people prefer a product, the more in demand that product will be. If consumers don't like a product, demand decreases. For example, each year, certain types of clothing become more popular while others become less so.

5. *Expectations about the Future* If a person expects the price of a product to increase, demand for that product may increase in the short term before the price increases. A baker, for instance, might buy 100 cans of pumpkin filling during the summer, when prices are low. That way, he can avoid the price increases that come as Thanksgiving approaches.

6. *Number of Buyers in the Market* The greater the number of buyers in the market, the greater the demand for all goods and services. As the number of buyers grows, more people have the ability to buy a product, increasing demand. Conversely, if the number of buyers is decreasing, the demand for all goods and services will decrease.

ANSWER THE TOPIC ESSENTIAL QUESTION

1. Why is there an inverse relationship between price and quantity demanded?

KEY TERMS

economic incentive	quantity demanded	change in demand
economic constraint	market demand	shift in the demand curve
market system	demand schedule	determinant of demand
economic agent	change in quantity	complementary good
property rights	demanded	normal good
demand	demand curve	inferior good
consumer decision-making	marginal utility	
law of demand	diminishing marginal utility	
own-price	substitution effect	
	income effect	

MULTIPLE-CHOICE QUESTIONS

1. Diminishing marginal utility means that a consumer's total satisfaction from consuming a good
   - (A) increases at a greater and greater rate
   - (B) increases at a constant rate
   - (C) decreases steadily over time
   - (D) decreases as the price of the product goes up
   - (E) increases at a decreasing rate

2. If Bryson Department Store has a sale on jeans,
   - (A) the quantity of jeans demanded will increase
   - (B) the quantity of jeans demanded will decrease
   - (C) the demand curve for jeans will shift to the left
   - (D) the demand curve for jeans will shift to the right
   - (E) the demand for a cheaper substitute will increase

3. Between 2012 and 2016, sales of cold cereal decreased and sales of yogurt increased. Which is the most likely explanation for both changes?

(A) Consumers thought that both cold cereal and yogurt were getting more expensive.

(B) Consumers viewed cold cereal and yogurt as complementary goods.

(C) Consumers felt their incomes were increasing, and they considered yogurt an inferior good.

(D) Consumers perceived cold cereal and yogurt as substitute goods, and the price of yogurt declined.

(E) Consumers expected the price of cold cereal to increase in the future and the price of yogurt to decrease.

FREE-RESPONSE QUESTION

1. Use the following table to answer the questions below.

Price ($)	Quantity Demanded
1	10
2	8
3	6
4	4
5	2

(a) Identify one reason for the slope of the demand curve shown above.

(b) If consumer income rises and sales of broccoli increase, would broccoli be considered as a normal or inferior good? Explain.

(c) Identify one reason for a decrease in demand for broccoli.

(d) A new, high-quality brand of frozen broccoli comes on the market. Identify the likely change in demand for broccoli.

THINK AS AN ECONOMIST: *DESCRIBE ECONOMIC CONCEPTS*

Demand is a consumer's interest in and ability to purchase a good or service. The desire to buy a product does not equal demand; a consumer must also have the economic resources to make a purchase. Market demand is the total demand of all consumers in a market for a particular good or service.

The quantity demanded varies according to price. Generally speaking, the quantity demanded of a good or service decreases as price increases and increases as price decreases.

Economists—and retailers—use charts and graphs to show the relationship between quantity demanded and price. You can see examples in this topic under the headings "Demand Schedule" and "Demand Curve." The demand curve transfers the information in a demand schedule into a graph. In the graph, the vertical axis shows various price points, ranging from low to high. The horizontal axis shows quantity demanded from low to high. To make a demand curve, you transfer each pair of data points on a demand schedule to the correct coordinates on the graph. Then you draw a line connecting the points to make the curve.

Apply the Skill

Below is a demand schedule for downloads from a music streaming service. Use the data in this schedule to create a demand curve for music downloads.

Quantity Demanded	Price of Downloads
1	$2.50
2	$2.25
3	$2.00
4	$1.75
5	$1.50
6	$1.25
7	$1.00
8	$0.75
9	$0.50
10	$0.25

Topic 2.2

Supply

"Demand and supply are the opposite extremes of the beam, whence depend the scales of dearness and cheapness; the price is the point of equilibrium, where the momentum of the one ceases, and that of the other begins."

French Economist Jean-Baptiste Say (1767–1832)

Essential Question: What factors affect the supply of a good or service in a market?

The produce section of your supermarket probably sells corn. It can be eaten alone, it goes well with all kinds of other foods, it is processed to use as an additive in many foods (corn starch, corn syrup, and so on) and it is also used as feed for cattle and other livestock. For many farmers, corn is central to their businesses. But in running their businesses, they face numerous decisions about supply. How much corn should they produce? How does the price of corn affect those decisions?

When the price of corn increases, the quantity that farmers grow also increases. That's because the rise in price gives farmers the **incentive** to increase the supply of corn. That incentive is known as **profit**, the difference between the cost of production and earnings. On the other hand, when the price of corn drops, a farmer will produce less because their profits are lower.

Source: commons.wikimedia.org

Farmers keep a close eye on the price of corn in making decisions about how much corn they should plant in the spring.

Law of Supply

Supply is the amount of a product or service that a producer is willing and able to provide at various prices during a specific period of time. A producer could be an individual, a company, or an organization that produces goods or provides services.

The amount of a product or service that a producer supplies depends on many factors, such as the availability of raw materials. In general, though, the most important factor in determining supply is the price of a good or service.

The **law of supply** holds that, all things being equal, the higher the price of a product, the greater the quantity supplied. Conversely, the lower the price of a product, the smaller the quantity supplied. Economists sometimes refer to the price of a good as the **own-price**—the price required for ownership of the product.

Quantity Supplied The specific amount of a product that a producer is willing to sell at a specific price and at a specific point in time is the **quantity supplied**. Suppose a homeowner's garage door needs a new belt, but belts are in short supply because the belt-making firm started making PPE masks because the price of PPE masks had risen so dramatically. The quantity supplied of masks had increased as the price of the masks increased.

Marginal Cost and Quantity Supplied In deciding whether to increase the quantity supplied of a product or service, a producer must consider **marginal cost**, which is the additional cost of producing one additional unit of a product. For example, to grow each additional acre of corn, the farmer needs more seeds, has to hire more workers, or has to purchase more machinery.

Because of the marginal cost, the farmer is willing to increase production of corn only if he or she receives a higher price for producing additional units. If the price falls, profits decline, giving the farmer an incentive to reduce the quantity supplied of corn.

To take another example, imagine you have an Aunt Rita who just sold a handcrafted necklace at a local fair for $20.85, and she believes she could sell many more at the same price. The cost of creating the necklace was $10. If Aunt Rita's marginal cost of producing the next necklace is $1, the total cost is $11. Will Aunt Rita increase production and therefore the quantity supplied? The answer is yes, because it costs Aunt Rita only an additional $1 to produce another necklace that will generate $20.85 in revenue. Aunt Rita's profit will be $9.85.

However, Aunt Rita finds that the cost of her raw materials, such as stones, is rising fast. The marginal cost of making an additional necklace is $12, increasing total cost to $23. At that point, Aunt Rita faces a decision. Should she raise the price of the necklace to cover the marginal cost? But, as you have learned, increasing the price will reduce the quantity demanded for the necklace. However, if Aunt Rita is able to increase the price of her necklaces, she may decide to continue producing them.

Aunt Rita, like all producers, knows it does not make much economic sense to produce a product if the price does not at the very least cover the cost of production. As prices increase, companies produce as much as they can because they don't mind paying a higher marginal cost if they're going to make more money. As a consequence, they'll increase the quantity supplied.

The Supply Schedule and Curve

A **supply schedule** shows the total amount of goods or services that manufacturers produce at various price levels. The first column lists the price for a product, while the second column lists the quantity supplied at each price.

Suppose that Tiana supplies farm-fresh tomatoes to several restaurants in your town. The first thing she does is create a supply schedule like the one that follows. The table shows the quantity of tomatoes Tiana is willing to supply each week to a restaurant at different prices. For example, at $1.00, Tiana is willing to supply 6 tomatoes. At $1.50, she's willing to provide 10 tomatoes. At $2.00, she's willing to supply 13 tomatoes.

SUPPLY SCHEDULE FOR TOMATOES	
Price of Tomatoes	Quantity of Tomatoes Supplied per Week (in pounds)
$0.50	0
$1.00	6
$1.50	10
$2.00	13
$2.50	15

Tiana can then use the supply schedule to create a **supply curve**, which provides a visual representation of the same information in the supply schedule:

- The quantity supplied of a product is shown on the horizontal axis.
- The price of a product is displayed on the vertical axis.

The upward slope of the supply curve shows that as price increases, the quantity supplied increases. Or looked at another way, as the price decreases, so does the quantity supplied. As you move your eye along the supply curve, you are tracing changes in quantity supplied

If you compare that supply curve to a demand curve, you will see that the two curves slope in opposite directions. Going from left to right, the supply curve slopes upward and the demand curve slopes downward. This probably makes sense. Consider how you react as both a producer and a conumser. If the price of something you make and sell goes up, you have incentive to supply a greater quantity of it. If the price of something you buy goes up, you have greater incentive to purchase a lower quantity of it.

SUPPLY CURVE FOR TOMATOES

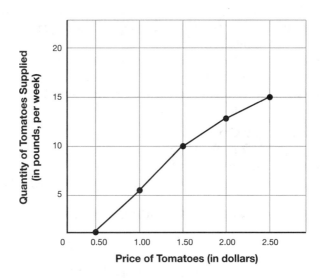

Source: commons.wikimedia.org
Credit: Hollie Adams/Bloomberg via Getty Images

The law of supply is an important concept to consider when producing goods and services.

Changes in Supply

Certain situations occur that cause a **change in supply**, which is an increase or decrease in the overall supply of a product or service *at all prices*. For example, in 1913, Henry Ford introduced the first assembly line to build automobiles. In the early days of the automobile industry, a worker worked on one car and performed all the steps in building that car. It took one worker about twelve hours to build a car.

But Ford had a better idea. Why not have each worker perform one simple step, such as installing the brake, on each car as it passed by on a conveyor belt? Because each worker was performing a simple step over and over, he could accomplish more in the same amount of time. Because of this innovation, a car that once took twelve hours to build now took two and a half hours. The supply of automobiles on the market increased practically overnight.

A change in quantity supplied is fundamentally different from a change in supply. With change in quantity supplied, price is the *only* variable that changes. When the price goes up, quantity supplied increases. When the price goes down, quantity supplied decreases.

With change in supply, though, the overall supply of a product or service changes because of factors besides price. Supplies can change because of many factors, including new technologies, changes in the supply of raw materials, or changes in how workers do their jobs.

Shift in the Supply Curve To show changes in supply, you can create a graph that shows a **shift in the supply curve**. In the graph, the entire supply curve shifts. When the curve shifts to the right, the supply is greater at *every price*. When the supply curve shifts to the left, the supply is less at *every price*.

A SHIFT IN THE SUPPLY CURVE

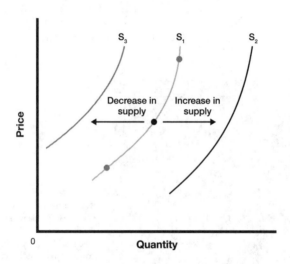

Determinants That Influence Supply

Economists have identified several **determinants of supply**, or factors that cause the supply curve to shift to the left or the right. They include:

- *An Increase or Decrease in Input Price* An input price is the cost that goes into manufacturing a product. Inputs include such things as raw materials, rent, labor, and equipment. If a factory's energy costs unexpectedly rise, for example, or the cost of steel increases, then the quantity supplied by that factory at every given price will decrease.

- *Improvement in Technology* Advances in technology are important determinants of supply, as they reduce the cost of production. As a result, the supply curve shifts to the right. For example, container ships have allowed businesses to transport their products all around the world, increasing the supply of products such as cars, machine parts, and clothes. The introduction of new fertilizers increases the food supply, allowing farms to bring more of their goods into the market.

- *Changes in Weather* Weather plays an important role in supply. When the weather is good in Florida, for example, orange juice companies increase their supply. But if an unexpected frost damages orange trees, the supply decreases. A hurricane that damages oil refineries in Texas will affect the supply of gasoline, resulting in shortages and higher prices. In such instances, the supply curve moves to the left, indicating a decrease in supply.

- *An Increase in the Number of Sellers* Just as the number of consumers can affect the demand curve, the number of producers can affect the supply curve. When more producers enter a market, supplies generally increase.

- *A Decrease in the Price of a Substitute Product* Suppose a farmer grows either soybeans or wheat. An increase in the market price of wheat will cause a farmer to substitute the production of wheat for the production of soybeans. If the market price of cheese decreases, then a dairy farmer will supply more milk to be used in the production of cheese because the farmer stands to make more of a profit.

- *An Increase in the Price of a Joint Product* Joint products are two or more products produced together. The production of one makes the other available. Crude oil and gasoline are good examples of joint products. If the price of crude oil increases, the supply of gasoline decreases.

- *Government Policies* Governments can have a major influence on supply. **Tariffs**, for example, are taxes on goods that a country imports from other countries. An increase in tariffs on manufactured goods, for example, will decrease the supply of a product, shifting the supply curve to the left. However, a government subsidy, or grant of money to help an industry or business, will increase the supply of a product, shifting the supply curve to the right.

Market Supply Curve You can use a **market supply curve** to show the combined total quantity of a particular product or service supplied by all individuals in a market. The market supply curve is the sum of all individual producers in the market.

Consider the following example of popular dog biscuits made using peanut butter. Initially, only one peanut butter supplier, Betty's Peanut Butter Company, supplied the biscuit maker. But after a time, a second suppler, Jolly Peanut Butter Company, joined the market. Jolly Peanut Butter Company supplies 10,000 gallons of peanut butter each year at a price of $10 a gallon. At $20 a gallon, it will provide 12,000 gallons.

For its part, Betty's Peanut Butter Company supplies 11,000 gallons of peanut butter annually at a price of $10 per gallon, while at $20 a gallon, the company supplies the market with 14,000 gallons. Together, the two firms supply 21,000 gallons of peanut butter each year at $10 per gallon and 26,000 gallons at $20 per gallon.

As you can see, although Jolly Peanut Butter Company supplies less peanut butter than Betty's, the market supply is much larger than it would be if only Betty's Peanut Butter Company were in the market. If a third company entered the market, supply of peanut butter in the market would be that much greater. As you can tell from the market curve below, an increase in the number of producers leads to a rightward shift of the supply curve.

MARKET SUPPLY CURVE

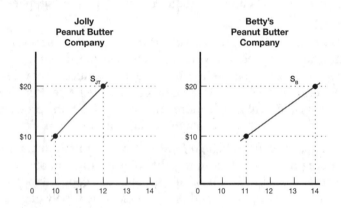

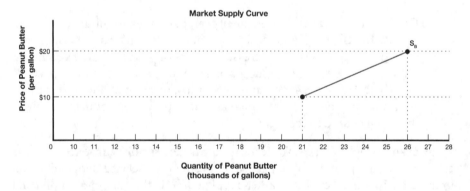

Market Supply Curve

Quantity of Peanut Butter
(thousands of gallons)

Recognizing Basic Economic Concepts The law of supply—along with the law of demand—are concepts that you encounter every day. They are important drivers of market economies and explain why prices and the quantity supplied rise and fall. The next time you go to the store to buy a gallon of milk, a pack of energy bars, or even dog treats, remember that the laws of supply and demand are important factors in how much you pay.

1. In one paragraph, explain the factors that affect the supply of a good or service in a market. Be sure to explain the difference between the quantity supplied of a good and the supply of a good.

KEY TERMS

incentive	quantity supplied	shift in the supply curve
profit	marginal cost	determinants of supply
supply	supply schedule	tariff
law of supply	supply curve	market supply curve
own-price	change in supply	

MULTIPLE-CHOICE QUESTIONS

1. The quantity supplied of a product or service usually increases after
   (A) the supply curve shifts to the left
   (B) the supply curve shifts upward
   (C) the price increases
   (D) the price decreases
   (E) the marginal cost increases

2. Which of the following is most likely to decrease the supply of crackers?
   (A) The cost of flour, an input for crackers, increases by 65 percent.
   (B) A new type of oven makes production more efficient.
   (C) The price of a joint product, such as salt, decreases.
   (D) New robots pack boxes of crackers more quickly at lower cost than people did.
   (E) Three new cracker factories open in six months.

3. If the price of apples decreases from $1.50 per pound to $1.00 per pound, which is most likely to occur?
   (A) The supply curve will shift to the left.
   (B) The supply curve will shift to the right.
   (C) The supply curve will become a straight horizontal line.
   (D) The quantity supplied will increase along a fixed supply curve.
   (E) The quantity supplied will decrease along a fixed supply curve.

MARKET SUPPLY CURVE FOR STRAWBERRIES

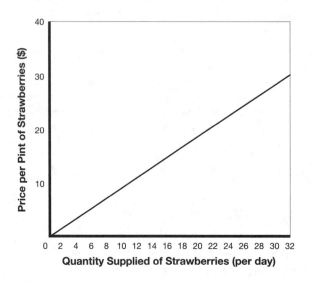

1. This graph shows the market for strawberries. Study the graph and answer each question.

   (a) What does the graph show about the relationship between price and quantity supplied?

   (b) Would this graph be more useful for showing a change in quantity supplied or a shift in supply? Explain.

   (c) At $30, what would the quantity supplied of strawberries be?

   (d) If the price of strawberries increases from $8 to $16, what will happen to the quantity of strawberries?

   (e) Suppose a freeze destroys a quarter of the strawberry crop. What would you expect to happen to the supply curve? What is the determinant of supply in this situation? Explain.

Economists use many kinds of graphs to show the relationships among variables. One common type is the line graph, which shows the relationship between two or more sets of variables. A market supply graph shows the relationship between the price of a good or service and the quantity that producers will provide at each price. To create a market supply graph, follow these steps:

1. Gather data into a supply schedule, which shows the quantities supplied at various prices.

2. Draw a horizontal axis, or x-axis, and a vertical axis, or y-axis.

3. Label the horizontal axis and the vertical axis. In a supply curve, economists typically label the horizontal axis "Quantity Supplied" and the vertical axis "Price."

4. Label the point at which the axes meet "0."

5. Plot the horizontal axis, or Quantity Supplied, with equal increments of numbers, using the supply schedule as a guide. Draw a vertical line that extends from each of the numbers.

6. Plot the vertical axis, with equal increments of numbers, using the supply schedule as a guide. Draw a horizontal line that extends from each of the numbers.

7. Using the supply schedule as a guide, plot the points that show the quantity produced for each price.

8. Connect the points with a line. This line will be the supply curve.

9. Give a title to your graph.

Apply the Skill

Create a line graph using the supply schedule below for smartphone apps

SUPPLY SCHEDULE FOR SMARTPHONE APPS	
Price of the App	**Quantity Supplied**
$5.00	100,000
$4.50	90,000
$4.00	80,000
$3.50	70,000
$3.00	60,000
$2.50	50,000
$2.00	40,000
$1.50	30,000
$1.00	20,000

Price Elasticity of Demand

"We've done price elasticity studies, and the answer is always that we should raise prices. We don't do that, because we believe—and we have to take this as an article of faith—that by keeping our prices very, very low, we earn trust with customers over time, and that that actually does maximize free cash flow over the long term."

Jeff Bezos, Chief Executive Officer of Amazon (b. 1964)

Essential Question: How do economists measure the responsiveness of demand after a change in a product's price?

You and your friends are standing with hundreds of others waiting for the phone store to open. A new model has finally arrived, and you have been waiting since 3 a.m. hoping beyond hope that when the store's doors finally swing wide, you will be able to rush in and get your hands on the device.

Why wouldn't you? No phone in the past decade has included so many upgraded or new features as this one. Several weeks ago, you made peace with knowing full well you're going to be at least $1,000 lighter by the time you get home today. *But you feel you just have to have this phone even if you have to pay twice that.*

On the other hand, if you suddenly had to pay twice the going price for a hamburger, you might not buy another one in your life. You would happily choose other items on the menu. The examples of the new phone and the hamburger demonstrate that how much a change in price affects your willingness to purchase a product varies. This is the basis of **elasticity**, a measure of how much the quantity demanded of products and services changes because of changes in price (also known as own-price), people's incomes, and the prices of similar products.

Some buyers will wait in in line to be among the first to purchase the new model of a phone or other new product.

Price Elasticity of Demand

The **price elasticity of demand** measures the responsiveness of the quantity demanded of a particular product to a change in price, when all other buying influences remain the same. Price elasticity of demand is, in essence, the percent change in quantity demanded brought about by a percent change in price. Economists and business executives use price elasticity of demand to understand how markets and economies work.

The demand for a product or service is very price **elastic** when price shifts can cause a substantial change in quantity demanded one way or another. Automobiles, for example, are highly price elastic goods. If a dealer increases the price of a pickup truck, for example, the quantity demanded will decrease. But conversely, if the dealer lowers the price, the quantity demanded will increase.

The demand for a product or service is more price **inelastic** when changes in price do not change the quantity demanded very much. Gasoline is a good example of a price inelastic product. No matter the price, people still need gasoline in their automobiles to get where they want to go. Even if oil prices rise, people will more often than not purchase the same amount of gasoline. Other price inelastic products are necessities like soap and prescription drugs. Regardless of cost, people will still demand them.

As you have learned, the law of demand holds that the higher a product's price, the less of that product will be demanded, while the lower a product's price, the more of it will be demanded. Still, the law doesn't explain how much quantity demanded would increase or decrease based on certain price changes. The price elasticity of demand measures the percentage in the quantity demanded that follows a percentage change in price. Economists define elasticity as a measure of the responsiveness of one **variable** to percent changes in another variable.

Calculating the Price Elasticity of Demand

To figure out the price elasticity of demand, you have to express the change in price as a percentage of the average price and the change in quantity demanded as a percentage of the average quantity demanded. Then you figure the magnitude (or amount) of the value of elasticity by dividing the percentage change in the quantity *demanded* by the percentage change in the price of the product. Write the equation like this:

$$\frac{\textit{percentage change in quantity demanded}}{\textit{percentage change in price}} = \textit{magnitude of the value of elasticity}$$

If the magnitude of the value of elasticity is greater than 1, then economists consider the demand for the product to be elastic. If the magnitude is less than 1, then economists consider the demand to be inelastic.

Suppose, for example, that the price of a video game rises by 10 percent (0.10). The quantity demanded drops by 50 percent (0.50). Use the equation to find the magnitude of the value of elasticity.

$$\frac{0.50 \ (percentage \ change \ in \ quantity \ demanded)}{0.10 \ (percentage \ change \ in \ price)} = 5$$

The magnitude of the value of elasticity for the video game is 5. The demand for the video game is elastic because the ratio of change in quantity demanded to change in price is greater than 1.

In contrast, look what happens with demand for another product, the cell phone. Suppose that the percentage change in quantity demanded is 20 percent (0.20). The percentage change in price is 50 percent (0.50). Use the equation to find the magnitude of the value of elasticity.

$$\frac{0.20 \ (percentage \ change \ in \ quantity \ demanded)}{0.50 \ (percentage \ change \ in \ price)} = 0.40$$

The magnitude of the value of elasticity for the cell phone is 0.4. The demand for the cell phone is price inelastic because the change in price causes a change in the quantity demanded that is less than 1.

Here's another example to calculate the elasticity of demand. Suppose the price of PPE rises from $5 to $10, resulting in quantity demanded falling from 30,000 to 20,000. To find the elasticity of demand,

{(30,000 – 20,000)}/{.5*(30,000 + 20,000)} / {(10 – 5)}/{.5*(10 + 5)}

which yields

(10,000/25,000) / (5/7.5) = 0.6. This indicates the demand for PPE is price inelastic because the elasticity coefficient is less than 1.

You might think that a decrease in either price or quantity demanded should be shown as a negative number. However, since economists focus on the magnitude of the change, not its direction, they conventionally report all the numbers in calculations on elasticity as positive ones.

Applying Price Elasticity of Demand If you're working in a business, how important is it whether demand is elastic or inelastic? It definitely can be important. Suppose, for example, that your sister runs a clothing manufacturer. Does it make sense for her to increase the price of a new line of dresses from $500 to $1,000? Probably not. Demand for the dresses is highly elastic because it's a **discretionary purchase**. In other words, the purchase is optional; people don't have to buy it. As a result, the quantity demanded for the dresses would fall by so much that the company's revenue would also fall.

However, she could lower the price for a line of $1,000 dresses to $500. The demand for that dress is elastic, meaning that quantity demanded will increase as price falls. The company's revenue might increase as the quantity demanded increases.

On the other hand, your cousin Joe, who has a dairy farm on the edge of town, knows that the price of milk is inelastic. People will buy about the same amount even if the price increases a little. While an increase in the price of milk would mean more money in Joe's pocket, a decrease in price would reduce total revenue. Yet he also has competitors, meaning that he can't raise the price too much, or consumers will buy milk from those competitors.

Factors That Influence the Price Elasticity of Demand

The price elasticity of demand for a product depends on a number of factors, including the following:

- *Nature of the Product* Consumers perceive some goods and services as more essential than others. Gasoline and basic medical care are commonly considered very important. Demand for these products tends to be inelastic. Items that people see as luxuries—diamond jewelry and gold watches—are less essential. Demand for luxuries tends to be highly elastic.

- *Availability of Substitutes* If the price of one product increases, people often substitute another, less expensive product. If you love an apple a day, but the price increases so much that oranges are less expensive, you might buy fewer apples and more oranges. Demand is more elastic when close substitutes are available. When no close substitute is available, demand is more inelastic.

- *Proportion of Income Spent on Goods* The greater the proportion of income spent on a good, the more elastic the demand tends to be. If the price of socks doubles, you will consume almost as many socks as before. The demand is inelastic because purchasing socks takes up only a small proportion of your income. On the other hand, if your landlord doubles your rent, you might look for a less expensive apartment. That's because housing takes up a significant portion of your income.

- *Time Elapsed Since Price Change* The longer the time period between changes in price, the more elastic demand becomes. With a longer time period, you have time to search for cheaper substitutes. In the 1970s, for example, oil prices skyrocketed, resulting in a huge increase in gasoline prices. Initially, people barely changed the amount of gasoline they bought because there were no close substitutes. Moreover, people needed their cars to go about their daily life chores. However, as the years passed, and more fuel-efficient automobiles came on the market, the quantity of gasoline demanded decreased. Americans changed their habits over time to reduce their consumption. As a result, gas prices fell over the next decade or so. The demand for gasoline became more elastic as more time passed after the huge price increase.

Five Categories of Price Elasticity of Demand

Because price elasticity of demand is such a useful concept for business owners, economists have divided price elasticities of demand into five categories:

- *Elastic* Elastic demand is one in which elasticity is greater than 1 and indicates a high responsiveness to a change in price.

- *Inelastic* Inelastic demand is one in which elasticity is less than 1 and indicates a low responsiveness to a change in price.

- *Perfectly Elastic* If the price elasticity of demand is infinite, or unlimited, then demand is **perfectly elastic**. For example, Farmer Smith and Farmer Rivera both grow corn. Corn is selling on the market for $4.00 a bushel. Farmer Smith, though, has to buy new irrigation equipment. Because of his increased expenses, he can't make a profit selling corn at $4.00 a bushel, so he raises his price to $4.50. However, Farmer Rivera can make a profit selling at $4.00 a bushel, and he continues to do so. In this case, the quantity demanded for Farmer Smith's corn falls to zero because he cannot compete with Farmer Rivera. In this case, the response to price is perfectly elastic.

Depending on the price, buying a dress straddles the line between an elastic and inelastic purchase.

- *Perfectly Inelastic* If the quantity demanded is 0 for any change in price, the demand is **perfectly inelastic**. Suppose the quantity demanded for pencils is 2 million boxes. The quantity demanded never changes regardless of price. Therefore, the demand for pencils is perfectly inelastic. If you were to graph this on a demand curve, the demand line would be a straight vertical line and not curved.

- *Unit Elastic* When the price of elasticity of demand is exactly 1, the good is said to be **unit elastic**. Here, the percentage change in price matches the percentage change in quantity demanded. For example, when Wentworth Bakery lowers the price of their loaves of bread by 5 percent, they find that the quantity demanded increases by 5 percent.

PRICE ELASTICITY OF DEMAND

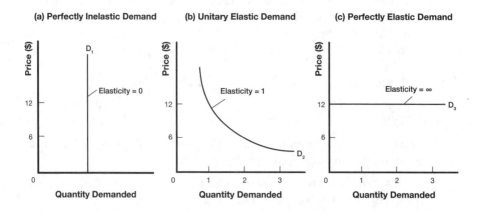

(a) Perfectly Inelastic Demand

(b) Unitary Elastic Demand

(c) Perfectly Elastic Demand

If you were to draw a demand curve for a perfectly inelastic product (illustration a.), the "curve" would be a vertical straight line. For a unitary elastic product (illustration b.), the elasticity is equal to 1. A perfectly inelastic demand curve is an infinite horizontal line.

Total Revenue and Elasticity

Knowing whether demand is elastic, inelastic, or unitary gives you a good idea of how businesses set their prices and how the market will react to shifts in demand. For example, raising prices will bring in more total revenue if demand is inelastic, but not if demand is elastic.

Economists define **total revenue** as the total value of sales of a product or service. Total revenue is equal to the price of that product multiplied by the quantity sold. You can figure out total revenue using this equation:

$$Total\ Revenue\ = Price\ X\ Quantity\ Sold$$

Price Effect and Quantity Effect With the exception of perfectly elastic or perfectly inelastic demand, when prices increase, two different consequences can occur. An increase in a good's price increases total revenue. This is known as **price effect**. In other words, after a price increase, each unit sold sells at a higher price, which tends to raise revenue.

However, when you increase the price of a good, you sell fewer units. This is known as the **quantity effect**. After a price increase, fewer units are sold, which tends to lower revenue.

If the price effect is stronger than the quantity effect, then total revenue will increase. If the quantity effect is stronger, then total revenue decreases. If the two are equal, the price increases do not change total revenue. By figuring the price elasticity of demand for a product, a businessperson can predict what will happen to the company's total revenue when prices change. For instance:

- If demand is unit elastic, an increase in price does not change total revenue. The price effect and quantity effect offset each other.

- If demand is elastic, an increase in price reduces total revenue because the quantity effect is stronger than the price effect.

- If demand is inelastic, a price increase increases revenue, because the price effect is stronger than the quantity effect.

Applying Price Elasticity of Demand To see how price elasticity of demand can help a person make economic decisions, consider the case of a touring company of a hit Broadway show traveling to smaller cities. In Pittsburgh, the company is scheduled to put on three performances. Assume all seats are the same price. What ticket price will maximize revenue?

- If critics have praised the show, producers might raise the price of tickets significantly with little or no decrease in quantity demanded and quantity sold. This decision would increase total revenue.

- If critics attacked the show, the producers might cut the price of tickets to get more people in the seats. Yet, they would only do so as long as the percentage drop in price would result in a larger quantity demanded, which would increase total revenue.

The key takeaway is that the show's producers, or any business for that matter, need to consider the price elasticity of demand in their decisions. Usually they learn how to apply price elasticity of demand over time and by experimenting with slightly higher or lower prices.

ANSWER THE TOPIC ESSENTIAL QUESTION

1. How do economists measure the responsiveness of demand after a change in the price of a product?

KEY TERMS

elasticity	variable	unit elastic
price elasticity of demand	discretionary purchase	total revenue
elastic	perfectly elastic	price effect
inelastic	perfectly inelastic	quantity effect

MULTIPLE-CHOICE QUESTIONS

1. When a good is determined to have an elasticity of demand coefficient of 3, demand is
   (A) unit elastic
   (B) perfectly elastic
   (C) perfectly inelastic
   (D) relatively elastic
   (E) relatively inelastic

2. A perfectly inelastic demand curve is a(n)
   (A) straight vertical line
   (B) upward sloping but not straight line
   (C) downward sloping but not straight line
   (D) straight horizontal line
   (E) sometimes upward and sometimes downward sloping line

3. Which of the following would cause the demand for a good to be relatively elastic?

(A) If the good is a necessity

(B) If the good is a luxury item

(C) If very few substitutes are available

(D) If the purchase of the good is a small proportion of the budget spent

(E) If the change in price occurred very recently, such as yesterday

FREE-RESPONSE QUESTION

PRICE ELASTICITY ALONG THE DEMAND CURVE

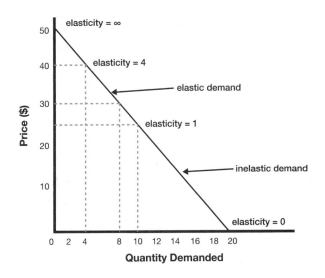

1. The price elasticity of demand changes along the demand curve. Study this demand curve and answer the following questions:

(a) Does elasticity of demand increase, decrease, or stay the same as you move down and to the right along the demand curve?

(b) Is elasticity of demand unit elastic, elastic, or inelastic if the coefficient for the elasticity of demand is found to equal 1?

(c) At what price point does demand start becoming inelastic?

(d) At what point along the curve does demand become perfectly elastic?

(e) When the price decreases from $40 to $30, the quantity demanded rises from 4 to 8. What is the price elasticity of demand over this range?

Economists use quantitative data and calculations to determine the effects of a change in an economic situation. Doing so requires them to answer three questions:

- What variable in the situation changed?
- What effect did that change have on economic outcomes?
- How did the degree of change in the variable compare to the degree of change in the outcome?

This process is useful in analyzing price elasticity of demand. For example, consider a basic demand schedule such as this:

Price of Fast-Food Breakfast	Percentage Change in Price	Quantity of Breakfasts Demanded	Percentage Change in Quantity Demanded
$1.00	n/a	100,000	n/a
$1.20	+20%	80,000	-20%
$1.44	+20%	64,000	-20%
$1.73	+20%	51,200	-20%
$2.08	+20%	40,960	-20%
$2.50	+20%	32,768	-20%
$3.00	+20%	26,214	-20%

An economist would note that with each price increase of 20 percent in fast-food breakfasts, consumer demand for those breakfasts drops by 20 percent. Using the formula for calculating elasticity of demand produces this result:

$$\frac{percentage\ change\ in\ quantity\ demanded}{percentage\ change\ in\ price}$$

$$\frac{0.20}{0.20} = 1$$

Since the price elasticity is 1, the fast-food breakfasts have unit price elasticity.

Apply the Skill

Look at the following demand schedule for video games. Using the percentage changes in price and in quantity demanded, calculate the price elasticity of demand. What can you conclude about the price elasticity of demand for the video game?

Price of Video Game	Percentage Change in Price	Quantity of Video Games Demanded	Percentage Change in Quantity Demanded
$35.00	n/a	50,000	n/a
$36.75	5	46,500	7
$38.59	5	43,245	7
$40.52	5	40,318	7
$42.54	5	37,403	7

Price Elasticity of Supply

I do know that homelessness is related to housing, and we haven't been producing housing in the numbers that our community requires —a lot of the escalating costs of housing is related to the fact that supply is way short [of] demand.

David Ige, governor of Hawaii (b. 1957)

Essential Question: How much does the quantity supplied of a product or service change in response to a change in price?

Suppose that your older brother is moving out of the house, and the two of you go across town to a new apartment complex, Trinity Acres, to help him look for an apartment. The three buildings are gorgeous, with balconies, ponds, two swimming pools, a tennis court, and apartments that overlook the river.

The manager, however, tells you all the units in the first tower have been rented. Still, she says, the second tower, with 500 additional units, will open next month, and the third, with the same number of apartments, the following month. The manager then says that when the first tower opened a few months ago, the building's owners were charging renters $750 a month, a good price for such nice apartments. People scooped up the flats as fast as they came on the market.

Now, the manager says, those wishing to live in the second tower will see their monthly rent increase to $950 a month. When the third tower opens, rent will climb to $1,250 a month. Your brother doesn't understand why as the price increases so does the supply of apartments.

Fortunately, you have an answer—the price elasticity of supply, which measures how a change in the price of a product or service affects the quantity supplied of the product or service.

In the long run, housing supply tends to be elastic. If rents rise, builders will increase the supply.

Sensitivity of Quantitied Supplies to Price

The **price elasticity of supply** measures the responsiveness of the quantity supplied of a particular product to a change in price, when all other production factors remain the same. The quantity supplied of some goods and services responds more than others to changes in price.

As you know, the law of supply holds that, all things being equal, the higher the price of a product, the greater the quantity supplied. Conversely, the lower the price of a product, the smaller the quantity supplied. The quantity supplied refers to the specific amount of a product that a producer is willing to sell at a precise price and at an exact moment in time. The law of supply, though, doesn't predict how much quantity supplied will increase or decrease based on price changes. That's where price elasticity of supply comes in.

If a price change brings about a large percentage change in the quantity supplied, then the quantity supplied for that product is price **elastic**. Televisions and other manufactured goods, such as car parts, are good examples of elastic products. If the price of a TV falls and demand rises, then factories can easily add more workers and production shifts to increase supply. If the manufacturer has a **surplus**, it can easily lower prices to reduce supply.

On the other hand, if a change in price brings about a small change in the quantity supplied, then the quantity supplied for that product is price **inelastic**. Farm goods, such as wheat, corn, or milk, tend to be price inelastic. For example, if the price of soybeans rises, a farmer can't easily increase quantity supplied. It takes time to lease additional land, prepare the land, and plant additional crops. The farmer may not be able to respond to the change in price for another growing season. The quantity supplied responds slowly to the change in price.

Price elasticity of supply is influenced by many factors, including how long the price change will last, the availability of substitutes from other producers, and the company's ability to increase production. This topic will explore these factors later.

Calculating the Price Elasticity of Supply

To figure out the price elasticity of supply, express the change in price as a percentage of the average price and the change in quantity supplied as a percentage of the average quantity supplied. Then you figure the magnitude (or amount) of the value of elasticity by dividing the percentage change in the quantity supplied by the percentage change in the product's price. The equation looks like this:

$$\frac{percentage\ change\ in\ quantity\ supplied}{percentage\ change\ in\ price} = magnitude\ of\ the\ value\ of\ elasticity$$

If the magnitude of the value of elasticity is greater than 1, then economists consider the quantity supplied for the product to be elastic. If the magnitude is less than 1, the economists consider the quantity supplied to be inelastic.

Suppose, for example, that the price of a video game rises by 20 percent (0.20). The quantity supplied increases by 40 percent (0.40). Use the equation to find the magnitude of the value of elasticity.

$$\frac{0.40 \ (percentage \ change \ in \ quantity \ supplied)}{0.20 \ (percentage \ change \ in \ price)} = 2$$

The magnitude of the value of elasticity for the video game is 2. The supply for the video game is elastic because the ratio of change in quantity supplied to change in price is greater than 1.

In contrast, look at what happens with quantity supplied for a bushel of corn. Suppose that the price of a bushel of corn increases from $4 to $5. That's a 25 percent (0.25) increase in price. The increase in price leads to a 10 percent (0.10) increase in quantity of corn supplied for that year. Use the equation to find the magnitude of the value of elasticity.

$$\frac{0.10 \ (percentage \ change \ in \ quantity \ supplied)}{0.25 \ (percentage \ change \ in \ price)} = 0.40$$

The magnitude of the value of elasticity of quantity supplied for corn is 0.4. The quantity supplied for corn is inelastic because the change in price causes a change in quantity supplied that is less than 1.

Because price and quantity supplied tend to change in the same direction (they increase or decrease together), the number indicating elasticity is normally positive.

One way to write the equation for the elasticity of supply is

{(QS1 – QS2) / (.5*(QS1 + QS2)} divided by {(P1 – P2) / (.5*(P1 + P2)}

In words, this is the difference in the quantities divided by the average of the quantities—all of which is divided by the difference in prices divided by the average of the prices.

For example, suppose that the price falls from $10 to $8 resulting in quantity supplied changing from 22,000 to 20,000. To calculate the elasticity of supply:

{(22000 – 20000) / (.5*(22000 + 20000)} divided by {(10 – 8) / (.5* (10 + 8)}

This results in 2,000 / 21,000 divided by 2 / 9

The elasticity of supply then would be .095 / .222 = 0.43

In this case, the supply of the produce is inelastic.

Applying Price Elasticity of Supply If you're working in or own a business, understanding the elasticity of supply of a product or service can be very important. Suppose, for example, that the quantity of video games supplied to a store in June was 2,000 units, with a price of $20. By the holiday shopping season, the quantity supplied increased to 30,000, and the price jumped to $30. The price of elasticity of supply is 4.375, which means the supply of video games is very elastic. Here's how the math works:

$$\% \text{ Change in Quantity Supplied} = \frac{(30,000 - 2,000)}{\{0.5*(30,000 + (2,000)\}} = \frac{28,000}{16,000} = 1.75$$

$$\% \text{ Change in Price} = \frac{(\$30 - \$20)}{\{0.5*(\$20 + \$30)\}} = \frac{\$10}{\$25} = 0.40$$

$$\text{Price Elasticity of Supply} = \frac{1.75}{0.40} = 4.375$$

Now suppose it's January and everyone is done with their holiday shopping. The quantity of video games supplied drops from 30,000 to 3,000, while the price drops from $30 back down to $20. In that instance, the price elasticity of supply is 4.09. At this ratio, the quantity supplied of the video game is still elastic.

Five Categories of Elasticity

Because price elasticity of supply is such a useful concept for business owners, economists have divided price elasticities of supply into five categories. The first two categories of elasticity are:

- **Elastic** Elastic supply is one in which elasticity is greater than 1 and indicates that a change in price results in a larger proportional change in quantity supplied.

- **Inelastic** Inelastic supply is one in which elasticity is less than 1 and leads to a smaller percentage change in quantity supplied.

If you were to graph both on a supply curve, the curves would look as follows. Line S1, Inelastic Supply, shows that the quantity supplied increases slowly as price rises. Line S2, Elastic Supply, shows that the quantity supplied increases rapidly as price rises.

ELASTIC AND INELASTIC SUPPLY CURVES

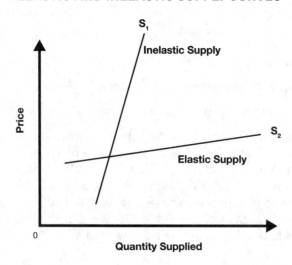

The other three categories of elasticity are:

- **Perfectly Elastic** When the smallest possible increase in price causes an infinitely large increase in quantity supplied, the supply is **perfectly elastic**. Suppose that the fishing rod industry pays its workers $20 an hour. One company wants to hire new employees to work on a new fly rod. If it offered potential workers less than $20 an hour, no one would be interested in working for that company. But if the company offered more than $20 an hour, the supply of applicants would increase. The reason is simple: prospective employees would rather work for a company that pays more than any other in the fishing rod industry.

- **Perfectly Inelastic** When the quantity supplied does not change at all in response to a change in price, economists say that product has a **perfectly inelastic** supply. Land is a good example. No one is producing more land, and regardless of price, the supply remains the same. The same is true for seating at sports stadiums. Yankee Stadium, for example, has 49,642 seats. The Yankees cannot increase the supply of seats no matter how expensive or inexpensive the tickets are. That supply is perfectly inelastic.

- **Unit Elastic** When the price of elasticity of supply is exactly 1, the supply of the good is **unit elastic**. In other words, the quantity supplied changes at the same percentage as the change in price.

If you were to graph all three elasticities along a supply curve, they would look like this.

THREE ELASTICITIES OF SUPPLY

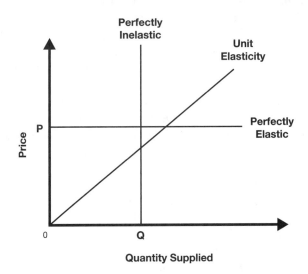

Marginal Cost

If a company can change the quantity supplied of a product quickly and at a low cost, it can respond more readily to changes in market conditions. To achieve this goal, companies try to lower their marginal costs. As discussed earlier, **marginal cost** is the additional cost a manufacturer incurs to produce one more unit of a particular good. As quantity supplied increases, the marginal cost of each unit tends to rise. As a result, a manufacturer will only spend extra money to produce more goods if it receives a higher price for the additional goods.

If marginal costs rise slowly with quantity supplied, then supply is extremely elastic. If marginal costs rise quickly with quantity supplied, then supply is extremely inelastic. So, if a company can lower the marginal cost of each new unit, it will gain elasticity of supply—and greater flexibility.

Applying the Concept In 2019, companies were making about 700 ventilators per week. The marginal cost of producing more did not justify higher output. But when the COVID-19 pandemic hit in early 2020, demand for ventilators increased quickly and producers responded. They shifted their facilities and workers from making other equipment to making ventilators, so they paid an opportunity cost. They also added new facilities and new staff, so they paid additional costs in money. But with strong demand from hospitals and support from government, producers were confident they could sell more ventilators. The increased marginal costs were covered by the increased sales. Within three months, companies had quadrupled production.

Determinants of Price Elasticity

Many factors affect whether the quantity supplied of a product is elastic or inelastic. Time is one of the most important factors. The more time a manufacturer has to respond to price changes, the more elastic is the quantity supplied. The less time a manufacturer has to respond, the less elastic is the quantity supplied. This phenomenon occurs because, in general, it is easier to shift resources over a longer period.

When the price of a product or service changes, the immediate quantity supplied is determined by the **momentary supply** of that good. Momentary supply, which is sometimes called market supply, is the amount currently available. Manufacturers are unable to respond immediately to changes in price.

Farmers, for example, deal with momentary supply every day. In most agricultural markets, they make decisions about planting crops months, sometimes years, before the crop actually heads to market. As a result, agricultural products tend to be inelastic and can sometimes even be perfectly inelastic. Look at a coffee bean grower. On any given day, regardless of price, coffee bean growers cannot change their output of coffee. They have already picked, packed, and shipped their beans to market. In other words, the quantity supplied for that day—its momentary supply—is fixed at whatever price.

However, some products have a perfectly elastic momentary supply. Every day, millions of people use the Internet at the same time. When many people connect to the Internet simultaneously, they create a huge demand for cable lines, Wi-Fi routers, computer servers, and other hardware. As the quantity supplied increases, the price of connecting to the Internet doesn't change. Internet carriers monitor fluctuations in demand and try to make sure that quantity supplied equals the quantity demanded without changing the price.

Short-Run and Long-Run Supply Manufacturers often find it easier to expand production and increase supply over a longer period than in a short interval. When it comes to **short-run supply**, many goods are inelastic. To increase supply in the short term, companies can pay workers to work overtime or hire additional employees. If a company has to scale back its supply in the short-term, they might lay off workers or reduce the number of hours their employees work.

For most goods, **long-run supply** is elastic. For instance, over time, a coffee grower can plant new fields and invest in new technology to increase supply. Moreover, it is much easier and more cost-effective to build a new shoe factory in the long run than in the short run. After all, it takes time to build the factory, hire employees, or even open new stores.

Other Factors of Price Elasticity of Supply

Other factors of price elasticity of supply include the following:

- *Price of Alternative Inputs* The inputs that go into creating a product include land, labor, capital, and entrepreneurship. A company can increase the elasticity of supply by looking for **alternative inputs**— inputs that are less expensive or more readily available. For example, fifty years ago, automobile parts were nearly all made from metal. Now many components are made of plastic, which is cheaper than metals and often more available from suppliers.

- *Ability to Store Supply* Goods, especially manufactured products such as refrigerators, dishwashers, furniture, and so much more are elastic because they can be safely stored or warehoused. The supply of other goods, such as fresh vegetables and other food items, are inelastic because they are perishable and can't be stored for a long time.

- *Factor Mobility* Factor mobility describes how producers can move factors of production, such as labor, from producing one product to producing another. If a manufacturer can easily switch between two different commodities, then the quantity supplied will be more elastic. For example, if a health food store can produce tuna salads and garden salads, the store's owner might switch from making tuna salads to only garden salads if the cost of producing tuna salads increases. As a result, the supply of garden salads is elastic.

- *The Size of the Firm or Industry* If a small bookbinding company gets a large, unexpected order, it could buy the materials it needs on short notice to increase its supply. The money the company pays for the materials probably won't affect the cost of each unit that greatly. On the other hand, a carmaker that buys large quantities of steel would have its unit cost greatly affected, along with its profitability, if the price of steel skyrockets. As you can see, the elasticity of supply is more elastic for the bookbinder than the carmaker.

- *Nature Constraints* Nature is always putting pressure on supply. An early freeze in Florida will greatly impact the supply and price of orange juice, for example. Almond trees need three years to grow enough to produce a large crop of almonds, so the supply of almonds does not increase quickly.

- *Availability of Substitute Inputs* How easy is it to change from one type of input to a different one? For example, when the minimum wage rises, labor becomes more expensive and capital becomes relatively cheaper. As labor costs have risen, fast food restaurants have substituted kiosks which consumers use to input their orders so the number of workers goes down. The easier it is to replace labor with capital makes the supply more elastic. In general, the more easily one input can be substituted for another input, the more elastic the supply of the good or service produced.

- *Definition of Product* The more narrowly a good is defined, the greater its elasticity of supply. For example, it's relatively easy to produce summer jackets with the resources usually needed to produce winter jackets. However, it is more difficult to shift the resources for summer jackets to producing women's skirts.

ANSWER THE TOPIC ESSENTIAL QUESTION

1. In a paragraph, explain why the quantity supplied of a product changes in response to a change in price.

KEY TERMS

price elasticity of supply	unit elastic
elastic	marginal cost
surplus	momentary supply
inelastic	short-run supply
perfectly elastic	long-run supply
perfectly inelastic	alternative input

MULTIPLE-CHOICE QUESTIONS

1. If the supply curve is a horizontal line for a specific price, then a firm will be willing and able to supply
   (A) as much as consumers demand at a lower price
   (B) as much as consumers demand at that price
   (C) as much as consumers demand at a higher price
   (D) only the amount the firm already produces, regardless of price
   (E) more than consumers demand at that price

2. Tricia owns an almond farm. When the price was $4 a pound, she supplied 500 pounds of almonds to a farmers' market. When the price of almonds rose to $10 a pound, she supplied 1,000 pounds of almonds. The price elasticity of supply of those almonds is
   (A) Elastic
   (B) Inelastic
   (C) Perfectly elastic
   (D) Perfectly inelastic
   (E) Unit elastic

3. The price of elasticity of supply of a product would most likely be greater than 1 if the producers
   (A) cannot easily switch from making other products to making it
   (B) cannot substitute one product for another
   (C) need natural resources that are hard to obtain
   (D) can safely store the product for only a very short period of time
   (E) have time to respond to price changes

FREE-RESPONSE QUESTION

1. In September, a grocery store received 2,000 pounds of apples with a price of $5 per pound. In October, the quantity supplied increased to 6,000 pounds, and the price increased to $7 per pound.
   (a) What is the percentage change in quantity supplied?
   (b) What is the percentage change in price?
   (c) What is the price elasticity of supply?
   (d) Is the price elasticity of supply elastic or inelastic? Why?
   (e) What is one factor that might limit the farmer's ability to increase supply even more?

Economists use quantitative data and calculations to determine the effects of a change in an economic situation. Doing so requires them to answer three questions:

- What variable in the situation changed?
- What effect did that change have on economic outcomes?
- How did the degree of change in the variable compare to the degree of change in the outcome?

This process is useful in analyzing price elasticity of supply. For example, consider a basic supply schedule such as this:

Price of Headphones	Percentage Change in Price	Quantity of Headphones Supplied	Percentage Change in Quantity Supplied
$40.00	n/a	100,000	n/a
$44.00	+10%	110,000	+10%
$48.40	+10%	132,000	+20%
$53.24	+10%	158,400	+20%
$58.56	+10%	190,080	+20%

In all these cases, changes in the variable price are related to changes in the outcome, quantity supplied. The degree of change varies, however. The initial 10 percent increase in price results in a 10 percent increase in quantity supplied. At each subsequent 10 percent step in price, however, the quantity supplied increases at a higher rate. Using the formula for calculating price elasticity of supply produces this result:

$$\frac{percentage\ change\ in\ quantity\ supplied}{percentage\ change\ in\ price}$$

$$\frac{0.20}{0.10} = 2$$

Since the price elasticity is 2, the headphones have price elasticity of supply. That is, the quantity supplied increases at a greater rate than increases in price.

Apply the Skill

Below is the supply schedule for another product. Use the quantitative data in the supply schedule to explain whether the supply of bananas is elastic or inelastic. Explain your answer.

Price of Bananas (per 50 pounds)	Percentage Change in Price	Quantity of Bananas Supplied (in 50-pound cases)	Percentage Change in Quantity Supplied
$3.00	n/a	20,000	n/a
$3.15	+5%	20,400	+2%
$3.31	+5%	20,808	+2%
$3.48	+5%	21,224	+2%

Other Elasticities

"With rising incomes, the share of expenditures for food products declines. The resulting shift in expenditures affects demand patterns and employment structures."

German economist Ernst Engel (1821–1896)

Essential Question: How do individuals and businesses respond to factors other than price that affect the demand for goods and services?

Tomorrow is your birthday, and many of your relatives will give you gifts of cash. What will you do with the extra money? Buy a set of wireless speakers that you have long wanted for your room? Save for your post-high school education? Something else? The infusion of money will shift your attitudes about what you can afford to purchase and what you can afford to save. Since this example is based on how one variable (how much money you have) is related to another variable (your demand for products), it is an example of elasticity.

For teenagers, birthdays can be a good way to boost your income. Unless you save your birthday money, you will probably use the cash to buy a good or a service. The income elasticity of demand is one reason why the quantity demanded for those products increases.

Income Elasticity of Demand

The greater your income, the more money you have to spend, so your demand for certain goods and services rises. On the other hand, the less money you have, the less money you have to spend, which decreases demand. **Income elasticity of demand** measures how much a change in a person's income affects that person's demand for a particular product.

Figuring Income Elasticity of Demand As you did earlier with the price elasticity of supply and the price elasticity of demand, you can use mathematics to determine the income elasticity of demand. Malika is a chef at a restaurant who earns $3,000 per month. She spends about $500 on food and $30 on going to plays monthly. After she gets a raise of 20 percent, or $600 per month, she has more money to save and spend. She already spends about as much as she wants to on food, but she does go out for meals more often, so her spending on food increases slightly, by 10 percent, or $50. She enjoys plays, so she increases her spending on them by 100%, or $30. Below is a summary of her income and expenses:

MONTHLY INCOME AND EXPENSES FOR MALIKA			
Item	Before Raise	After Raise	Percentage Change
Income	$3,000	$3,600	20%
Spending on Food	$500	$550	10%
Spending on Plays	$30	$60	100%

Her decisions indicate that her spending on plays was far more sensitive to a change in income than was her spending on food. You can measure the difference using simple equations. You divide the percentage change in the quantity demanded for a product by the percentage change in income. The equation looks like this:

$$\frac{percentage\ change\ in\ quantity\ demanded}{percentage\ change\ in\ income} = income\ elasticity\ of\ demand$$

Plugging the numbers for food into the formula produces this equation:

$$\frac{10\ (percentage\ change\ in\ quantity\ demanded)}{20\ (percentage\ change\ in\ income)} = 0.5$$

A ratio of less than 1.0 results when a percentage change in income results in a smaller percentage change in spending. This type of demand is called **income inelastic**.

Plugging the numbers for plays into the formula produces this equation:

$$\frac{100\ (percentage\ change\ in\ quantity\ demanded)}{20\ (percentage\ change\ in\ income)} = 5.0$$

Since the ratio is greater than 1.0, it indicates that the percentage change in income results in a larger percentage change in spending. It is **income elastic**.

Types of Income Elasticity Using this ratio of change in quantity demanded to change in income, economists have identified four types of income elasticity of demand:

- *Positive Income Elasticity* A rise in income leads to an increase in the quantity demanded. In other words, the demand for the product is income elastic.

- *Negative Income Elasticity* A rise in income leads to a decrease in the quantity demanded. Inferior goods, which you will learn about in a bit, have a negative income elasticity.

- *Unitary Elasticity* A rise in income is proportional to the increase in the quantity demanded. If income increases by 15 percent and demand also increases by 15 percent, then demand would be unitary, or equal to 1.0.

- *Zero Income Elasticity* Regardless of whether income changes, the quantity demanded is the same.

Normal Goods and Inferior Goods Although an increase in income may lead to an increase in demand for many goods, it does not necessarily cause an increase in demand for all goods. Economists classify goods as normal or inferior, depending on how the demand for those goods changes in response to changes in income.

Normal goods are products or services for which the demand rises as income increases. For example, your mother just got a new job that pays significantly more than the last, giving her the economic resources to buy a new washing machine. In this instance, the demand for the washing machine, a normal good, has a positive income elastic relationship to your mother's income. The following graph shows the relationship between income and demand for normal goods. In the graph, as income rises from Y_1 to Y_2, the demand for a normal good rises from Q_1 to Q_2.

DEMAND FOR NORMAL GOODS

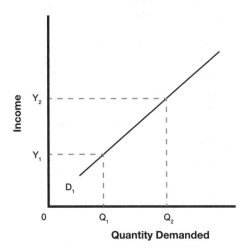

On the other hand, **inferior goods** are those for which the demand decreases when income rises. Inferior goods have a negative income elasticity. Older used cars are good examples of inferior goods. When people don't have much money to spare, they might buy an older used car, which provides basic transportation. But as their incomes rise, they might choose to buy new cars. Consequently, as income rises, the demand for older used cars declines.

Inferior goods do not reflect the quality of the product. Nor does it mean they are a bad purchase. If your income is low, and you're living on a budget, inferior goods, like an inexpensive used car, are a great way to lower costs.

Source: Getty Images

Frozen pizza would be considered an inferior good, but not because all frozen pizza is bad. It's not. However, when people's incomes rise, demand for a less expensive item such as frozen pizza decreases versus demand for a more expensive item, such as pizza delivered from a pizzeria. Delivery pizza would be considered a normal good. When people's incomes rise, the demand for pizzeria pizza increases. In other words, consumers may order it two or three times a month, rather than just once.

Coffee is also an inferior good. Because you're on a budget, you might not be able to afford the pricey grande white chocolate mocha at the high-end café on the corner. However, you can afford to buy an inexpensive cup of coffee at the local convenience store. If your income increases, you might start buying the higher-priced coffee. Now you have more money to spend, and the quantity demanded for inferior goods decreases.

Necessities and Luxuries Income elasticity also comes into play when goods are either necessities or luxuries. **Necessities** are goods you feel you can't do without, such as medicine, gasoline, or milk. These goods have an income elasticity between 0 and 1 because demand does not increase or decrease much with changes in income. In other words, you'll purchase these items regardless of your income level. As your income rises, the total proportion of money you spend on a necessity typically declines.

Electricity is an example of a necessity. Regardless of your income, you still need electricity to turn on the lights, power your TV, and cook. Although your income might have risen, it doesn't necessarily mean you will use more electricity. If your income went up 10 percent, chances are your quantity demanded for electricity did not increase by 10 percent.

Luxuries are goods that you feel you can do without more easily. If your income is low, you are less likely to purchase a luxury item. However, if your income is high, you are more likely to purchase a luxury item. Luxury goods tend to be income elastic. Traveling overseas is a luxury, as is a second home, expensive cars, and jewelry. If your income went up 10 percent, chances are that your quantity demanded for rings would go up more than 10 percent.

Remodeled bathrooms, as well as second homes and jewelry, are luxury goods. The income elasticity of demand for luxury items is usually greater than 1. That is, the percentage of increase in demand tends to be higher than the percentage of increase in income.

Cross-Price Elasticity of Demand

Elasticity of demand is also affected by the price of other, related goods that are either substitutes or complements. That "cross" effect on demand can be measured by the **cross-price elasticity of demand**, which measures the responsiveness of the demand for a good to a change in the price of a substitute good or a complementary good.

Substitutes Goods that can replace one another, such as butter and margarine, are **substitutes**. When two goods are substitutes, the cross-elasticity of demand is positive, or greater than zero. That is, when the price of one good increases, the demand for the substitute good also increases. Similarly, when the price of one good decreases, the demand for the substitute good also decreases.

For example, if the price of whole milk increases, consumers may switch to less expensive 2 percent milk. When the price of butter increases, the demand for margarine is likely to rise as consumers seek a cheaper substitute.

To determine the cross-price elasticity of demand, take the percentage change in the quantity of one good and divide it by the percentage change in price of the second good, as shown in the following equation:

$$\frac{percentage\ change\ in\ quantity\ B\ demanded}{percentage\ change\ in\ price\ of\ A} = cross\text{-}price\ elasticity\ of\ demand$$

Suppose, for example, that the price of grape juice has increased over the past week by 10 percent because cold weather killed a large number of grapes. As a result, the demand for cranberry juice, a substitute, has increased by 12 percent. Use the equation above to determine the cross-price elasticity of demand.

$$\frac{12\ (percentage\ change\ in\ quantity\ demanded\ of\ cranberry\ juice)}{10\ (percentage\ change\ in\ price\ of\ grape\ juice)} = 1.20$$

The cross-price elasticity of demand is 1.20. Because the cross-price elasticity of demand is positive, the products are considered substitutes.

Complementary Goods Goods that are related in their use are **complementary goods**. Cars and gasoline are complementary products, as are batteries and flashlights. When the price of one product rises, the quantity demanded for the other decreases. In other words, the relationship between complementary products is an inverse one.

To determine the cross-price elasticity of demand for complementary products, use the same equation that you did for substitute products. However, for complementary products, the ratio will be negative, or less than zero. Suppose, for example, that the price of flashlights increases by 50 percent. As a result, the demand for batteries decreases by 20 percent.

$$\frac{-20 \ (percentage \ change \ in \ quantity \ demanded \ of \ batteries)}{50 \ (percentage \ change \ in \ price \ of \ flashlights)} = -0.40$$

The cross-price elasticity of demand is -0.40. When the cross-price elasticity of two products is negative, they are considered to be complementary products.

Many products and services are **not related**. That is, increases or decreases in the price of one product have no impact on the demand for another product. For example, an increase in the price of books has no effect on the demand for snow shovels. The cross-price elasticity of demand for unrelated products and services is zero.

Usefulness of Cross-Price Elasticity Business owners can use cross-price elasticity in determining the prices at which they sell their products. For example, businesses often introduce new products that are intended to be substitutes for existing products. Suppose that Theta Beverages just released a lemon-flavored drink to compete with Athletic Fluids's orange-flavored drink. Theta's drink is intended to be a substitute for Athletic's. Athletic Fluids decides to compete with Theta's new product by reducing the price of its orange-flavored drink by 10 percent in the coming month.

By figuring out the cross-price elasticity, Theta Beverages can predict how much the demand of its product will decline in response to the change in the price of Athletic's product. Theta can then decide how to keep revenue up.

Now suppose a company produces both tennis rackets and tennis balls, which are complementary goods. The rise in price of either product will result in a fall in quantity demanded for both. For example, if the price of tennis balls jumps sharply, people might switch from tennis to other sports. If people play less tennis, they will buy fewer rackets. So, before this company raises the prices for tennis balls, it will consider the possible impact on sales of rackets as well. They will try to determine if the increased revenue from one product is worth the possible overall decrease in revenue from the two products together.

ANSWER THE TOPIC ESSENTIAL QUESTION

1. In two paragraphs, explain how factors besides price affect the demand for products and services.

MULTIPLE-CHOICE QUESTIONS

1. Which statement best defines positive income elasticity of demand?

   (A) A rise in income comes with an increase in quantity demanded.

   (B) A rise in income comes with a decrease in quantity demanded.

   (C) A rise in income is proportional to the increase in quantity demanded.

   (D) A decrease in income comes with an increase in quantity demanded.

   (E) Regardless of income, quantity demanded remains the same.

2. A product for which the quantity demanded decreases when income rises is known as a(n)

   (A) inferior good

   (B) normal good

   (C) luxury good

   (D) substitute good

   (E) complementary good

3. Marie received a 5 percent increase in salary. She had been seeing one concert a month, but now she is seeing two concerts a month. Marie's demand for concerts demonstrates

   (A) negative income elasticity

   (B) unitary elasticity

   (C) cross-price elasticity

   (D) zero income elasticity

   (E) positive income elasticity

RELATIONSHIP BETWEEN INCOME AND QUANTITY DEMANDED

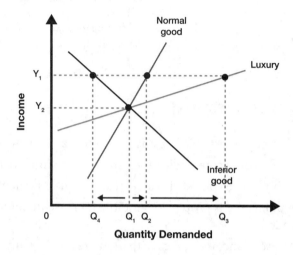

1. This graph illustrates the relationship between quantity demanded and income for the three types of goods: Q1, Q2, Q3. As you can see, the demand for all three kinds of products is different in response to the same change in income from Y to Y1.

   (a) Based on this curve, what conclusion can you draw about luxury goods?

   (b) Based on your answer to the first question, is the demand for luxury goods income elastic or income inelastic? Explain your answer as it relates to the slope of the curve.

   (c) Based on this curve, what conclusion can you draw about inferior goods?

   (d) Based on your answer to question (c), is the demand for inferior goods income elastic or income inelastic? Explain your answer as it relates to the slope of the curve.

   (e) Use this curve to answer the following question: The more luxurious the good, is the income elasticity greater or lesser?

THINK AS AN ECONOMIST: *DETERMINE THE EFFECTS OF AN ECONOMIC CHANGE USING CALCULATIONS*

Elasticity of demand measures how constant the demand for a good is in relation to economic changes. As you have learned, some goods have price elasticity of demand and others do not. Elasticity of demand can also be affected by changes in the price of complementary goods—goods for which the use is related.

To determine whether goods have the cross-price elasticity demonstrated by complementary goods, economists use a formula:

$$\frac{percentage\ change\ in\ quantity\ A\ demanded}{percentage\ change\ in\ price\ of\ B} = cross\text{-}price\ elasticity\ of\ demand$$

A negative result indicates that the quantity demanded for the second good has an inverse relationship to a change in price of the first good, meaning they are complementary goods. A positive result means the goods are not complementary.

Apply the Skill

Use the data in the table to calculate the relationship between change in price for Good A and the change in demand for three possible complementary goods—B, C, and D. Which good(s) are complementary and which are not?

	Percentage Change in Price	Percentage Change in Quantity Demanded
Good A	+12%	
Good B		-2%
Good C		0%
Good D		+4%

Market Equilibrium and Consumer and Producer Surplus

"We know, in other words, the general conditions in which what we call, somewhat misleadingly, an equilibrium will establish itself: but we never know what the particular prices or wages are which would exist if the market were to bring about such an equilibrium."

Friedrich August von Hayek, Austrian-British economist (1899–1992)

Essential Question: How does the market for a product or service reach equilibrium between supply and demand?

Joaquin owns a deli across the street from the main classroom building of a community college. Each evening, at 9:00 p.m., as students leave class, many stop by to pick up a late dinner or snack. Selling sandwiches for $6.50 each, he has a few sandwiches left over, but he makes a good profit. However, when another deli opened up just a block away that sold sandwiches for just $5.50 each, Joaquin suddenly found himself with far more unsold sandwiches at the end of the evening. He was losing business and with it, his profits.

In the face of more competition and a greater supply of sandwiches for the student consumers, he lowers his price to $6.00. Sales increase enough that even at the lower price, his business is profitable. He considered cutting prices again, but estimated that doing so would just reduce his revenue without increasing sales much.

The owner of the new deli, who was selling sandwiches at $5.50, was so busy that he completely used up his supplies each night. Hoping to increase profits, he raised his prices to $6.00. Though he sold fewer sandwiches, because of the higher price, he increased his profits overall.

Soon, both Joaquin's deli and the new deli were selling similar sandwiches for the same price and making similar profits. On a typical day, they could estimate demand well enough that they rarely made too many sandwiches and rarely had supplies left over.

When a new deli, or any type of firm, opens, existing firms need to adjust their strategies for how much to produce and how much to charge. New competitors are just one of many factors that firms need to consider in order to operate profitably.

Market Equilibrium

The amount of a good or service available to consumers is the **market supply**. It fluctuates constantly, as new suppliers enter or leave a market and existing suppliers change the quantity of products they produce. **Market equilibrium** is the point in a perfectly competitive market in which supply is equal to demand. Generally, when an oversupply of goods exists, prices fall and quantity demanded increases. Moreover, when a shortage of goods exists, prices rise and quantity demanded decreases. The price point at which quantity supplied and quantity demanded intersect is called the **equilibrium price**. The quantity bought and sold at the equilibrium price is known as the **equilibrium quantity**.

Market equilibrium occurs most readily in a market that is perfectly competitive. **Perfect competition** is a theoretical market structure in which competition is at its greatest possible level. Perfect competition assumes that a large number of manufacturers will produce the same goods that will be consumed by a large number of buyers. It also assumes that new producers can enter and exit the market quite easily.

When markets are in equilibrium, prices will not change unless a new factor changes supply or demand. That's what happened to Joaquin. Before the new deli opened, he was selling out his **inventory**, or stock of sandwiches, at $6.50 a sandwich—the equilibrium price at that time. After the new deli opened, he had to adjust. The quantity of sandwiches he was willing to supply exceeded the quantity demanded by the students. To reduce the surplus of sandwiches, he reduced production and prices, eventually finding a price that students were willing to pay—the equilibrium price, at a quantity he could make and still have a profit.

The equilibrium price of a product provides information that helps producers allocate their resources efficiently. Two important signals are the existence of shortages or surpluses in a market.

Shortages Go back to the example of Joaquin's sandwich shop. If the price of each sandwich were to fall below equilibrium, the quantity demanded would outpace the quantity supplied, creating a **shortage**, which is an undersupply of products in a market. Because of the low price of the sandwiches, cash-strapped students lined up to buy the sandwiches until the supply ran out.

In that event, what would Joaquin have done? Because demand was now greater, he might have decided to raise prices. If he did, quantity demanded would fall as the quantity supplied increased. Eventually, supply and demand would find equilibrium again.

Surpluses Yet if Joaquin raised prices too much, his customers would go to his competitors for their sandwiches, leaving Joaquin with a **surplus**, or an oversupply of sandwiches.

To understand the impact of surpluses on a market, consider this real-life example. In 2016 in the United States, the grocery store shelves, not to mention warehouses and distribution centers, were brimming with milk, eggs, and vegetables. The surplus was the result of increases in production and a decrease in exports. U.S. dairy farmers were on the front lines that year, producing 24 billion gallons of milk, a record amount. As a result, consumers had more milk to sip and more butter and cheese to eat.

It was a great time for consumers because prices for these and other food staples took a nosedive. Farmers, on the other hand, were less happy because they were selling their products for less money, which ate into their profits. Two years earlier the exact opposite had happened. The price of milk, eggs, poultry, and other food staples was high, putting more money in the pockets of farmers.

These events reflected the cyclical world of **market surplus**. A market surplus occurs when quantity supplied is greater than quantity demanded, creating a glut of goods on the market. When market surpluses happen, prices are higher than the equilibrium price. As a result in 2016, farmers weren't able to sell off their goods, just as Joaquin couldn't sell his sandwiches.

Examples such as these abound every day for products that consumers want more of during one time of the year than another. Many of these are weather related, such as snow shovels in the winter, baseball gloves in the spring, and leaf rakes in the autumn. Others are related to special events that come regularly. After the holidays each December, stores often sell surplus gift wrap at rock-bottom prices. Store managers know that lowering prices will increase the quantity demanded. As a result, the surplus is reduced until it hits the equilibrium price. Swimsuits in the summer, baseball gloves, and leaf

Graphing Market Equilibrium To determine market equilibrium visually, combine a supply curve with a demand curve on the same graph. The price at which the two intersect is the equilibrium price. The following supply and demand schedule shows the quantity of sandwiches students demanded and the quantity Joaquin was willing to supply at various prices. At $5.00 a sandwich, the quantity of sandwiches demanded was 30 and the quantity supplied was zero, leaving a shortage of 30 sandwiches. At $5.50, the quantity demanded was 25 and the quantity supplied is 21, leaving a shortage of 4 sandwiches, and so on.

SUPPLY AND DEMAND SCHEDULE FOR JOAQUIN'S DELI			
Price per Sandwich	Quantity Demanded	Quantity Supplied	Shortage (-) or Surplus (+)
$5.00	30	0	-30
$5.50	25	15	-10
$6.00	20	20	0
$6.50	10	28	+18

To find the equilibrium price, plot the numbers on the following line graph. You can see clearly that the equilibrium price is $6.00 a sandwich. At that price, Joaquin is willing to make 20 sandwiches, which is the same as the quantity demanded.

MARKET EQUILIBRIUM PRICE FOR SANDWICHES

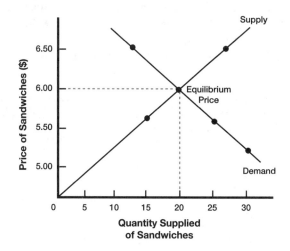

Efficient and Inefficient Markets

As was explained earlier, the equilibrium price gives information to economic decision makers to help them achieve allocative efficiency, which is the efficient allocation of resources. As it applies to supply and demand, efficiency occurs in a market when the optimal amount of each good is being produced and consumed.

Economists define an **efficient market** as one in which it is impossible to improve the economic situation of one party without imposing a cost on another. For example, at $6.00 a sandwich, the market is operating efficiently. Joaquin and his competitors are making just enough sandwiches for the market. But if Joaquin raised his price to $6.50, his price would be above the equilibrium price. He would probably lose customers.

In contrast, in an **inefficient market**, it is possible to benefit one party without imposing a cost on another. At $5 a sandwich, a shortage occurs. The price is so low that Joaquin would not meet the demand for sandwiches. The shortage is a signal that the market is not operating efficiently.

Consumer Surplus, Producer Surplus, and Market Efficiency

To explain market efficiency further, economists use the concepts of consumer surplus and producer surplus. **Consumer surplus** is the difference between the price consumers pay and the price they are willing to pay. For example, when Joaquin began selling his sandwiches at the community college, assume that all students were willing to pay $6.50 apiece. But when the deli down the street selling sandwiches for $5.50 opened, the market for sandwiches changed. There was a difference between what students were willing to pay and what they did pay:

$$\$6.50 - \$5.50 = \$1.00$$

If the consumer surplus for one sandwich was $1.00 for every consumer, and Joaquin sold 10 sandwiches, the total consumer surplus would be $10.00.

However, not all consumers were willing to pay $6.50. The amount of consumer surplus would decrease as the amount they were willing to pay decreased. The table below shows this relationship at a few prices to demonstrate this pattern.

EXAMPLES OF CONSUMER SURPLUS FOR ONE SANDWICH		
Price a Consumer Was Willing to Pay	Actual Price	Amount of Consumer Surplus
$6.50	$5.50	$1.00
$6.49	$5.50	$0.99
$6.48	$5.50	$0.98
$5.52	$5.50	$0.02
$5.51	$5.50	$0.01
$5.50	$5.50	$0.00

On a graph, this is the triangular portion with its corners at the highest price, the actual price, and the actual (or equilibrium) quantity. So, to more accurately estimate the actual total consumer surplus, calculate the area of this triangular portion using this calculation:

(highest price -the actual price) X quantity supplied at the actual price X 0.05

Economists talk about consumer surplus whether referring to individuals or total consumer surplus. They, and you, can graph consumer surplus on a demand curve. Suppose that at the price of $700, consumers demand a total of 500,000 tablets of a medication. If you look at the following demand curve, the shaded area above the $700 price is the consumer surplus. Some consumers are willing to pay more than $700, but the quantity demanded above that price decreases.

CONSUMER SURPLUS

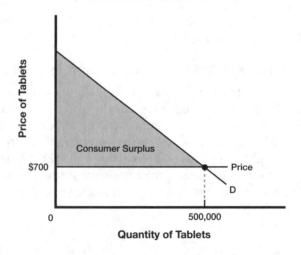

Producer Surplus Seen from the supplier's point of view, the **producer surplus** is the difference between the price for which the producer is willing to sell the product and the market equilibrium price. Joaquin would sell his sandwiches for $5.50, but since students are willing to pay more, he charges $6.50.

$$\$6.50 - \$5.50 = \$1.00$$

The producer surplus for one sandwich for one consumer, then, was $1.00.

When you add it all together, Joaquin makes $130 for selling all his sandwiches at $6.50. Had he sold the sandwiches for $3.25 apiece, his total revenue would have been $64.50. You determine producer surplus by taking the amount that he received —$130 —and subtracting the amount that he was willing to sell the sandwiches for—$64.50.

$$\$130 - \$64.50 = \$65.50$$

Joaquin's producer surplus, then, is $65.50—the difference between what he actually received and the lesser amount that he was willing to sell the sandwiches for. As the market price for a product changes, so does the level of producer surplus.

You can graph producer surplus on a supply curve like the one that follows. A producer is willing to sell the product at the lower price, P_1, but the quantity supplied would be only Q_1. However, the equilibrium price turns out to be P_E and the equilibrium quantity sold is Q_E. The difference between the quantity sold at P_1 and the quantity sold at P_E is the producer surplus—the shaded area on the graph. As you can see, the greater the increase in quantity supplied and market price, the larger the producer surplus. Conversely, as market price and quantity supplied decreases, so does the producer surplus.

PRODUCER SURPLUS

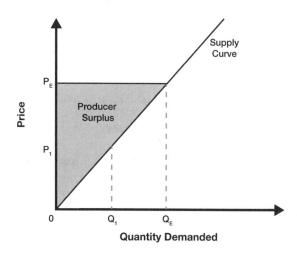

Total Economic Surplus When you add together consumer surplus and producer surplus, you get **total economic surplus**, which is often referred to as total surplus. When a market is at equilibrium price and equilibrium quantity, the total surplus is larger than it would be at any other quantity. The market is operating at its most efficient level. As was explained earlier, efficiencies allow one party to improve its situation without imposing a cost on another party. As it relates to supply and demand, efficiencies allow for the production of goods at the cost and in quantities that consumers demand.

For example, say there is a DVD that you are willing to pay $40 for, but you find it on sale for $20. The consumer surplus—the amount you paid compared to the amount you were willing to spend—is $20.

This exchange was good for both you and the store. Suppose it cost the store's owner $5 to purchase the DVD from the supplier. The store sold it to you for $20. The store's owner likes the exchange because she made a $15 profit. In economic terms that $15 was the producer surplus.

You like the exchange because you got an extra $20 of value, and the store made $15 in profit. The combination of both is the benefit that society garnered during the trade. It's the total economic surplus. To understand how society benefitted when you bought the DVD, all add consumer surplus and producer surplus, in this case $20 + $15= $35. You can graph total surplus on a supply/demand graph like this:

TOTAL ECONOMIC SURPLUS

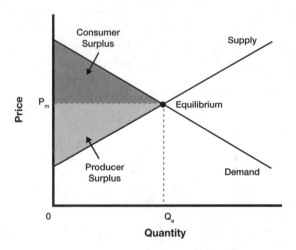

In the above graph, P_m is the market price and Q_e is the equilibrium quantity. The two shaded areas, together, represent the total economic surplus.

When consumer surplus and producer surplus are maximized, or at their highest level, a market is operating most efficiently. The market is perfectly competitive. Producers are free to enter and leave markets and to set prices. Likewise, consumers are free to buy or not buy and to decide whether a price is fair. In conclusion, perfectly competitive markets are efficient.

1. If you own a business, why is it important to determine what the market equilibrium is for a product or a service?

KEY TERMS

market supply	inventory	inefficient market
market equilibrium	shortage	consumer surplus
equilibrium price	surplus	producer surplus
equilibrium quantity	market surplus	total economic surplus
perfect competition	efficient market	

MULTIPLE-CHOICE QUESTIONS

1. The price point at which quantity supplied and quantity demanded intersect is called
   (A) market surplus
   (B) market equilibrium
   (C) equilibrium price
   (D) equilibrium quantity
   (E) market supply

2. You are willing to pay $35 for a book but bought it on sale for $28.50. It cost the store $10 to buy from a supplier. What would be the total economic surplus?
   (A) $6.50
   (B) $18.50
   (C) $25.00
   (D) $35.00
   (E) $35.60

3. In the example in item 2, what would be the consumer surplus?
   (A) $6.50
   (B) $18.50
   (C) $25.10
   (D) $35.00
   (E) $35.69

1. Customers are willing to pay $2.50 for a bottle of a new brand of energy drink. The supermarket down the street is willing to sell the energy drinks for that price, but puts it on sale for $1.50 a bottle. It cost the supermarket $1 to buy each energy drink from the supplier. Across the street, the convenience store originally sells the same energy drink for $1.75, but puts it on sale for $1.25. It also costs the convenience store $1 to buy each bottle from its supplier. Assume that each store sells only ten bottles of the new energy drink.

   (a) What is the consumer surplus for the energy drink sold by the convenience store before it went on sale?

   (b) What is the total surplus if customers bought the drink at the convenience store before it went on sale?

   (c) What is the total surplus if customers bought the drink at the supermarket?

   (d) At the sale price, what is the producer surplus at the supermarket?

   (e) At the sale price, what is the producer surplus at the convenience store?

Economists use economic models to analyze situations and explain how economic outcomes occur. To do so, they take these steps:

- Identify what specific economic behaviors are taking place in a particular situation.

- Use an economic model to explain how those economic outcomes have occurred.

For example, economists note that producers will reduce production when they see that their quantity supplied exceeds the quantity demanded by the consuming public. If they have an excess of supply already on hand, they will lower prices, recognizing that when they do, quantity demanded will rise until it meets the quantity they have in supply. Producers make these choices because supply and demand work together to reach market equilibrium—the price at which supply and demand are equal.

Apply the Skill

A local market for fruit smoothies saw a sharp increase in demand after a local celebrity spoke on an interview show about how healthy he felt drinking a smoothie every day. Noting the increased demand, two coffee shop chains added smoothies to their menus. With increased competition, smoothie providers found they had to lower smoothie prices to prevent being stuck with rotting fruit at the end of the day. An economist used the supply-and-demand graph shown here to visualize what happened. Using the graph, explain how the economic outcomes occurred in terms of supply and demand.

SMOOTHIE MARKET GRAPH

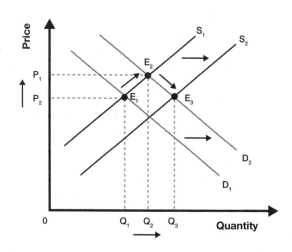

Topic 2.7

Market Disequilibrium and Other Changes in Equilibrium

"[Financial markets] are in continuous disequilibrium."

George Soros, investor and philanthropist (b. 1930)

Essential Question: What factors cause supply and demand to fall out of balance with each other?

The United States is the world's largest producer of soybeans. Businesses and government have spent millions of dollars making the country's grain industry more robust. They have invested in research to increase yields and new storage and railway facilities to get the crop to market. Individual farmers in the Midwest and Great Plains have done the work of planting, tending, and harvesting. Because of these combined efforts, soybean production in the United States increased dramatically between 1924 and 2018:

- Average harvest per acre increased from 11 bushels to 52 bushels.
- Total production increased from 5 million bushels to almost 5 billion bushels.

However, in the summer of 2019, soybean farmers found themselves hurting. China, the world's top soybean importer, stopped buying American soybeans for a second consecutive year in response to a trade war with the United States. As a result, the demand for soybeans plummeted. With the collapse of that market, the country's farmers were unable to sell their supplies at a profit.

During the back-and-forth between U.S. and Chinese trade negotiators, prices for soybeans fell well below their previous **market price**. Even with the lower prices, some farmers were unable to sell a single bean from the preceding fall harvest. To make matters even worse, farmers could not sell soybeans from the upcoming harvest. Historically, they would have already committed to selling 50 to 70 percent of their crop before they had planted a single bean.

As a result, a surplus of soybeans sat unsold in silos and warehouses, the victim of **market disequilibrium**. In other words, the quantity supplied of soybeans exceeded the quantity demanded at the current market price. In this topic, you will learn about the serious effects that market disequilibrium can have on people and businesses—and the factors that cause quantity supplied and quantity demanded to fall out of balance.

American farmers were hard hit when China stopped soybean imports when trade talks with the United States bogged down. Because the Chinese stopped buying the crop, prices dropped, creating a market surplus.

Market Disequilibrium

Market disequilibrium occurs when various factors force markets to become imbalanced. Specifically, market disequilibrium occurs when the price demanded for a product is not equal to the supply price, and the quantity demanded is not equal to the quantity supplied.

Market disequilibrium causes quantity and price to change. When the quantity supplied (Qs) and quantity demanded (Qd) are out of balance, the result is a shortage or surplus, at current market prices.

- A **shortage** is a situation in which not enough goods or services exist to meet market demand (Qd > Qs).

- A **surplus** is a situation in which too many goods or services are on the market, exceeding the quantity demanded (Qs > Qd).

Shortages and surpluses usually lead to changes in price. Shortages create pressure for prices to increase, while surpluses create pressure for prices to decrease.

For example, when the U.S. trade war with China began in May 2019, the quantity demanded of soybeans fell, creating a surplus on the market. To try to sell their surplus, farmers and traders who owned soybeans became willing to accept less money in exchange for their product. The price of soybeans declined from $9.20 a bushel at the end of January to $8.03 in May.

To better understand what was happening, study the supply and demand graph that follows. It shows visually how basic economic principles work in a market economy.

MARKET DISEQUILIBRIUM

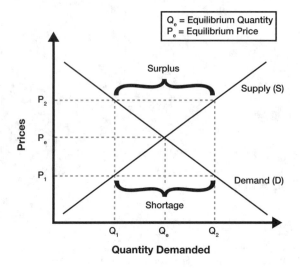

As you can see, the price in which demand and supply are in sync is the **equilibrium price** (P_e), which occurs at the equilibrium quantity (Q_e). In other words, the quantity demanded and the quantity supplied are balanced at a particular price. Because of the trade war, the quantity demanded of soybeans declined from the equilibrium quantity to a lower quantity, indicated by Q_1, yet farmers did not have time to reduce the quantity supplied of soybeans. Consequently, a surplus of soybeans resulted, as shown in the area labeled "Surplus" on the graph.

Over time, farmers could respond to the disequilibrium in a number of ways. As has already been shown, they lowered the price of soybeans in response to the reduced demand. They could also look for other international markets besides China, such as Europe or Brazil. Finally, they could adjust supply by growing fewer soybeans and more of another crop, such as corn or vegetables.

Because shortages and surpluses occur frequently in market economies, they are worth examining in greater depth.

Shortages The shortage of a good or service is usually a temporary condition. During a shortage, prices will tend to rise in response to the declining supply of a good or service. Producers will increase their production, causing the shortage to disappear over time. Gradually, the market regains equilibrium.

Don't equate a shortage with scarcity, however. Scarcities occur when products cannot be replenished. For example, France has very little oil in the ground. No matter how much it increases the price of oil, it cannot create more oil. Consequently, the country imports almost all of this important resource.

Shortages can occur because of weather. For example, in the summertime, when temperatures are hot, the demand for electricity rises as people turn on their air conditioners. Many times, power companies cannot meet this unexpected demand for energy. The shortage of electricity generally ends as the weather cools off.

Natural disasters such as tornadoes and hurricanes can also cause shortages for essential products such as food, water, and housing, leading to higher prices. If an unexpected freeze in Florida destroys much of the state's orange groves, then a massive reduction in the supply of orange juice will result.

Government policies, such as price ceilings and tax increases, can result in shortages. Price ceilings are a type of price control in which the government sets the maximum amount a seller can charge for a product. The role of government in market disequilibrium will be explored later in this topic.

When orange groves unexpectedly freeze in Florida, it can result in a shortage of orange juice.

Surpluses In contrast to shortages, surpluses occur when quantity demanded is less than quantity supplied at the market price. Remember Joaquin, the sandwich maker from Topic 2.6? When the new deli down the road from the college opened, it cut into Joaquin's business. The equilibrium price of sandwiches shifted downward because of the increase in quantity of sandwiches supplied. As a consequence, the quantity demanded for Joaquin's sandwiches dropped because his prices were higher than those of his competitor. As a result, Joaquin had a surplus of sandwiches on his hands. Eventually, Joaquin eliminated his surplus by lowering the price of his sandwiches. In other words, Joaquin adjusted to the new equilibrium price.

Surpluses don't just affect individual producers like Joaquin. As you remember from Topic 2.6, consumers can also have a surplus. Remember that a consumer surplus is the difference between the price consumers pay and the price they are willing to pay. A producer surplus is the difference between what the producer is willing and able to pay to supply a good and what the producer actually receives. If you add the two together, you get a total economic surplus.

Surpluses usually occur because of an imbalance between supply and demand. Suppose a toy manufacturer has introduced a new doll on the market. If the doll maker overprices the toy, demand for it will decrease, creating a surplus. In that instance, the doll maker may choose to lower the price, spurring demand and reducing the surplus.

Surpluses are generally good for consumers but not for producers. The surplus of soybeans in North Dakota, for example, created immense economic pressure on farmers and other businesses. A company that overestimates future demand for a particular product can be financially hurt if it creates too many unsold units, which will eventually eat into profits. A surplus of perishable goods, such as milk, wheat, and soybeans, could spoil and become unsellable, resulting in an economic loss. Even goods that don't perish quickly can result in an economic loss because they are costly to store.

Market Disequilibrium and Price Elasticity

When a market is in disequilibrium, producers have to make decisions about how to respond. Should they raise or lower prices? Should they increase or decrease supplies? One factor they must consider is the price elasticity of demand, which you learned about in Topic 2.3. According to this principle, the demand for some goods responds readily to changes in prices, but the demand for other goods does not respond so readily.

When prices do not respond readily to changes in demand or supply, the market has **sticky prices**. Price stickiness, also known as price rigidity, is a situation in which prices adjust slowly when the supply and demand curve shifts. According to the laws of supply and demand, when prices rise, quantity demanded drops and when prices decrease, quantity demanded goes up. However, those laws don't necessarily apply to certain products. In those instances, prices either remain constant or, at the very least, are slow to adjust. Haircut prices are sticky because they rarely change. The price of gasoline, on the other hand, is not sticky, because those prices go up and down constantly with changes in both supply and demand.

Producers also consider the price elasticity of supply. In other words, the supply of some goods responds readily to changes in price, while the supply of other goods does not respond so readily. For example, during the Great Recession of 2008–2009, millions of people could not afford to keep up the mortgage payments on their homes, and they lost their homes. As a result, the housing market experienced a major surplus of homes on the market. Yet home prices were highly elastic, and the prices plummeted. In response, consumers began to buy homes at the lower prices, and the surplus gradually decreased. Over the next ten years, the housing market slowly recovered and came closer to equilibrium.

Causes of Market Disequilibrium

In a market economy, the forces of supply and demand pressure producers and consumers toward equilibrium, but rarely reach it. Several factors cause market disequilibrium, some of which have been mentioned already.

Difficulty in Predicting Behavior Moreover, social factors, such as changes in fashion, and the tastes and preferences of consumers, can influence the production of goods, causing market disequilibrium. How many people will want to fly from Chicago to Atlanta on July 1? What kinds of cars will consumers value more next year: smaller, fuel-efficient models or larger models? Will this new toy become wildly popular or not? Producers have sophisticated models to predict demand, but no one can do it perfectly. That's why you see end-of-year sales at bargain prices.

Further, producers rarely know the behavior of their competitors. If one sock company accurately perceives that consumers want fewer cotton socks and more wool socks, that producer can shift production. However, if every producer perceives the same shift and all increase production, the growing market might be overwhelmed, pushing prices down sharply.

Changes in Economic Conditions Cyclical fluctuations in economic conditions can also cause market disequilibrium. An **economic recession** occurs when a country experiences a decline in economic activity. An **economic depression** is a deep and prolonged recession. During these bad economic times, consumers purchase fewer goods, stores sell less, and factories reduce output. Demand falls for many goods and services, and a surplus of goods often occurs. The result is market disequilibrium.

Population Shifts Population growth or decline can also cause market disequilibrium. If the total population of a country increases, a country will need to grow or import more food. Beginning in the 1950s, as millions of Americans moved from the Midwest and Northeast to the warmer climates of the South, sales of air conditioners increased overall, but particularly in states such as Arizona and New Mexico.

Government Intervention Government can result in disequilibrium, often intentionally as a local city council, a state legislature, or the federal government tries to balance economic goals with other goals. These interventions are described in Topic 2.8.

How to Resolve Market Disequilibrium

As you now know, a number of things can cause a market to fall into disequilibrium. But how do markets fall back into equilibrium? The answers are many. Remember Joaquin and his sandwiches? He resolved his disequilibrium problem by lowering the prices of his sandwiches. In other words, market forces resolved Joaquin's disequilibrium.

Innovations in manufacturing technology can help put supply and demand back in sync by lowering a product's price. The new equilibrium might be one in which the company's supply is not only greater, but its cost of bringing products to market is lower. The development of the personal computer in the 1980s, for example, allowed companies in many businesses, including publishing and film production, to lower production costs.

ANSWER THE TOPIC ESSENTIAL QUESTION

1. Explain what factors cause supply and demand to fall out of balance with each other.

KEY TERMS

market price	equilibrium price
market disequilibrium	sticky price
shortage	economic recession
surplus	economic depression

MULTIPLE-CHOICE QUESTIONS

1. On a demand/supply graph, a surplus occurs when
   - (A) the current price is below the equilibrium price
   - (B) the current price is above the equilibrium price
   - (C) the equilibrium price is equal to the disequilibrium price
   - (D) markets are efficient
   - (E) shortages are greater than the equilibrium price

2. On a demand/supply graph, a shortage occurs
   - (A) when the current price is below the equilibrium price
   - (B) when the current price is above the equilibrium price
   - (C) to the right of the supply curve
   - (D) to the left of the supply curve
   - (E) to the left of the demand curve

3. Which of the following correctly describes the effects of an increase in demand when the market features a downward sloping demand curve and an upward sloping supply curve?
   - (A) price increases, quantity decreases
   - (B) price increases, quantity increases
   - (C) price stays the same, quantity stays the same
   - (D) price decreases, quantity decreases
   - (E) price decreases, quantity increases

FREE-RESPONSE QUESTION

1. Study the Supply and Demand Schedule for Apples and answer the questions that follow.

SUPPLY AND DEMAND SCHEDULE FOR APPLES		
Price of Apples per Pound	Quantity Demanded	Quantity Supplied
$0.50	100	30
$1.00	75	40
$1.50	50	50
$2.00	40	100
$2.50	35	150
$3.00	30	175

(a) At which price or prices do shortages exist from excess demand?

(b) At the price of $1.00 per pound, is the market in equilibrium or disequilibrium? Why?

(c) What price is the market equilibrium price?

(d) At which price or prices do surpluses exist from excess supply?

(e) A storm ruins one-quarter of the apple crop. How would this event likely throw the apple market into disequilibrium? Explain.

Economists use models to analyze markets and explain the outcomes of economic situations. To do so, they take these steps:

- Identify what factors are causing the economic situation.

- Use an economic model to explain the outcome of the situation.

For example, economists note that market forces push a market toward equilibrium. When disequilibrium occurs, producers and consumers change their behavior until supply and demand meet at the market price again.

Apply the Skill

Suppose a natural disaster devastates the coffee-growing region of Brazil. That country is a major supplier of coffee beans to American coffee producers. Use the model shown here to explain how producers and consumers will respond initially to this development. Then suggest at least one way that the market can return to equilibrium.

SUPPLY AND DEMAND FOR COFFEE

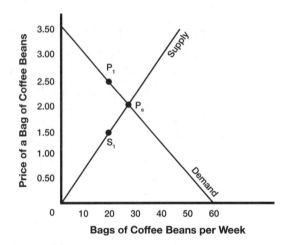

Topic 2.8

The Effects of Government Intervention in Markets

"I have never been a proponent of intervention, and I just think we have an unprecedented situation here and it calls for unprecedented action. There's no way to stabilize the markets other than through government intervention."

Henry Paulson, U.S. Secretary of the Treasury, in 2008

Essential Question: How and why do government policies influence consumer and producer behavior and therefore affect market outcomes?

In late 2007, the housing market in the United States collapsed and the entire economy was in freefall. The Great Recession, the greatest economic calamity since the Great Depression of the 1930s, had just begun. Unemployment ballooned to 10 percent by the fall of 2009. Home prices fell, on average, 30 percent from 2006 to 2009. The country's gross domestic product, a measure of all goods and services produced, took a nosedive.

The government intervened to counteract the collapse. Through a combination of tax cuts, loans, and regulations, in 2009, the U.S. economy began to recover, then grow. Businesses once again started hiring workers. For the following ten years, the country enjoyed an expanding economy. Most economists credit these steps by the government with preventing the Great Recession of 2007 from becoming as bad as the Great Depression.

But most government economic activity is not nearly so dramatic. Even though governments do not control most investment decisions (businesses do), nor most purchasing decisions (individual consumers do), government carries out vital functions that make a market economy run smoothly. In the most successful market economies in the world, government accounts for 30 to 60 percent of all economic activity. As noted in Topic 2.1, government protects property rights by enforcing laws. In addition, it promotes competition by preventing one or two companies from controlling an industry. It provides roads and schools that make operating a business easier and more profitable. It encourages consumption by providing aid to people in need. It uses regulations to provide consumers with confidence that the food they buy is safe to eat and the banks where they save their money are sound. Later topics provide more details about these activities of government.

But like all economic activity, government actions have both benefits and costs. Unlike most private actions, though, government actions are hotly debated in public. This topic will explore why governments intervene in economies, how they intervene, and what the effects are.

Source: www.apimages.com
Credit: Associated Press/Mel Evans

In January 2009, the Great Recession had a firm grip on the American economy. Crowds of people stood in line to talk to potential employers during a job fair at Rutgers University in New Jersey. At the time of the job fair, unemployment had risen to 7.2 percent.

Price and Quantity Regulations

Some of the most direct forms of government intervention target the price for goods and services. Other interventions focus on the quantity of products supplied.

Price Floors A minimum price for a good or service established by government is called a **price floor**, or price support. By giving producers confidence that even if demand decreases, the price they receive will not fall below a certain level, price floors can give incentives to producers to increase supply.

One economic sector where government has often used price floors is agriculture. Because Congress has determined that a reliable supply of food is in the national interest, it has instituted price supports for crops such as wheat and corn. Congress wants to give incentives to farmers to produce food even when the free market price would make doing so unprofitable.

But the most common use of price floors is for labor. The **minimum wage** is the lowest amount of money an employer can legally pay workers to purchase their labor. Benefits of the minimum wage include providing low-wage workers better pay and promoting economic growth by giving more money to individuals to spend. One cost, though, is that by raising the cost of labor, it provides a disincentive for businesses to hire workers. Below is a supply/demand graph for a price floor (P_f). As you can see, a surplus occurs because the price ceiling is above the equilibrium price (P_e).

PRICE FLOOR AND MARKET DISEQUILIBRIUM

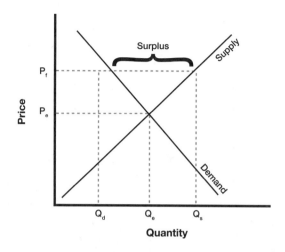

If a price floor is set less than the market price, it has no effect because the price is already higher than the floor and is called a nonbinding price floor. For example, many employers are not directly affected by the minimum wage law because they choose to pay higher wages to attract the employees they want. A price floor set higher than the market price that does affect prices is called a binding price floor.

Price Ceilings A maximum price for a good or service established by government is called a **price ceiling**. If it is set lower than the market equilibrium price, it can provide incentives to consumers to purchase more of a product. A government usually sets a price ceiling in response to a serious problem such as a war or environmental crisis that causes a sudden, sharp reduction in the quantity of a product supplied. For example, during a war, the military might be using so many resources that prices for civilians would skyrocket without a ceiling.

Critics point out that price ceilings reduce the incentive for producers to increase the supply. For example, in the aftermath of a hurricane, a government might limit the price companies can charge for bottled water. While this might keep the available water affordable for more people, it might not allow the price to rise enough to make it profitable for companies to ship more water to the affected community.

One controversial use of price ceilings is on rent. In response to a shortage of apartments that consumers can afford, some communities have limited rent increases. Opponents of these limits argue that they reduce incentives for investors to develop additional housing units. Below is a supply/demand graph for a price ceiling (P_c). As you can see, a shortage occurs when the price ceiling falls below the equilibrium market price (P_e).

PRICE CEILING AND MARKET DISEQUILIBRIUM

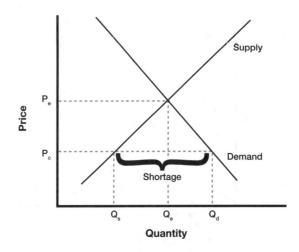

Similar to price floors, price ceilings can be binding or nonbinding. Ones set above the market price have no effect and are called nonbinding. Ones set below the market price do have an effect. They are called binding price ceilings.

Other Forms of Price and Quantity Regulations Markets normally rely on price to limit, or ration, consumption. However, governments can also use non-price rationing to regulate consumption and production. During World War II, the government wanted to reserve gas and oil supplies for the military. To limit the use of these resources by civilians, people had to purchase them with coupons they received from the government. This policy helped win the war—but it also created an illegal market in selling rationing coupons.

Taxes and Subsidies

Price ceilings and price floors are very direct interventions by the government, with taxes and subsidies almost as direct. They change incentives that result in shifting supply and demand curves.

Taxes Government can impose **taxes**, which are compulsory payments that individuals and firms make to governments. Three of the most common taxes are on income, sales, and property. They provide the revenue that federal, state, and local governments use to pay for everything from national defense to roads to elementary schools. The government also collects revenue through **user fees**, such as hunting licenses, fishing licenses, restaurant licenses, and car registrations.

Taxes can affect both supply and demand. Reducing taxes on businesses, for example, might spur those businesses to invest in new factories and technologies, which will bolster the economy by creating more products that consumers will demand. Lowering taxes on workers' incomes can also have a positive economic effect, not only for the worker but also for society in general. The more money workers have in their pockets, the more money they will spend on goods and services, increasing both supply and demand. Raising taxes can fund government so it can fix roads and bridges, invest in cutting-edge research, and improve education.

While the primary purpose of most taxes is to raise money to pay for public services, taxes also change incentives by making some products or activities more expensive. Hence, government sometimes imposes taxes primarily to influence behavior. For example, as people became more aware of the cancer and death caused by smoking cigarettes, governments increased taxes on them to discourage smoking. By 2016, taxes made up about half of the cost of a pack of cigarettes.

Governments also use taxes to allocate costs of **externalities**, costs or benefits that arise from the production or consumption of a good that falls on neither the producer nor the consumer, but on a third party. For example, factory pollution might not affect the company or those who buy its products, but it might cause health problems and lower property values for those who live near the factory. A taxation on pollution emissions could be used to provide health care for people in the neighborhood of the factory. (Externalities are covered in more detail in Topic 6.2.)

Subsidies Governments can increase incentives for economic activity by providing businesses or individuals with **subsidies**, or assistance that decreases costs or increases benefits. The stated goal of subsidies is to benefit the public overall. Subsidies take many forms.

Reduction in taxes, known as tax expenditures, reduce the disincentive for certain economic actions. They are sometimes called loopholes. For example, in 2019, one of the largest tax expenditures for individuals, about $25 billion, was to encourage home ownership by allowing homeowners to deduct interest paid on a home mortgage loan. In 2018, tax expenditures reduced the revenue from the federal income tax by over $4,000 per person.

Direct payments of money to individuals, businesses, universities or other units of government can support specific activities. One of these is research. Government-funded research at state universities starting in the mid-1800s was one reason for the miraculous increase in agricultural productivity. In 2020, in response to COVID-19, the federal government allocated $9 billion dollars to develop a vaccine. Most of this money went to large private pharmaceutical companies doing research. Through the Supplemental Nutrition Assistance Program (SNAP), the government provides money to help people in low-income households purchase food.

SNAP RECIPIENTS IN 2019	
Category of Families	**Percentage**
With children	66%
With members who are elderly or disabled	36%
With someone who is employeed	42%

Source: U.S. Department of Agriculture

Another form of subsidy is a guarantee. In 1965, the federal government began to guarantee loans made to students to finance their education. With confidence that the loan would be repaid, banks could charge lower interest rates on these loans.

The impact of subsidies on prices depends on the price elasticity of demand for that product. Subsidies on solar panels, a product with high price elasticity, greatly increased the quantity demanded.

Allocative Efficiencies

One cost of government intervention is that it can decrease **allocative efficiency**, the level of production at which the price of a product equals the marginal cost of production. That is, government actions that are done for non-market reasons might lower the overall output of the economy.

For example, in 1956, the U.S. government passed the National Interstate and Defense Highways Act, which built the interstate highway system, connecting cities and regions throughout the country. The system greatly expanded use of cars and trucks for long-distance transportation. Yet at the same time, the highways devastated the passenger rail system, which had previously moved people in efficient ways. By subsidizing auto and truck transportation, the government weakened the rail system. The total effect was a less efficient economy. However, as the name of the act suggested, the government had another purpose besides allocative efficiency: national defense. Transporting military troops along multiple highways rather than a small number of rail lines was safer and more flexible.

Hence, government intervention presents citizens and policy with a tradeoff. People might decide that government intervention to fight a war, provide health care, or reduce pollution might be useful, but price and quantity controls, taxes, and subsidies will decrease allocative efficiency. Whether achieving these other goals is worth making the economy less efficient is a judgment based on what people value.

Deadweight Loss

A decrease in total surplus that results from an inefficient level of production is a **deadweight loss**. This deadweight loss occurs when consumers choose not to pay for a specific good because the utility for that good is no longer worth the price. As you may remember, utility is a measure of how much a person enjoys a good or service.

Government intervention in the economy can cause deadweight losses. For example, consider sales taxes. Suppose your family decides for you to take a trip to Miami, Florida, to visit a college. You are willing to pay the cost of the ticket simply for the cost of flying there and back. However, government then adds taxes in order to pay for operation of the Miami airport. The tax increases the cost of the flight enough that you decide not to make the trip. The lost economic activity that your trip would have generated is a deadweight loss caused by the higher tax.

Determining Who Taxes and Subsidies Affect

Depending on where you live, if you buy a shirt at a clothing store, you might be charged a little extra to cover a tax on the sale. You give the store money to cover the tax, which the store collects and sends to the government. In one sense, you are paying the tax because the money comes from you. In another sense, the store is paying because they actually send the money to the govverment. The **incidence of tax** describes who pays extra money because of the tax, regardless of who actually submits it to the government.

Determining tax incidence can be complicated. For example, if property taxes increase for a business, its cost of supplying goods increases. If the business passes the cost along to consumers through higher prices, then the incidence of the tax falls on the consumers. If the business absorbs the extra cost, then the incidence falls on them. Whether, or how much, a business passes a tax along depends on the mixture of elasticity of supply and elasticity of demand for a particular product:

- If supply is perfectly inelastic, there is no change in the cost of production and suppliers cannot raise the price. Thus, incidence of the tax is entirely on the seller.

- If supply is perfectly elastic, the cost of production will change by the amount of the tax and suppliers can pass the entire amount of the tax on to consumers. Thus, incidence of the tax is entirely on the buyer.

- If demand is perfectly inelastic, consumers do not respond at all to price changes and continue to purchase the same amount. Suppliers can pass all costs along to consumers. Thus, incidence of the tax is entirely on the buyer.

- If demand is perfectly elastic, suppliers cannot pass any of the tax on to consumers. Thus, incidence of the tax is entirely on the seller.

As with taxes, the incidence of government subsidies is determined by who ultimately benefits from the subsidy. In the first decades of the 21st century, both college tuition and government aid to students increased. The incidence of the subsidy provided by this aid was unclear. Did the subsidy mostly help individual students because it made college costs more affordable? Or did the subsidy mostly help colleges because it allowed them to increase tuition as they became aware that students could afford to pay more? The answers to these questions shaped the debate about whether the government should increase financial aid for students.

ANSWER THE TOPIC ESSENTIAL QUESTION

1. Explain how and why government policies influence consumer and producer behavior and therefore affect market outcomes.

price floor   subsidy
minimum wage   allocative efficiency
price ceiling   deadweight loss
tax   incidence of tax
user fee
externality

MULTIPLE-CHOICE QUESTIONS

1. Governments often intervene in free market economies to address
   (A) efficiencies
   (B) inefficiencies
   (C) deadweight loss
   (D) market supply
   (E) market demand

2. Which is the clearest example of a government subsidy?
   (A) A school district's allocation of money to construct a new public high school
   (B) A city government's expenditures to run theater programs in parks
   (C) A county government purchases snowplows to clear roads
   (D) A state government's refunds of money to people who overpaid their income tax
   (E) The federal government's payments to farmers to encourage them to grow corn

3. A price ceiling is most likely to create inefficiencies when it is set
   (A) below the market price, so it reduces the quantity supplied the producers will provide
   (B) above the market price, so it increases the amount that consumers will purchase of a good
   (C) the same as the market price
   (D) above the market price, so it encourages producers to raise prices
   (E) above the market price, so it discourages consumers from purchasing a good

1. Read this news article and then answer the questions that follow.

Council Approves New Waterfront Development

The City Council last night voted to approve a $120 million waterfront development. The developers of the project plan to construct a shopping complex, a business park, and affordable housing units.

To get the project off the ground, the city promised the developers to postpone five years' worth of property taxes. The city also mandated that the developers employ at least 500 local residents during construction. The city also stipulated that those workers would have to be paid at a minimum $25 an hour.

The project's manager told the council that her firm will construct more than 250 affordable housing units. She said the federal government has agreed to allocate more than $400,000 in housing grants to qualified tenants each year.

The owners of one of the restaurants to be located in the complex has promised that the dinners on the menu will not exceed $15.50. Moreover, City Council members mandated that the project's developers pay to set up a job training center for teenagers in an adjacent neighborhood.

(a) Which statement describes a government subsidy?

(b) Which statement describes a government incentive?

(c) Which statement describes a price ceiling?

(d) Which statement describes a price floor?

(e) If the city wanted to further help potential tenants, would the city implement a price floor or price ceiling on housing?

Economists can demonstrate the effects of a change by using an accurately labeled graph. Doing so requires them to answer three questions:

- What variable in the situation changed?
- What effect did that change have on economic outcomes?
- How can we illustrate that change and the effect on a visual?

For example, suppose a news article reports a new scientific study that links a particular vegetable to heart health. Consumers rush to their grocery stores to buy packages of the miracle veggie. Store owners raise prices. Economists can explain and illustrate these events using a supply and demand curve for the equilibrium price of the vegetable. The rise in demand pushes the demand curve to the right, which shifts the equilibrium price from E_1 to E_2—a higher level.

MIRACLE VEGGIE EQUILIBRIUM

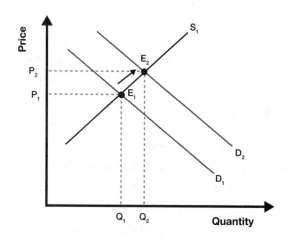

Apply the Skill

Economists are also called on to explain the effects of government interventions in the economy. Sometimes those interventions are not deliberate efforts to affect the economy but secondary effects of government actions taken for policy reasons. For public health reasons, Congress passes a law imposing a tax on e-cigarettes. A year later, supply of that product has dropped, prices have risen, and demand has fallen. Explain these results and illustrate them with a graph.

Since the passage of the first antitrust laws more than a century ago, federal government regulation of U.S. businesses has expanded dramatically. Today, an alphabet soup of agencies including the EPA, the FDA, the SEC, OSHA overlook businesses practices.

Opposing Regulation Historically, businesses have generally opposed regulation, focusing on the additional costs the requirements impose. They have relied on several arguments against government regulations:

- Regulations drive up prices for consumers. Compliance with regulations costs firms money, which they must pass on to consumers. In some cases, the cost of compliance may drive existing firms out of business and create barriers that prevent new firms from entering the market.

- Regulations deter business investment and stifle innovation and entrepreneurship by leading to confusion and uncertainty. Concern about possible regulations can make investors and entrepreneurs reluctant to invest time and money in new ventures.

- Government regulations are unnecessary, since the free market regulates itself. According to this view, businesses will provide quality goods and services, and those that fail will be forced to adapt or go out of business.

Supporting Regulation Businesses, like consumers, often support regulations that protect the public interest. In addition, businesses sometimes see greater regulation in their self-interest.

- Ethical business owners often want regulations to keep out competition from unethical business owners.

- Small start-ups might want stricter enforcement of anti-trust laws so that they can enter a market more easily.

- A firm that operates nationwide might prefer to have one set of federal regulations, even if they are strict, over a mixture of state regulations that vary widely.

- An established company might want tougher rules that are more expensive to comply with in order to create higher barriers for potential rivals who want to enter a market.

Businesses sometimes reject efforts to ease regulations. During the Trump administration, the government attempted to rollback regulations aimed at reducing pollution and slowing climate change. However, several large businesses, including auto manufacturers, utility companies, and tech firms, ignored the rollbacks. Some wanted to be ready to meet higher standards if they were reinstated and others wanted to woo potential customers. At some companies, the leaders simply thought that complying with the higher standards was the right thing to do.

Topic 2.9

International Trade and Public Policy

"Trade is the oldest and most important economic nexus among nations. Indeed, trade along with war has been central to the evolution of international relations."

—Robert Gilpin, American professor of politics and international affairs, 1930–2018

Essential Question: How do government policies involving international trade affect consumer behavior, producer behavior, and market outcomes?

On January 1, 1994, the United States, Canada, and Mexico entered into one of the largest free market trading partnerships in history. Known as the North American Free Trade Agreement, or NAFTA, the treaty eliminated **tariffs**, which are taxes on goods that are imported or exported. The result was an explosion in trade. Trade quadrupled between 1993 and 2019. Consumers benefitted from lower prices on imported goods and manufacturers could hire workers at lower wages. For most people in the United States, freer trade was a benefit. However, a minority suffered greatly. Between NAFTA and new technology, hundreds of thousands of manufacturing workers in the United States lost their jobs. In 2019, the three countries updated NAFTA with a new trade deal called CUSMA, the Canadian-United States-Mexico Agreement.

NAFTA and CUSMA are examples of how **international trade** can affect the economies of nations. International trade is the exchange of services and goods between countries. By 2020, total world trade accounted for over half of the world's economy.

The CUSMA agreement between Canada, the United States, and Mexico (also sometimes referred to as NAFTA 2.0) officially came into effect on July 1, 2020. It focused primarily on automotive production, steel and aluminum trade, intellectual property issues, and the dairy, egg, and poultry markets.

The Effects of International Trade

International trade clearly is why you can buy a banana grown in Ecuador, a car assembled in Germany, clothes made in India, and appliances manufactured in China.

Countries use international trade as a way to expand their markets. Countries also trade with one another when they cannot satisfy their own needs because they lack the resources. In such situations, no domestically-made substitutes exist, which makes importing products essential. As a result, imports may be less expensive to buy. When countries trade with one another, it gives consumers exposure to goods that are perhaps not available in their own countries, or which would be more expensive to produce domestically.

In Topic 1.4, you learned about one of the most important concepts in international trade, **comparative advantage**. This principle suggests that countries will trade with one another and export goods that each has a relative advantage in producing.

Impact on Equilibrium Price

Trade has wide-ranging effects on the supply, demand, and prices of products and services. It can, for example, affect the equilibrium price of a product or a service. As you recall, market equilibrium is the point at which supply is equal to demand. Trade can also fill the gap between domestic supply and demand.

Take the example of coffee. It grows well in the South American country of Colombia. However, in the United States, it grows only in small regions in Hawaii, California, and Puerto Rico. Without international trade, Colombia could produce so much coffee that the equilibrium price would be very low. In the United States, the equilibrium price would be very high. With trade, companies can buy less expensive coffee in Colombia and sell it at a higher price in the United States. This benefits the large number of coffee growers in Colombia and coffee drinkers in the United States. Coffee drinkers in Colombia would pay more and coffee growers in the United States would face competition. However, each of these groups might benefit from other forms of trade.

As this example shows, trade tends to have the following effects:

- Supply tends to increase because more producers are selling products into a market.

- Prices tend to decrease because supplies are increasing, and more companies are competing for a market.

- Quantity demanded tends to increase because of lower prices.

The graph that follows shows the impact of trade on equilibrium price. (Pt is price with trade; Pnt is price with no trade.) International trade causes prices to decrease and quantity demanded to increase (point A), as opposed to conditions without trade (point E).

TRADE IMPACT ON EQUILIBRIUM PRICE

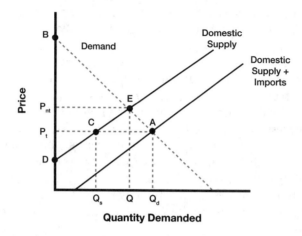

Conditions Under Autarky Autarkic economies are those that are closed from trade, such as North Korea. In other words, autarkic economies don't participate in international trade. Autarky is an extreme form of protectionism. Such societies are self-sufficient, which means they make all the goods and services within their borders.

Impact on Consumer Surplus, Producer Surplus, and Total Surplus

International trade affects **consumer surplus** and **producer surplus**, which you learned about in Topic 2.6. To review, consumer surplus is the difference between the price consumers pay and the price they are willing to pay. If international trade results in imports of more oranges, then domestic consumers will pay a lower price than they are used to paying. The consumer surplus will grow because there is a bigger difference between what consumers are willing to pay and what they actually pay.

Producer surplus is the difference between the price that a producer is willing to sell a product for and what he or she actually receives for the product. Trade can benefit producers by increasing the producer surplus. For example, farmers may be able to export wheat for a higher price than they can receive on the domestic market, increasing the producer surplus.

When you add together consumer surplus and producer surplus, the result is total economic surplus. Total economic surplus tends to increase with international trade. To understand why, consider the example of the computer industry. Companies based in the United States dominate the industry. By exporting computers, a U.S. manufacturer can outcompete rivals in other countries and charge higher prices. The producer surplus grows. At the same time, because the computer manufacturer is building more computers, each computer costs less to build. As a result, the manufacturer is able to offer computers to the domestic market for somewhat lower prices, and the consumer surplus grows. Put together, the computer manufacturer has increased the total economic surplus.

Tariffs

Sometimes governments will impose restrictions on international trade. That's what happened beginning in July 2018, when the United States fired the first salvo of an economic trade war with China. President Donald Trump imposed tariffs on $34 billion worth of Chinese goods. Within hours, the Chinese government struck back, levying $34 billion of its own tariffs on American cars, soybeans, beef, seafood, dairy, and other products.

Within a month, the United States had slapped China with an additional $16 billion in tariffs, forcing China to respond in kind. The purpose of the escalating trade war, at least from the perspective of the Trump administration, was to force China to stop its "unfair trade practices," which Trump believed were harming U.S. manufacturers.

Governments use tariffs for a variety of purposes, such as to raise revenue, protect domestic industries, and respond to tariffs imposed by other countries. Tariffs are considered a form of **protectionism**, an official government policy that restricts imports from other countries. Tariffs can have multiple effects on consumers, companies, and the entire economy of a country. They affect the prices of domestic products, the quantities produced of products, government revenues, consumer surplus, producer surplus, and total economic surplus.

Domestic Prices Tariffs tend to raise the price of imported goods, affecting consumers' pocketbooks. As a result, people are less likely to purchase those imported products because they are too expensive. Because imported goods are now more expensive, domestic manufacturers may feel that they can raise the prices of their own goods to maximize profits. For example, after President Trump placed a 25 percent tariff on imported steel in 2018, domestic manufacturers were able to raise their prices but still kept the prices below the levels of imported steel.

Quantities Supplied Tariffs can have two effects on quantities in a market: (1) increase quantities supplied by domestic producers but (2) decrease total quantities supplied to a market. The following graph shows why. The equilibrium price (P_E) is where domestic demand (Demand) intersects with supply before any trade or tariffs. Study the graph to see how tariffs affect prices and supply:

- Imports before tariffs bring the price down from P_E to Pw. At this price, the total quantity supplied to the market is Q_{W1}. Of that total, domestic manufacturers supply quantity Q_{D1}. Importers supply the rest of the goods to the market.

- The government imposes a tariff. The price of each good rises from P_W to P_T. The quantity supplied by domestic manufacturers increases from Q_{D1} to Q_{D2}. But the total quantity consumed decreases from Q_{W1} to Q_{W2} because of the higher prices resulting from the tariffs.

With tariffs, domestic manufacturers benefit. They sell more goods. But consumers pay more, and they consume fewer goods overall. With tariffs, the total amount supplied in the market will decrease.

IMPACT OF TARIFFS

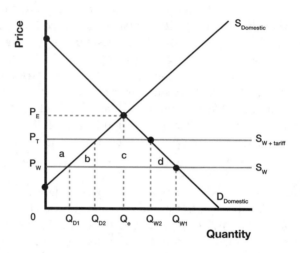

Increased Government Revenues Tariffs increase government revenues. In fact, during the 19th century, taxes on imports accounted for about half of all U.S. government revenues. The ratification of the Sixteenth Amendment in 1913 permitted the federal government to assess an income tax. Since then, the federal government has relied far more on the income tax than on tariffs for its revenues. Even so, since the Trump administration raised tariffs on a wide variety of imports in 2018, those revenues have risen from about $30 to $40 billion a year to about $75 billion a year.

Impact on Consumer Surplus, Producer Surplus, and Total Surplus As you learned earlier in this topic, international trade tends to increase consumer surplus, producer surplus, and total economic surplus.

Tariffs, though, tend to reduce consumer surplus—transferring it, instead, to the government. With tariffs, consumers pay more for a product than they would without tariffs. Consequently, the higher price reduces the difference between the highest price the consumer is willing to pay and the price that the consumer is actually paying.

At the same time, tariffs tend to increase producer surplus for domestic manufacturers. Because domestic manufacturers are protected by a tariff, they can charge a higher price than before the tariffs. Remember, for example, that U.S. steel manufacturers raised their prices after the Trump administration put tariffs on imported steel. With the higher prices, a producer increases producer surplus—the difference between the minimum it is willing to charge and the actual price.

Yet the total economic surplus may be less than it was before the tariffs. If you will look back at the graph "Impact of Tariffs," you will see why. Because of the tariffs, the overall quantities supplied have been reduced. As mentioned earlier, this reduced the amount of consumer surplus.

Economists want to know where this lost consumer surplus goes. The "Impact of Tariffs" graph shows where this loss goes.

- The loss of consumer surplus equals the areas a, b, c, and d.
- Area a is a transfer of consumer surplus to producer surplus.
- Area c is the amount of consumer surplus transferred to government in the form of tariff revenue.
- Areas b and d are areas of deadweight loss created by the tariff.

The deadweight loss indicates that with a tariff companies do not realize allocative efficiency. This also shows that the amount of total economic surplus is smaller with a tariff than with free trade.

The shipping of manufactured goods from China took a severe hit on August 1, 2019, when President Trump hit China with tariffs on $300 billion worth of goods.

Quotas

Like tariffs, quotas are a form of protectionism. **Quotas** are restrictions that limit the number of goods a country can import or export during a specific moment in time. The idea behind setting quotas is to provide a domestic industry with economic support by shielding it from foreign competition.

Quotas help domestic manufacturers because the restrictions regulate the volume of trade between countries. Sometimes governments set quotas on specific products not only to reduce imports, but to increase domestic production. A government can impose several types of quotas on another country, including:

- *Absolute Quotas* These simply set a limit on the number of products.
- *Tariff-rate Quota* This allows a country to import a certain number of goods at a reduced tariff rate.
- *Voluntary Restraints* These are also known as VER. They limit the amount of exports for a particular type of good.

The following graph shows how a trade quota would look if you graphed it on a supply and demand curve. The line Sw shows what the market would be when there are no tariffs nor quotas on imports. The market price (Pw) is the same for all quantities supplied. With free trade and domestic demand curve D, Q_4 is the amount of the good consumed. The quota is the difference between the domestic supply (Sd) and the domestic supply including the quota imported from abroad (Sdq). To make the analysis comparable to the tariff, assume that the amount of the quota equals the amount of imports under a tariff.

Now, assume a trading partner imposes a quota that equals the amount of goods which would be imported if a tariff had been imposed. What will happen? Basically the same thing as under a tariff.

- Price rises to Pq.
- Quantity purchased goes from Q_4 to Q_3.
- Imports equal $Q_3 - Q_2$.
- Domestic producer supply Q_2.
- Consumer surplus goes down the same as in the tariff graph.
- Area a is a transfer from consumer surplus to producer surplus.
- Areas b and d are still deadweight loss.
- Area c in the tariff graph (tariff revenue) now becomes a transfer of consumers surplus that goes to importers.

IMPACT OF QUOTAS

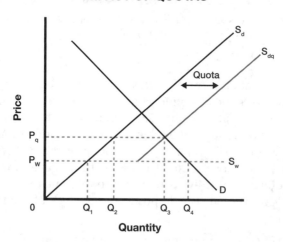

To summarize the graph, quotas will often lead to higher prices for consumers and limit the choices of goods that they can purchase. Because consumers are paying higher prices, their consumer surplus will be reduced. For producers, their producer surplus will increase, as they are able to charge higher prices. However, as with tariffs, the total economic surplus will decrease because the companies in the protected market are not operating at peak efficiency. In other words, they are not achieving allocative efficiency.

Japan's Experience One of the best examples of quotas in action came during the 1980s when Japan and the United States were locked in a bitter trade war. When the 1960s began, Japan's auto industry had grown so robust that it was exporting 10,000 vehicles a year for sale overseas. That number climbed to 1 million by the beginning of the 1970s. The country's gross domestic product surged year after year.

By the time the 1980s dawned, Japan had become an economic powerhouse, with the second-largest economy in the world. That success, in part, was due to the quotas the Japanese government placed on foreign imports. Those quotas gave Japan an advantage over foreign competitors, especially in the auto industry, as the country restricted the number of foreign-made vehicles coming into its country.

The restrictions were keenly felt in the United States. U.S. auto companies were limited in the number of cars they could sell in Japan. When Ronald Reagan became president in 1981, his administration began pressuring Japan to open its markets. To protect the U.S. auto industry, the Reagan administration capped the number of cars the Japanese could export to the United States.

Over time, the quotas forced the Japanese to rethink their decision. A number of Japanese automakers opened up factories in the United States, creating thousands of jobs for Americans and allowing the Japanese to participate more fully in the American market. Ultimately, the U.S. and Japan reached a trade accommodation, chiefly through Japanese concessions, including allowing more American-made goods to enter the country. The trade war ended when both sides realized that their economies relied on one another.

Source: www.apimages.com

Credit: Associated Press

In this photo members of the United Autoworkers Local 588 of the Ford Motor Co. stamping plant wield sledgehammers and bars on a 1975 Toyota Corolla on March 3, 1981, during a rally against buying foreign-made products.

International Trade Opens Markets Most wealthy countries today grew wealthy using tariffs and quotas to help their young industries compete with better established foreign firms. Great Britain, the United States, and Germany all used protectionist policies in the 19th century and part of the 20th century. Japan, South Korea, and other East Asia countries were protectionist in the late 20th century. However, the world has moved toward freer trade since the end of World War II in 1945. One benefit of this is that when companies have to compete in a global marketplace, they have greater incentive to innovate. As consumers, individuals benefit from greater access to products from all over the world that might be less expensive or better made than products in their own country. However, as workers, individuals might suffer unemployment as their jobs are transferred to countries with lower wages or fewer regulations.

ANSWER THE TOPIC ESSENTIAL QUESTION

1. Explain how government policies involving international trade affect consumer behavior, producer behavior, and market outcomes.

KEY TERMS

tariffs	comparative advantage	total economic surplus
international trade	consumer surplus	protectionism
capital	producer surplus	quota

MULTIPLE-CHOICE QUESTIONS

1. Which statement best defines the strategy of a government policy of protectionism?
   (A) To increase imports from other countries
   (B) To increase exports to other countries
   (C) To decrease the exchange rate
   (D) To limit exports to other countries
   (E) To limit imports from other countries

2. An example of a tariff is a 20 percent tax on
   (A) imported steel
   (B) domestically grown oranges
   (C) water-use
   (D) cable TV services
   (E) books printed in the United States

3. Which is the most likely effect of quotas on the purchasing power of consumers?
   (A) Increases their purchasing power
   (B) Decreases their purchasing power
   (C) Keeping purchasing power stable
   (D) Changing only the price of imported goods
   (E) Changing only the price of exported goods

FREE-RESPONSE QUESTION

1. Study the graph below, which illustrates the impact tariffs can have on the importation and sale of U.S.-made baseball hats. Then answer the questions that follow.

TARIFFS ON U.S. BASEBALL CAPS

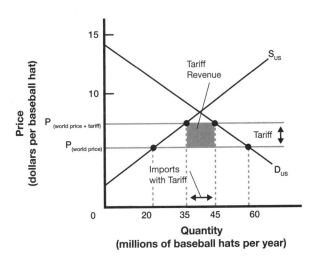

(a) When countries engage in free trade, the world price for hats is _____ than if a tariff were imposed.

(b) What is the price for each hat prior to a U.S. tariff being enacted?

(c) How much does the U.S. government collect in the tariffs per hat?

(d) With free trade, how many hats do Americans buy per year?

(e) With a tariff, domestic production of hats (increases, decreases, remains the same), while U.S. purchases (decrease, increase, remain the same).

THINK AS AN ECONOMIST: *DEMONSTRATE THE EFFECT OF A CHANGE ON A GRAPH*

Economists can demonstrate the effects of a change by using accurately labeled visuals. Doing so requires them to answer three questions:

- What variable in the situation changed?
- What effect did that change have on economic outcomes?
- How can we illustrate that change and the effect on a visual?

For example, suppose a country that had previously been closed to world trade opens its markets to foreign goods that are less expensive than domestically produced goods. Doing so would add a new supply line available to domestic consumers, pushing supply to Q_2. The influx of cheaper goods would lower the equilibrium price to P_1. Domestic producers' market share would fall from Q to Q_1. Economists could graph these changes as follows.

OPENING DOMESTIC MARKET

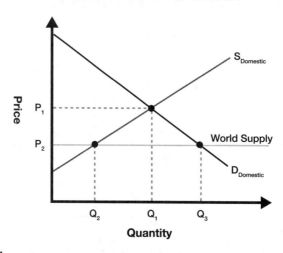

Apply the Skill

Now suppose that the government is alarmed by the impact of these changes—the imports--on its domestic industries. The country imposes a tariff on imported goods that raises the price of those imports. The new situation could be graphed as shown here.

MARKET WITH TARIFFS

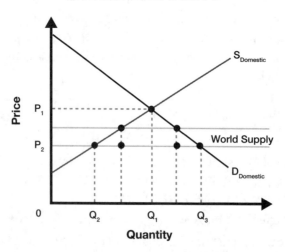

Copy the graph onto another paper and label it correctly. Write a brief description of how the domestic and world markets changed as a result of the tariffs.

1. The graph below depicts the perfectly competitive bagel market in a community. The main ingredient in bagels is wheat.

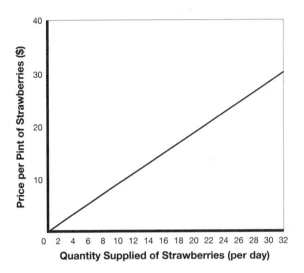

(a) What is the equilibrium price and quantity?

(b) At the equilibrium price you stated in part (a), what is the total consumer surplus? Show your work.

(c) What is the situation created at $7? Identify how many units are demanded, supplied, and either in surplus or shortage at that price. Show your work.

(d) If the price of wheat increases drastically, would the equilibrium price increase, decrease, or stay the same? Explain.

(e) Assume the price per bagel increases from $2 to $3.

   i. Calculate the elasticity of demand. Show your work.

   ii. Based on your answer in part (e) i., is demand perfectly elastic, relatively elastic, unit elastic, relatively inelastic, or perfectly inelastic?

   iii. Calculate the elasticity of supply. Show your work.

(f) Assume the government places a price floor at $7. Will the price floor result in a shortage, surplus, or neither? Explain.

(g) Assume the world price for the bagel market is currently $4. Would this community import or export bagels at this price? Explain.

UNIT 3

Production, Cost, and the Perfect Competition Model

In his 1776 book The Wealth of Nations, Adam Smith described the self-regulating nature of a market economy in which when producers and consumers compete against each other. Even though no single person or agency tells everyone what to produce and what to consumer, they do so as if guided by an "invisible hand." The result, Smith argued, was the most efficient economic system possible.

Today, economists create models to explain how this "invisible hand" works. Economic models are simplified versions of reality designed to provide an understanding of economic behavior. They generally consist of a set of equations that describe an economic theory. The supply-and-demand model is a simple economic model. Other economic models can be very complex, taking many variables into consideration. Businesses and policymakers use economic models to help them make decisions.

While they are based on reality, most economic models make assumptions that are not completely realistic. One of the most common is the assumption that consumers have "perfect information"—that is, that they know everything they need to know about a product or service. Another assumption is that consumers make rational decisions when making choices. In reality, people do not have perfect information and they sometimes make decisions based on emotion rather than reason.

In this unit, you will learn about the perfect competition model. In theory, this is the opposite of a monopoly, in which a firm can charge whatever it wants since there are no alternatives available. The perfect competition model makes two assumptions: that goods for sale are essentially indistinguishable from each other, and that there are so many buyers and sellers that supply and demand remain constant. Even though this conditions rarely if ever occur completely, the model provides a useful way to understand how people do make economic decisions.

"It's fine to discover cures, but, remember, chronic conditions are our bread and butter."

Topic Titles and Essential Knowledge

Topic 3.1 The Production Function

- The production function explains the relationship between inputs and outputs both in the short run and the long run.
- Marginal product and average product change as input usage changes, and hence, total product changes.
- Diminishing marginal returns occur as the firm employs more of one input, holding other inputs constant, to produce a product (output) in the short run.

Topic 3.2 Short-Run Production Costs

- Fixed costs and variable costs determine the total cost.
- Marginal cost, average (fixed, variable, and total) cost, total cost, and total variable cost change as total output changes, but total fixed cost remains constant at all output levels, including zero output.
- Production functions with diminishing marginal returns yield an upward-sloping marginal cost curve.
- Specialization and the division of labor reduce marginal costs for firms.
- Cost curves can shift in response to changes in input costs and productivity.

Topic 3.3 Long-Run Production Costs

- In the long run, firms can adjust all their inputs, and as a result, all costs become variable.
- The relationship between inputs and outputs in the long run is described by the scale of production—increasing, decreasing, or constant returns to scale.
- The long-run average total cost is characterized by economies of scale, diseconomies of scale, or constant returns to scale (efficient scale).
- The minimum efficient scale plays a role in determining the concentration of firms in a market and the market structure.

Topic 3.4 Types of Profit

- Firms respond to economic profit (loss) rather than accounting profit.
- Accounting profit fails to account for implicit costs (such as cost of financial capital, compensation for risk, or an entrepreneur's time), which, if fully compensated, result in normal profit.

Topic 3.5 Profit Maximization

- Firms are assumed to produce output to maximize their profits by comparing marginal revenue and marginal cost.

Topic 3.6 Firms' Decisions to Enter or Exit Markets

- In the short run, firms decide to operate (i.e., produce positive output) or shut down (i.e., produce zero output) by comparing total revenue to total variable cost or price to average variable cost (AVC).
- In the absence of barriers to entry or exit, in the long run (i.e., once factors that are fixed in the short run become variable), firms enter a market in which there are profit-making opportunities and exit a market when they anticipate economic losses.

Topic 3.7 Perfect Competition

- A perfectly competitive market is efficient. Firms in perfectly competitive markets face no barriers to entry and have no market power.

- In perfectly competitive markets, prices communicate to consumers and producers the magnitude of others' marginal costs of production and marginal benefits of consumption and provide incentives to act on that information (i.e., price equals marginal cost in an efficient market).

- In perfectly competitive markets, firms can sell all their outputs at a constant price determined by the market.

- At a competitive market equilibrium, firms are price takers and select output to maximize profit by producing the level of output where the marginal cost equals marginal revenue (at the price).

- At a competitive market equilibrium, the price of a product equals both the private marginal benefit received by the last unit consumed and the private marginal cost incurred to produce the last unit, thus achieving allocative efficiency.

- In a short-run competitive equilibrium, price can either be above or below its long-run competitive level resulting in profits or losses, motivating entry or exit of firms and moving prices and quantities toward long-run equilibrium.

- In a long-run perfectly competitive equilibrium, productive efficiency implies all operating firms produce at efficient scale, price equals marginal cost and minimum average total cost, and firms earn zero economic profit.

- Firms may be in a constant cost, increasing cost, or decreasing cost industry. Long-run prices depend on the portion of the long-run cost curves on which firms operate.

- A perfectly competitive market in long-run equilibrium is allocatively and productively efficient.

The Production Function

"As it is with an individual, so it is with a nation.
One must produce to have, or one will become a have-not."

U.S. political economist Henry George (1839–1897)

Essential Question: What is the production function, and how do businesses use it?

Every company faces important decisions about how much of a product it should produce. If you managed a company making smartphones, for example, you need to decide how many units to produce and how to do so efficiently. How many workers should you hire? What technology should you use?

To make such decisions, companies analyze the **production function**, an equation that shows the relationship between inputs and outputs. (In economics, *function* refers to a mathematical equation with one or more variables.)

The production function helps businesses compare the quantities of **inputs**, or productive factors such as land, capital, and labor, against **outputs**, or the amount of product the company produces. The production function determines the amount of product that can be obtained from every possible combination of factors, assuming that businesses use the most efficient methods of production available.

The production function is a powerful tool for businesses, as it can answer questions about how any tweak in inputs will change the outputs. Businesses can also use the production function to determine the most efficient combination of factors necessary to produce the desired level of output.

The owner of a business that creates custom flower pots must consider several factors when determining how to produce the pots in the most efficient way possible

Factors of Production

Suppose Emily owns a custom flower pot operation and wants to maximize the number of flower pots she's able to produce from a certain amount of inputs. Should she hire more workers? How much clay should she keep on hand? Does she need more potter's wheels? Does she need another kiln? To make such decisions, she needs to consider several factors.

First, Emily considers the **factors of production**, or the inputs needed to produce a desired output—in this case, the flower pots. The three classic factors of production are:

- Land
- Capital
- Labor

A fourth factor, entrepreneurial talent, is sometimes considered a factor of production as well. In the case of the flower pot operation, Emily's inputs include clay (land), a potter's wheel and kiln (capital), her own work and that of any employees she hires to make flower pots. Her own entrepreneurial talent can also be a factor. When she decides how to design the pots and sell them, she is using her entrepreneurial talent. Emily is also using her entrepreneurial talent when she decides which and how much of the other inputs to use.

Using the Production Function

Once businesses have determined their own factors in production, they are able to plot specific data on the production function. In the example, Emily knows exactly how long it takes her to create one flower pot on her wheel. She also knows how long each pot must be in the kiln to become a finished flower pot. The amount of time required for each raw piece of clay to be shaped and fired by her working alone is a fixed amount of time.

If she decides that she wants to produce more flower pots, she must alter the factors of production. Obtaining more clay may be very easy and take little time. But without additional wheels, kiln space, or artists to create the flower pots, the amount of extra clay doesn't matter because Emily does not yet have more potter's wheels on which workers can make pots.

Factors of production that take longer to obtain are known as **fixed inputs**. Most often, this is capital. If a car manufacturer decides to increase production of a popular pickup truck, for example, the managers must first obtain thousands of different parts, which are considered capital. The process might take months or even years.

Short-run In the **short run,** when considering how many flower pots she can produce right away, the owner must account for at least one fixed input to determine how many flower pots she's able to create. For example, if she can hire another worker in a week, she has come up with a short-run solution. In the short run, there is at least one fixed factor of production. For Emily, the fixed factors are the potter's wheel and the kiln.

Long-run In the **long run,** when considering how many flower pots Emily can produce over a longer period of time, no input is fixed. She must think beyond the longest fixed input. If she takes a month to purchase a new wheel and a new kiln, then her long-run consideration must extend beyond one month.

Plotting the Production Function

The relationship between output and inputs in production is predictable. The production function helps explain the shape of the supply curve and find a producer's marginal costs of producing goods and services. (Additional details about the production function are provided later.)

When Emily opens Emily's Flower Pot Shop, she has no additional help. She completes all steps in production herself. She can make 10 pots in a given time period. But if she hires another worker or two, everyone can specialize. Working together, everyone can be much more productive.

Adding more workers will increase production, but the space she rents might start to get crowded. She might not have quite enough room to store materials and finished pots. At some point, the workers might start to get in each others way.

If she continues to hire people, at some point the shortage of space will become so severe that total production will start to go down. This changing relationship between the number of worker and production is summarized in the following table.

Number of Workers (Input)	Number of Flower Pots Made (Total Output or TO)	Marginal Product of Each Additional Worker (ΔTO/Δ Input)	Average Product (TO/Input)
0	0	-----	-----
1	10	10	10
2	30	20	15
3	60	30	20
4	80	20	20
5	95	15	19
6	108	13	18
7	119	11	17
8	128	9	16
9	126	-2	14
10	120	-6	12

This data can be shown in a graph. The following graph illustrates these three phases by showing the relationship of three variables:

- The solid line represents **total product**, or the overall quantity of an output that the firm produces.

- The dashed line represents **marginal product**, or the change in total output as inputs are added to the firm's production. The equation for total product is as follows:

$$MP = \frac{\Delta TO}{\Delta Input}$$

- The dotted line represents **average product**, or the amount of output that is produced per unit of input, assuming all other inputs are fixed. The average product is calculated by dividing the total product by the quantity of the variable input.

$$AP = \frac{TO}{Input}$$

For example, when Emily hires a second worker, the marginal product equals the change in total output (20) divided by the change in input (1), which equals 20. The average product equals the total ouput (30) divided by the input (2), which equals 15.

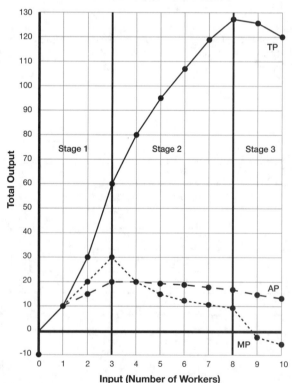

PRODUCTION FUNCTION

Three Stages in Production

The table and graph show that Emily goes through three distinct phases with her flower pot shop that are typical for firms. Known as the **stages of production,** they apply to short-term factors of production, such as an increase in the number of workers.

Stage 1: Increasing Marginal Returns In this stage, total output increases, as does marginal product, the additional output that a firm gains from increasing the input by one unit. For example, when Emily increased the number of workers from one to two, the output increased from 10 to 30. With the help of an extra worker, the group could produce 20 more pots, so this was the marginal product resulting from adding that person. Since the two workers together made 30 pots, the average product was 15.

By adding one more person, each worker could specialize in certain tasks. They became more productive as they gained experience, knowledge, and skills, and spent less time transitioning from one task to another. The increases in output, marginal product, and average product continued with the addition of a third employee.

Stage 2: Diminishing Marginal Returns However, adding additional inputs, whether it is more workers or more raw materials, does not increase total product endlessly. Firms are constrained by the law of **diminishing marginal returns**, which states that firms reach a point at which additions to input lead to progressively smaller—or diminishing— increases in output.

The table and the graph show that Emily reaches this point when she hires a fourth employee. Total output increases from 60 to 80 flower pots, but the increase in marginal product and the average product are smaller than when she added a third employee. Her returns are dimishing and continue to diminish as she hires up to her eighth employee.

Stage 3: Negative Marginal Returns At some point, inputs can be so high that they actually cause production to decrease. That is, the firm has negative marginal returns. Imagine a workspace so filled with people, raw materials, finished products, or tools that workers did not have enough space to work. If Emily hired nine or ten workers, they would get in one another's way and drag down total production.

Applying the Model Models shown in charts and graphs make the stages look very clear. In practice, though, business owners face a challenge in deciding when to expand production. They perpetually vary their short-run and long-run inputs to consider how best to achieve the output they think will maximize profits.

ANSWER THE TOPIC ESSENTIAL QUESTION

1. In two to three paragraphs, explain the production function and how businesses use it to help maximize output.

production function   long-run
input   stages of production
output   total product
factors of production   marginal product
fixed inputs   average product
short-run   diminishing marginal returns

MULTIPLE-CHOICE QUESTIONS

1. Which of the following inputs is the hardest to adjust in the short run?
   (A) Amount of sugar used to make lemonade
   (B) Size of an automobile manufacturing plant
   (C) Amount of water used by a health club
   (D) Number of salespeople in a paper company
   (E) Amount of dirt used by a landscaping company

Questions 2 and 3 refer to the following table.

Labor	Total Product	Average Product	Marginal Product
0	0	0	0
1	x	20	20
2	50	25	30
3	75	25	25
4	84	y	9
5	90	18	z
6	84	14	-6

2. What numbers would go in the blank spaces labeled above?
   (A) x = 20; y = 9; z = 18
   (B) x = 20; y = 18; z = 9
   (C) x = 20; y =6; z = 21
   (D) x = 20; y = 21; z = 6
   (E) x = 25; y = 21; z = 0

3. Where do diminishing marginal returns begin and why?

(A) With worker number 2 because marginal product reaches its highest value

(B) With worker number 3 because marginal product begins to decline

(C) With worker number 5 because total product reaches its highest value

(D) With worker number 6 because total product begins to decline

(E) With either worker number 2 or 3 because average product reaches its highest value

FREE-RESPONSE QUESTION

Use the table below to answer the questions that follow.

1. The workers on the Shanley's Pineapple Farm can pick the following number of pineapples per day.

Labor	Output (pineapples per day)
0	0
1	100
2	220
3	300
4	360
5	400
6	420
7	430

(a) What is the marginal output of the 5th worker? Show your work.

(b) What is the average output of the 6th worker? Show your work.

(c) With which worker does diminishing marginal returns set in? Explain.

(d) Which workers represent diminishing marginal returns?

(e) Why will diminishing returns always exist in the short run?

THINK AS AN ECONOMIST: *DESCRIBE ECONOMIC PRINCIPLES*

Economics is founded on several important principles or laws that describe the results of economic behavior. Being able to accurately describe these principles is an essential part of understanding them. To describe a concept, answer these questions about it.

- What is the definition?
- What are examples of the principle?
- How does it relate to other principles?
- Why is it important in the field of economics?

For example, consider the principle of the law of demand. According to this principle, consumers' demand for a good or service increases as the price decreases. For example, a movie theater that cuts the price of a ticket for a movie will see more customers buying tickets. This law bears an important relationship to the law of supply, which states that as price increases, the quantity that producers are willing to supply increases. The law of demand is essential to understanding economics because it is a fundamental feature of consumer behavior and thus affects producers' production decisions.

Apply the Skill

In this topic you learned about another principle, the law of diminishing returns. Answer these questions to demonstrate your understanding of this principle.

1. What is the definition of the principle of diminishing returns?
2. What is an example of diminishing returns?
3. How does the law of diminishing returns relate to the production function?
4. Why is the law of diminishing returns important in the field of economics?

Topic 3.2

Short-Run Production Costs

"The Band-Aid solution is actually the best kind of solution because it involves solving a problem with the minimum amount of effort and time and cost."

Malcolm Gladwell, *The Tipping Point*

Essential Question: Why should firms consider short-run production costs?

Suppose you own a restaurant. Over time, nearby businesses grow significantly and hire more staff, attracting more people to shop on your street. With more people in your area, your business also grows. As a result, your one cook and three waitstaff are overwhelmed. Ideally, you would like to remodel your building to expand the kitchen and the dining area. However, those changes would take at least two years to accomplish. For now, they can't be changed. They are fixed, or unchanging, in the short run.

What you can do right away is to hire another cook and at least one more part-time waitstaff. The additional expense of hiring extra staff is an example of a **short-run production cost,** one that can be adjusted quickly.

Types of Short-Run Production Costs

As was discussed in the previous topic, the point of diminishing marginal returns is the point when the marginal product begins to decline. A number of short-run production costs affect if and when businesses reach this point. Firms must consider and weigh each of them. In most cases, a profitable business is one in which the short-run production costs are minimized in relation to output.

Variable Costs and Fixed Costs Consider, for example, the owner of a clothing company. The owner is considering whether he should produce more pants to meet a seasonal increase in quantity demanded. He first considers his **variable costs,** or those that can be changed quickly and relatively easily. Variable costs tend to relate to an amount of a particular item. This particular owner may consider whether to order more fabric and buttons or whether he should hire additional seasonal employees. His variable costs will depend on the number of pants he ultimately hopes to produce. The more pants the owner wishes to make, the more his variable costs will increase. His **total variable cost** (TVC) will be the sum of all the variable costs, from fabric to buttons to employees and everything in between.

The opposite of a variable cost is a **fixed cost**, or one that cannot be changed quickly or easily. While variable costs depend on the quantity of items produced, fixed costs are not. Fixed costs are incurred even if the factory makes no clothes at all. The clothing factory owner may have purchased a factory with a 30-year mortgage, or he may rely on a team of salaried employees with contracts. It would be much more difficult for him to alter those fixed costs than his variable costs.

Total Costs and Marginal Costs The owner's **total fixed costs** are the sum of all of the fixed costs—the mortgage, the salaried employees, loan payments taken out to purchase machinery, taxes on the building, and so on. The total fixed costs remain constant at all output levels, including zero output. In other words, even if a factory is idle, the owner must still pay fixed costs.

The factory owner must consider other costs as well. His **marginal cost** is the cost to produce one additional unit of a single good. In this case, the marginal cost is the amount it will cost to produce one more pair of pants. To determine marginal cost, the clothing factory owner will move around his variable costs until he finds the right combination. For example, he might weigh the cost of buying more fabric and buttons against the cost of hiring additional seasonal employees necessary to make more pants.

To determine his **total cost**, the clothing company owner adds all the variable costs (VC) and the fixed costs (FC). The equation for total cost (TC) is as follows:

$$TC = VC + FC$$

Average Costs The owner can take this a step further and determine his **average total cost** (ATC), or the total cost divided by the total output (TO). The equation for average cost is as follows:

$$ATC = \frac{TC}{TO}$$

In this case, if the owner spends $100 in total costs to produce an output of 20 pairs of pants, then the average cost to produce one pair of pants is $5, because $100/20 = $5. For this reason, average total cost is also referred to as the "per unit total cost."

The **average variable cost** (AVC) is determined by dividing the total variable cost by the total output, as expressed in the following equation:

$$AVC = \frac{TVC}{TO}$$

For example, say the total variable cost to produce 20 pairs of pants is $50. Then the average variable cost to produce one pair of pants is $2.50.

The **average fixed cost** (AFC) is determined by dividing the total fixed cost by the total output:

$$AFC = \frac{TFC}{TO}$$

For example, if the fixed cost of producing in the clothing factory is $50 and total output is currently 20 pants, then the average fixed cost to produce one pair of pants is also $2.50. Average fixed costs are considered to be a sunk cost, meaning that they are not considered in production decisions such as whether to shut down or remain open.

SHORT-RUN PRODUCTION COSTS	
Type of Cost	**Description**
Variable Cost	• Factors that can be easily and relatively quickly changed • Volume-related, such as the number of hourly employees or the amount of a raw material • Depends on the size of the output
Total Variable Cost	• Sum of a business's variable costs • Changes as total output changes
Fixed Cost	• Opposite of variable costs • Cannot be easily or quickly changed • Time-related, such as number of salaried employees or a monthly lease • Does not depend on the size of the output
Total Fixed Cost	• Sum of a business's fixed costs • Affected by short-run decisions, but most closely associated with long-run costs
Marginal Cost	• Additional cost to produce one more unit of a single good • Involves the manipulation of variable costs • Includes any additional inputs required to produce the next unit • Mostly affected by costs that vary with production, so associated with variable cost
Total Cost	• Determined by adding variable costs and fixed costs
Average Total Cost	• More than simply a sum of costs • Found by dividing the total cost by the total output • Example: If it costs $100 in total costs to produce an output of 20 items, the average cost is $5 per item. • Also referred to as "per unit total cost"
Average Variable Cost	• Found by dividing the total variable cost by the total output • Example: If it costs $50 in total variable costs to produce an output of 20 items, the average variable cost is $2.50 per item.
Average Fixed Cost	• Found by dividing the total fixed cost by the total output • As output increases, average fixed cost will always decline.

Short-Run Production Revenue

In theory, firms are in business to maximize profits. Profits are determined by the **revenue** the firm earns and the costs of production. You have already learned how costs are calculated, but how are revenues determined? Note that revenue is not the same as profit, which will be discussed in Topic 3.4.

In the short run especially, firms are concerned with marginal revenue. Similar to marginal cost, which is the cost to produce one additional item, **marginal revenue** is the additional revenue that can be earned by producing one more of that same item. Suppose the clothing factory owner is able to produce 10 pairs of pants each hour. The number of pairs of pants is the quantity (Q), and the market price of each pair is the price (P). The following equation is used to calculate total revenue (TR):

$$P \times Q = TR$$

Suppose he is able to sell each pair of pants for $20. In this case, the revenue is 10 pairs of pants multiplied by $20, or 10 × $20 for total revenue of $200 per hour. Recall that marginal revenue is the additional revenue received from selling one more unit of output. The formula for marginal revenue is the change (Δ) in total revenue (TR) divided by the change in quantity (Q).

$$\frac{\Delta TR}{\Delta Q} = MR$$

For example, if the total revenue of producing 10 pairs of pants is $200 as shown above, when the company sells its 11th pair of pants, the total revenue would be 11 × $20 for a total revenue of $220. Now, to calculate marginal revenue, you must take the change in total revenue ($220 − $200) divided by change in total output (11 − 10) to get result of $20 ($20/1).

Short-Run Production in Practice

Business owners manipulate different short-run costs in order to achieve a desired output. They take actions to affect their short-run production costs and reduce their marginal costs. Consider once again the owner of a clothing company.

Specialization In an attempt to reduce the marginal cost necessary to produce shirts, the business owner might choose to focus on specific aspects of production. By utilizing this type of **specialization**—or a limited scope that leads to improved efficiency—the business owner will likely improve output. He may decide, for example, not to produce every kind of shirt but to specialize only in long-sleeve dress shirts. Specialization would help the owner limit variable costs such as fabric and other supplies necessary for the other kinds of shirts.

Division of Labor The owner of the clothing company may reduce average costs throughout his company and increase revenue through **division of labor,** splitting the production process into different stages in order to allow employees to focus on individual tasks. A classic example of this practice is the automobile assembly line, but the idea is used in many industries, including ones that provide services as well as those that produce goods. For example, high schools often divide the work of teaching among people who each specialize in one specific subject area, such as math, biology, language arts, or physical education.

Shutdown of Production If the total revenue received from the sale of the shirts does not even cover the variable costs of production, then the factory owner would have a greater loss from producing the shirts than by not producing anything at all. If the owner expected this to continue, the rational decision would be to choose a **shutdown of production**. The business would still be losing money, but by not producing any shirts, the factory losses would be only the fixed costs, not the variable ones.

The owner of a clothing producer considers many factors in order to achieve a desired output most efficiently.

Short-Run Cost Curves

To see the effects of altering various short-run production costs, firms may plot the information on a graph like the one on the following page. **Short-run cost curves** show the minimum cost impact of specific output changes. They also show the optimal combination of inputs necessary to produce a desired output. Cost curves can accordingly shift in response to changes in input costs and productivity.

SHORT-RUN COST CURVES

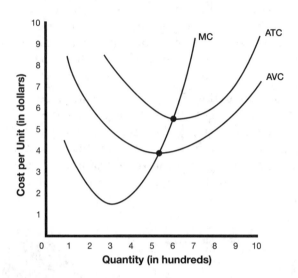

A typical short-run cost curve diagram shows marginal cost (MC), average total cost (ATC) and average variable cost (AVC). Short-run cost curves tend to be U-shaped because of the law of diminishing marginal returns:

- In the short run, capital is more fixed because fewer changes can be made.
- After a certain point, adding workers may lead to a decline in marginal production of each worker and thus an increase in the marginal cost of producing each additional unit of output. As firms employ more workers, therefore, marginal costs can increase.
- The average will eventually rise again when marginal cost is once again above the average cost, leading to the U-shaped curves of ATC and AVC.

The marginal cost always passes through the lowest point on the average total cost curve and through the lowest point on the average variable cost curve, as well. On the preceding graph, the marginal cost line intersects the lowest average total cost of about $5.50 per shirt and the average variable cost curve at its minimum at about $4.00. Over time, a series of production functions with diminishing marginal returns will slowly but surely create an upward-sloping marginal cost curve. This concept is explored further in the following topic on long-run production costs.

Business owners must consider a host of short-run production costs in order to determine how each may help or hinder output goals. They can utilize a variety of strategies and tools to affect those costs and ultimately prevent shutdowns and revenue declines.

1. In a paragraph, explain the tools firms may use to consider various types of short-run production costs.

KEY TERMS

short-run production cost	total cost	specialization
variable cost	average total cost	division of labor
total variable cost	average variable cost	shutdown of production
fixed cost	average fixed cost	short-run cost curve
total fixed cost	total revenue	
marginal cost	marginal revenue	

MULTIPLE-CHOICE QUESTIONS

1. Which of the following is an example of a cookie factory's marginal cost?

   (A) The cost of additional sugar

   (B) The cost of a new commercial oven

   (C) The cost to produce an additional box of cookies

   (D) The cost associated with delayed shipping

   (E) The cost per unit of multiple varieties of cookies

2. If a flower shop incurs $450 in total costs to produce an output of 10 flower arrangements, what is the average cost per arrangement?

   (A) $450

   (B) $440

   (C) $45

   (D) $44

   (E) $10

3. A coffee shop had a very busy Saturday morning, and the owner wishes to calculate her revenue. If she sold 200 cups of coffee at $2 per cup, what would the total revenue for that morning be?

   (A) $100

   (B) $200

   (C) $300

   (D) $400

   (E) $500

1. Laszlo's Lawn Rangers produces one product—lawn mowers for golf courses. Fixed costs for Laszlo's Lawn Rangers include rent on the building, interest payments to the bank, insurance costs and property taxes and are $4,000 per month. The following represents a short-run production cost schedule for Laszlo's Lawn Rangers. Use it to answer the questions that follow.

Output per Month	Total Cost per Month (in dollars)
0	4,000
10	10,000
20	14,000
30	23,000
40	34,000
50	47,000
60	62,000
70	88,000

(a) When output is 50 units, AFC is _____.

(b) The marginal cost of producing 40 lawn mowers instead of 30 is _____.

(c) When output is 60, AVC is _____.

(d) What is the total variable cost of producing 70 units?

(e) Will AFC increase or decrease as more lawnmowers are produced? Explain.

Producer costs generally increase with increased output. To produce more and more birthday cakes, a bakery owner must buy more ingredients, hire more bakers, and expand capacity by installing more ovens. As long as output rises, costs rise, which means that basing production decisions on total cost is pointless—costs inevitably go up. To make rational production decisions, producers must determine how much costs go up per unit of output. This is the marginal cost—the cost of producing an additional unit of output.

Producers incur two types of costs—fixed costs, which do not change per unit of output, and variable costs, which do change per unit of output. In the short term, variable costs greatly affect total costs since they are determined by factors that are easier to manipulate in a short period of time. The bakery owner can more easily hire more bakers than she can install new ovens.

To make short-term production decisions, producers look at the average costs, or costs per unit. They must consider average total cost because that determines their total outlay for production. Since variable costs have more impact than fixed costs in the short term, producers focus on this component of total costs as well. From the average total cost and the average variable cost, they can determine the marginal cost—the increase in costs generated by each additional unit of output.

Apply the Skill

The following table shows the bakery's output, fixed and variable costs, marginal cost, average total cost, and average variable cost. (All costs listed are in dollars.) Use the data to plot the last three columns on a graph, labeling each line and circling the optimal point of production.

Output	Fixed Costs	Variable Costs	Total Cost	Marginal Cost	Average Total Cost	Average Variable Cost
16	160	80	240	5.00	15.00	5.00
40	160	160	320	3.30	8.00	4.00
60	160	240	400	4.00	6.60	4.00
72	160	320	480	6.60	6.60	4.40
80	160	400	560	10.00	7.00	5.00
84	160	480	640	20.00	7.60	5.70

Topic 3.3

Long-Run Production Costs

"But this long run is a misleading guide to current affairs. In the long run we are all dead. Economists set themselves too easy, too useless a task, if in tempestuous seasons they can only tell us, that when the storm is long past, the ocean is flat again."

John Maynard Keynes, *A Tract on Monetary Reform* (1923)

Essential Question: How do firms consider long-run production costs?

The previous topic discussed how firms manipulate capital, land, and labor in the short run in order to achieve production goals. A bakery can buy more eggs, sugar, and flour. A florist can buy more roses, tulips, and daisies. Recall that a producer is able to adjust short-run costs like these fairly quickly and easily.

Other costs, though, are fixed and take longer to change. For example, Fred has started a company that manufactures printers for computers, and sales are rising quickly. He needs more space to manufacture the product, so he must either lease or buy the space.

Fred is considering his long-run production costs. Economists define the **long run** as the time period when all costs are variable. In the long run, a producer can adjust all inputs. The long run is not a set period of time. Rather, it is the length of a firm's longest fixed cost.

After a firm has reached the point of its longest fixed cost, such as the length of a lease of property, much can happen. After that point, a firm is free to adjust all its inputs, and all costs become variable. The long run typically includes costs like new factories and the hiring of salaried employees—investments that are significant and that may take time to implement.

Business owners must plan for the long run in order to achieve their capital goals.

Long-Run Inputs

A firm's long run is defined by the period of time in which all inputs, including its lengthiest, can vary. If a business has signed a 12-month lease, for example, and it has no obligations longer than that, then its long-run period is anything longer than a year.

Similarly, no costs are fixed in the long run. Given time, a firm can explore other options. If a firm decides that it is unhappy with its current location, it can choose not to renew that 12-month lease and consider moving to other locations. If it owns old equipment, it can purchase other more advanced or newer **production technologies**, or any machinery necessary to make a business's specific good or service.

Consider, for example, a factory that produces solar panels. If the business owner wants to increase production in the long run, she may choose to hire more workers to build more panels. She may also choose to invest in large-scale machinery that will automate most of the work. She performs calculations such as those below to determine when she should invest in employees and when she should invest in technology.

Option	Number of Worker	Number of Machines
A	10	2
B	6	5
C	2	8

Option A uses the most workers and the least amount of machinery, while Option C uses the fewest workers and the most amount of machinery. The business owner would consider how any of these inputs may change over time in order to determine whether it would be wise to invest in more machinery. A change in wages, for example, would likely lead to different conclusions about investments in technology. The following two charts show how the relative costs of labor and machinery can affect long-run decision-making.

SITUATION A. INPUTS OF $10/WORKER AND $20/MACHINE			
Option	Labor Cost	Machine Cost	Total Cost
A: 10 workers, 2 machines	10 workers × $10 = $100	2 machines × $20 = $40	$140
B: 6 workers, 5 machines	6 workers × $10 = $60	5 machines × $20 = $100	$160
C: 2 workers, 8 machines	2 workers × $10 = $20	8 machines × $20 = $160	$180

SITUATION B. INPUTS OF $40/WORKER AND $20/MACHINE			
Options	Labor Cost	Machine Cost	Total Cost
A: 10 workers, 2 machines	10 workers × $40 = $400	2 machines × $20 = $40	$440
B: 6 workers, 5 machines	6 workers × $40 = $240	5 machines × $20 = $100	$340
C: 2 workers, 8 machines	2 workers × $40 = $80	8 machines × $20 = $160	$240

In this example, as wages rise, the firm will spend less money in the long run by adding machines than by adding employees. As one input, labor, becomes more expensive, firms can shift to another input, machines, that are less expensive.

Companies tend to have more options in the long run than in the short run. A solar power manufacturer may choose to operate in a country where labor is less expensive, or it may choose to remain in its current market and invest in technology. Either way, firms will always seek to choose the most profitable combination of inputs in the long run.

Scale of Production

Business owners manipulate many variables to determine how to achieve the most desirable outcome for their firm. This relationship between inputs and outputs in the long run is described by the **scale of production**, which is the quantity of output. In the example above, the scale of production would be the number of solar panels produced. Changing the scale of production can lead to three different outcomes.

Increasing Returns to Scale occur when output increases by more than the proportional change in all inputs. For example, imagine the solar panel manufacturer doubles all her inputs and can then produce three times the number of panels. This could occur if each input is used more efficiently.

Decreasing Returns to Scale are the opposite of increasing returns to scale. For example, imagine the solar panel manufacturer doubles all her inputs, but the number of panels she is able to produce increases by only half. Then she has experienced a decreasing return to scale. Her output may have increased, but not in proportion to her inputs.

Constant Returns to Scale occur when an increase in inputs leads to the same proportional increase in output. Constant return to scale, or **efficient scale**, occurs when increasing the number of inputs leads to an equivalent increase in the output. If the solar panel manufacturer doubles all inputs and produces twice the number of panels, it has a constant return to scale.

Long-Run Costs

Scale of production is one way to study inputs and outputs. It focuses on the quantity of production. Another way is to focus on costs. A firm's **long-run average total cost (ATC)** is the cost-per-unit of the product being created. In the long run, the ATC can vary in three ways.

Economies of Scale occur when the long-run average total cost decreases as the quantity of output increases. A producer often gains relative cost advantages by increasing the **scale**, or size, of a firm's operation. Often, a larger factory can produce output at a lower average cost than a smaller factory can—possibly because division of labor and specialization are at play. Companies that deal in large volume, such as warehouse stores, effectively use economies of scale. The following graph illustrates how the average cost of producing a product—in this case, solar panels—drops as the quantity of output rises.

ECONOMIES OF SCALE

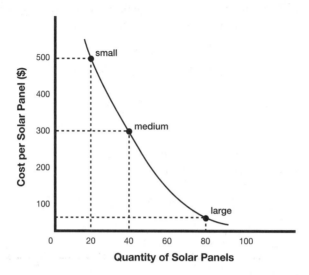

Diseconomies of Scale are the opposite of economies of scale. As the quantity of output increases, the long-run average total cost also increases. In other words, as companies produce output beyond a certain point, the cost to make each unit increases.

Diseconomies of scale often occur as businesses grow. If the solar panel manufacturer were to vastly increase her output, she would have increased **coordination issues**, or people and resources to coordinate and manage. That additional coordination could make the firm less efficient. At an even larger scale, the manufacturer may not be able to find more people willing to work at a certain hourly wage. The owner's machinery may also not be able to handle the increased volume, resulting in the need to invest in new machinery. Regardless of the reason, diseconomies of scale typically result in a higher per-unit cost.

Minimum Efficient Scale

The **minimum efficient scale** is the lowest point at which a firm stops realizing economies of scale. In other words, it is the quantity at which a firm's long-run average total cost curve is at its lowest value. At this point, the company achieves its greatest efficiency in production, so is is called **productive efficiency.**

Minimum efficient scale plays a role in determining whether a market has a large number of firms or a small number. A large minimum efficient scale is associated with more **market concentration**, or the extent to which one or more similar businesses are all able to enter the market. Minimum efficient scale is also the minimum point at which a firm must run in order to be competitive.

For example, a pizza restaurant can achieve economies of scale fairly quickly. Pizzas are easy to make, the ingredients are readily available, and a parlor owner can quickly train workers to make pizzas. A parlor can reach the minimum efficient scale quickly. In contrast, to build a car requires about 30,000 parts and highly trained workers. An auto manufacturer takes a long time to reach the minimum efficient scale. Because of these contrasting conditions, the United States supports more than 75,000 pizza restaurants, but only a handful of auto manufacturing companies.

MINIMUM EFFICIENT SCALE

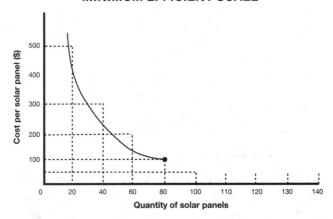

Minimum Efficient Scale and Competition

Once a business has achieved minimum efficient scale, it can be more competitive. Minimum efficient scale also affects the structure of the market. If the price of a certain input increases unexpectedly or if the quantity demanded suddenly drops, firms that have achieved minimum efficient scale will be more likely to survive. Those that have not reached that point may ultimately experience diseconomies of scale.

Firms try to reach the point at which they can produce goods at a lower enough cost that they can offer them at a competitive price. This makes them more financially able to weather unexpected costs. If the solar panel manufacturer is producing panels as efficiently as possible, it will be able to sell the panels at the most competitive price, even in a crowded market. If one of the company's inputs should unexpectedly increase, then it should still be secure enough to be able to produce output.

The curve on the graph above shows the solar panel company's long-run average cost. The point at which the company reaches its minimum efficient scale is 80 solar panels.

Business owners are not as constrained in the long run as they are in the short run. They are freer to consider a wide variety of inputs and manipulate them through a number of scales. Ultimately, companies aim to find the point at which they are most efficient and most likely to weather or adapt to economic downturns, competition from new firms, and other unforeseen circumstances.

1. In one paragraph, explain how firms take long-run production costs into consideration.

KEY TERMS

long run	economies of scale
production technology	scale
scale of production	diseconomies of scale
increasing return to scale	coordination issues
decreasing return to scale	minimum efficient scale
constant returns to scale	productive efficiency
efficient scale	market concentration
long-run average total cost	

MULTIPLE-CHOICE QUESTIONS

1. If a bread company increases production of its products and notices that its long-run average total cost decreases, it is experiencing
   (A) decreasing returns to scale
   (B) constant returns to scale
   (C) economies of scale
   (D) diseconomies of scale
   (E) none of the above

2. The concept that as the quantity of a certain product increases and the associated long-run average total cost stays the same is defined as
   (A) increasing returns to scale
   (B) decreasing returns to scale
   (C) constant returns to scale
   (D) economies of scale
   (E) diseconomies of scale

3. The graph below shows a company's production of windmills. At what quantity will the company reach its minimum efficient scale?

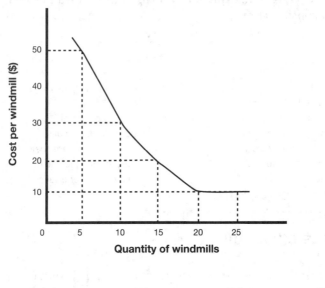

(A) 5   (B) 10   (C) 15   (D) 20   (E) 25

FREE-RESPONSE QUESTION

1. Owings Airplane Corp. produces planes based on the table below. The company has three different plant sizes to choose from in the long run. Current order amounts include plans for two planes produced per day. The plant cost refers to the total cost of the factor per day. The per plane costs include all labor and inputs to produce one plane.

Plant Size	Plant Cost	Per Plane Costs	Long-Run Average Total Cost (LRATC)
1	20,000	100,000	
2	50,000	80,000	
3	100,000	60,000	

(a) If Owings uses plant size 1, what would the long-run average total cost be?

(b) If Owings uses plant size 2, what would the average total cost be?

(c) If Owings uses plant size 3, what would the average total cost be?

(d) At plant size 2, is LRATC increasing or decreasing?

(e) If orders increase to 4 planes per day, what plant size would Owings use?

THINK AS AN ECONOMIST: *DESCRIBE THE SIMILARITIES AND DIFFERENCES OF ECONOMIC CONCEPTS*

Describing the similarities and differences of economic concepts involves comparing and contrasting. That is, you explain the features that two or more concepts have in common and those that make each one distinct. In economics, it is particularly helpful in describing concepts to use real-world examples to clarify them.

For example, you can compare and contrast fixed and variable costs. Both involve the cost of inputs in production, and both contribute to total cost. Fixed costs do not change with the amount of output over a given period of time. They refer to factors like the cost of the plant and the yearly salaries of certain executives. Variable costs do change, increasing as output increases and decreasing as output decreases. Examples of variable costs are the costs of labor, which increase if workers are added to boost production, and of raw materials, which are needed to generate greater output.

As business owners think about long-term operations, they think about the relationship of the average cost of operations to output. In doing so, they seek the minimum efficient scale—the lowest point at which they can experience economies of scale.

Apply the Skill

In evaluating long-term operations, business owners can identify one of three conditions—economies of scale, diseconomies of scale, and constant return to scale. What are the similarities and differences between economies and diseconomies of scale? In writing your description, be sure to use real-world examples.

Types of Profit

"Civilization and profits go hand in hand. It is out of the surplus of our efforts that progress is made."

Calvin Coolidge, November 27, 1920

Essential Question: How do firms calculate different types of profit?

In 1971, Frederick W. Smith believed he could build a company that could deliver packages throughout most of the United States overnight. That year, he founded Federal Express and the company invested heavily in trucks and airplanes to fulfill its promise. The idea worked, yet FedEx, as the company came to be known, didn't turn a profit until 1975.

Like FedEx, every firm selects inputs to achieve desired outputs in an attempt to realize as much financial gain as possible. The owner of a small grocery store, for example, may decide to charge less for sparkling water in an attempt to sell more bottles. She may also search for a different sparkling water supplier, so she can lower her own cost.

Profit is the basic difference between the amount of money a business spends to create a good or service and the amount of money the company receives for it. Firms consider various types of profit and how to calculate each.

Business owners track various types of profit to determine how they will ultimately be most successful.

Accounting Profit vs. Economic Profit

Accountants and economists think about profit very differently. The main difference is the way in which members of each profession treat costs.

Accounting Profit Most people, including accountants, focus on **accounting profit.** This is the difference between revenue and **explicit costs**, or any payments by a firm for tangible resources such as supplies, labor, and rent. Any typical operating expense is considered an explicit cost. All explicit costs are recorded within a company's financial statements. Consider the following simplified example of a bakery's pre-tax accounting profit for one year.

BAKERY ACCOUNTING PROFIT

Revenue	$400,000
Explicit Cost #1: Ingredients	($100,000)
Explicit Cost #2: Labor	($25,000)
Explicit Cost #3: Rent	($50,000)
Accounting Profit	$225,000

The baker's revenue for the year is $400,000. After explicit costs of ingredients, labor, and rent, she has an accounting profit of $225,000.

Economic Profit Economists, on the hand, look at **economic profit**, which is more than a series of expenses. Rather, it tells firms whether or not it makes sense to run the business in the manner in which they are running it.

Economic profit considers explicit costs, but it also considers **implicit costs**, or any costs that have already occurred but may not have been reported as expenses. Implicit costs are **opportunity costs**, or those opportunities a company misses when it decides to focus on one product over another.

For example, most U.S. automobile companies face the choice whether to produce electric vehicles, for which the market is expected to grow. If a company decides not to invest in developing electrical vehicles, its opportunity cost is potential sales of electrical vehicles. Implicit costs include several items:

- Cost of financial capital is money necessary to invest to make a product or offer a service. Financial capital can be in the form of debt, such as interest paid to a bank for a small business loan. It can also be in the form of capital, such as any necessary equipment.

- Compensation for risk is the theory that firms may be more careful when they sense greater risk. Any associated costs would be an implicit expense. For example, if a hot dog vendor could save money by buying buns in bulk, but only buys the minimum number, the difference in cost to purchase buns at the last minute would be an implicit cost.

- Entrepreneur's time is the amount of time an entrepreneur spends in activities such as meeting with investors or training new employees. Time spent on any such activities is an implicit cost.

If a company runs an economic loss, it will consider shifting resources to other products or services, or it may determine ways to produce its current products more efficiently. So, economic profits help guide the decisions that a business's managers make.

The following table illustrates how the same bakery would calculate its economic profit to determine if it is being run effectively.

BAKERY ECONOMIC PROFIT

Revenue	$400,000
Explicit Costs (ingredients, labor, rent)	($175,000)
Implicit Cost #1: Wages lost from other work	($125,000)
Implicit Cost #2: Time taken to train new employees	($25,000)
Implicit Cost #3: Cost of financial capital	($100,000)
Economic Profit	**($25,000)**

Because of the baker's implicit costs (wages lost, time taken from other possible work, financial capital), her bakery has an economic loss of $25,000. (Economic losses are shown between parentheses, as in the preceding chart.) As this example shows, a firm can have a negative economic profit even if it has a positive accounting profit.

If the difference between a company's revenues and its explicit and implicit costs is zero, the company earns a **normal profit.** In other words, the company's revenues match its explicit and implicit costs. A normal profit means the firm is using its resources as efficiently as possible.

Responding to Profit

The manner in which firms respond to profit opportunities will ultimately determine their success. A firm's motivation to operate in a manner that maximizes its profits is called **profit motive**. Since the purpose of a company is to make a profit, a business has little reason to exist if it does not do so.

Profits and losses also send signals about resource allocation to individuals and firms:

- If a company is making a profit, it knows it is taking scarce resources and turning them into something that society values more highly. Profits are a signal to continue.

- If a company is losing money (making a negative profit) it is taking scarce resources and turning them into something that society values less highly. The losses tell the firm to stop.

If a firm is making higher-than-average profits, it also provides a signal to other firms to enter the market. Television shows often demonstrate this pattern. In 1993, a comedy about six single friends in their 20s and 30s living in New York City aired. Titled *Living Single*, it was successful enough to inspire another show the following year about a different group of six friends in New

York City. The second show, *Friends*, became one of the most successful series in television history. After it ended in 2004, its legacy lived on in numerous other comedies about groups of young friends that it inspired.

If a firm is losing money, its owners try to predict whether those losses will continue. They might be able to stand losses temporarily, but losses that are not likely to end are a signal they should leave the market. However, sometimes losses are expected. In particular, new businesses often have high initial start-up costs that are not likely to be replicated in future years. As a result, many firms exist for years before they produce a profit. Amazon, for example, was founded in 1994 but did not see a profit until 2001. By 2020 it was one of the largest companies in the world.

ANSWER THE TOPIC ESSENTIAL QUESTION

1. In two to three paragraphs, explain how firms respond to different types of profit.

KEY TERMS

accounting profit

explicit cost

economic profit

implicit cost

opportunity cost

normal profit

profit motive

MULTIPLE-CHOICE QUESTIONS

1. Which of the following is an explicit cost?

   (A) Time taken to attend a business seminar

   (B) Lost wages from another job

   (C) Hours spent training new employees

   (D) Store lease payments

   (E) Meetings with potential investors

2. Assume that a firm's total revenue is $500 and its total costs are $150. Calculate its accounting profits.

   (A) $150

   (B) $350

   (C) $500

   (D) $650

   (E) $750

3. Assume that a bakery's average cost to produce one muffin is $2, and the price it charges for each muffin is $5. If the bakery sells 50 muffins, what will its profit be?

(A) $50

(B) $100

(C) $150

(D) $250

(E) $500

FREE-RESPONSE QUESTIONS

1. Ruben is considering the option of opening a restaurant instead of working as a teacher. Use the following information to answer the questions that follow. All numbers are for the year.

Current Teaching Salary	$100,000
Expected Revenue from Restaurant	$350,000
Restaurant Rent and Bills	$100,000
Restaurant Labor Costs	$125,000
Restaurant Ingredient Costs	$50,000

(a) What is the implicit cost of starting the restaurant?

(b) What is the total explicit cost of opening the restaurant?

(c) What is the total accounting profit of the restaurant?

(d) What is the total economic profit of opening the restaurant?

(e) Based on your answer in part (d), should Ruben open the restaurant or continue teaching? Explain.

In a market economy, business owners seek profits. Profits are their incentive for doing business—the reward for success.

As you have read, profits come in different types. While all profits are based on revenues and costs, each is calculated in a different way depending on which set of revenues and costs are included. Accounting profit and economic profit differ.

- Accounting profit considers explicit costs, or any payments by a firm for operating expenses that are recorded in a company's financial statements.

- Economic profit considers both explicit and implicit costs, including costs incurred that may not have been reported as an expense on the company's financial statements.

Apply the Skill

A regional pharmacy chain is trying to determine the long-term viability of opening ten new outlets. The management team has the following estimates of revenues and costs. Use them to calculate both accounting profit and economic profit for the new stores. Then explain the difference between the two and identify the economic principle that the chain's managers should use to make their decision.

Revenue	$12 million
Explicit Costs	
Rent	$2 million
Equipment	$500,000
Inventory	$4 million
Labor	$2.5 million
Depreciation on equipment	$150,000
Implicit Costs	
Opportunity cost (interest earned from investing cash instead of expanding)	$300,000
Training new employees	$300,000

Topic 3.5

Profit Maximization

"Production for sale in a market in which the object is to realize the maximum profit is the essential feature of a capitalist world-economy."

Immanuel Wallerstein, historian, 1979

Essential Question: How do firms maximize profit?

The COVID-19 pandemic created turmoil throughout the food industry. In general, people consumed less food in restaurants and cafeterias and consumed more at home. This shift led to dramatic changes in prices between February and June of 2020:

- Peanut butter prices increased almost 8 percent. Consumers stocked up on a good source of protein they could store in a cabinet so quantity demanded increased.

- Butter prices decreased more than 3 percent. Apparently restaurants and cafeterias use more butter to prepare foods than do people cooking at home, so quantity demanded fell.

- Beef prices increased more than 20 percent. Several meat packing plants had to shut down because so many workers caught the virus, so quantity supplied decreased.

- Prices for beef stew decreased about 1 percent. As firms shifted production from individual cuts of meat that they could sell to restaurants to canned goods desired by consumers, the quantity supplied increased.

To make matters more confusing, overall food costs increased in the United States but they declined globally.

Despite all these ups and downs in prices, one core question remained constant for firms. How could they increase (or at least reduce any decrease) in their profit? This is one of the most basic questions for a firm in a market economy. Providing food is not a firm's reason to exist. Rather, food is the product a firm provides to make a profit. This focus on profit provides firms a clear goal, even in the most confusing times.

It may seem that firms should be able to maximize profit by producing more or by charging more. But the formula is more complex than that. **Profit maximization** is the process by which a business or company applies specific economic principles to earn maximum profit at minimum cost. It considers a variety of factors and is the chief target of any business. One item that firms must consider is the best level of production to maximize profits.

Firms analyze costs to determine the point at which their marginal costs equal marginal revenue.

Profit-Maximizing Rule

Firms can use a formula to decide how to make the most profit they can. This formula, the **profit-maximizing rule**, states that firms should produce at the point where marginal cost (MC) is equal to marginal revenue (MR) and where the marginal cost curve is rising. (See the graph "Profit Maximization" on p. 195, which illustrates how marginal costs often initially fall but later rise.)

Recall that marginal cost is the increase in cost by producing one more unit of a single good. Recall also that marginal revenue is the change in total revenue as a result of increasing sales by a single unit and that marginal revenue can also be calculated as follows:

$$MR = \frac{Change\ in\ total\ revenue}{Change\ in\ quantity\ of\ output}$$

The profit maximization rule can therefore be written mathematically as MR = MC.

Consider an example of a jewelry designer. Assume that the designer makes a bracelet whose unit price is $40, which means that the marginal revenue for bracelets in this competitive market is also $40. The jewelry designer must decide how many bracelets to produce at that price in order to maximize profit. If the marginal revenue is higher than the marginal cost, then the designer will bring in net money with the sale of each bracelet and profits will rise. If the marginal cost is greater than the marginal revenue, however, then the designer will add more to total cost than is added to total revenue. Thus, the designer will see profits decrease.

At the point where marginal cost equals marginal revenue, the jewelry designer will maximize profits. After that point, it may cost $41 to produce the next bracelet, but the next bracelet can only be sold for $40, so the designer would lose money by selling the next bracelet. The designer would need to scale back production accordingly to ensure that production occurs at the point where the marginal cost to make a bracelet is equal to the marginal revenue the designer takes in when the bracelet is sold.

The profit maximizing rule delineates how much output the firm should produce in order to maximize its profits, but it does not quantify how much those profits will be. Recall from unit 3.4 that profits may be defined in different ways. When economists talk about profits, they are referring to economic profits—meaning the revenue left over after all costs, both explicit and implicit, are subtracted or are accounted for.

To determine the amount of economic profit, revenues and costs must be determined first. Total revenue (TR) is the total amount of revenue a firm generates from selling a good or service. Total revenue is found by multiplying the price of product by the number of items sold. The formula for this is:

$$TR = P \times Q.$$

Another revenue concept that is often used is average revenue (AR), or the revenue from selling a good or service on a per unit or average basis. The formula for AR is

$$AR = \frac{TR}{Q}.$$

Substituting the formula for TR into the formula for AR,

$$AR = \frac{(P \times Q)}{Q}$$

which results in

$$AR = P$$

The graph below illustrates this point of profit maximization. Marginal revenue (MR) remains constant throughout, at $40. Marginal cost (MC), however, shows an initial decline, then an upward curve. The average total cost (ATC) is the cost of producing each unit of output, on average. Average total cost is calculated by taking the total cost and dividing by quantity. Another way to express this is that total cost (TC) equals the average total cost (ATC) multiplied by quantity (Q). In a formula,

$$TC = ATC \times Q$$

and by rearranging the terms,

$$ATC = \frac{TC}{Q}.$$

PROFIT MAXIMIZATION

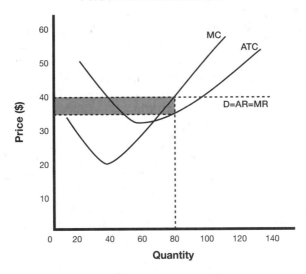

The point at which MR intersects MC shows the designer the price and quantity combination at which profit is maximized. The shaded area shows how much economic profit the designer will earn.

Rational Choice Theory

When exploring how best to maximize profit, firms employ the **rational choice theory**, which states that individuals will always make rational choices based on calculations and outcomes in line with their own personal objectives. **Rational economic agents**, therefore, are hypothetical consumers making rational choices in a free market.

By applying rational choice theory to formulas meant to achieve maximum profit, firms expect to achieve outcomes that provide the greatest financial benefit. In the case of the jewelry designer, she will attempt to maximize the profits from selling bracelets. So how many bracelets will the designer sell and how much profit will be earned?

Profit Maximizing Levels of Production

Applying the profit maximizing rule of MR = MC, the designer will produce 80 bracelets. This competitive market sets a price of $40 so the total revenue is $40 × 80 = $3,200. Since each additional bracelet sells for $40, the marginal revenue is also $40. Further, since every bracelet sells for $40, the average revenue in this market is also $40.

According to the graph, if the designer sells 81 bracelets, $40 is added to revenues, but the total cost increases by more than $40. This means that profits must go down. Also, according to the graph, if the designer sells only 79 bracelets, profits will also decrease. Why? According to the marginal cost curve, producing one fewer bracelets reduces costs by less than $40, but selling one fewer bracelets also means total revenues go down by $40. This means that profits must also go down.

How much profit does the designer earn? Again, using the profit maximizing rule of MR = MC, the designer produces 80 bracelets at a price of $40 each. Total revenue is $40 × 80 = $3,200. According to the graph, when quantity is 80, average total cost is $35. Thus, total cost (TC) = ATC × Q = $35 * 80 = $2,800. To calculate profit, subtract the total cost from the total revenue to find that profit = $3,200 – $2,800 = $400. The formula for profit is

$$Profit = TR = TC$$

Another way to calculate profit is to recognize that price (P) equals the average revenue (AR). Using the average approach, the average profit, also called the profit per unit sold, is AR – ATC = $40 – $35 = $5. To determine the total profit, multiply (AR – ATC) by the quantity (Q) to find that the designer's profit will be ($40 – $35) × 80 = $400. The formula for profit in this method is

$$Profit = (AR - ATC) \times Q \ or$$
$$Profit = (P - ATC) \times Q.$$

Either approach will lead to the same result.

Firms work to determine the optimal level at which their level of production leads to benefits that exceed total costs. But they are careful not to overproduce. This balancing act compares marginal benefits and marginal costs to achieve the highest profit-maximizing formula.

ANSWER THE TOPIC ESSENTIAL QUESTION

1. In two to three paragraphs, explain how firms determine if they have maximized their profit.

KEY TERMS

profit maximization

profit-maximizing rule

rational choice theory

rational economic agent

MULTIPLE-CHOICE QUESTIONS

Use the graph below to answer the following three questions.

PROFIT MAXIMIZATION

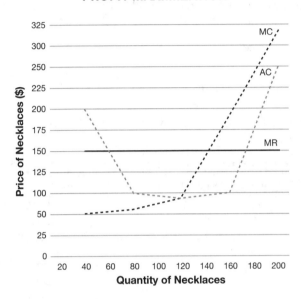

1. The point on the graph where the jeweler will maximize profit is where the marginal cost

   (A) is at its lowest point
   (B) intersects average cost
   (C) equals marginal revenue
   (D) results in maximum revenue
   (E) is at its highest point

2. What is the maximum number of necklaces the jewelry designer should produce in order to maximize profits?

   (A) 120
   (B) 130
   (C) 140
   (D) 150
   (E) 160

3. If a firm finds that its current marginal cost is $15 and current marginal revenue is $20, what should the firm do in the short run?

(A) Decrease production to increase profits.

(B) Increase production to increase profits.

(C) Continue current production level of the profit maximizing quantity.

(D) Increase plant size.

(E) Raise the price.

FREE-RESPONSE QUESTION

1. Below shows a table for a local jewelry designer who sells bracelets in a competitive market.

Quantity of Bracelets	Marginal Revenue	Marginal Cost	Average Total Cost
1	$30	$6	$13.00
2	$30	$12	$11.00
3	$30	$18	$12.33
4	$30	$24	$14.50
5	$30	$30	$17.00
6	$30	$36	$19.37
7	$30	$42	$22.43

(a) What is the profit of producing 3 bracelets?

(b) If the designer decides to sell 4 units, should she produce more, produce less, or is she maximizing profits? Explain.

(c) What is the number of bracelets the designer should sell if she wishes to maximize her profits? Explain your answer.

(d) How much profit would the jewelry designer earn at the quantity that maximizes profit?

(e) If demand for bracelets increased which caused the price to increase, would the designer now likely decide to increase or decrease production in order to maximize profits?

THINK AS AN ECONOMIST: *USE ECONOMIC PRINCIPLES TO EXPLAIN HOW TO ACHIEVE A SPECIFIC OUTCOME*

Economists use economic principles to explain what decisions economic actors should make.

- Identify what specific economic behaviors are taking place in a particular situation.
- Use an economic principle to explain how to achieve a specific outcome.

For example, economists explain why an individual is willing to risk opening a business. The reason is that he or she has the incentive of potential profits if the business succeeds, which makes the risk worthwhile.

Apply the Skill

Jermaine has a hair salon. She is trying to decide how many stylists to hire based on how many haircuts they can perform each day. Jermaine figures that each additional stylist could do 25 haircuts a day. Based on her materials, supplies, overhead, and other costs, Jermaine calculates her marginal revenue (MR), marginal cost (MC), and average cost (AC) as shown here:

Quantity	MR	MC	AC
25	250	60	200
50	180	70	100
75	130	80	85
100	100	100	90
125	80	200	140

Using the model for profit maximization, graph the marginal revenue (MR), marginal cost (MC), and average cost (AC) curves and explain how many stylists Jermaine should hire and why.

"The Social Responsibility of Business Is to Increase Its Profits." That title sums up an influential article by economist Milton Friedman that appeared in in *The New York Times Magazine* in September 1970. His article was written in response to Campaign GM, a movement founded by a group of Washington lawyers headed by Ralph Nader to pressure the General Motors Corporation to become more socially responsible. Campaign GM demanded that a committee be set up to study areas of public concern, such as safety and pollution.

The "Friedman Doctrine" Friedman's essay called demands that businesses be socially responsible "pure and unadulterated socialism." He argued that corporate executives' only responsibility is "to conduct the business in accordance with their desires, which generally will be to make as much money as possible while conforming to the basic rules of the society, both those embodied in law and those embodied in ethical custom."

Friedman's ideas influenced a generation of executives, as well as the policies of leaders such as U.S. President Ronald Reagan and British Prime Minister Margaret Thatcher. In the words of Darren Walker, president of the Ford Foundation, Friedman's ideas became "theology—the intellectual scaffolding that allowed its disciples to justify decades of greed-is-good excess." On the 50th anniversary of Friedman's essay, *The New York Times* asked a group of more than 20 experts to respond to all or parts of Friedman's essay. The respondents included economics professors, corporate executives, and Nobel laureates.

The "Friedman Doctrine" Reconsidered Nobel laureate Joseph Stiglitz recounted having given a talk at the University of Chicago around the time Friedman's essay appeared. In his talk, he presented an early version of his research that showed that "firms pursuing profit maximization did not lead to the maximization of social welfare." He argued that Adam Smith's "invisible hand" does not in reality lead to the well-being of society. He claims that his analysis, not Friedman's, has stood the test of time. Another University of Chicago economics professor, Marianne Bertrand, pointed out that "perfect markets [such as the ones envisioned by Smith and Friedman] exist only in economics textbooks."

Like many modern corporate executives, former Starbucks CEO Howard Schultz believes that a company's social and environmental responsibility does not come at the expense of profits but actually increases them. He repeatedly stood up to shareholders who suggested that Starbucks's policies hurt profits, telling them that they were free to sell their shares if they thought they could do better elsewhere.

Former Chief Justice of the Delaware Supreme Court Leo Strine Jr. and Allbirds (a company that makes athletic shoes) co-founder Joey Zwillinger pointed out that Friedman's essay appeared at a time when there was widespread prosperity and Black Americans were taking strides toward inclusion. "Since then, the United States has gone backward in economic equality and security."

Topic 3.6

Firms' Decisions to Enter or Exit Markets

"Nobody buys a farm based on whether they think it's going to rain next year. They buy it because they think it's a good investment over 10 or 20 years."

Warren Buffett, investor, 2018

Essential Question: How do firms decide how much to produce and whether they should enter or exit a market?

So far, Unit 3 has outlined the various costs that firms consider, both in the short run and long run. It has also outlined different types of profit and how firms work to maximize those profits. This topic illustrates firms' short-run decisions about how much output—if any—they should produce. It also illustrates long-run decisions to enter or exit a market.

Short-Run Decisions

Keep in mind that the goal of firms is to maximize their profits (or minimize losses). This profit-maximizing decision occurs where marginal revenue is equal to marginal cost. Once this point is determined, firms make one of two decisions. They may choose to continue to operate and produce a product, which is called a **positive output**. Alternatively, they may choose to shut down and produce nothing at all, which is called a **zero output**.

To make this decision, firms compare their total revenue to total variable cost in order to determine if they are making a profit. They may also compare price to average variable cost. Recall from Topic 3.2 that revenue is the total income that a business receives from its normal business activities, and variable costs are those that can be changed quickly and relatively easily.

Consider, for example, a coffee roasting company. The owner needs to determine if she should stay open through a slow period. Her total revenue for this same period last year was $5,000. She adds all her upcoming variable costs and finds they will total $400. Since her variable costs are less than her anticipated revenue, she decides to stay open. She may also compare her price to her average variable costs. Shipping prices have gone up, but packing prices have gone down. Her average variable cost, therefore, remains relatively constant. The price she is able to charge during this slower period is still likely to bring in more profit than the average variable cost, so she will likely maintain her current pricing. There are three basic outcomes for the firm:

1. *Price (P) is greater than or equal to average total cost (ATC), or $P \geq ATC$.* In this case, the firm is making zero economic profits or positive economic profits. So, the firm would produce positive output.

2. *Average total cost is greater than price, and price is greater than or equal to average variable cost (AVC), or $ATC > P \geq AVC$.* In this case, the firm would continue to produce because the total revenue would pay for all the fixed costs and at least some of the variable costs. This would minimize losses in the short run.

3. *Average Variable Cost is greater than price, or $AVC > P$.* In this case, the firm would shut down; in other words, it would produce nothing. This is a zero-output decision. When $AVC > P$, total revenue is not sufficient to cover the fixed costs plus any of the variable costs, so the best decision is to produce nothing. The firm has economic losses equal to the amount of the total fixed costs when it produces zero output. If the firm produces positive output, it would use all of its revenues to pay some of the fixed costs but would have no revenues to pay any of the variable costs. The firm would have economic losses equal to its fixed costs plus economic losses from additional variable costs. Thus, the firm is better off producing zero output and having economic losses equal to the total fixed costs.

Positive Output Level The point at which either profit is maximized or loss is minimized so that it makes sense to continue to produce output is referred to as the **positive output level**. In the example above, the coffee roaster compares revenue or price against variable costs to determine her greatest capacity to both maximize profit and minimize loss. If she is able to do this, she will be able to earn a profit and stay open. Consider this example.

Case 1: Price > ATC. Suppose P = $12, output = 12, so total revenue =$144. TFC=$50 and TVC = $75 so total costs are $125 and economic profits would be $19. Obviously, the firm would produce. If the price fell to $11 and output fell to $11, total revenue would be $121. If output falls, the TVC will also fall, say to $71, and total costs will be $50 + $71 = $121, so the firm breaks even or has economic profit of zero.

Case 2: ATC > P but P ≥ AVC. Let P = $10, Q = 10, so TR = $100. Fixed costs are still $50, average variable costs are $6, making total variable costs $60. Thus, total costs are $110 (and ATC = $11). In this case, the firm earns negative economic profits or losses of $10 if the firm produces positive output. If the firm produces zero output—the firm shuts down—the firm still has to pay its fixed costs of $50, so its losses would be $50. Firms don't like to lose money, but losing $10 in the short run is much better than losing $50 in the short run. Thus, when $ATC > P \geq AVC$ the firm is better off to produce than to shut down.

Case 3: AVC > P. Let P = $6 and output = 6 for total revenue of $36. Fixed costs are the same $50, average variable costs are $7 so total variable costs would be $42. Total costs are now $92 and ATC are 92/6 = $15.33. Economic losses would be $56 if the firm produced 6 units of output, but the firm is better off producing zero output (shutting down) and would have economic losses of only $50, the amount of the total fixed cost.

Before businesses can consider these types of short-run decisions, however, they must first determine when—and if—they should enter the market in the first place.

The owner of a coffee roasting company compares her total revenue to total variable cost and her price to average variable cost to determine if she should continue roasting coffee or shut down.

Long-Run Decision to Enter

Determining when and if to enter a market can be complicated. Some markets are more saturated than others. Some are less tested. Ultimately, someone making the long-run decision to enter a market looks for profit-making opportunities, or any opportunity a firm has to make a profit.

The decision to enter a market is not a decision made solely by new businesses. An existing business that only sells in one state or country may investigate whether or not there would be profit-making opportunity by selling in another. A firm that makes only one type of product may investigate whether or not there is profit-making opportunity in making another. Once firms determine such profit-making opportunities in the long run, they may begin to provide that particular output.

The coffee roaster, for example, may currently only sell in the Midwest. In determining whether to branch out into other markets, she considers the profit-making opportunities in other regions. The coffee market in the Pacific

Northwest may be too saturated for her small business, but she may find opportunity in the South. Once she does find an opportunity for profit, she will be able to increase her output. Firms enter a market when the total revenue (TR) is greater than total cost (TC). Mathematically, this is written as TR > TC.

Long-Run Decision to Exit

The long-run decision to exit a market is similar to the decision to shut down in the short run. The decision to exit a market completely is just more permanent than a temporary shutdown. Both are a response to a lack of profit-making opportunity.

While the decision to shut down temporarily is often a response to a slow period, the decision to exit a market completely is a response to a long-run inability to turn a profit. For example, a restaurant may choose to close at lunch every day, because it doesn't have enough customers to offset its variable costs of food and wages at that time of day. This type of shutdown does nothing to save long-run costs, however, such as rent and kitchen equipment. Those costs are **sunk**, or are costs that have already been incurred and cannot be altered or recovered. Firms may choose not to shut down during slow periods in order to cover such long-run fixed costs. If the restaurant's profits throughout the day fail to offset both variable costs and fixed costs, then it will likely choose to exit the market completely by going out of business.

If the coffee roaster expands into the South, she may also increase long-run costs in that region. This may alter her short-run decision to stay open through slow periods. If her overall profits fail to offset the new variable costs from the new market in the South, then she may choose to leave that market altogether. Firms exit a market when the total revenue (TR) is less than total cost (TC). Mathematically, this is written as TR < TC.

Long-Run Supply Curves

When one firm has realized economic profit in the short run, it stands to reason that other firms would likely follow them into the market. A market in which such expansion does not affect input prices is called a **constant-cost industry**. The long-run supply curve in a constant-cost industry is a horizontal line.

How does this work? Suppose we start from a long-run equilibrium in the market. This means that economic profits are zero. This is shown in part (a) of the graph on the following page. Demand for the product grows for whatever reason resulting in a higher price for the product. This is shown in part (b) of the graph. With no increase in costs, economic profits become positive. These profits attract new firms who enter the market. These new firms cause an increase in supply of the product, driving the price of the product down. The decrease in price results in economic profits going down and eventually returning to zero at the original price. This results in a horizontal long-run supply curve of a constant-cost industry, which is shown in part (c) of the graph on the following page.

Consider that the coffee roaster from the example finds success in the South. Other Midwestern coffee roasters may follow her. Now suppose there are underutilized resources in the South that could be purchased at the going market rate. Also suppose all inputs are purchased in a competitive input market at the current market rate. This would mean that all inputs purchased by the new coffee roasters would have no effect on the price of these resources, and the cost of producing coffee in the South would remain the same. This results in a long-run supply curve that would simply be a horizontal line, as in the example below.

LONG-RUN SUPPLY CURVE

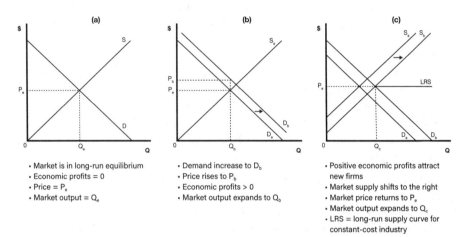

- Market is in long-run equilibrium
- Economic profits = 0
- Price = P_e
- Market output = Q_e

- Demand increase to D_b
- Price rises to P_b
- Economic profits > 0
- Market output expands to Q_b

- Positive economic profits attract new firms
- Market supply shifts to the right
- Market price returns to P_e
- Market output expands to Q_c
- LRS = long-run supply curve for constant-cost industry

On the other hand, a market in which expansion does affect input prices is called an **increasing-cost industry**. In this industry, production costs increase as output rises.

Consider that if resources are fully employed, then the influx of new coffee roasters would lead to an increase in demand for coffee beans, roasting machines, experienced employees, and several other inputs. This results in higher prices for coffee beans and roasting machines, and employees realize they are able to demand higher wages. These factors mean increased costs for the firm. The resulting long-run supply curve would no longer be a horizontal line but instead would look like an upward-sloping supply curve.

In other words, the roasters will all supply more coffee, but they will do so at a higher price. The coffee market in the South has achieved a new long-run equilibrium point where zero economic profits are being made, so there is no incentive for firms to enter or exit the market. Because the demand for inputs has risen, the price of those inputs has risen, driving the costs of production higher. Thus, the market will supply more coffee but at a higher price.

Outside Factors

Some additional outside factors may also affect a firm's decision to either enter or exit a market. Barriers to entry and barriers to exit are the most important of these factors.

Barriers to Entry from Other Firms Factors that make it difficult for a firm to enter a market are known as **barriers to entry**. They can make a market less competitive by allowing for fewer firms. If barriers to entry are extremely high, then the market will become a monopoly, in which there is only one supplier. (Monopolies will be discussed in greater detail in Topic 4.2.)

Some of the coffee roaster's barriers to entry in the Pacific Northwest may have been brand loyalty to the many other coffee companies already flourishing there. The area may already be controlled by one or more popular, well-established coffee businesses. Such a business is known as a **first mover**, or the first firm to dominate a market.

Economies of scale, which were discussed in Topic 3.3, are another important barrier. Recall that economies of scale represent the stage of output where a firm's long-run average total cost decreases as its output increases. Since economies of scale tend to favor large firms that may have a cost advantage because of their size, they may also discourage smaller firms from entering a market, since they may not be able to be competitive.

Barriers to Entry from Government Other barriers to entry may result from government actions or policies. Many of these are intentional, either to promote innovation or to protect public health.

The clearest government barriers are patents and copyrights. They are a way to reward people who develop new ideas in some way. When the government grants a person or business a patent, it confers exclusive right for that entity to use or produce the process, design, or invention in question for a certain number of years. A U.S. patent for an invention lasts 20 years, although the payment of periodic fees is required to maintain it. If the coffee roaster were to patent an innovative roasting process that helped to create better tasting coffee, faster and at a cheaper price, this might act as a barrier to entry to other roasters looking to enter the market.

A copyright is like a patent. However, it applies to artistic works, such as novels, poems, songs, and the like. Only the creator may benefit from a copyrighted during his or her lifetime, and then the creator's beneficiaries can benefit for an additional 70 years. The creator is free to license his or her creation, allowing others to use it for a fee. When the copyright expires, the work is then part of the public domain, which means that people can use it without charge.

Government regulations to protect the public health include environmental regulations to keep the air and water clean. Others include ones to ensure that firms are producing clean food, reliable pharmaceutical drugs, and safe medical devices. Compiling with these regulations can be expensive enough to prevent people from starting up new companies.

A large, industrial coffee roaster, able to buy and roast coffee in large quantities using expensive equipment, may present a barrier to entry to smaller roasters hoping to break into a market.

Barriers to Exit Factors that make it difficult for a firm to exit a market known as **barriers to exit**. Typical barriers include highly specialized assets such as machinery or experienced personnel, both of which may be difficult to sell or relocate. Other barriers include exit costs such as legal fees and the loss of customer goodwill.

If the coffee roaster wishes to leave the Southern market, she may be burdened by the expensive coffee roaster she purchased or an contracts with specialized labor force that she hired to provide coffee in that part of the country.

ANSWER THE TOPIC ESSENTIAL QUESTION

1. Write a paragraph to explain how firms decide how much to produce in the short run. Write an additional two paragraphs to explain how they decide to enter or exit a market.

KEY TERMS

positive output	increasing-cost industry
zero output	barrier to entry
sunk	first mover
constant-cost industry	barrier to exit

MULTIPLE-CHOICE QUESTIONS

1. The short run in economic terms refers to the time period when _____ input(s) is/are variable and _____ input(s) is/are fixed.
   (A) all; none
   (B) none; all
   (C) none; none
   (D) many; at least one
   (E) none; at least one

2. The short-run decision to shut down is based on
   (A) low fixed costs.
   (B) high sunk costs.
   (C) high fixed costs
   (D) price being greater than average variable costs.
   (E) price being less than average variable costs.

3. The long-run decision to enter a market by a firm is based upon _____ being greater than _____.
   (A) total revenue; total cost
   (B) price; average fixed cost
   (C) price; total revenue
   (D) total revenue; average fixed cost
   (E) total cost; total revenue

FREE-RESPONSE QUESTION

1. A local cookie store's total revenue for January was $2,500. Its variable cost was $2,700. The cookie store makes 2,500 cookies per month and sell all of them throughout the month.
   (a) What is the average price for the sale of a cookie?
   (b) If total fixed costs are $1,000, what is the store's profit if it produces positive output?
   (c) Should the store remain open or shut down in the short run? Explain using the numbers above.
   (d) If a successful advertisement effectively increases demand and the store is able to charge $2 for all of the cookies produced, what would total profit be?
   (e) Based on your answer in part (d), will other cookie stores enter or exit the market?

THINK AS AN ECONOMIST: *USE ECONOMIC MODELS TO EXPLAIN HOW TO ACHIEVE A SPECIFIC OUTCOME*

Economists use economic models to explain what decisions economic actors should make. They have devised models to determine both short-term and long-term economic viability.

- Firms remain open in the short run when total revenue is greater than total variable cost.
- Firms exit a market when the total revenue is less than total cost.

Apply the Skill

Smith's Computer Services is a small business that provides computer services and repairs to other businesses and consumers. The business has been struggling lately as more and more people are buying computers and service packages from big-box stores. Val Smith, the company's owner, is trying to determine whether to close the business. To do so, she considers her monthly revenues and costs at different levels of performance:

Total Revenues	Total Fixed Costs	Total Variable Costs
$7,000	$5,000	$10,000
$8,000	$5,000	$9,000
$9,000	$5,000	$8,000
$10,000	$5,000	$5,000
$11,000	$5,000	$4,000

Using the short-term and long-term models, determine what Val should do about her computer store.

Perfect Competition

"In economic life, competition is never completely lacking, but hardly ever is it perfect."

Austrian political economist Joseph A. Schumpeter, 1942

Essential Question: What is a perfectly competitive market?

Perfectly competitive markets rarely, if ever, exist. **Perfect competition** is an abstract state of the market in which buyers and sellers are so numerous and well informed that all market prices are beyond the control of any individual buyer or sellers. That is, the market controls all prices and every buyer is fully informed. Economists create this model state because it helps them understand how real markets work by understanding how variations from it are significant. Insights from studying a perfectly competitive market are therefore directly applicable to real markets, even though the markets are not perfectly competitive.

Some industries come close to achieving perfect competition, even if none achieve it fully. Farms that all grow a specific type of crop, for example, are in nearly perfect competition. In such an industry, there are many buyers and sellers, all of whom know exactly what is being grown. Both the farmers and all of the customers know how much the product is being sold for. But most industries do not operate that way.

What Happens in Perfect Competition?

Perfect competition is allocatively efficient. Every firm is selling an identical product or service. Every customer is paying the same amount for that product or service. Every firm knows how much all other firms are charging, and every customer knows how much the other customers are paying. There is complete transparency in a perfectly competitive market. Every agent in the market—buyers, sellers, producers, and consumers—have perfect information regarding all aspects of the market.

As such, there are no questions or variables in perfect competition. All prices are determined in a large market in which all firms compete for the same buyers. Firms in perfect competition are therefore **price takers**, meaning they have no influence on the price of the product they produce and sell. Firms in perfectly competitive markets have no market power. **Price makers**, on the other hand, produce goods that are differentiated in some way from competitors' products. Price makers do not exist in a perfectly competitive market.

Very few industries, if any, actually operate in perfect competition. Farming comes close.

Firms in perfectly competitive markets also face no barriers to entry. Recall from the previous topic that a barrier to entry is any obstacle that may prevent new competitors from entering a market.

Consider a farmer growing carrots on a small farm in the Midwest. The farmer's carrots are sold to local grocery stores and restaurants. In a perfectly competitive market, she would know exactly how the carrot is being grown, transported, sold, and purchased at every other farm that produces the same type of carrot. Her customers also have this same set of information. No variable is unknown in perfect competition.

Even in a fairly competitive market in which farmers are growing and selling the exact same type of carrot, the market is still not perfectly competitive. There are always variables and barriers. Some farms may use a different kind of fertilizer or sell to a specific kind of customer. Barriers to entry include the land needed to grow the carrots, the resources necessary to grow and harvest the crop, and customers in different markets demanding different prices.

What Does Perfect Competition Look Like?

In a perfectly competitive market, the price is set by the market. If a firm were to charge more than the market price, it would lose revenues and profits. Hence it would have no incentive to charge above-market prices. Thus, every firm in such a market sells at the **equilibrium price**, the price of a good or service when the supply of it is equal to its demand. The equilibrium price is pictured in the graphs on the following page.

PERFECT COMPETITION MARKET AND FIRM

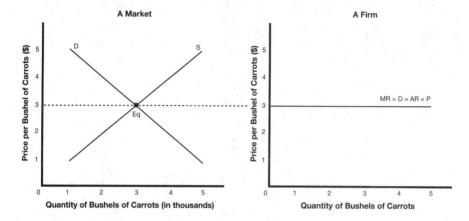

The supply curve is an upward sloping line in perfect competition. The demand curve is the opposite line. Together, they form an intersection, which is the rational point for firms to set their price:

- From the point of intersection, you can draw one line down to the horizontal "Quantity" axis. This line determines the **equilibrium market quantity**.

- From the point of intersection back you can draw a second line to the vertical "Price" axis. This line determines the **equilibrium market price**.

Equilibrium is discussed in greater detail in the next section. It is one of the most important concepts in economics. Market forces tend to push prices to the level at which the the amount consumers will purchase and the amount that producers will supply match. Because of constant changes in consumer demand and the costs of production, prices constantly fluctuate, but they are usually moving toward equilibrium.

Note that the graph on the right shows that the farmer's marginal revenue is an extension from the point at which supply and demand intersect. On every perfect competition graph, marginal revenue also equals demand, which equals average revenue, which equals price. This relationship is shown in the following equation:

$$MR = D = AR = P$$

In other words, all these factors remain constant in perfect competition. In the case of the carrot farmer, each additional bushel of carrots grown will sell for the same price and yield the same revenue because demand and price are always the same.

Even when adding marginal cost (MC) and average total cost (ATC) curves, as illustrated in the graphs at the top of the following page, all these factors remain the same in perfect competition. This is one of the features of this market.

PERFECT COMPETITION COST CURVES

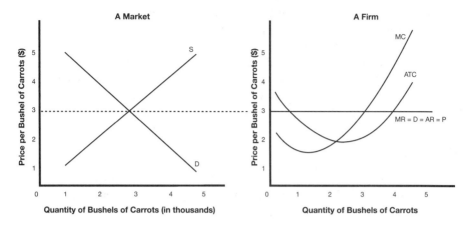

Note that the profit-maximizing quantity of carrots remains unchanged. As long as firms are price takers, as they must be in a perfectly competitive market, these four factors will always be equal. The intersection point will always remain the same.

To find the total cost in this perfectly competitive scenario, economists multiply the average cost per unit by the quantity of units. On the graph below, note the line drawn from the point at which marginal cost intersects price down to the quantity axis. The resulting shaded area below the ATC curve shows the firm's total cost. The smaller area above that total cost shaded area and below the MR = D = AR = P curve shows the economic profit that this firm would earn. Both shaded areas together are the firm's total revenue.

PERFECT COMPETITION COST CURVES WITH COST AND PROFIT

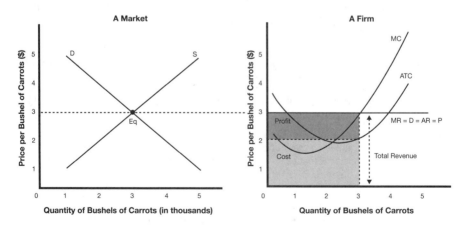

In this example, the farmer would only earn a profit if she sold two or three bushels of carrots. She would lose an opportunity for profit if she sold fewer and she would grow more than she could sell if she produced more.

Competitive Market Equilibrium

The intersection point seen in all three of the preceding pairs of graphs is called **market equilibrium**. Note that this is the point at which the supply curve crosses the demand curve.

At a competitive market equilibrium, firms select output to maximize profit by producing the level of output where the marginal cost equals marginal revenue, as was shown on the graph above. When a market is at this equilibrium point, the price will not change unless an external factor changes the supply or demand. This results in a disruption of the equilibrium and a disruption to perfect competition.

For example, if the carrot farmer is growing and selling carrots in perfect competition, she would reach the point of market equilibrium when her supply of carrots is equal to consumers' demand for them. She is a price taker as the market determines the equilibrium price she can charge for her carrots. She selects the number of bushels of carrots to grow and sell by determining where the marginal cost of growing one bushel of carrots equals the marginal revenue she is able to earn from that bushel. If any outside factors such as bad weather, crop disease, or distribution problems were to disrupt this equilibrium, then the market would adjust accordingly.

Short-Run Market Equilibrium The fact that prices can fluctuate above or below the long-run competitive level illustrates **short-run market equilibrium**. This results in profits or losses, which motivate firms either to enter or exit a market. It also motivates them to move their prices and quantities toward the long-run equilibrium.

Long-Run Market Equilibrium When all firms are operating at an efficient scale, they are experiencing **long-run market equilibrium**. Price equals marginal cost, as well as minimum average total cost. Firms in a state of long-run market equilibrium earn zero economic profit. In this equilibrium, firms may also fall into one of three industries.

Industry	Definition	Example
Constant Cost Industry	The ratio of units produced to production costs remains the same, regardless of volume or demand.	More consumers are buying more carrots. More farmers grow more carrots to meet the demand, and prices stay the same.
Increasing Cost Industry	The cost of production increases as the number of firms increases.	As more farmers grow more carrots, the demand for land, equipment, and other factors of production increases. The price to purchase carrots increases as the cost to grow carrots increases.
Decreasing Cost Industry	The cost of production decreases as the number of firms increases.	As more farmers grow more carrots, the industry becomes more efficient. The price to purchase carrots decreases as the cost to grow carrots decreases.

Long-run prices will ultimately depend on which portion of the long-run cost curves a firm operates in. For example, carrots produced in an increasing cost industry will be more expensive than carrots produced in a decreasing cost industry. Similarly, in an efficient market with no barriers to entry—as carrot farming is in this example—many new firms see a chance to make profits and quickly enter the market. This increase in competition increases the supply of carrots, which consequently shifts the market equilibrium.

Efficiencies

A perfectly competitive market in long-run equilibrium achieves a perfectly efficient allocation of resources. In fact, it is so efficient that it is only found in this type of market. This efficiency comes in two forms:

Allocative Efficiency When a firm produces at the output level where price is equal to marginal cost, or P = MC, **allocative efficiency** is reached. At this output level, firms produce the exact amount that demand requires. Producing any more or less would be inefficient and would therefore not be in perfect competition.

At the competitive market equilibrium described above, the price of a product equals both the private marginal benefit received by the last unit consumed and the private marginal cost incurred to produce the last unit. This is how allocative efficiency is achieved.

In the case of the carrot farmer, she would need to sell each of her bushels of carrots for the same price as the marginal benefit she earned from the last bushel of carrots purchased. She would also have to sell each bushel at the same private marginal cost that she spent to produce it.

Productive Efficiency is reached when a good is being produced at the lowest possible cost. The price equals the minimum average total cost (ATC). Mathematically, this is written as follows:

$$P = minimum\ ATC$$

Productive efficiency implies two things:

- All firms produce at an **efficient scale**, or the output level where a firm makes best possible use of all its inputs.

- Price equals both marginal cost and minimum average total cost and that firms earn zero economic profit.

Recall that zero economic profit is not a bad thing, but simply the point at which a firm has used all its resources most efficiently.

The Model A perfectly competitive market in long-run equilibrium is both allocatively and productively efficient. These might not completely exist in reality, but they provide a useful standard against which to compare actual markets.

A carrot farmer in a perfectly competitive market can only sell her carrots at levels of allocative and productive efficiencies.

Marginal Costs and Benefits

Prices tell a story in perfectly competitive markets. They tell both consumers and producers the magnitude of others' marginal costs of production. They also tell all parties the marginal benefits of consumption. Consequently, prices provide incentives for both firms and consumers to act on that information. Price equals marginal cost in an efficient market.

Private Marginal Benefit The benefit enjoyed by the individual consumers of a particular good is known as the **private marginal benefit**. It is measured by the amount individuals are willing to pay for the additional unit of a good or service.

Private Marginal Cost The change in the total cost to produce a good as impacted by the production of one additional unit of a good or service is known as the **private marginal cost**. Private marginal cost is also called **marginal cost of production**. For example, if the price to grow a single bushel of carrots rises from $1.00 to $1.05, the private marginal cost would be $0.05.

The inherent passivity required for perfect competition seems contrary to the notion of firms undercutting each other in fierce competition. But in perfectly competitive markets, where firms are price takers, they must sell all their outputs at a constant price determined by the market, not by the firms themselves.

1. Write a paragraph that describes the components of a perfectly competitive market.

KEY TERMS

perfect competition	long-run market equilibrium
price takers	allocative efficiency
price makers	efficient scale
equilibrium price	private marginal benefit
market equilibrium	private marginal cost
short-run market equilibrium	marginal cost of production

MULTIPLE-CHOICE QUESTIONS

1. A donut shop in a perfectly competitive market is earning a positive economic profit. This indicates that the market price for a donut is

   (A) greater than the price the donut shop is charging for the exact same donut

   (B) less than the price the donut shop is charging for the exact same donut

   (C) greater than the price the donut shop is charging for a similar donut

   (D) less than the price that the donut shop is charging for a similar donut

   (E) equal to the price that the donut shop is charging for the exact same donut

2. If a firm operating under the conditions of perfect competition earns a positive economic profit in the short run, how will the market adjust in the long run?

   (A) Firms will exit and the market price will increase.

   (B) Firms will exit and the market price will decrease.

   (C) Firms will exit and the market price will remain the same.

   (D) Firms will enter and the market price will decrease.

   (E) Firms will enter and the market price will increase.

3. If a firm operating in a perfectly competitive market in the short run realizes that its price is $5 at a quantity of output of 10 units and its marginal cost is $7, what must be true about the perfectly competitive firm?

(A) It is maximizing profit.

(B) It is operating in economies of scale.

(C) It is operating in diseconomies of scale.

(D) It is decreasing production in order to maximize profits.

(E) It is also operating in a long-run equilibrium.

FREE-RESPONSE QUESTION

1. David's Corn Farm is a profit-maximizing firm operating in a perfectly competitive market earning positive economic profits. Draw and correctly label side-by-side graphs of the market for corn and for David's Corn Farm.

(a) Label the market price and quantity as P_m and Q_m respectively.

(b) Label David's Corn Farm's price and profit-maximizing quantity as P_d and Q_d respectively.

(c) Label the firm's allocatively efficient quantity as Q_e.

(d) Shade in the area of total cost for the firm.

(e) In the long run, will firms enter or exit the corn market?

In a market with perfect competition, buyers and sellers are so numerous and well-informed that all market prices are beyond the control of any individual buyer or sellers. In such a situation, the market determines the price since no individual buyer or seller has enough clout to influence price.

Two different graphs illustrate what a market with perfect competition looks like. One illustrates how the supply and demand curves determine the equilibrium market price. The other carries that information out for each individual firm in the market.

The market for single-scoop ice cream cones in Paradise has perfect competition. The market supply and demand curves look like this:

PERFECT COMPETITION

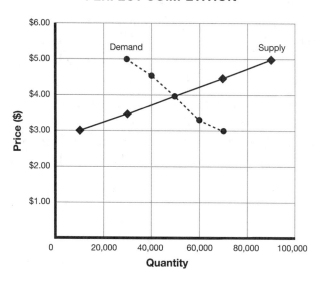

Apply the Skill

Draw a graph showing the equilibrium price for each firm in this market. Explain what the line you draw represents, and why that is the case.

1. Rice is produced in a perfectly-competitive constant-cost industry. Grand Farm is a typical firm in the rice industry earning a positive economic profit.

   (a) Would the price charged by Grand Farm be less than, greater than, or equal to the price in the rice market?

   (b) Using correctly labeled side-by-side graphs for the rice industry and Grand Farm, show each of the following in the short run.

      i.   The industry price and quantity, labeled PM and QM

      ii. Grand Farm's demand curve labeled DF

      iii. Grand Farm's quantity of output, labeled QF

      iv. Grand Farm's profit, shaded completely

   (c) Is Grand Farm allocatively efficient, productively efficient, or both? Explain.

   (d) In the long run, what happens to each of the following?

      i.   The number of firms in the industry. Explain.

      ii. In the long run, does the market price increase, decrease, or remain the same relative to PM ?

   (e) After the adjustment to the new long-run equilibrium, is Grand Farm now allocatively efficient, productively efficient, or both?

UNIT 4

Imperfect Competition

In the real world, the conditions of perfect competition rarely if ever exists. Hence, almost all competition is imperfect to some degree. One important form of imperfect competition is an oligopoly, a market in which a few companies dominate an industry. The U.S. airline industry is an example of an oligopoly. Over the years, the number of major carriers has dwindled as a result of mergers.

A second form of imperfect competition is a monopoly, a market in which one company dominates an industry. Utilities such as electricity and natural gas are often monopolies because they are the only providers in their respective regions.

The degree of competition in an industry shifts over time. Fifty years ago, the television industry was an oligopoly. Three large television networks dominated it: NBC, CBS, and ABC. As new technology developed, cable companies and streaming services emerged and competition increased. Then, with consolidation among companies, the degree of competition began to decrease again.

Another way that imperfect competition differs from perfect competition is in prices. Under perfect competition, all sellers of the same product would charge the same price for that product. However, under imperfect competition, prices vary for a product. The identical computer might sell for a higher price at one store than it does at another. Further, one seller often charge consumers different prices for the same product. For example, a movie theater might charge people under 18 and over 65 less than it charges people between those ages.

"Are there several doctors in the house, so we can have a little managed competition?"

Topic Titles and Essential Knowledge

Topic 4.1 Introduction to Imperfectly Competitive Markets

- Imperfectly competitive markets include monopoly, oligopoly, and monopolistic competition in product markets and monopsony in factor markets.
- In imperfectly competitive output markets and assuming all else is constant, a firm must lower price to sell additional units.
- In imperfectly competitive markets, consumers and producers respond to prices that are above the marginal costs of production and/or marginal benefits of consumption (i.e., price is greater than marginal cost in an inefficient market).
- Incentives to enter an industry may be mitigated by barriers to entry. Barriers to entry—such as high fixed/start-up costs, legal barriers to entry, and exclusive ownership of key resources—can sustain imperfectly competitive market structures.

Topic 4.2 Monopoly

- A monopoly exists because of barriers to entry.
- In a monopoly, equilibrium (profit-maximizing) quantity is determined by equating marginal revenue (MR) to marginal cost (MC). The price charged is greater than the marginal cost.
- In a natural monopoly, long-run economies of scale for a single firm exist throughout the entire effective demand of its product.

Topic 4.3 Price Discrimination

- A firm with market power can engage in price discrimination to increase its profits or capture additional consumer surplus under certain conditions.
- With perfect price discrimination, a monopolist produces the quantity where price equals marginal cost (just as a competitive market would) but extracts all economic surplus associated with its product and eliminates all deadweight loss.

Topic 4.4 Monopolistic Competition

- In a market with monopolistic competition, firms producing differentiated products may earn positive, negative, or zero economic profit in the short run. Firms typically use advertising as a means of differentiating their product. Free entry and exit drive profits to zero in the long run. The output level, however, is smaller than the output level needed to minimize average total costs, creating excess capacity. The price is greater than marginal cost, creating allocative inefficiency.

Topic 4.5 Oligopoly and Game Theory

- An oligopoly is an inefficient market structure with high barriers to entry, where there are few firms acting interdependently.

- Firms in an oligopoly have an incentive to collude and form cartels.

- A game is a situation in which a number of individuals take actions, and the payoff for each individual depends directly on both the individual's own choice and the choices of others.

- A strategy is a complete plan of actions for playing a game; the normal form model of a game shows the payoffs that result from each collection of strategies (one for each player).

- A player has a dominant strategy when the payoff to a particular action is always higher independent of the action taken by the other player. Dominant strategies can be eliminated from each player's action set and can sometimes lead to an equilibrium outcome.

- A Nash equilibrium is a condition describing the set of actions in which no player can increase his or her payoff by unilaterally taking another action, given the other players' actions.

- Oligopolists have difficulty achieving the monopoly outcome for reasons similar to those that prevent players from achieving a cooperative outcome in the Prisoner's Dilemma; nevertheless, prices are generally higher and quantities lower with oligopoly (or duopoly) than with perfect competition.

Introduction to Imperfectly Competitive Markets

"It is no secret at this point that the American economy has a concentration problem. Nearly every American industry has experienced an increase in concentration in the last two decades, to the point where . . . sectors dominated by two or three firms are not the exception, but the rule."

—Asher Schechter, editor of "ProMarket," University of Chicago Business School, 2019

Essential Question: What is an imperfectly competitive market?

The previous unit discussed the economic principle of perfect competition. Recall that perfect competition is an abstract state of the market in which every party is perfectly informed and prices are beyond the control of any of them. Perfect competition is so abstract that it rarely exists in a real market, if it exists at all.

Imperfect competition is how markets typically operate. **Imperfect competition** refers to any economic market that does not qualify as a perfectly competitive market. In imperfect competition, companies sell different products and services, set their own prices, fight for market share, and are often hindered or protected by barriers to entry and exit. Consumers are also not perfectly informed, as they would be in a perfect competition market. One example of imperfect competition is the airline industry. Prices fluctuate constantly, even several times per day. Companies encounter huge barriers to entry, and consumers are left without complete information.

The airline industry operates in an imperfectly competitive market.

Imperfectly Competitive Market Structures

Imperfectly competitive markets can be divided into two main types of market structures: the product market and the factor market.

- The **product market** produces output for people to consume. This can be a tangible output such as clothes or other physical goods or a service such as snow-removal or plumbing repair.

- In the **factor market,** the factors of production are bought and sold. Recall that the three factors of production are land, labor, and capital. Examples could include a farm that grows corn for the ethanol industry or an architectural firm that provides plans for renovating a kitchen. These are discussed in the next topic.

Product markets can be compared to each other on a spectrum based on how competitive the market structure is.

Most competitive   **Least competitive**

Perfect competition   Monopolistic competition   Oligopoly   Monopoly

Perfect competition (see Topic 3.9) is not common. Neither is **monopoly** (see Topic 4.2), which is when a company and the product it makes utterly dominate a market. Most product markets feature either **monopolistic competition**, wherein many firms offer similar products or services that are not perfect substitutes, or **oligopoly**, in which a few firms, rather than just one, dominate. Characteristics of each type of market structure are summarized in the following chart.

CHARACTERISTICS OF MARKET STRUCTURES				
Characteristics	**Perfect Competition**	**Monopolistic Competition**	**Oligopoly**	**Monopoly**
Number of Firms	• Unlimited	• Many	• Few	• One
Barriers to Entry	• None	• Low	• High	• Very high
Control over Price	• None	• Low	• High	• Very high
Number of Buyers	• Unlimited	• Many	• Many	• Many
Close Substitutes Available to Buyers	• Unlimited	• Many	• Few	• None
Level of Market Power for a Firm	• None	• Low	• High	• Very high
Examples	• Corn	• Hotels	• Airlines	• Water
	• Wheat	• Restaurants	• Automobiles	• Electricity

Market Power The type of market structure influences the level of market power each firm in the industry has. The key to the market power of a monopoly is not only the lack of competition, but also the high barrier to entry to keep it that way.

What Does Imperfect Competition Look Like?

In imperfectly competitive output markets—assuming all else is constant—a firm must lower its price in order to sell additional units. In other words, firms face a downward sloping demand curve. This contrasts with the horizontal line that shows perfectly elastic demand under perfect competition. In the airline industry, for example, carriers offer less expensive tickets for less desirable flights, such as those in the middle of the night or at a slow time of year.

Incentives to enter an industry may be mitigated by barriers to entry. Barriers to entry—such as high fixed or start-up costs, legal barriers to entry, and exclusive ownership of key resources—can sustain imperfectly competitive market structures. Again, the airline industry fits this model. Both the start-up costs and legal barriers are large. The materials and space needed are just two huge investments, as are the legal requirements of the Federal Aviation Administration and other oversight entities. Industries such as utilities also often include companies that are the sole owners of necessary resources.

Inefficient Markets

Imperfectly competitive markets tend to operate with less efficiency than a perfectly competitive market would. Under perfect competition, the price that consumers pay would equal the marginal cost of production (P = MC). Each firm would have so little market power that it could not charge more than the marginal cost of production. If it did, it would lose all of its sales as consumers would choose to purchase from other firms.

By contrast, in a monopoly, the market power of one firm would be very high. Hence, it could charge prices far in excess of the marginal cost (P > MC). Such a market would be inefficient. While it might lead to higher profits, it would also decrease consumer demand.

ANSWER THE TOPIC ESSENTIAL QUESTION

1. Write a paragraph that describes each of the imperfect competitive market structures.

KEY TERMS

imperfect competition	monopoly
product market	oligopoly
factor market	monopolistic competition

MULTIPLE-CHOICE QUESTIONS

1. A bakery sells its one-of-a-kind rye bread in a monopoly market. Which of the following is true?
   (A) There is at least one other bakery in the market also selling rye bread.
   (B) There are no, or low, barriers to entry.
   (C) The bakery can charge any price it wants.
   (D) This is the only bakery selling this product with no close substitutions.
   (E) The bakery is successful because it is the only employer in town.

2. The best example in the United States of monopolistic competition is the market for
   (A) soybeans, because there many producers that offer identical products
   (B) legal services, because many providers offer varied products
   (C) cell phone service, because a few large firms dominate the market
   (D) internet searches, because 90 percent of searches are done with one engine
   (E) fighter planes, because the U.S. government is the only purchaser

3. Which is true about production in an imperfectly competitive market?
   (A) More is produced than is optimal.
   (B) The amount produced minimizes costs.
   (C) Less is produced than is optimal.
   (D) The amount produced maximizes costs.
   (E) The amount produced is the same as in perfect competition.

FREE-RESPONSE QUESTION

1. Companies in various industries operate and compete differently depending on market structure characteristics.
   (a) Identify one major difference between a perfectly competitive market and a monopolistically competitive market.
   (b) Identify the two market structures that have many buyers and many sellers as a market characteristic.
   (c) If the government provides exclusive access to a key resource to one company because of high entry costs, identify the type of market structure this firm would compete in.
   (d) Identify two characteristics of an oligopoly market structure.
   (e) Identify the market structure with the least power over price.

Perfectly competitive markets cannot be found in the real world. Instead, economists observe different types of imperfectly competitive markets based on the number of competitors.

To describe the differences in economic markets, focus on these criteria:

- How do the numbers of competitors in the markets differ?
- How do the numbers of buyers in the markets differ?
- What is the degree of control that competitors exert over price?
- What barriers of entry limit the appearance of new competitors?

A perfectly competitive market has a large number of competitors and a large number of buyers for whom the producers compete equally. Producers have little control over price, which is set by the market, and there are low barriers to entry, which opens the market to fresh competitors.

Apply the Skill

Using the four criteria, contrast a monopoly to a market with monopolistic competition, and give an example of an industry in each type of market. Use examples that are different from those in the chapter.

Monopoly

"I think it's wrong that only one company makes the game Monopoly."

—Steven Wright, comedian

Essential Question: What is a monopoly?

As has been shown in previous topics, market structure will always constrain and influence prices, output, and efficiency. This is particularly the case in a monopoly. A **monopoly** is a market structure in which an entire industry is composed of a single firm. In a monopoly, there are no close substitutions for consumers. Monopolies influence price, output, and efficiency because they have such control over the market. In the natural gas industry, for example, where there is often just one supplier in a given market, companies are able to set price, control output, and determine exactly how efficient they need to be. Such monopolies are legal and often supported by the government.

The natural gas industry is one industry where a monopoly could occur.

One measure of how close an industry is to being a monopoly is the **concentration ratio**, which is the ratio of the number of firms in an industry to the industry as a whole. A ratio nearing 100 percent, or one in which there is only one firm in the industry, characterizes a true monopoly. A low concentration ratio indicates greater competition among firms in the industry.

Nature of a Monopoly

Recall from the previous topic that economic market structures fall on a spectrum. On the far-left end is the idealized notion of perfect competition.

On the far-right side—the complete opposite of perfect competition—is monopoly.

Further recall that firms in perfect competition act as price-takers. All consumers and the numerous firms have full knowledge of who is selling which product and for what amount. Perhaps most significantly, firms in perfect competition have no barriers to entry or exit. The other extreme is a monopoly. Instead of several firms, there is only one. Instead of acting as price-takers, monopolies are price-setters or price-makers. They control the price of the product, because they are the only one selling it. Finally, instead of no barriers to entry or exit, the barriers in a monopoly are practically insurmountable, especially to enter the market.

There are several such barriers to entry, each of which is significant enough to create a monopoly.

BARRIERS TO ENTRY IN A MARKET		
Type	**Description**	**Example**
Government Intervention	A local, state, or federal government may grant sole production rights to a single firm.	State-owned petroleum companies in oil-rich nations
Economies of Scale	Large firms are able to produce more, so their long-run average total costs decrease. They are able to price competition out of the market.	Warehouse stores that are the exclusive carrier of a product
Legal Protections	One firm holds the necessary copyright or patent to produce a product.	A drug company with a patent on a new medical drug
Control of Resources	A firm is the only entity with access to a necessary resource.	Diamond companies with access to diamond mines

Any of these factors may lead to a monopoly, but having sole control of a necessary resource may be the most likely.

Natural Monopoly When a monopoly is the direct result of high start-up costs or powerful economies of scale necessary to conduct a business in a specific industry, it is called a **natural monopoly**. Natural monopolies often arise in industries that require unique raw materials or specific technologies to operate. Consider the natural gas industry. The costs to construct a system of pipes to deliver the product are exceedingly high in that industry. The barriers to entry are so extremely high that competitors are naturally kept from entering the market. Due to these high start-up costs, firms operating as a natural monopoly may actually be able to offer a product at a lower price to consumers than if it had competition. In order to maintain natural monopolies, firms' long-run economies of scale must exist throughout the production and distribution of their products.

Marginal Revenue and Demand

Recall that in perfect competition, many factors are equal—as shown in the equation $MR = D = AR = P$. In a monopoly, however, the demand curve is not perfectly elastic. Rather, marginal revenue is less than demand, or $MR < D$. If a natural gas company is operating as a monopoly in its market and it wants to sell more units, it must lower its price for all buyers. When price decreases in this way, the additional marginal revenue received decreases faster than price. The table and graph below both illustrate how marginal revenue and demand work together in a monopoly.

PRICE AND MARGINAL REVENUE			
Price ($)	Quantity	Total Revenue	Marginal Revenue
6	0	0	–
5	1	5	5
4	2	8	3
3	3	9	1
2	4	8	–1
1	5	5	–3

NATURAL GAS MONOPOLY

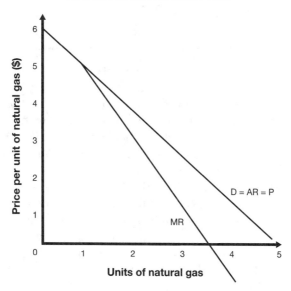

Note that as monopolies continue to lower prices to sell more units, the marginal revenue eventually becomes negative. A monopoly will no longer produce its product once it reaches this range. There are other, more detailed factors to consider when plotting a monopoly on a graph.

Profit Maximization in a Monopoly

Recall that firms in an imperfect market are price-makers (rather than price-takers). In addition, a firm that holds a monopoly is the entire industry. This means that it has greater ability to influence price than do firms in other markets. A firm operating as a monopoly still needs to determine how much of its product to supply in order to achieve the maximum possible profit. The graph below illustrates how a firm in a monopoly market performs such a calculation.

NATURAL GAS MONOPOLY

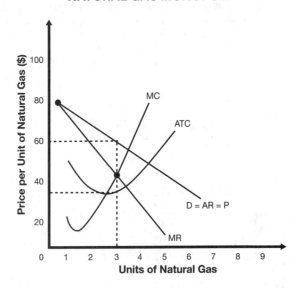

First, the firm determines its ideal level of output. On the graph above, that is first the point where the marginal revenue equals the marginal cost, then down to the quantity axis below. The point where the dotted line hits the quantity axis is the ideal level of output. This natural gas company should produce three units of its product.

Next, the firm determines what price to charge for each unit. A rational firm will charge what the market is willing to pay. That point is illustrated by again finding the point where marginal revenue equals marginal cost, then following the dotted line up to the demand curve and straight back to the price axis. The point where the dotted line hits the price axis is the price to charge to maximize profits. This natural gas company should charge $60 for each unit of its product in order to earn a maximum profit.

Finally, the firm calculates its total profit by drawing a final line from the point at which the line down to quantity intersects with the average total cost. A line from there back to the vertical axis creates a box that represents the economic profit.

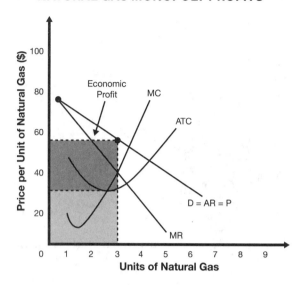

NATURAL GAS MONOPOLY PROFITS

Mathematically, the economic profit can be calculated with the following equation:

$$(P - ATC) \times Q$$

Another way to calculate the economic profit is to subtract the total cost from total revenue:

Note that the demand curve on the earlier graph is still equal to price and average revenue, even if it is no longer equal to marginal revenue as it was in perfect competition. This is why it is now sloping downward as opposed to being a straight horizontal line. This is also the key difference between the graph of a monopoly and the graphs of other economic principles discussed earlier in this text.

The graph here, and similar graphs that illustrate a monopoly, all assume that the monopoly firm is charging the same price to all customers. In many cases, however, this does not happen. The monopoly might adjust its prices so that people who are willing and able to pay more will do so, and others will pay less. This concept, called price discrimination, is discussed in more detail in the following topic.

Deadweight Loss

Topic 2.8 introduced the concept of deadweight loss, or the losses that occur when supply and demand are not in balance. Deadweight loss also leads to a reduction of consumer and producer surpluses. It is illustrated in the following graph, which is similar to the graph above, by shading the area where these losses occur.

NATURAL GAS MONOPOLY DEADWEIGHT LOSS

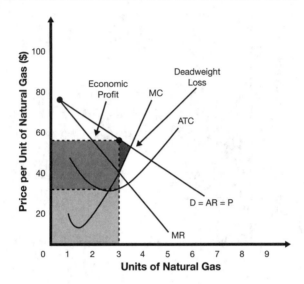

This area would not be shaded in a graph for a perfectly competitive market. Only in a monopoly is this area not part of either the consumer or product surplus. In this sense, the monopoly is inefficient:

- It is not allocatively efficient, as it does not produce the amount of output society demands. Price is greater than marginal cost.
- It is not productively efficient either, as it does not produce products at the minimum average total cost.

Regulation of Monopoly

Monopolies generally do not benefit consumers. Without sufficient choices, resources are not allocated effectively throughout the market. Because monopolies produce less than the socially desired quantity, government policymakers respond to monopolies in a variety of ways.

Increase Competition Government officials try to make an industry more competitive by passing **antitrust laws**, which are laws that seek to protect consumers by limiting the concentration in an industry. If the two largest providers of mobile phone service in the United States wanted to merge, for example, U.S. government regulators might decide that such a merger would reduce competition in this business to the point that it would affect the economic well-being of the country as a whole. The federal government could go to court to attempt to stop such a merger.

Regulate Prices Policymakers may also attempt to set or modify the prices charged by a monopoly. This is common in the case of natural monopolies such as power companies, where government regulators can set firms' prices. Government regulators may force the monopoly to have **socially optimal**

pricing, or allocatively efficient pricing where price is equal to marginal cost (P = MC). However, if the socially optimal price is below the firm's average total cost of production, firms will eventually run out of money and go out of business.

To keep firms in business, the government can subsidize them with tax dollars. Or it can set prices at a level high enough to insure service for everyone. For example, because of differences in population density, providing electricity is less expensive in cities than in rural areas. If a state that regulated the electricity market set the same rate for everyone, people in cities would be subsidizing people in rural areas.

Setting prices and providing subsidies might insure that all people can afford service, but it gives monopolies no incentive to reduce costs. In a competitive market, firms try to reduce costs to increase profits. But if a regulated monopoly knows that its prices will be lowered whenever costs fall, it will not benefit from lower costs and will therefore have less reason to innovate.

Regulators may also attempt to regulate a monopoly's pricing with **fair-return pricing**, which is the price of a product that enables its producer to obtain a normal profit on top of the cost of production. The equation for this is P = ATC. A fair-return price is higher than a socially optimal price but less than the price that a monopoly could charge without regulation.

Take Public Ownership Policymakers can decide that the public, through a government agency, should own a monopoly. When they do, they take on the responsibility of running the monopoly. Many European countries, for example, operate some or most of the utility industry. In the United States, the federal government owns and operates the Postal Service. Because the Postal Service is run by the government, it is responsible for delivering mail even to the most remote, costly-to-reach communities in the country.

Remain Uninvolved Finally, government regulators might decide that costs of increasing competition, regulating prices, or owning a company outweigh the benefits of trying to control a monopoly. Or they might believe that the monopoly might be temporary, as innovations will soon allow new firms to compete in the market. As a result, they may decide to allow the monopoly to continue. In an unregulated monopoly, firms produce at a point where marginal revenue equals marginal cost. Mathematically, this is written as MR = MC.

ANSWER THE TOPIC ESSENTIAL QUESTION

1. Write a paragraph that describes the elements of a monopoly.

KEY TERMS		
monopoly	natural monopoly	socially optimal pricing
concentration ratio	antitrust laws	fair-return pricing

A lumberjack is operating as a monopoly for firewood in her area. Use the figure below to answer questions 1 and 2 about the lumberjack's firewood monopoly.

FIREWOOD MONOPOLY

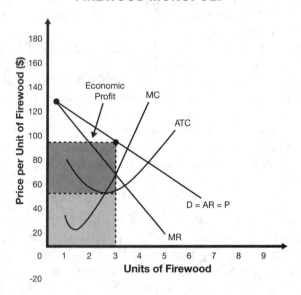

1. What is the price charged by the profit-maximizing monopolist?
   (A) $60
   (B) $70
   (C) $80
   (D) $90
   (E) $95

2. What quantity of firewood should this lumberjack cut down in order to maximize her profits?
   (A) 2
   (B) 3
   (C) 4
   (D) 5
   (E) 6

3. Which of the following is true about monopolies?

(A) They are price-makers.

(B) Price is less than the minimum average total cost.

(C) They cannot be regulated.

(D) Marginal revenue equals demand.

(E) Profit is calculated by multiplying quantity by price.

FREE-RESPONSE QUESTION

1. Draw a correctly labeled graph of a single-price monopoly earning positive economic profits and show each of the following.

(a) The quantity that maximizes profit labeled as Q_m.

(b) The price charged by the profit maximizing monopolist labeled as P_m.

(c) Shade in completely the area that represents profit.

(d) If the monopolist is maximizing profits, would deadweight loss be created? Explain.

(e) If the monopolist is maximizing profits, would the firm be producing in its elastic, inelastic, or unit elastic portion of its demand curve?

THINK AS AN ECONOMIST: *DEMONSTRATE UNDERSTANDING OF AN ECONOMIC SITUATION ON AN ACCURATELY LABELED VISUAL*

Economists calculate the profits of a monopoly by subtracting the average total cost (ATC) from the price the monopolist charges and multiplying that figure by the quantity produced. In other words, Profit = (P − ATC) x Q. As long as consumers are willing to pay the price the monopolist sets, the firm can continue to make a profit.

Apply the Skill

Nature's Cup Coffee has a successful monopoly on the coffee market. It enjoys a steady profit of $2 per pound of coffee sold at a price of $6 per pound. In 2025, however, the company's costs soar as the price of coffee beans doubles from $4 per pound to $8 due to a natural disaster in the growing area of its major supplier. What happens to Nature's Cup if it doesn't raise its price to consumers? Draw a graph and explain the outcome.

Topic 4.3

Price Discrimination

"In my high school economics class, my students asked me to explain why there are sales on 'Black Friday.' The class period was over, so I only had time to blurt out 'price discrimination' without getting into an explanation of what it is and why it explains sales."

—Arnold Kling, economist (b. 1954)

Essential Question: What is price discrimination?

In 2012, the e-commerce travel retailer Orbitz was showing more expensive hotel options to users with a Macintosh computer than to other users. Orbitz knew that such users were willing to pay as much as 30 percent more for their hotel rooms and adjusted those users' search results accordingly.

Orbitz was using a form of price discrimination to increase its profits. **Price discrimination** occurs when firms sell the same goods to different customers for different prices, even though the cost of producing the good is the same. Price discrimination is not possible when a good is sold in a highly competitive market, since many firms are selling the same good at competing prices. No firm wants to charge a lower price than another, and if any firm tried to charge too much, every consumer would buy from another firm. Firms operating as monopolies especially have enough market power to price discriminate, though price discrimination can happen anywhere.

The type of computer you use to purchase items or services online might affect how much you pay for them.

The Principles of Price Discrimination

Like Orbitz, firms commonly practice price discrimination to increase profits. They use different **price elasticities of demand**, or a measure of the change in demand in relation to a change in price. If a profit-maximizing firm has the market power to be able to charge more for the same product in a different market, it would be rational for it to do so.

To understand why a firm would choose to price discriminate, consider an example of a music production company. Assume it pays a recording artist for the right to produce, record, and sell his or her latest output. The production company knows that enthusiastic fans will pay $25 for their favorite artist's new music. They also know that other, significantly less-enthusiastic fans are willing to pay only up to $10 for the same music.

Assume that the marketing department of the production company does further research and discovers that almost all the enthusiastic fans live in the United Kingdom. In response, the production company can charge $25 for the music in the United Kingdom and $10 for the same product everywhere else. In this way, the company engages in price discrimination to maximize its profits.

Firms can price discriminate in other ways as well.

- They can discriminate based on quantity. The music production company can charge record stores that purchase 1,000 units of a new album less for each album than stores that purchase only 100 albums.

- They can also discriminate based on time of use. Movie theaters do this by charging less for a matinee than for an evening show of the same movie. Similarly, movie theaters may also choose to price discriminate based on age, charging less for students or senior citizens than they would charge the general population to see the same movie at the same time.

- They can discriminate based on the time of purchase. The airline industry is constantly adjusting fares, even changing prices from one time of day to another for tickets on the same flight.

Common Examples of Price Discrimination

Price discrimination is not a one-size-fits-all practice. Firms charge different prices for a product for many reasons:

- A firm charges different prices depending on the quantity sold. A fifty-pound bag of dog food often will cost less per pound than a ten-pound bag.

- A firm charges a different price to different consumer groups. Movie theaters commonly sell discounted tickets to students and senior citizens.

- A firm charges different prices for off-peak usage. Electrical companies typically charge less for power used in the evenings and on weekends than during the business day.

Perfect Price Discrimination

In theory, a firm could maximize its profits if it knew exactly how much each consumer would be willing to pay and could charge them that exact amount. This would be **perfect price discrimination,** also called first-degree price discrimination. Rarely does a firm have enough market power to be able to charge a different price for every unit consumed. Usually, only monopolies can practice perfect price discrimination.

Graphing Price Discrimination

A graph that depicts price discrimination looks like the monopoly graphs from the previous topic. Consider a scenario in which an orange juice company produces a special kind of juice that allows it enough of a market share to charge higher prices in certain markets. Maybe the company's juice has a distinctive flavor, an unusual type of packaging, or simply a reputation as being more presigious than other juices sold in the sam emarket. The company should still produce a quantity at the point where marginal revenue intersects with marginal cost.

According to the table below, the company should produce 200 gallons of orange juice. But because this company is able to price discriminate, it should also charge more for its juice in some markets than in others.

ORANGE JUICE PRODUCTION IN PRICE DISCRIMINATION			
Quantity in Gallons	Marginal Revenue	Demand	Marginal Cost
0	50	50	10
100	40	45	15
200	20	30	20
300	-10	20	50
400	-20	10	90

Consumer Surplus The graph that follows also illustrates why the company should produce 200 gallons of orange juice in order to maximize its profit. Note that the lowest price the company should charge is the point on the demand curve directly up from the point where marginal cost and marginal revenue intersect. Any cost in the area above that point is called the **consumer surplus,** where consumers are receiving more benefit for the orange juice but are still paying the same price.

If this orange juice company were to engage in price discrimination, it would charge bands of customers in the shaded consumer surplus area a higher price. The correlating price on the vertical axis would help the company determine the higher pay bands.

ORANGE JUICE PRODUCTION IN A TYPICAL MONOPOLY

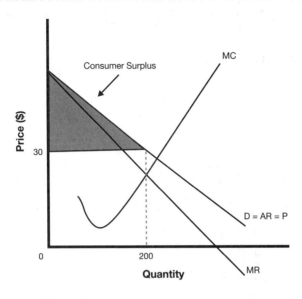

In perfect price discrimination, the orange juice company not only accounts for that consumer surplus, but it also charges each consumer exactly what they are willing to pay. This is extremely rare, as very few firms, if any, have enough market power or data to charge consumers in this way. A monopoly would be the only firm with enough market power to charge each consumer separately for the same gallon of orange juice. Note on the table below that a monopoly practicing perfect price discrimination has a marginal revenue equal to demand.

ORANGE JUICE PRODUCTION IN PERFECT PRICE DISCRIMINATION			
Quantity of Gallons	Marginal Revenue/ Demand	Marginal Cost	Average Total Cost
0	50	5	10
100	30	10	10
200	20	20	12
300	10	30	15
400	5	50	10

Again, even with a monopoly on production, the orange juice company still produces 200 gallons; it just charges specific consumers different amounts for each of those gallons.

By charging each consumer the most they are willing to spend, perfect price discrimination leads to much higher profits, as demonstrated by the shaded area on the graph below.

ORANGE JUICE MONOPOLY IN PERFECT PRICE DISCRIMINATION

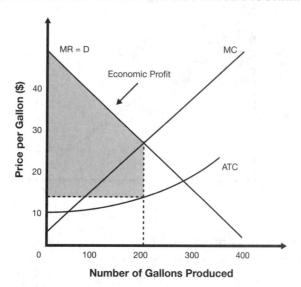

Note that marginal revenue (MR) equals demand (D) on the graph as well. Also note that even with the change in appearance of the perfect price discrimination graph, this orange juice company still produces 200 gallons of juice, the point where MR intersects with marginal cost (MC). It is just able to extract every bit of economic surplus above that point.

To eliminate consumer surplus completely, an orange juice company operating as a monopoly can engage in perfect price discrimination.

Elimination of Deadweight Loss By increasing or decreasing prices based on what consumers will pay, a firm can increase its profits. It also provides consumers products at the price they are willing to pay. In effect, then, adjusting the prices transfers consumer surplus to the producer. In this way, the use of price discrimination reduces deadweight loss as producers start to produce a quantity where P = MC.

ANSWER THE TOPIC ESSENTIAL QUESTION

1. Write a paragraph that describes how price discrimination works.

KEY TERMS

price discrimination
price elasticities of demand

perfect price discrimination
consumer surplus

MULTIPLE-CHOICE QUESTIONS

1. Which of the following best describes perfect price discrimination?
   (A) The ability to charge one group of buyers a different price than another group
   (B) The ability to set a single price for a good based on buyer characteristics
   (C) The illegal practice of charging some groups of buyers a different price than others
   (D) The ability to charge different buyers the exact amount they are willing to pay for a good or service with identical production costs
   (E) The need to charge each customer less than the marginal cost of production

2. If a single-price monopoly were now able to perfectly price discriminate, deadweight loss would _____.
   (A) exactly double
   (B) increase a little
   (C) be eliminated
   (D) not change
   (E) decrease by 50 percent

Use the following graph to answer question 3.

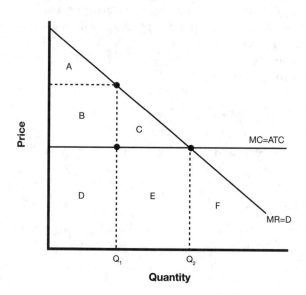

3. The firm above is a monopoly earning positive economic profits practicing perfect (sometimes called first-degree) price discrimination. If the firm is maximizing profits, the quantity the firm would produce would be _____, while the area of profit would be designated as _____.

(A) Q1; AB
(B) Q2; ABC
(C) Q1; ABD
(D) Q2; BCDE
(E) Q2; CE

1. Draw and label the graph of a profit-maximizing monopoly practicing perfect price discrimination earning positive economic profits. Draw and label the firm's demand curve, marginal revenue curve, marginal cost curve, and average total cost curve.

   (a) Label the quantity produced by the monopoly as Q_p.

   (b) Shade in completely the area of profit.

   (c) What is the dollar value of consumer surplus?

   (d) Assume instead that the firm, with the same cost structure, was not able to price discriminate and would have to charge a single price to all consumers.

      (i) Would the amount produced now be greater than, less than, or equal to Q_p?

      (ii) Would profits increase, decrease, or stay the same?

THINK AS AN ECONOMIST: *DEMONSTRATE THE EFFECT OF A CHANGE ON AN ACCURATELY LABELED VISUAL*

Economists can demonstrate the effects of a change by using accurately labeled visuals. In doing so, they must answer three questions:

- What does the visual show?
- What variable in the situation must have changed to produce that visual?
- What effect did that change have on economic outcomes?

For example, look back at the graph showing perfect price discrimination in the topic text. The visual shows perfect price discrimination because the first has absorbed all consumer surplus. In a competitive market, the equilibrium price would be $30 at a quantity supplied of 100 units. A firm's profit would be the rectangular area formed from $30 down to the bottom of the vertical axis and from 100 quantity to the left. Once the firm engages in perfect price discrimination, its profit covers a much larger area.

Apply the Skill

Draw correctly labeled diagrams and explain the differences between a single-price monopoly and one that can perfectly price discriminate. How are they different? How are they similar?

Separately, compare and contrast the perfectly price discriminating monopoly diagram you drew to a perfectly competitive diagram you studied in the previous unit.

Topic 4.4

Monopolistic Competition

"In the marketplace, differentiation is everywhere. Everybody—producer, fabricator, seller, broker, agent, merchant—tries constantly to distinguish his or her offering from all others."

—Theodore Levitt, professor, Harvard Business School, 1980

Essential Question: What are the effects of monopolistic competition?

Recall from previous topics that perfect competition and monopoly are at two ends of an economic spectrum that runs from complete to nonexistent competition. Firms in industries with nearly perfect competition have very low barriers to entry and are complete price-takers, while firms that are nearly monopolies have extremely high barriers to entry and are primarily price-makers. Further recall that neither end of this spectrum occurs very often, if ever, in an actual market.

Monopolistic competition has characteristics of both perfect competition and a monopoly. It is a type of imperfect competition in which many producers sell products that are slightly differentiated from one another and are therefore not perfect substitutes. A firm in monopolistic competition has a monopoly over its specific differentiated product, but eventually, other firms will make close enough substitutes to begin to chip away at that first firm's market share. For example, Apple introduced a tablet computer, the iPad, in 2010 and has held a monopoly over iPad production. No other tablet computer is exactly like it. However, other companies, such as Samsung and Lenovo, make similar tablets that compete with the iPad.

The family restaurant industry is another example of monopolistic competition. Several national or regional chains sell similar food, but each one is slightly different from its nearest competitor in some way. Different chains might have a Western theme or offer an impressive assortment of pies or emphasize that it is great for kids. Because of these differences, each restaurant chain has its own piece of monopoly power. But since there are so many other family restaurants selling other types of food, the market is still competitive. Thus, the market is one of monopolistic competition.

Characteristics of Monopolistic Competition

Besides featuring firms that compete with firms that offer similar but not quite identical products, monopolistic competition has other elements. The market is also structured in a way that many other firms may also decide to sell a similar product to the same group of consumers. All monopolistic competition markets, therefore, have the same three attributes: competition, differentiation, and low barriers to entry and exit.

Many markets share this list of attributes. Firms selling shoes, music, books, or computers all have attributes of monopolistic competition, as do restaurants, bakeries, and nail salons.

All of these markets have similar characteristics and are very easy to enter or exit. It takes relatively little initial capital to open a karate studio, for example. When a new studio opens, it decreases the demand for other karate lessons in that area. When a studio closes, it increases the demand for the other studios still offering lessons. Such intense competition results in a very elastic demand curve, or one that appears nearly horizontal.

Issues of Price Monopolistic competition firms have some degree of market power, though obviously not nearly as much as a monopoly. Firms can therefore raise prices slightly without losing all their customers, and they can lower prices without starting a **price war**, or a fierce competition to cut prices. These firms have such market power because they have few enough competitors and a product that is just different enough.

Firms engaging in monopolistic competition often rely on **non-price competition,** or strategies to increase sales and attract customers through methods other than adjusting prices. For example, one of the karate studios may advertise at local elementary schools and focus on youth classes in an attempt to differentiate itself from its competition.

A local karate studio engages in monopolistic competition when it advertises its unique class offerings.

Product Differentiation When firms selling in a monopolistic competition environment sell products that have real or perceived non-price differences, they are said to be competing via **product differentiation**. These differences are not so great as to eliminate other goods as substitutes. Rather, they typically have subtle differences, such as quality, reputation, or appearance, which distinguish them from each other just enough for there to be enough space in the market for all of them. Firms often focus their advertising on these distinguishing elements in order to differentiate their product from their competitors' product.

For example, the basic function of the karate studios in a single town is the same, but one might be open at a specific time when all others are closed. Another might offer more advanced classes. A studio may offer courses just for women, just for children, or just for senior citizens. The basic function of every studio is the same—to teach karate—but there are enough small differences for each studio to have its own monopolistic share of the market. Any advertising done by a firm that focuses just on the broad benefits of karate attracts students for studios in general, but by focusing on these small differences, a studio can attract students to itself in particular.

Monopolistic Competition in the Short and Long Run

Another attribute of monopolistic competition is how differently firms earn profit in the short run and the long run. In the short run, there are dynamic shifts in demand, due to the low barriers to entry. Some firms may see a huge spike in profits as demand for their product initially increases, though other firms may earn negative or even zero economic profit in the short run.

Assume that a firm in such a market does see an initial spike in its profits. In the short run, firms are often able to maximize profits by producing a quantity where marginal revenue equals marginal cost and where price is based on the average total revenue curve. The market power of monopolistic competition means that such a firm will also face a downward sloping demand curve. Note in the graph below that the curve is highly elastic, though not entirely flat.

SHORT-RUN PROFITS IN MONOPOLISTIC COMPETITION

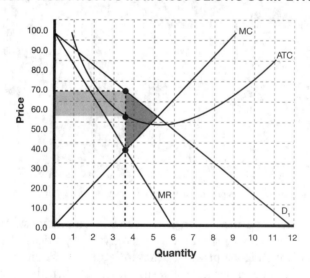

In the long run, however, firms typically show zero economic profit. There is such room to freely enter and exit a monopolistic competition market that profits are ultimately driven to zero in the long run. The graph below shows that the firm is still producing at the point where marginal cost intersects marginal revenue, but the demand curve has shifted as other firms entered the market and increased competition. This means that the output level is smaller than the output level needed to minimize average total costs. This creates **excess capacity**, or a situation in which the demand for a good or service is less than the firm's capacity to produce it.

Note that the price on this graph is also greater than marginal cost, which would create allocative inefficiency. Recall from previous topics that allocative inefficiency occurs when costs exceed what consumers are willing to pay. The graph, therefore, shows that this firm is no longer selling its product above average cost, and can no longer claim an economic profit.

LONG-RUN ADJUSTMENTS IN MONOPOLISTIC COMPETITION

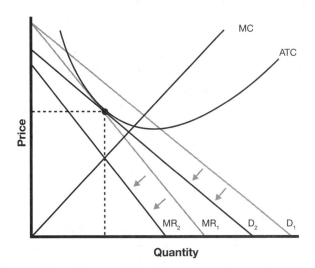

To see this shift from the short run to the long run in monopolistic competition, consider once again the example of a karate studio. When it initially enters the market, one karate studio might create its own monopoly by being the only studio in town to offer karate classes specifically for elementary school girls. Other studios offer other classes, even other classes for specific groups, but this is the only studio to offer this specific type of class to this specific group.

In the short run, the karate studio offers an optimal number of classes to meet demand and charges the highest rate that the market will allow. Demand for the class increases.

However, the profits of the one studio attract new firms to enter the market. Other karate studios begin to take notice of the increase in demand for this particular type of class. They may choose to offer classes for girls in a specific elementary school grade or classes for elementary school girls wishing to learn a specific karate skill. They can then heavily market this slight differentiation and take demand away from the first studio to offer classes specifically to elementary school girls.

In the long run, the demand for classes for elementary school girls at the first studio will decrease. Eventually, the classes' economic profit will also decrease to the point where the studio is earning zero economic profit for its classes, even if elementary school girls are still enrolling.

Drawbacks to Monopolistic Competition

The markets for most products feature monopolistic competition because this structure has many benefits for both firms and consumers. However, these benefits come with some possible costs:

Excess Advertising Firms commonly spend between 10 and 15 percent of their revenue on advertising to attract customers. But their ads focus on the very small differences between their products and those of their competitors. Some economists argue that if companies focused only on large, important differences among products, they could reduce their advertising expenses. Then, they could invest more in innovation or lower the cost of their products.

Excess Capacity As discussed in the previous section, monopolistic competition can generate excess capacity. When this happens, total output is less than the output that is socially desirable. Since production capacity is not fully realized, production resources go unused. Production levels in monopolistic competition, therefore, are often below capacity. Between 1972 and 2018, industry produced at about 80 percent of their full capacity and unemployment was often above 5 percent.

Limited Innovation Firms want some product differentiation, but not so much that they lose consumers. Critics say this leads to a saturation in the market by products that are indistinguishable. Further, it discourages innovation by existing companies, so big changes come only when a new firm enters a market that is willing to take a risk on a highly differentiated product. For example, IBM was a leader in the computer industry when computers filled entire rooms. However, the innovations that resulted in laptops, tablets, and smartphones were introduced to consumers by tiny upstart firms such as Microsoft and Apple, and outsider firms such as Nokia, a Finnish company that started in the wood pulp industry.

Possible Inefficiency Firms are inefficient if they charge a price that exceeds marginal costs when they are at their optimum level of output. The market power of a firm in monopolistic competition means it will actually have a net loss of consumer and producer surplus at its profit-maximizing level of production.

The ultimate effects of monopolistic competition are felt both in the short run and the long run as firms easily enter the marketplace, flooding consumers with niche products and services, and inundating them with advertising in an attempt to showcase the differences.

ANSWER THE TOPIC ESSENTIAL QUESTION

1. Write a paragraph that describes the short- and long-term effects of monopolistic competition.

KEY TERMS

monopolistic competition   price war   excess capacity
non-price competition   product differentiation

MULTIPLE-CHOICE QUESTIONS

1. Which of the following is a difference between perfect competition and monopolistic competition?
   (A) In perfect competition, there are many buyers and sellers, but in monopolistic competition there are only a few buyers and sellers.
   (B) In perfect competition, all products are the same, but in monopolistic competition goods are differentiated slightly.
   (C) In perfect competition, firms cannot earn positive economic profits in the long-run, but in monopolistic competition firms can earn positive economic profits in the long-run.
   (D) In perfect competition, firms set their own prices, but in monopolistic competition firms cannot set their own prices.
   (E) In perfect competition, the barriers to entry are low, but there are no barriers to entry in monopolistic competition.

2. Which of the following is a similarity between a monopoly and monopolistic competition?
   (A) Both have high barriers to entry.
   (B) Both have just one firm.
   (C) Both have just a few buyers.
   (D) Both have excess capacity in the long run.
   (E) Both can raise prices indiscriminately.

3. Which of these characteristics describes a firm in monopolistic competition?
   (A) Significant barriers to entry
   (B) Only a few buyers
   (C) Only one or two sellers
   (D) Slightly differentiated products
   (E) An inelastic demand curve

1. Draw and label the graph of a profit-maximizing monopolistically competitive firm operating in the short-run with positive economic profits. Include the Demand curve, Marginal Revenue curve, Marginal Cost curve, and Average Total Cost curve.

   (a) Identify the profit maximizing quantity labeled as Q_1.

   (b) Identify the allocatively efficient quantity as Q_2.

   (c) Identify the productively efficient quantity as Q_3.

   (d) Shade completely the area of economic profits.

   (e) Shade completely the area of deadweight loss.

According to economic principles, firms in a market marked by monopolistic competition can enjoy high profits in the short run. That very success invites competition, however. Increased pressure from competitors reduces demand for a firm's goods or services. That pushes its price down until the firm's profits stabilize at a normal level. Each of these situations can be shown graphically.

Apply the Skill

The graph below shows current market conditions for Fryers and Fries, a restaurant that specializes in fried chicken. The graph is missing the labels. Add the missing labels and describe what stage of the restaurant's life span the graph represents.

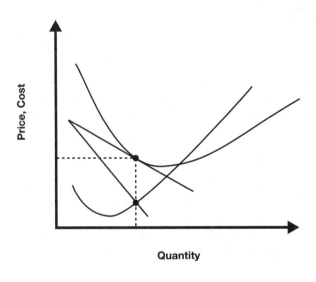

Topic 4.5

Oligopoly and Game Theory

"The United States has nowadays nearly abandoned scrutiny of oligopoly behavior, leaving consumers undefended. That's a problem, because oligopolies do an awful lot that's troubling."

—Tim Wu, Professor of Law, Science, and Technology,
Columbia Law School, 2013

Essential Question: What are the effects of oligopoly and game theory on consumers?

Topic 4.2 identified steps that governments can take to regulate monopolies. But governments hardly ever take steps to regulate oligopolies, even though economists believe that they have the potential to be almost as harmful for consumers.

An **oligopoly** is an inefficient market structure in which there are a very small number of firms with market dominance. Oligopolies tend to have high barriers to entry, and the few firms that are involved often act together interdependently. The effects of such a structure often mean that what is best for the firms often comes at the expense of what may be the best for consumers. If a market is dominated by only two firms, it is called a **duopoly.** For example, in 2019, Visa and Mastercard accounted for about 90 percent of the credit card market.

The U.S. mass media market operates as an oligopoly, with approximately 90 percent of U.S. media outlets owned by six firms.

How Oligopolies Work

The success of oligopolies is partly because rival firms depend on each other. The output and price decisions of one firm closely affects the decisions of others. The U.S. passenger airlines industry is an oligopoly. In 2019, the country's four largest airlines—American, Delta, Southwest, and United—more or less evenly split two-thirds of the domestic travel market. As each other's chief rivals, they were fiercely competitive. Each spent millions of dollars a year to convince consumers that their product was superior to the others.

Because of this competition, the airlines often acted similarly. For example, Southwest sometimes offered low-priced fares for certain routes or time periods, and its three main competitors then followed. American, Delta, and United did not want to be undercut by Southwest and lose market share.

One of the reasons an oligopoly involves so few firms is the extremely high barrier to entry. Starting a commercial passenger airline is an overwhelmingly capital-intensive endeavor. This and other barriers help explain why the last time a new U.S.-based airline entered the market was 2007. The advantage of large size is one reason that between 2008 and 2013, the number of competing companies in the industry decreased significantly. Each of the big four airlines engineered mergers that swallowed up U.S. Airways (American), Northwest (Delta), AirTran (Southwest), and Continental (United). These mergers reduced competition in the U.S. airline business, and fares began to rise.

Collusion occurs when oligopolies stop competing and start acting together like a monopoly. While governments tend to not intervene in oligopolies, they may choose to get involved and regulate if they suspect collusion. One example of government intervention took place in 2006. U.S. government investigators found that British Airways (BA) had engaged in collusion with Virgin Atlantic. The two had worked together to fix levels of fuel surcharge fees tacked onto customers' ticket prices. In the end, the U.S. Department of Justice (DOJ) fined BA $300 million for its illegal actions.

As shown in previous topics, government regulators usually push markets toward perfect competition. This does not always mean DOJ investigations and massive fines. Regulators will steer markets away from collusion and toward more efficient production and more total surplus for consumers.

Cartels Firms in an oligopoly have a natural incentive to collude, or work together, to avoid competition that can drive prices down or costs up. A **cartel** is a group of firms that have a formal agreement to reduce competition with each other. One of the best-known examples of a cartel is the Organization of Petroleum Exporting Countries, or OPEC. Each country in OPEC acts like a single firm because it has a state-run oil business. It was founded by five countries in 1960. By 2018, OPEC had more than doubled that number, and it controlled roughly 72 percent of the world's total crude oil reserves and produced 42 percent of the world's total crude oil output. As OPEC grew, member countries signed formal agreements to restrict output to keep the price at a level they desired. This level of coordination helped the countries act as a monopoly over the crude oil industry. As in every successful cartel, members saw the benefits of collaboration among everyone over the costs of economic competition with everyone.

Still, each member also had a large incentive if it, but it alone, broke the agreement:

- If it produced more oil and no other country did, it could sell more and increase its own income.
- If it reduced its price for oil and no other country did, it could again sell more and increase its own income.

If multiple countries undercut the agreement by increasing production or reducing their price, the cartel would fall apart. In general, then, the benefits for one country or one firm to break a cartel agreement means that for a cartel to succeed, it needs an effective way to enforce the agreement.

Game Theory

Game theory is the study of how firms and individuals act strategically in the context of a game. It can be used to analyze anything from a friendly game of checkers to determining the price of crude oil. In any game, a certain number of individuals take actions, and the payoff for each individual depends directly on both the individual's own choice as well as the choices of others. Each player acts with a strategy in mind and considers potential payoffs and tradeoffs from every action and every reaction.

When playing any game, a player often has a **dominant strategy,** the best choice for that player, regardless of what the other players choose to do. In other words, the payoff of a particular action is always better than—or independent of—the action taken by the other players. But just because a strategy is dominant does not necessarily mean it is the one that will guarantee the highest payoff. It's simply the strategy with the best guarantee.

This conundrum of weighing a guaranteed strategy against the strategy with the highest potential payoff is called the **prisoners' dilemma**. The table below helps to illustrate why. The number on the left of each quadrant belongs to Neal, and the number on the right belongs to Angela. Assume that Angela and Neal have both been arrested. The prosecution has offered them deals independently of each other, one for confessing and one for staying silent, and a different coordinating deal if their partner either confesses or stays silent.

The Prisoners' Dilemma

		Angela	
		Confess	Stay Silent
Neal	Confess	Neal: 4 years / Angela: 4 years	Neal: 0 years / Angela: 10 years
	Stay Silent	Neal: 10 years / Angela: 0 years	Neal: 6 months / Angela: 6 months

Note that if Angela chooses to confess, she will either get four years in prison if Neal confesses or no time in prison if Neal stays silent. Similarly, if Angela chooses to stay silent, she will earn ten years in prison if Neal confesses, and six months in prison if Neal stays silent.

Even if Angela and Neal agreed before they were arrested that they would both stay silent, Angela now has no guarantee that Neal will stay true to his word. If Angela stays silent and Neal confesses, Angela will be faced with ten years in prison. But if Angela confesses and Neal confesses, Angela will face only six months in prison. The guarantee of only six months in prison is better than the high-risk choice of either ten years or no time. So, Angela confesses.

On this matrix, Angela's dominant strategy is to confess. It may not be her ideal strategy—especially if Neal also stays silent—but it is her dominant one. It is the choice with the best outcome, regardless of what the other party chooses to do.

A similar situation often occurs in an oligopoly. Boeing and Airbus may decide to collude and both increase prices in order to increase their profit on the airplanes they produce. But after the agreement is reached, both firms have an incentive to cheat on their agreement. For example, if Boeing maintains its high prices while negotiating with a major airline and Airbus goes back on the agreement and undercuts Boeing's price, Airbus's profits will ultimately increase while Boeing's will decrease. Real firms often encounter the prisoners' dilemma, which is why collusion in an oligopoly is so hard to maintain.

Nash Equilibrium The point of the matrix at which both firms have reached their respective dominant strategies is known as the **Nash equilibrium.** It describes a set of actions in which no player can increase a payoff by unilaterally taking another action, given the other players' actions. (The Nash equilibrium is named after John Nash, the Princeton professor and Nobel Prize winner who developed the concept.) In the example of prisoners Angela and Neal, the Nash equilibrium is reached in the upper left corner when they both confess. Note that the Nash equilibrium is not necessarily the best choice overall, just the best choice given the other party's possible choices.

Oligopolists might want to work together to achieve the benefits of a monopoly. But doing so would violate the antitrust laws. These laws are designed to protect and promote competition. In general, cartels and other forms of collusion among competing companies are illegal.

ANSWER THE TOPIC ESSENTIAL QUESTION

1. Write a paragraph that describes the effects of oligopoly and game theory on firms and consumers.

KEY TERMS

oligopoly	cartel	prisoners' dilemma
duopoly	game theory	Nash equilibrium
collusion	dominant strategy	

MULTIPLE-CHOICE QUESTIONS

1. Which of the following is a key difference between monopolistic competition and oligopoly?

   (A) Monopolistic competition produces identical goods but oligopoly produces slightly differentiated goods.

   (B) Monopolistic competition has an opportunity for long-run profits, but oligopoly does not.

   (C) Monopolistic competition is allocatively inefficient but oligopoly is allocatively efficient.

   (D) Monopolistic competition is illegal, but oligopolies are legal.

   (E) Monopolistic competition has more firms than oligopoly.

2. When a group of firms colludes in order to act as a cartel, what kind of industry is the cartel trying to emulate?

   (A) monopolistic competition

   (B) monopoly

   (C) oligopoly

   (D) monopsony

   (E) perfect competition

Two farmers are the only two suppliers of turkey bacon in their small village. Each has a choice either to go to market in the next village, or stay home and sell only in their village. The numbers listed in the table below refer to the total profit of each of the farmers. The number in the upper-right corner of each box refers to the profits of Farmer 1. The number in the lower-left corner of each box refers to the profits of Farmer 2.

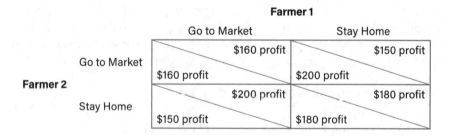

3. Which of the following best describes each farmer's dominant strategy?

(A) Farmer 1's dominant strategy is to go to market; Farmer 2's dominant strategy is to stay home.

(B) Farmer 1's dominant strategy is to stay home; Farmer 2's dominant strategy is to go to market.

(C) Farmer 1's dominant strategy is to go to market; Farmer 2's dominant strategy is to go to market.

(D) Farmer 1's dominant strategy is to stay home; Farmer 2's dominant strategy is to stay home.

(E) Neither Farmer 1 nor Farmer 2 has a dominant strategy.

SHORT FREE-RESPONSE QUESTION

1. YourCar and Pinto are the only two car-rental companies serving a small town. Each company can choose to set a high price or a low price for a daily car rental. The payoff matrix below shows the daily profits for each combination of prices that the two companies could choose. The first entry shows YourCar's profits, and the second entry shows Pinto's profits. Answer the following questions, assuming that both shops know the information shown in the matrix.

		Pinto	
		High Price	Low Price
YourCar	High Price	$210, $220	$80, $260
	Low Price	$240, $160	$125, $140

(a) Does YourCar have a dominant strategy to set a high price, a dominant strategy to set a low price, or does it have no dominant strategy? Explain.

(b) Does Pinto have a dominant strategy to set a high price, a dominant strategy to set a low price, or does it have no dominant strategy? Explain.

(c) If the two companies do not cooperate on price, what will the profit be for each shop?

(d) Based on your answer in part (c), is this a Nash equilibrium? Explain.

(e) The local city council is concerned that it is too expensive to rent a car. It decides to give a daily subsidy of $40 to any car-rental company that chooses to set a low price to rent from its fleet of vehicles. Redraw the payoff matrix under this subsidy program.

THINK AS AN ECONOMIST: *INTERPRET AN ECONOMIC OUTCOME USING QUANTITATIVE DATA*

Game theory is a useful tool for determining the best outcome for participants in an oligopolistic market. Firm managers can use it to find their best option vis-a-vis the potential actions of a competitor.

An important concept of game theory is the Nash equilibrium. This is the position of the decision matrix at which no firm can increase its advantage by changing its decision in light of a competitor's decision. This option ensures that each participant in the game—or competitor in the market—enjoys the optimum outcome regardless of the choice made by the other player.

Apply the Skill

Competitors in an oligopolistic market have products that are only narrowly differentiated from one another. They typically use advertising to try to increase consumers' perception of their differentiation. Two car dealers, Shao Auto and Sorich Motors, sell the same make of vehicles and are vying for market share in a small city. Since they sell the same cars with the same manufacturer's incentive plans, they must differentiate in some way. The two dealers consider whether or not to advertise. The matrix shows their potential weekly profits in each scenario, with Shao Auto's profits listed first in each case.

		Shao Auto	
		Advertise	Don't Advertise
Sorich Motors	Advertise	$11K, $12K	$8K, $15K
	Don't Advertise	$20K, $9K	$15K, $13K

Which cell in the matrix represents the Nash equilibrium? Why? Use quantitative data to explain your response.

In an article in the magazine The Atlantic in 2019, finance professor Thomas Philippon compared the United States with Europe in 1999 and in 2019. In 1999, nearly everything in the United States was cheaper than in Europe. By 2019, Internet service, wireless cellphone plans, and plane tickets are much more expensive in the United States than in Europe and Asia. Philippon argued that it was no coincidence that these are three industries in which there was little real competition in the United States. Each was an oligopoly. Each was dominated by a few firms and, though acting independently, the firms kept prices high.

Since 1999, as a result of mergers and acquisitions, a number of industries became dominated by a small handful of companies. Philippon argued that oligopolies had emerged as the rule rather than the exception in a significant number of U.S. industries. The resulting decline in competition cost American consumers billions of dollars a year in higher prices. In addition, the dominant companies were able to control employment, wages, supply chains, and market share. This led to increased inequality as labor's share of income fell. It stifled innovation and resulted in sluggish productivity growth. It also contributed to rising healthcare costs.

What Happened? One explanation of the rise of oligopolies is a change in government policy. Influenced by the economists known as the Chicago School, U.S. regulators began to take a more hands-off approach toward mergers. They argued that monopolies were temporary because high profits would attract new competitors. Critics responded that this might have been true in the past, but since about 2000 high profits reflected greater barriers to entry. In short, the Chicago School underestimated the many ways in which large firms could stifle competition.

At the same time, as national economies in the European Union became more integrated, firms faced greater competition. When Germany's Siemens and France's Alstom tried to merge their rail services in 2017, both countries wanted the merger approved. However, the EU's competition commissioner, Margrethe Vestager, concluded that such a merger "would have significantly reduced competition" by depriving customers of a choice of suppliers and products. The European Commission blocked the merger.

Should Something Be Done? Some economists argue that the government should continue its hands-off approach to mergers. They suggest that either oligopolies are not as big a problem as greater government oversight or that eventually market forces will undercut the dominance of a few firms.

Another response is that the government should take stronger steps to encourage competition. As part of this policy, in October 2020, the Justice Department sued Google for violating antitrust laws. Philippon strongly believes that making markets more competitive will reduce prices for consumers, increase income for labor, and encourage economic growth.

1. Laila's Widget Factory has been granted a government permit to operate as the only provider of widgets and is currently earning economic profits in the short run.

   (a) Identify the market structure that Laila's Widget Factory operates in. Explain.

   (b) Use a correctly labeled graph, show each of the following.

      i.   Laila's profit maximizing Quantity and Price, labeled as Q* and P* respectively.

      ii. The area of economic profits, shaded clearly and completely.

      iii. The allocatively efficient quantity, labeled as Qe.

      iv. Would profit increase or decrease if the firm produced at Qe rather than Q*?

   (c) Assume that Laila's Widget Factory can now effectively price discriminate.

      i.   Would the quantity produced now by Laila's Widget Factory increase, decrease, or remain unchanged? Explain.

      ii. Is this new quantity now productively efficient?

      iii. What is the value of consumer surplus?

   (d) Now instead assume that government removes the government permit and now allows for increased competition which leads to the market becoming monopolistically competitive. Would the demand for Laila's widgets become more elastic or less elastic due to these changes? Explain.

UNIT 5

Factor Markets

When most people think of markets, they think of the product markets in which business offer goods or services to consumers. But businesses have to produce these goods and services, and in order to do so, they must use the factors of production. Businesses compete with each other for the factors of production in factor markets. These markets, like product markets, are also affected by the laws of supply and demand.

The most crucial factor of production is labor. Generally, the higher the salary or wages offered by a business, the less the quantity of labor demanded and the higher the quantity of labor supplied. Conversely, lower wages lead to an increase in the quantity of labor demanded but to a lower quantity of labor supplied. But there are other factors to consider besides quantity of labor. One of them is the quality of the labor force.

For example, a tech company may have the option of building a new facility in a rural area, where the cost of living is low, or building it in a major urban area where the cost of living is high. Building in the rural area may be less expensive, but the labor force may be inadequate—too few people with the necessary skills or knowledge to do the job, and too few amenities to attract qualified workers. Building in the urban area will probably be more expensive, but there will likely be a better qualified labor pool. The company may also have to pay a higher wage rate because of the higher cost of living. These are some of the trade-offs businesses must consider.

"We're agreed then - no more purring or
tail wagging until our demands are met."

Topic Titles and Essential Knowledge

Topic 5.1 Introduction to Factor Markets

- Factors of production (labor, capital, and land) respond to factor prices (wages, interest, and rent), and employers' (firms') decision to hire is based on the productivity of the factors, output price, and cost of the factor.
- The quantity of labor demanded is negatively related to the wage rate, while the quantity of labor supplied is positively related to the wage rate in a given labor market, other things constant.

Topic 5.2 Changes in Factor Demand and Factor Supply

- Changes in the determinants of labor demand, such as the output price and the productivity of the worker, cause the labor demand curve to shift.
- Changes in the determinants of labor supply (such as immigration, education, working conditions, age distribution, availability of alternative options, preferences for leisure, and cultural expectations) cause the labor supply curve to shift.

Topic 5.3 Profit-Maximizing Behavior in Perfectly Competitive Factor Markets

- In a perfectly competitive labor market, the wage is set by the market and each firm hires the quantity of workers, where the marginal factor (resource) cost (wage) equals the marginal revenue product of labor. A typical firm may be a perfect competitor in the labor market even if it is an imperfect competitor in its output markets.
- A typical firm hires labor in a perfectly competitive labor market as long as the marginal revenue product of labor is greater than the market wage.
- To minimize costs or maximize profits, firms allocate inputs such that the last dollar spent on each input yields the same amount of marginal product.
- Marginal revenue product of a factor of production is the change in total revenue divided by the change in that factor of production, which is also equal to the marginal physical product of that factor multiplied by the marginal revenue ($MRP = MP \times MR$). Firms in a perfectly competitive output market will have marginal revenue product of labor that is equal to the value of the marginal product of labor ($VMPL = MPL \times P$) because marginal revenue for each unit of output is equal to price.

Topic 5.4 Monopsonistic Markets

- In a monopsonistic labor market, a typical firm hires additional labor as long as the marginal revenue product is greater than the marginal factor (resource) cost (the wage of a new unit of labor plus the wage increase given to all existing labor).
- When a typical firm hires additional workers in a monopsonistic labor market, the marginal factor (resource) cost is greater than the supply price of labor.

Introduction to Factor Markets

"Labor is the true standard of value."

—Abraham Lincoln, 1861

Essential Question: What effects do factor prices have on people and businesses?

Think of where you buy goods and services that you consume. Maybe you love peanuts and like to keep some handy for a snack. So, you regularly buy bags of peanuts at a nearby grocery store. The place where you buy peanuts to eat is an example of a product market because it sells products for consumers to use.

But many economic activities happen so that you can buy those bags of peanuts. The grocery store has rent or buy a building to operate in, hire people to stock the shelves and run the cash register, and buy the peanuts from a distributor. Behind each of these activities are others. Construction workers built the building, truckers transported the peanuts from a warehouse to the store, and a farmer grew the peanuts. Something a business uses to produce the goods and services for consumers is a **factor**. The place where firms purchase what they need to produce goods and services is the **factor market**. The items they need are the **factors of production** that were described in Unit 1:

1. Labor is both physical and mental labor performed by people.

2. Capital is all of the machinery, tools, equipment, buildings, and other similar things that are used to produce goods and services.

3. Land is another name for natural resources. Among these are plots of ground, crops, minerals, and water.

4. Entrepreneurship is the work done by an individual, called an entrepreneur, who takes the risk of combining the other three factors of production to produce the goods and services demanded by consumers and society.

Understanding Factor Markets

The basic principles that shape product markets also shape the markets for labor, capital, land, and entrepreneurship. Participants in factor markets try to use the factors of production as efficiently as possible. Firms purchase labor, land, capital and entrepreneurial ability in some combination to meet their specific goals, needs, and objectives. Just like a demand curve in the product market, the demand curve for a factor of production is downward sloping. That is, if the price of the factor goes up, the quantity demanded of the factor decreases.

In a similar fashion, there is a supply of these factors, and as the price of the factor increases, the quantity supplied of the factor increases. In other words, the factor supply curve is upward sloping. (Later you will see a special case where the labor supply curve may be "backward bending," but generally, the supply curve has a positive slope.) If you get a job waiting tables, then you are selling your labor into the labor market. If your family has a business and uses machinery to produce a good or service, then that machinery is considered capital, and someone supplied that capital into the capital market. If you lease land to a farmer, you have supplied land into the land market.

Understanding Factor Prices The demand and supply of factors in the factor market can be analyzed by using the same tools of demand and supply used in the product market. When economists talk about a **factor price**, they are referring to how much a firm pays to acquire the labor, land, or machinery that is part of creating a good or service. Each factor price has a specific name:

- *Wages* are money that a person or business pays to others for their labor, time, and effort. You might earn wages from working in a store, office, or factory. Many businesses pay wages by the hour. Other workers may be paid a salary which is a fixed payment to an employee without regard to hours worked. Your teacher is most likely paid a salary. In either case, these are considered wages, a payment made to labor.

- *Interest* is the "price" associated with the use of capital. Since most firms borrow money to finance capital, the interest rate firms pay to borrow money is a good estimate of this price. Alternatively, firms that use their own funds, instead of using loans, give up the interest they could have earned by lending this money to someone else.

- *Rent* is how much a person or business pays for temporary use of tools, equipment, or office space in order to create goods or services.

- *Profit* is the payment made to entrepreneurs for combining the other three factors of production to produce goods and services, for managing these resources, and as a reward for taking the risk to produce those goods and services for customers and society.

Understanding the Decision to Hire Consider why firms decide to hire workers to create goods and services. Firms always have imperfect information, so they sometimes make the decision to hire people based on guesswork or a hunch that adding employees will increase profits. More often, though, the decision is based on three concepts:

- **Productivity** This is a measure of how much the employer can get out of the hire. For example, if someone hires you by the hour, they might keep track of how many meals can you cook, or how many boxes can you assemble, or how many computer issues can you troubleshoot per hour.

- **Output Price** This is the amount a business can charge for a finished good or service.

- **Factor Cost** This quantifies how much a person or business must spend to get those inputs for the business to produce those goods and services.

Each of these three factors affects the other two. For example, if an employer installs new equipment or adopts better training methods that allow workers to do the same work in less time, then employees' productivity will increase. The cost per unit will decrease in the product or output market.

In the factor market, this increase in productivity can either increase or decrease employment. The firm might choose to reduce labor costs by laying off workers. Or, the firm might see each worker as more valuable. Depending on the market demand for the worker's labor, the worker might be able to negotiate a higher wage. In this case, because of higher productivity, both the employer and the employee might benefit.

How Wage Rates Affect Employment When wages in a market increase, assuming that everything else stays the same, then the quantity demanded for that labor will decrease. Higher wages for employees mean higher costs for employers, which the employer may pass along to consumers in the form of higher output prices, or they may pass backward to the owners of the firm in the form of lower profits. In purely economic terms, the quantity of labor demanded is negatively related to the wage rate. This is very similar to the demand curve in the product market.

How Wage Rates Affect Labor Supply An increase in wages has other results. More people will enter the labor market, meaning that the quantity of labor supplied will increase. In other words, the quantity of labor supplied is positively related to the wage rate in a given labor market, assuming that other things stay constant.

As you will see later, this is not the case all the time. But for now, and most of the time, generally, the supply curve of labor does have a positive slope.

A "Now Hiring" sign suggests that at the current market wage, the quantity demanded exceeds the quantity supplied.

What Factor Prices Convey It's important to understand that factor markets involve complex interactions between productivity, cost, and many other issues. It's worth studying factor markets because of two vital lessons that you can learn from them.

1. *Factor prices provide incentives to people and businesses.* For example, if you make jewelry to sell at local markets, and you improve your productivity, then you can reduce the cost per item that you produce. The additional profit you make per necklace or bracelet can be a strong incentive to work harder and improve your processes.

2. *Factor prices convey information to people and businesses.* Say you have the option to landscape people's yards or groom dogs, and the wages for landscaping are twice as high as the wages for dog grooming. The wage for each job tells you how much your local labor market values those skills.

Calculating Marginal Revenue Product and Marginal Resource Cost

It's one thing to understand how factor prices affect factor markets in general. It's another to be able to calculate a practical, real-life effect, such as when a business should hire more workers and when it should stop hiring. In other words, where does the demand meet the supply in the input market?

Understanding Marginal Revenue Product Remember that in economics, *marginal* means "one more unit" and *revenue* means "income or benefit." **Marginal revenue product** (MRP) is the change in income or benefit received from the addition of one extra unit, assuming that everything else stays the same. You learned about marginal analysis in Topic 1.6, and marginal revenue product is an important part of this technique. Businesses use marginal revenue product to figure out how many employees the firm can hire in order to maximize the profits of the firm. Here's the formula for marginal revenue product:

marginal revenue product = marginal product of labor × marginal revenue

The *marginal product of labor* is the number of products that each extra worker produces. You learned in Topic 4.2 that *marginal revenue* is how much more a business or individual makes by producing one more unit of a good or service. In a competitive product market, the price of the good or service is the marginal revenue, but in imperfectly competitive markets, the price is greater than the marginal revenue.

Calculating Marginal Revenue Product To apply this formula to a practical scenario, say that a business is trying to decide how many snow cones to produce each day. The figures below show how much more the business could make by hiring one extra snow cone maker.

MARGINAL ANALYSIS OF PRODUCTION OF SNOW CONES (DAILY)				
Units of Labor Hired	Total Product (in number of snow cones produced)	Marginal Product of Labor (in number of snow cones)	Marginal Revenue (in dollars)	Marginal Revenue Product (in dollars) (MRP = MP MR)
1	50	50	2	100
2	110	60	2	120
3	160	50	2	100
4	200	40	2	80
5	230	30	2	60

To understand why the marginal revenue product initially increases but then begins to decrease, recall that MRP = MP × MR. Marginal product of labor (MP) is the additional output resulting from an additional unit of labor. In the snow cone case, when a second worker is employed, MP rises. This is because of increasing marginal returns; two workers may work better together, each specializing in specific tasks, increasing efficiency and output.

If a third worker is hired, MP declines. This is the point where diminishing marginal returns begin. Since MP is beginning to decline, and because marginal revenue is constant, MRP must also decline beginning with the third worker. Because marginal revenue (MR) is constant, this firm is selling its product in a perfectly competitive output market. If the snow cone maker were in an imperfectly competitive output market, the firm would have to lower its price to sell more output, which would result in marginal revenue also declining and, further, would result in MRP decreasing even faster.

To summarize, MRP will decline for two reasons:

- when MP is declining
- when MR is declining

If the firm is in a perfectly competitive output market, only MP will decline. If the firm is in an imperfectly competitive market, both MP and MR will decline.

Calculating Marginal Resource Cost Producing more of something seems like it should increase profits. It often does. But whether it does or not is based on the **marginal resource cost** (MRC). This is the extra cost a person or business incurs to make one more unit of the good or service. The MRC is sometimes referred to as the marginal factor cost, or MFC. To calculate the MRC, use this formula:

$$\text{marginal resource cost} = \frac{\text{change in total cost}}{\text{change in quantity of labor}}$$

The change in total cost is the additional monetary amount it takes to produce one more unit of a good or service. The change in quantity of labor is the amount in additional wages or other costs that the employer must expend to achieve that change in total costs. Most businesses want to maximize profits. So, they use marginal revenue product to pinpoint the best output to make the most profit.

Comparing Marginal Revenue Product and Marginal Resource Cost If marginal revenue product (MRP) is the same as the marginal resource cost (MRC), then the firm or business is hiring the optimal or equilibrium amount of that resource. If marginal revenue product is greater than marginal resource cost, then that is even better for the company. It will bring in more money and can increase profits by hiring more workers.

But if the marginal revenue product is less than the marginal resource cost, then the company should not produce that extra product or hire that extra person because doing so will cost the company profits. These decisions can be expressed in formulas:

- MRP > MRC = producer will hire more labor which will result in more output produced
- MRP < MRC = producer will hire fewer workers which will result in fewer units of output produced
- MRP = MRC is an equilibrium level of hiring

The optimal level of production can vary over time, even if the same producer is making the decision.

These formulas can help you analyze the snow cone example. Suppose the snow cone firm currently employs three workers and produces a total of 160 snow cones per day. This means that the MRP is 100. Thus, the maximum daily wage would be $100, which is the marginal resource cost.

Now, suppose that wages rise to $120 per day. This raises the MRC to $120, which results in only two workers being hired because the MRP equals 120 when just two workers are hired. Similarly, if wages fall to $80 per day, assuming no other changes, the firm can hire four workers because, at four workers, the MRP is $80.

The rule that firms try to follow is to purchase a resource as long as the MRP is greater than or equal to the MRC. If firms follow this rule, they hire the optimal number of workers.

ANSWER THE TOPIC ESSENTIAL QUESTION

1. In one to three paragraphs, explain how factor prices provide incentives and convey information to people and businesses.

factor	rent	marginal revenue product
factor market	profit	(MRP)
factors of production	productivity	marginal resource cost
wages	output price	(MRC)
interest	factor cost	

MULTIPLE-CHOICE QUESTIONS

1. On a hot day, you buy two boxes of ice cream treats, head to the park, and sell the individual treats to friends. You spend $6 for each box of 12 ice cream treats, and you sell each treat for $2. In this scenario, what economic label applies to the $2?

   (A) Marginal resource cost

   (B) Marginal revenue product

   (C) Quantity

   (D) Output price

   (E) Cost

2. What is the relationship between the quantity demanded of labor and the wage rate in a labor market? Assume that all other factors remain constant.

   (A) Positive—when wage increases, quantity demanded increases

   (B) Negative—when wage increases, quantity demanded decreases

   (C) Equal—wage and quantity stay the same in most economies at most times

   (D) Unrelated—wage has no impact on quantity supplied

   (E) Exponential—when the quantity of labor increases, the wage rate increases twice as much

3. What is the relationship between the quantity supplied of labor and the wage rate in a labor market? Assume that all other factors remain constant.

   (A) Positive, because when wage increases, quantity supplied increases

   (B) Negative, because when wage increases, quantity supplied decreases

   (C) Equal, because wage and quantity stay the same in most economies at most times

   (D) Unrelated, because wage has no impact on quantity supplied

   (E) Exponential, because when the quantity of labor increases, the wage rate increases twice as much

1. You decide to provide a service helping elderly neighbors. You plan to have workers help with chores and charge $2 per chore. You plan to pay each worker $10 for their labor.

OPTIONS FOR HIRING NEIGHBORHOOD HELP	
Number of Workers You Hire	**Total Number of Chores Completed**
0	0
1	12
2	36
3	42
4	45
5	44

(a) Calculate the marginal product of labor for hiring the 2nd worker. Show your work.

(b) When hiring the 2nd worker, are you experiencing diminishing marginal returns? Explain.

(c) Calculate the marginal revenue product (MRP) of hiring the 3rd worker. Show your work.

(d) Assuming you want to maximize profits, how many workers will you hire? Explain.

(e) If demand increases for your service and you are now able to charge $3 per chore, will you now hire more workers, fewer workers, or the same number of workers?

Economists use economic principles to explain economic behavior. Being able to apply an economic principle to a situation—or to contrast two different situations—demonstrates comprehension of an economic principle. Applying an economic principle means answering these questions:

- How does the situation involve that principle?
- How does the principle apply to the situation?

For example, a company's decision concerning how much to produce involves the principle of the maximization rule. A company will choose the level of output at which marginal cost equals marginal revenue and the marginal cost curve is rising. That level of production is ideal because it represents the most efficient use of the company's productive resources.

Apply the Skill

In this topic, you learned about the principles that guide decisions in the labor market. Consider these two situations:

1. A local convenience store owner decides not to hire another worker after the state increases the minimum wage.
2. A free-agent professional football player signs a new contract worth $100 million.

What principles of the factor market influence the outcomes in these two situations?

ECONOMICS PERSPECTIVES: *HOW DOES A MINIMUM WAGE INFLUENCE THE LEVEL OF EMPLOYMENT?*

In 2019, economist Ben Zipperer testified before the U.S. House of Representatives, which was considering a new minimum wage act. He pointed out that the federal minimum wage had reached its high point in 1968, at $1.60 an hour. In 2020 dollars, that would be over $12. But in 2020 the federal minimum wage was only $7.25, which had not changed since 2009. In other words, minimum wage workers had experienced a net loss in buying power. The House of Representatives went on to pass the Raise the Wage Act of 2019, which would have raised the federal minimum wage to $15 an hour by 2024. After that, the minimum wage would be indexed to median wages so that it would automatically be adjusted each year.

Who Might Benefit When Zipperer testified, two-thirds of the working poor in the United States earned the minimum wage. Most were adults. They were disproportionately women and people of color. The largest percentage were employed in service occupations. The states with the highest percentage of workers making the minimum wage or less were in the South. While the primary beneficiaries would be low-wage workers, business would also benefit from increased consumer spending.

Who Might Suffer Opponents of raising the minimum wage argued that unemployment would rise. They pointed out that a higher wage would help only the workers who don't lose their jobs. A 2021 report by the Congressional Budget Office concluded that raising the minimum wage to $10 an hour would not affect employment. Raising it to $12 an hour would likely cause a small temporary rise in unemployment. Raising it to $15 an hour could result in a net loss of about 1 million jobs, about 0.6 percent of the workforce.

Taking the Initiative According to the organization Business for a Fair Minimum Wage, research shows that raising the minimum wage does not necessarily increase unemployment. Unemployment went from 3.8 percent in 1967 to 3.6 percent in 1968, when the federal minimum wage was raised by 20 cents to $1.60 an hour. Unemployment also fell after the minimum wage was raised in 1996 and 1997.

One reason the impact of a higher federal minimum wage on employment might be limited is that many states and cities have higher minimums than the federal government requires. As of November 2020, 28 states and the District of Columbia had minimum wages higher than the federal minimum wage. In addition, 48 cities and counties had minimum wages higher than their state's minimum wage. Washington, California, and Massachusetts had the highest state minimum wages.

In addition, many large companies have an internal minimum wage that is higher than what their competitors pay. They argue that the higher wages attract more capable candidates who then work more productively and leave at a lower rate. In March 2021, Costco raised its internal minimum wage to $16 per hour. The company's CEO Craig Jelinek stated that the move "isn't altruism." He explained, "We know that paying employees good wages . . . constitutes a significant competitive advantage for us. It helps us in the long run by minimizing turnover and maximizing employee productivity."

Topic 5.2

Changes in Factor Demand and Factor Supply

"I don't pay good wages because I have a lot of money; I have a lot of money because I pay good wages."

—Robert Bosch, German industrialist, (1861–1942)

Essential Question: How do changes in the labor market affect the supply of workers and the demand for those workers?

More than 1 million restaurants operate in the United States, and they employ more than 5 percent of the entire population. So, the odds are good that you know someone who works in, or has worked in, a restaurant. The food business is very tough. Four out of five restaurants go out of business within five years of opening. One challenge is that labor costs change frequently. A restaurant in northern Minnesota might need more help during the summer months when vacationers are visiting. One in a college town might need less help in the summer when fewer students are in school. Other forces, such as immigration laws, the development of training programs in community colleges, and the existence of other employers nearby affect the number of people who will choose to work in a restaurant.

In addition, many restaurants have a very high rate of staff turnover. They hire more teenagers than any other industry, and many of them work only a short time before returning to school or moving on to another job. Even older and full-time staff move frequently, taking higher paying jobs at other restaurants or leaving the industry altogether.

Labor is one of the basic factors of production, along with land, capital, and entrepreneurship. Economists study how restaurants and other firms adjust their demand for labor and the other factors as well as reasons the supply of each one increases or decreases. Understanding how factor demand and factor supply change helps explain why wages go up or down.

Changes in Determinants of Labor Supply

The labor market is vital in any modern economy. Economists study **determinants of labor supply**, the forces that influence how many hours workers are willing and able to supply their labor at a certain wage rate. Economists study these determinants at the local, regional, and national scale. The information is extremely valuable to businesses (who want to know the best places to build new offices or factories) and to governments (who want to promote their workforces to businesses that are looking for new places to expand). But it's difficult to track because so many aspects of labor supply change constantly. Each of the following is a determinant of labor supply.

Education One important determinant of labor supply in a market is the education level of individual workers. For example, in 2010, studies showed that the country had a shortage of experienced nurses and that based on current patterns, the shortage would worsen in the following decades. But becoming a successful nurse requires certain intellectual, emotional, and physical skills that not everyone has. Further, it takes years of education and training. So, hiring qualified nurses is difficult, which is why they earn high salaries relative to most of the population.

Conversely, jobs that require little education or training often pay less. Because they require less preparation, there is likely to be a larger number of people who are willing and able to complete the tasks that the job requires. In most cases, it is easier for employers to find, hire, train, and replace workers in low-skilled jobs.

Electricians require years of schooling and on-the-job training to master their trade, and an aptitude and background in STEM studies is a must. For these reasons, like nurses, electricians earn above-average wages.

Immigration It can take years to train a new nurse, doctor, lawyer, or technician. However, if qualified people exist outside the country and are willing to move, then immigration can significantly affect the supply of available labor in certain sectors of the economy. The United States, Germany, Japan, and many other countries have allowed "guest workers" to immigrate temporarily to work. In 2018, the United States approved visas for about 180,000 guest workers who were highly skilled workers, such as software developers and technical consultants.

In addition, the United States approved more than 700,000 visas for lower-skilled guest workers. Many performed agricultural labor. Though paid low wages for hard work, they provided the foundation of the country's food system.

Working Conditions People's attitudes vary greatly about whether a particular job is pleasant or unpleasant. For example, some workers prefer jobs that are done outdoors while others prefer jobs inside. Some workers are risk-averse while others are risk-takers. In general, if all other factors are the same, the more unpleasant or dangerous a job is, the labor supply for it is probably lower. Hence, workers who take these jobs should be able to get higher pay.

Age Distribution When you apply for a job, you might think about the other people who are applying for it. But an economist thinks about the entire pool of people who are looking for work. Whether they are young, in the middle of their careers, or near the end of their careers and considering retirement can be important. Economists analyze the age distribution of a population and use it to project the likelihood of people entering, staying in, or leaving the workforce.

Availability of Alternative Options Why do people work at jobs they dislike? It may be because there are few other jobs to be had in that neighborhood, career, or region. Economics is the study of choices, and one choice that workers want is the ability to choose between different jobs and careers.

One example of a workforce that has few alternative options is the residents of a company town. In a company town, an employer builds not only factories and offices but also homes for workers. The employer is also the landlord and owns the stores where workers shop. Company towns are often in isolated locations—for example, mining camps or logging camps. Some company towns offer schools, churches, and libraries.

Preferences for Leisure In 1890, the U.S. government began tracking how long employees worked. Back then, workers in factories averaged 100 hours per week. Labor unions put pressure on the government to restrict the amount of time employers could require people to work. Today, polling indicates that the average American employed full time works between 44 and 47 hours per week. Employers may offer overtime pay to those who work extra hours, but some employees choose to spend time with their families or simply rest instead.

Cultural Expectations and Discrimination Sometimes a person is qualified for a job and available to perform it, but the employer refuses on the grounds that the person is inappropriate for the job based on race, gender, age, disability, or for some other reason. Or the qualified person may not even consider applying because a certain job is "not for people like me."

Changes in Determinants of Labor Demand

Like workers seeking jobs, employers seeking workers also have economic incentives and constraints that affect their behavior. Economists call these **determinants of labor demand**.

Output Price You learned in Topic 5.1 that an output price is the amount a business can charge for a finished good or service. In general, if a business raises its output price for an item because sales are increasing, then it will have an incentive to hire more workers to produce that item. Conversely, if a business reduces its output price because sales are falling, then it will not have an incentive to hire more workers. Rather, it will have an incentive to lay off some or all workers. In short, output price is directly related to marginal revenue which, in connection with marginal product, impacts marginal revenue product.

Productivity To an economist, productivity means how much of a good or service a worker can produce in a certain period of time. Several factors affect productivity. A highly skilled labor force is more productive than a lightly skilled or unskilled one. The tools and machinery that a worker can use also affect productivity. And the technology of production methods also makes a difference. For example, a factory that uses a production line, with workers specializing in different parts of the manufacturing process, will be more productive than a factory in which each worker builds a product individually from top to bottom.

Workers and managers can develop ways to become more productive. However, some changes in productivity happen because of national or global changes. For example, the U.S. Bureau of Labor Statistics has calculated that between 1995 and 2000, labor productivity in the United States grew 2.5 percent per year—more than double the rate of growth in the period from 1975 to 1995. That is largely because computers and the Internet allowed people and teams to work more efficiently. In recent years, labor productivity has grown at a slower rate—about 1.1 percent—as workers and businesses have adjusted to these technologies. A significant technological breakthrough could send productivity rates soaring again.

Responses to Changes in Incentives

The discussion of determinants of labor supply earlier in this topic did not cover the impact of a change in wages. One would assume that if a business raises its wages, then its workers will work more hours, but this is not necessarily true. In either case, it is possible to track these changes using graphs.

The Labor Supply Curve The **labor supply curve** is relatively simple: as wages rise, more people will be willing to work. This makes sense because working takes time and effort, and if wages are low enough, then most people are not motivated to work more hours unless they have no savings.

The Labor Demand Curve Think about what you have already learned about output prices. If a business owner raises wages, then he or she probably has to raise output prices. And if goods and services are more expensive, then fewer people are likely to buy them. So, the **labor demand curve** is generally the opposite of the labor supply curve: as wages rise, employers hire workers for fewer hours.

How the Labor Supply Curve Works in Practice A person who gets a job as a trainee at a local factory will initially need help from coworkers to complete even the simplest tasks. As a result, the employer might pay a trainee a wage that is greater than that person is worth at the moment. Over time, this employee will be able to complete tasks without coworkers having to spend time checking them. Based on this improved productivity, the employee will become worth more to the company and might be able to negotiate for a higher wage.

If the employee is paid a higher wage, this employee will have an incentive to work more. This is a **substitution effect** because the worker has an incentive to substitute labor for leisure time, thus spending more hours on the job.

If an employee has been working at a job for a while and has become skilled enough to train other employees and check their work, the employee is more valuable to the employer. To dissuade the employee from seeking another job elsewhere, the employer might raise the individual's wages again.

In some cases, though, higher wages decrease the incentive to work. Individuals sometimes decide that the extra income lets them afford to work less and have more leisure time. This is an **income effect** because the higher wage increases income that the worker would now prefer to use and spend. Some people reach this point at a young age, either because they have accumulated enough wealth or have adopted a simple enough lifestyle that they can afford to live the life they want. For most people, it happens later in life. They cut back on work or retire completely. The decrease in the labor supply resulting from an increase in wages appears as a backward bend on the labor supply curve.

LABOR SUPPLY CURVE

The backward-bending labor supply curve illustrates the two effects of a wage increase on labor supply. The positive sloping portion of the labor supply curve illustrates the substitution effect. The negative sloping portion illustrates the income effect.

As discussed in the example, as a person's hourly wage rises, he or she usually works more hours at first but then gradually cuts back to have more leisure time. Economists call this the **labor-leisure tradeoff**.

Putting It All Together The labor supply curve above is for one person. However, the entire labor market also has a labor curve. When there is a change in the determinants of labor supply (such as immigration, age distributions, and so on), then the labor supply curve shifts. When there is a change in the determinants of labor demand (such as output price and productivity levels), that shifts the labor demand curve. When either or both of these curves shift, a new equilibrium point is created. This new equilibrium point for the new wage and quantity of labor can be analyzed just like the new price and quantity in the product market. For example, if the demand for labor rises while labor supply does not change, both the wage rate and the amount of labor will rise.

1. In one to three paragraphs, describe the determinants of labor demand and the determinants of labor supply, and explain how these determinants cause the labor supply curve and the labor demand curve to shift.

KEY TERMS

determinants of labor
  supply
determinants of labor
  demand

labor supply curve
labor demand curve
substitution effect

income effect
labor-leisure tradeoff

MULTIPLE-CHOICE QUESTIONS

1. An airport invests in new trucks that de-ice airplanes during cold weather. The new trucks are better insulated than the old ones were, turning one of the most-hated jobs at the airport into one of the most pleasant. What is the economic term for this situation?

   (A) Continuation of the labor demand curve

   (B) Input price disruption

   (C) Output price disruption

   (D) Change of determinant of labor supply

   (E) Change of determinant of labor demand

2. In 1890, full-time factory workers averaged 100 hours per week on the job. Today, they work about 40 hours per week but wages have also increased over that same period. Which of the following best explains both changes?

   (A) A decrease in the demand for the products that factory workers produced caused wages to increase.

   (B) Increases in the number of people who want to work caused companies to spread the work.

   (C) Increases in the population made more workers available so individuals had to work less.

   (D) Increases in the labor supply curve caused wages to increase.

   (E) Increases in productivity allowed workers to negotiate for higher wages.

3. If the demand for the final product produced by a labor market increases due to successful advertising campaigns, how might an economist expect the labor market to change?

(A) An increase in the demand for labor causing wage to increase

(B) An increase in quantity demanded for labor

(C) A decrease in quantity demanded for labor

(D) A decrease in the supply of labor causing wages to increase

(E) A change in working conditions

FREE-RESPONSE QUESTIONS

1. Consider a labor market with an upward sloping supply curve and a downward sloping demand curve.

(a) What is the effect on the labor market of a drastic increase in immigration?

(b) Based upon your answer in part (a), what will happen to both wage and quantity at equilibrium?

(c) What is the effect on the labor market of an increase in worker productivity? Explain.

(d) What is the effect on the labor market of a decrease in output price of the product produced by the labor?

(e) What situation will be created by an effective minimum wage placed in the market?

THINK AS AN ECONOMIST: *DETERMINE THE EFFECT OF A CHANGE ON OTHER MARKETS*

Changes in the determinants of labor supply can have a significant effect on the labor market. An increase in qualified workers shifts the labor supply curve to the right. This change moves the labor supply curve toward more hours worked and lower wages. Producers—eager to take advantage of the surplus of labor—then have the opportunity of employing workers at lower wages and more hours.

But what is the effect of these changes on other markets—such as the output market for the goods that workers produce? To determine that effect, economists must answer these questions:

- What is the nature and extent of the change in the labor market?

- What is the effect of that labor market change on producer output?

- What is the effect of changes in producer output on the output market?

In this example of a competitive labor market, the increased supply of workers causes wages to fall and more hours are worked. Everything else the same, this means that more output can be produced, increasing the supply of output and shifting the output supply curve to the right, which results in lower prices and more output being consumed.

Apply the Skill

Consider what happens when there is a change in a determinant of labor demand. Suppose clever inventors provide athletic shoe producers with a new machine that can cut and assemble raw materials into a shoe 20 percent faster than before. What effect does this change have on the labor market? What is the effect of this change on athletic shoe output and on the output market for athletic shoes?

Topic 5.3

Profit-Maximizing Behavior in Perfectly Competitive Factor Markets

"If you're the founder, entrepreneur, starting a company, you always want to aim for monopoly and you want to always avoid competition. And so hence competition is for losers."

— Peter Thiel, German-American investor (b. 1967)

Essential Question: How does a business decide how many workers to hire in a market where no single buyer or seller has the power to influence all prices?

In the 2019–2020 National Basketball Association season, Los Angeles Lakers' player LeBron James was not a typical worker. He earned a salary of $37 million, about 740 times the median salary of U.S. workers. Still, the decision by the Lakers to pay James $37 million reflected the same market forces that shaped what other firms paid for labor. The Lakers decided that if they paid James that amount of money, his labor would bring them more than that amount in return. The same reasoning guides firms such as a book store hiring a clerk for minimum wage or a law firm hiring a new lawyer who just graduated from a prestigious law school. They all make hiring decisions with the goal of maximizing their profits.

Characteristics of Perfectly Competitive Factor Markets

The labor market is an example of a factor market, the market where businesses and individuals buy what they need to produce goods and services. In a **perfectly competitive factor market,** no buyer and no seller has enough power to affect what everyone else will charge. While no market is completely competitive, understanding how a perfectively competitive factor market works in theory will help you understand how they work in practice.

Many Buyers and Sellers If a large number of people or businesses are buying and selling a particular product, and each of those people and businesses are acting independently, then a market may be close to perfectly competitive. When there are many buyers and sellers, goods and services go for what economists call the market price or the equilibrium price.

In the labor markets, when there are many people seeking work and many companies seeking workers, then workers and employers accept that they must live with the market price if they want to stay in the industry. In other words, the market sets the wage.

Similar Skills and Abilities In a perfectly competitive labor market, all the workers have similar skills and abilities, and all will be paid the same. If the market wage is $25 per hour and an individual worker wants to be paid $26 per hour, he or she will not find an employer willing to make the hire. If an employer wants to pay only $24 per hour, they will find no one to hire.

Profit-Maximizing Behavior of Firms Buying Labor

A graph can show how forces in a perfectly competitive factor market interact.

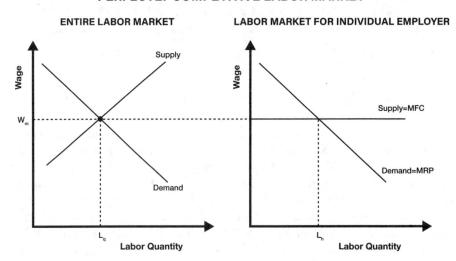

PERFECTLY COMPETITIVE LABOR MARKET

First, look at the graph on the left, which shows an entire labor market that is perfectly competitive. As the wage rate increases, the quantity demanded of labor decreases but the quantity supplied of labor increases. But this is a perfectly competitive market, so neither the employers nor the employees can do much to change wages. The market sets the wage, which is the dotted horizontal line (W_m) on the graph, and the quantity of available labor, the vertical dotted line (L_q).

The graph on the right shows the curves for an individual employer in this market. The employer must accept the wage the market sets (assuming the employer wants to continue in this line of work). But the employer controls how many workers he or she hires. The supply curve of labor (the horizontal line on the graph) shows that the employer can hire each additional worker for the same cost. That is, the wage rate is the same as the marginal factor cost.

The employer will continue to hire until the marginal factor cost equals the marginal revenue product of labor. This can be written as an equation:

$$MFC = MRP$$

Marginal Costs and Products The **marginal factor cost** (MFC) is the extra money the employer must spend to hire one more worker. The **marginal revenue product of labor** (MRP) is the extra money the employer gets from adding one more unit of a resource. Once MFC becomes larger than MRP, the employer stops hiring more workers. On the left-hand graph, that point is the intersection of labor demand and labor supply. As long as the MRP is greater than the MFC, the employer will keep hiring workers. These can be expressed in equations:

- MRP > MFC = employer will increase the number of employees
- MRP < MFC = employer will decrease the number of employees
- MRP = MFC = employer will keep the equilibrium number of employees

The Labor Market vs. Output Markets Does a business in a perfectly competitive labor market have to sell its products for the same prices its competitors do? No, because a labor market and an output market are different. An output market is where businesses sell the goods and services they produce. A company can be a perfect competitor in the labor market and other factor markets and an imperfect competitor in the different output markets where it sells its products.

One good example might be a business that makes protein bars. The business owners are in a perfectly competitive labor market, with plenty of factory workers available to make the bars and plenty of similar businesses hiring. But maybe this company makes healthier, tastier protein bars than its competitors do. In that case, the output market is not perfectly competitive, because the products are not all identical. Hence, the business may be able to sell its products for a little more than the average market price for similiar products.

Calculating Profit-Maximizing Behavior

Most firms seek to maximize their profits. Calculating the marginal revenue product of labor (MRP) can help them determine the optimal mix of factors for this goal.

Spending on Inputs Each input is a good or service that a company uses to create another good or service. For example, if you decided to start a business detailing cars, your inputs might include items such as sponges, cloths, brushes, cleaning products, wax, polish, and a vacuum cleaner. You might decide to hire people, maybe just as part-time staff, to help you do the detailing work, advertise your business, or help with bookkeeping. To pay for everything you need to open your business, you might need to borrow money from a bank or a relative.

A rational business owner allocates inputs so that the last dollar spent on each input brings in the same amount of **marginal product,** the extra unit of output you get from that input.

As discussed in Topic 1.6, economists often focus on the last dollar spent. That is, they calculate on the margins. A rational business owner thinks about the cost of adding one more unit rather than thinking about the total costs that he or she has already spent.

Calculating Marginal Revenue Product You already learned in this topic that marginal revenue product is the extra money an employer gets from adding one more unit of a resource. You saw MRP in a graph earlier in this topic. You can also calculate it with this formula:

$$MRP = MP \times MR$$

In the equation, MRP means the marginal revenue product of a factor of production. To find out how much extra money this is, find out the marginal physical product (MP) of that factor. The marginal physical product is just another name for the marginal product—it's the one extra unit of visible, tangible output that you get from that input. So, for a business that makes furniture, a marginal physical product might be one more chair or table. Then multiply MP by the marginal revenue (MR). The result, the marginal revenue product, is the extra revenue the employer gets from adding one more unit of a resource.

Calculating VMPL and MRP in a Perfectly Competitive Market When a product market is perfectly competitive, as is the case with the examples used in this topic, the formula for calculating marginal revenue product is a little different. Because the price equals the MR in a competitive output market, the MRP can be written as:

$$MRP = MPL \times P$$

When using this formula with P instead of MR, the result is the **value of the marginal product of labor (VMPL),** the worth (in dollars or some other currency) of the last unit produced by the last worker the employer hired. To find this, you would multiply the marginal product of labor by the price of that last good or service that the last worker created.

$$VMPL = MPL \times P$$

What is different about a perfectly competitive market? In such a market, each business has a marginal revenue product of labor that is the same as the value of the marginal product of labor. That is because the marginal revenue for each unit of output is the same as the price of that unit of output. This, too, can be expressed in equations.

- VMPL > Unit Price = employer will increase the number of employees
- VMPL < Unit Price = employer will decrease the number of employees
- VMPL = Unit Price = employer will keep the equilibrium number of employees

1. In one to three paragraphs, explain what a perfectly competitive factor market is, and describe how a business operates in one. How does the business decide how many workers to hire?

KEY TERMS

perfectly competitive factor market	marginal product
marginal factor cost	value of the marginal product of labor
marginal revenue product of labor	(VMPL)

MULTIPLE-CHOICE QUESTIONS

1. Which of these describes a perfectly competitive factor market?
   (A) one buyer, many sellers, few workers have similar skills and abilities
   (B) few buyers, many sellers, few workers have similar skills and abilities
   (C) many buyers, few sellers, all workers have similar skills and abilities
   (D) many buyers, one seller, no workers have similar skills and abilities
   (E) many buyers, many sellers, all workers have similar skills and abilities

2. Emmanuel owns Emmanuel's Widget Factory which hires both labor and capital in perfectly competitive factor markets and sells the widgets in a perfectly competitive product market for $0.50 each. Emmanuel currently has three employees who produce a total of 100 widgets. He is considering hiring a fourth worker. This worker increase total production to 125 widgets. The cost of labor is $20. Calculate the marginal product of the fourth worker, the marginal revenue product if the fourth worker is hired, and the total labor costs (TLC) for four workers.
   (A) MP = 25; MRP = $12.50; TLC = $60
   (B) MP = 50; MRP = $25.00; TLC = $80
   (C) MP = 25; MRP = $25.00; TLC = $80
   (D) MP = 25; MRP = $12.50; TLC = $80
   (E) MP = 50; MRP = $25.00; TLC = $60

3. Sam owns a taco stand. She hires workers in a perfectly competitive labor market and sells her tacos in a perfectly competitive product market. She considers hiring an extra worker. The extra worker can produce 20 tacos per hour, and Sam sells the tacos for $2.00 each. With local minimum wage laws of $15 per hour, Sam _____ the extra worker because the worker's _____.

(A) should hire; MRP is greater than the wage

(B) should hire; wage is greater than the MRP

(C) should not hire; MRP is greater than the wage

(D) should not hire; wage is greater than the MRP

(E) should hire; wage and MRP are equal

FREE-RESPONSE QUESTIONS

1. Syndergaard's Danish Bakery sells cupcakes in a perfectly competitive product market at a price of $2. The bakery also hires labor in a perfectly competitive factor market. Assume that labor is the only cost. Use the table below to help answer the questions that follow.

Number of Laborers Hired	Total Quantity Produced
0	0
1	32
2	59
3	82
4	97
5	107
6	112
7	110

(a) What is the marginal product (MP) of the fifth worker hired? Show your work.

(b) Calculate the marginal revenue product (MRP) of the fourth worker hired. Show your work.

(c) If workers are hired at a wage of $16, how many workers would be hired? Explain.

(d) If a minimum wage is instituted at $25, will the number of workers hired increase, decrease, or stay the same? Explain.

(e) Assuming instead that wage stays at $16 but the demand for cupcakes decreases and cupcakes now sell for $1, how many workers should now be hired?

THINK AS AN ECONOMIST: *INTERPRET AN ECONOMIC OUTCOME USING CALCULATIONS*

Producers are constantly competing for employees, seeking to use the incentive of wages to convince individuals to work for them. They must pay high enough wages to attract these individuals. At the same time, they try to minimize wages in order to minimize costs—and maximize profits.

Producers make these decisions using marginal analysis, comparing each additional unit of labor to the marginal output provided by that labor and the marginal revenue generated by that output. In a purely competitive job market, the value of a marginal product of labor equals the marginal revenue product. That figure is found by multiplying the marginal physical product by the marginal revenue. As long as that value equals or is greater than the marginal factor cost, the employer keeps hiring.

Apply the Skill

Consider the situation of three producers in different purely competitive labor markets. Producer A makes nutritional supplements, Producer B makes cupcakes, and Producer C sells auto insurance. Review the data in the chart and make the necessary calculations to determine if each producer should continue hiring.

	Producer A	Producer B	Producer C
Marginal physical product	5,000 supplements per hour	5 dozen cupcakes/hour	1 sale per 2 hours
Marginal revenue	$1.99 per 1,000 supplements	$0.25/cupcake	$37.50 fee per sale
Marginal cost of labor	$12.00/hour	$15.00/hour	$20.00/hour

Monopsonistic Markets

"We're recruiting the cream of society. Your personality must be optimistic, your work diligent."

— Recorded message played on loudspeakers outside the entrance to a factory complex in Zhengzhou, China, that made half the world's iPhones (2017)

Essential Question: What is a monopsony, and how does it affect wages?

On April 12, 1961, Soviet astronaut (also known as a cosmonaut) Yuri Gagarin became the first human to travel into outer space. Within a month, U.S. astronaut Alan Shepard followed. In the early years of space travel, it was so expensive and the financial returns were so unlikely that only national governments were willing to take the risk to finance space ventures. Not until 2020 did a private company first launch people into space, and even then, the astronauts were still employees of the U.S. government space agency, NASA. In the United States, then, if you wanted to be an astronaut, you had only one possible employer—the federal government. Since there was only one buyer for labor, this was an example of a factor market that was **monopsonistic.**

Source: Wikimedia

Caption: Alan Shepard was one of the first astronauts for the only employer of people in his profession, the United States government.

Monopsonies in the labor market are rare. Other examples include communities with only one major employer. When monopsonistic labor markets do exist, the firm can use its power to maximize profits, just as other firms do. However, unlike other firms that have to compete for workers, a monopsonistic firm has far more power to control wages.

Characteristics of Monopsonistic Markets

In a monopoly, there are many buyers but only one seller. In a **monopsony**, there are many workers (or potential workers) but only one employer. In both cases, a lack of competition makes the market less efficient. Another way to think a monopsony is that a firm has a monopoly on labor.

MONOPOLIES VS MONOPSONIES

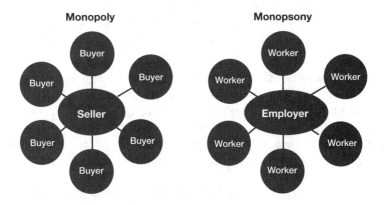

Monopoly

Buyer · Buyer · Buyer · Seller · Buyer · Buyer · Buyer

Monopsony

Worker · Worker · Worker · Employer · Worker · Worker · Worker

Monopsonies and Wages Consider the incentives for employers in a monopsony. Compared to employers in a competitive market, they would have less incentive to increase their workers' wages or to improve working conditions or benefits. If a worker's options are to work for the one company in town, move to another area, or stop working, then the worker is likely to keep his or her job—even if conditions are poor. In Topic 5.3, you learned that the market sets the wage in a perfectly competitive market. But in a monopsony, the employer sets the wage.

For most of the 20th century, major league baseball was a monopsony. When a team signed a contract with a player, the player was "reserved" to that team. Even when his contract ended, he could not sign with another team. Players had almost no negotiating power with owners, so they had to accept the salary they were offered. In 1967, the average salary of a player was about $19,000, about the wage of an experienced chemist. In 1969, outfielder Curt Flood challenged the reserve clause in court. He lost, but the players' union picked up the issue. In 1975, the union successfully won the battle to overturn the reserve clause. Salaries skyrocketed. In 2020, the average salary of a major league player was about $4.4 million, about 37 times a typical salary for a chemist.

Monopsonies and Power A monopsony has other powers besides the ability to control wages. Monopsonies are usually large, which means they can pressure suppliers for more competitive prices on raw materials. And because monopsonies employ such a high percentage of people in an area, they can pressure local governments to grant them tax credits, land grants, or other perks in exchange for keeping jobs in the community. For instance, to keep the iPhone manufacturer Foxconn in China, a Chinese province paved new roads, built new power plants, and paid tens of millions of dollars in bonuses.

Near-Monopsonies Even if other employers are hiring the same type of worker in the same area of the country, a large and powerful company can exercise considerable influence on workers, competitors, and governments.

For example, when Amazon announced it wanted to open a second corporate headquarters, more than 200 cities offered proposals. The city of Newark, New Jersey, offered up to $7 billion in tax breaks—but Amazon still said no. Instead, Amazon chose Virginia, which offered far less in financial incentives, but had one of the best-educated workforces in the country.

Monopsonies and Competition Remember that monopsony applies to the labor market, not the product market. A monopsony can still face competition and experience pressure to lower prices, even if it has a great deal of control over the labor market and some control over local government. For example, a manufacturer in a one-factory town might face stiff competition from manufacturers in other regions of the country or in other countries.

Profit-Maximizing Behavior in Monopsonistic Markets

You already know that for-profit companies seek to maximize their profits. Monopsonies have that goal—and in many cases it is easier for them to achieve than it would be if they were in a competitive labor market. The following graph pinpoints how a monopsony maximizes profit.

HOW A MONOPSONY MAXIMIZES PROFITS

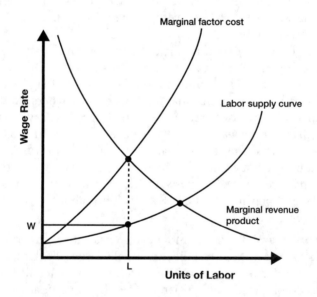

What the Graph Means As wages rise, the number of workers who make themselves available for work rises too. And as the employer hires more workers (or employs the same number of workers for more hours), the marginal revenue product decreases. Remember from Topic 5.3 that the marginal revenue product of labor is the extra money the employer gets from adding one more unit of a resource.

Advantages of a Monopsony How does this graph differ from the ones you saw in Topic 5.3? In this case, the employer (not the market) sets the wage. The wage is the black horizontal line marked with a W on the graph. So, the employer has more of an advantage than it would in a competitive labor market.

In a monopsony, the marginal factor cost is greater than the supply price of labor. That means the monopsonist has the chance to make substantial profits. If the market becomes competitive, or if the employer is paying low wages and a local or national government sets a minimum wage, then that horizontal line denoting the wage could be considerably higher on the graph.

Pressure to Pay Higher Wages In spite of the clear advantages to a firm of being a monopsony, there are some disadvantages. If a monopsony wants to keep hiring, then it will be necessary to pay higher wages. And if the employer has to pay those new employees more, then it will most likely have to pay those same higher wages to the employees who were hired earlier. Remember from Topic 5.3 that the marginal factor cost is the extra money the employer must spend to hire one more worker. In a monopsony, the marginal factor cost is the wage of the new unit of labor plus the wage increase the employer gives to all existing labor. That is why the marginal factor cost rises much faster than the labor supply curve does, as you can see on the graph.

Suppose the labor supply curve shows that the first worker can be hired for a wage of $16. To attract one more worker with the same qualities you have, the labor supply curve shows a wage of $18. If you were the first worker and you learned that the next person hired was paid $18, you might be able to argue successfully that you should get a wage of $18 as well. For the employer then, the marginal factor cost, the extra cost of hiring the next worker, will be the total of the $18 paid to the second worker plus the additional $2 paid to you, the first worker. Similarly, each additional worker hired might lead to increased wages for the previously hired workers. A simple example is shown in the table below.

Quantity of Labor Supplied	Wage Rate	Additional Costs	Marginal Factor Cost
1	$16	• $16 paid to the first worker	$16
2	$18	• $18 paid to the second worker • $2 more paid to the first worker	$20
3	$20	• $20 paid to third worker • $2 more paid to the first worker • Plus $2 more paid to the second worker	$24
4	$22	• $22 paid to fourth worker • $2 more paid to the first worker • $2 more paid to the second worker • $2 more paid to the third worker	$28

Calculating Profit-Maximizing Behavior in a Monopsony The employer will keep hiring workers as long as the marginal revenue product—the extra money the employer gets from adding one more unit of a resource—is greater than the marginal factor cost. In the example shown in the table above, assume the MRP is $25. Employing three workers increases profits, but hiring a fourth worker would decrease profits. So, to maximize profits, the employer would hire just three people. The hiring decisions of an employer can be summarized in three equations:

- MRP > MFC: the employer has incentive to hire more labor
- MRP < MFC: the employer has incentive to hire less labor
- MRP = MFC: the employer will maintain the equilibrium quantity of labor

ANSWER THE TOPIC ESSENTIAL QUESTION

1. In one to three paragraphs, explain what a monopsony is and describe how a business operates in one. How does the business decide how many workers to hire?

KEY TERM

monopsony

MULTIPLE-CHOICE QUESTIONS

1. Imani owns a factory that is the only employer in town. She finds out that someone else is going to build a factory in the same town as hers. What would an economist predict about how Imani's business will change?

(A) She will face increased competition for workers so her business will change from a monopsony to a monopoly.

(B) She will lose her monopsony, but increased competition will most likely drive wages down.

(C) She will lose her monopsony and will most likely have to raise wages because of increased competition for workers.

(D) She will keep her monopsony, but only if the new factory employs workers who have similar skill sets to the employees she hires.

(E) She will keep her monopsony, but only if she and the owner of the new factory agree to compete with each other for workers.

2. In a monopsonistic labor market, a profit-maximizing firm would continue to hire workers as long as the extra money the firm gets from adding workers would be

(A) greater than the extra money the employer would spend to hire one more worker

(B) greater than the average amount of money the employer pays existing workers

(C) equal to the average amount of money the employer pays existing workers

(D) less than the average amount of money the employer pays to existing workers

(E) less than the extra money the employer would spend to hire one more worker

3. Would the average worker prefer to work in a monopsonistic market or in a competitive market?

(A) a monopsonistic market, because a monopsonist workforce is likely to have a greater variety of skills and abilities than a workforce in a competitive market

(B) a monopsonistic market, because a monopsonist employer is likely to expend more effort to attract and retain high-quality workers

(C) a monopsonistic market, because his or her hourly wage is likely to be higher and working conditions are likely to be better

(D) a competitive market, because his or her hourly wage is likely to be higher and working conditions are likely to be better

(E) a competitive market, because competition is likely to raise the price of the goods or services the worker produces

FREE-RESPONSE QUESTIONS

1. Only Shop Batteries is a company that specializes in providing batteries to auto companies. Only Shop hires labor as a monopsonist as the only job provider in town. The table shows the labor supply for the company. Assume that all other inputs are fixed.

LABOR SUPPLY FOR ONLY SHOP BATTERIES	
Number of Workers (also called Quantity of Labor, or QL)	Wage Paid per Hour (also called Wage Rate, or WR)
0	$0
1	$5
2	$10
3	$15

(a) Calculate the total labor cost for Only Shop to hire 2 workers. Show your work.

(b) Calculate the marginal factor cost for Only Shop to hire the 2nd worker. Show your work.

(c) Explain why the marginal factor cost calculated for the 2nd worker in part (b) is different from the wage rate paid to 2 workers.

(d) Assume that a minimum wage is instituted at $10. Would the marginal factor cost of the 1st worker increase, decrease, or stay the same?

(e) Assume instead that a minimum wage is instituted at $5. Would the marginal factor cost of the 1st worker increase, decrease, or stay the same?

Economists use economic concepts to explain what decisions economic actors should make. They use one of those concepts to predict the behavior of monopsonistic employers, who enjoy great control over the labor factor market. They say that a monopsonistic firm keeps hiring workers as long as marginal revenue product is greater than marginal factor cost. If MRP is equal to or less than the marginal factor cost, the firm stops hiring.

Apply the Skill

Look at the following chart with details on Fly-by-Night Enterprises labor factor market and costs. Study the chart and answer the questions.

Number of Workers (QL)	Wage Paid (WR)	Total Variable Cost (QL × WR)	Marginal Factor Cost (change in TVC ÷ change in QL)
0	$0	$0	0
5	$15	$75	75 ÷ 5 = $15
10	$18	$180	105 ÷ 5 = $21
15	$21	$315	135 ÷ 5 = $27
20	$25	$500	185 ÷ 5 = $37
25	$30	$750	250 ÷ 5 = $50
30	$36	$1,080	330 ÷ 5 = $66

1. What marginal revenue product would Fly-by-Night need to have to justify hiring 20 workers and earning a profit of $5 per unit?

2. How many employees could the firm employ if its marginal revenue product was $28?

3. What per-unit profit would it earn at that level?

1. Below is the production function for Bryana's Delivery Corporation which is a perfectly competitive firm hiring workers in a perfectly competitive labor market. Assume that the current price of deliveries is $8 and hires workers at $150 per day.

Quantity of Workers	Number of Deliveries/Day
1	30
2	70
3	95
4	115
5	130
6	135

(a) What is the marginal product (MP) of the 4th worker? Show your work.

(b) Based on your answer in part (a), what is the marginal revenue product (MRP) of the 4th worker? Show your work.

(c) What is the marginal resource cost (MRC) of hiring each worker?

(d) How many workers would Bryana's Delivery Corporation hire to maximize profits? Explain.

(e) Assume now that due to increased demand for deliveries, the firm can now charge $10/delivery.

   i. Will the marginal product (MP) of each worker increase, decrease, or remain the same?

   ii. Will the marginal revenue product (MRP) of each worker increase, decrease, or remain the same? Explain.

   iii. Will Bryana's Delivery Corporation now hire more workers? Explain.

UNIT 6

Market Failure and the Role of Government

At times, markets face inefficiencies or other problems that are significant enough that they are considered market failures. In these cases, governments often intervene. One such market failure occurs when one company so dominates an industry that the industry has little competition. Without competition, the business can set prices and has less incentive to innovate. In response, the government sometimes breaks up a company like this in an attempt to restore competition in a market.

Another common market failure is that people make economic decisions that have costs for other people. For example, in the course of its production, a manufacturing facility might produce air pollution that increases the rate of lung disease for people living near the facility. To limit the dangers of pollution, government regulates emissions into the air and water.

Finally, markets might produce results that people find unacceptable, such as extreme economic inequality. The government uses its power to tax to provide care for people who are not able to work productively enough to be able to afford food and shelter. During the 2020 COVID-19 pandemic, almost all businesses and workers suffered, but travel and hospitality businesses, restaurants and bars, theaters and sports venues, and salons and gyms were particularly hard hit. In order to prevent economic collapse, governments in many countries, including the United States, paid workers to stay home and provided grants or loans to large and small businesses.

"Wasn't this blue back in 1947?"

Topic Titles and Essential Knowledge

Topic 6.1 Socially Efficient and Inefficient Market Outcomes

- The optimal quantity of a good occurs where the marginal benefit of consuming the last unit equals the marginal cost of producing that last unit, thus maximizing total economic surplus.
- The market equilibrium quantity is equal to the socially optimal quantity only when all social benefits and costs are internalized by individuals in the market. Total economic surplus is maximized at that quantity. [See also PRD-3 and POL-3.]
- Rational agents can pursue private actions to exploit or exercise market characteristics known as market power.
- Rational agents make optimal decisions by equating private marginal benefits and private marginal costs that can result in market inefficiencies.
- Policymakers use cost-benefit analysis to evaluate different actions to reduce or eliminate market inefficiencies.
- Market inefficiencies can be eliminated by designing policies that equate marginal social benefit with marginal social cost.
- Equilibrium allocations can deviate from efficient allocations due to situations such as monopoly; oligopoly; monopolistic competition; negative and positive externalities in production or consumption; asymmetric information; and insufficient production of public goods.
- Producing any non-efficient quantity results in deadweight loss.

Topic 6.2 Externalities

- The socially optimal quantity of a good occurs where the marginal social benefit of consuming the last unit equals the marginal social cost of producing that last unit, thus maximizing total economic surplus.
- Externalities are either positive or negative and arise from lack of well-defined property rights and/or high transaction costs.
- In the presence of externalities, rational agents respond to private costs and benefits and not to external costs and benefits.
- Rational agents have the incentive to free ride when a good is non-excludable.
- Policies that address positive or negative externalities include taxes/subsidies, environmental regulation, public provision, the assignment of property rights, and the reassignment of property

Topic 6.3 Public and Private Goods

- Private goods are rival and excludable, and public goods are non-rival and non-excludable.
- Due to the free rider problem, private individuals usually lack the incentive to produce public goods, leaving government as the only producer.
- Governments sometimes choose to produce private goods, such as educational services, and to allow free access to them.
- Some natural resources are, by their nature, non-excludable and rival and therefore open access. Private individuals inefficiently overconsume such resources.

Topic 6.4 The Effects of Government Intervention in Different Market Structures

- Per-unit taxes and subsidies affect the total price consumers pay, net price firms receive, equilibrium quantity, consumer and producer surpluses, deadweight loss, and government revenue or cost. The impact of change depends on the price elasticity of demand and supply.

- Lump-sum taxes and lump-sum subsidies do not change either marginal cost or marginal benefit; only fixed costs will be affected.

- Binding price ceilings and floors affect prices and quantities differently depending on the market structures (perfect competition, monopoly, monopolistic competition, and monopsony) and the price elasticities of supply and demand.

- Government intervention in imperfect markets can increase efficiency if the policy correctly addresses the incentives that led to the market failure.

- Government can use price regulation to address inefficiency due to monopoly.

- A natural monopoly will require a lump-sum subsidy to produce at the allocatively efficient quantity.

- Governments use antitrust policy in an attempt to make markets more competitive.

Topic 6.5 Inequality

- Income levels and poverty rates vary greatly both across and within groups (e.g., age, gender, race) and countries.

- The Lorenz curve and Gini coefficient are used to represent the degree of inequality in distributions and to compare distributions across different countries, policies, or time periods.

- Each factor of production receives the value of its marginal product, which can contribute to income inequality.

- Sources of income and wealth inequality include differences in tax structures (progressive and regressive tax structures), human capital, social capital, inheritance, effects of discrimination, access to financial markets, mobility, and bargaining power within economic and social units (firms, labor unions, and families).

Socially Efficient and Inefficient Market Outcomes

"These social losses may take the form of damages to human health; they may find their expression in the destruction or deterioration of property values and the premature depletion of natural wealth. . . ."

—K. William Knapp, German American economist (1910–1976)

Essential Question: How do perfectly competitive markets allocate resources efficiently, while imperfect competition often results in market inefficiencies?

In the 1970s, air pollution produced in power plants and factories in the Midwest was drifting eastward. As it did, it was ruining the scenic mountains, lakes, and streams of northern New York and New England. The pollution caused toxic precipitation, called acid rain, that was killing fish and destroying forests. It was so harsh that it was damaging the limestone facades on buildings. One of the country's premier destinations for camping, hiking, and fishing was being destroyed. Besides harming the natural environment, it was damaging the tourist industry of an entire region of the country.

But the cost to the owners of the Midwestern plants and factories of reducing the pollution would be high. It would far exceed any benefits they would get themselves. As a result, they had no economic incentive to fix the problems they were causing. A coalition of people concerned about the environment and business interests in New York and New England organized to stop acid rain. They successfully pressured the federal government to intervene and require the plants and factories to reduce the emissions that were causing so much damage.

Adding scrubbers to capture the pollutants before they were released increased the costs of operation for the power plants and factories. In a narrow sense, these regulations made the economy less efficient.

However, in a broader sense, by protecting the environment and the jobs in another region, the regulations increased **social efficiency**, the optimal distribution of resources in society, taking into account both the private and social costs and benefits of an economic action. Often, when one type of efficiency conflicts with another, the government becomes involved to resolve the difference.

During the 1970s, power plants and heavy industries in the Midwest billowed pollution that created acid rain in the Northeast. The federal government forced the power companies to remediate the problem.

Social Efficiency

The interplay between free markets and social efficiency manifests itself in many ways, every day. People drive cars and fly in airplanes for both work and pleasure, but emissions from cars and airplanes contribute to air pollution. Pollutants harm the health of people and damage the environment. Farmers use pesticides to save their crops from insects and other harmful organisms, but those pesticides often contaminate soil and water.

Manufacturers try to keep the **private cost** of production (materials, wages, and utilities) as low as possible to maximize profits. Their success in doing so reflects their **market power,** their ability to influence prices by adjusting the supply of or demand for their products.

However, private costs do not equate with the social costs (private costs plus external costs). As a consequence, what is efficient for making a profit for one individual or firm in a competitive market might be inefficient for the general welfare of the larger society.

Economic efficiency optimizes all resources to benefit all those in a free market. It involves the efficient consumption and production of goods of both individual economic agents and the society overall:

- **Marginal social benefit** (MSB) includes the private benefits from a transaction plus the additional benefits to society from the transaction.

- **Marginal social cost** (MSC) includes the private costs from a transaction plus the additional costs to society from the transaction.

Social efficiency, or the socially optimal level of output, occurs when marginal social benefit equals marginal social cost. On a graph, this is the point at which the MSB and MSC lines intersect.

Don't confuse marginal social benefit and marginal social cost with **marginal private cost** (MPC) and **marginal private benefit** (MPB). MPC is the change in a manufacturer's total cost when producing an additional unit. For example, if the production cost of producing an additional baseball rises from $5 to $6, the MPC is $1. MPB is the additional benefit of consuming one more unit of a good.

When acid rain was harming the Northeast, the marginal social cost to the region was high because the power plants did not install pollution cleaning devices. Assume that each $100 worth of electricity produced by a power plant also caused $25 worth of damage to the environment. The MSC would be the cost of production plus the external cost of the pollution: $100 + $25 = $125.

External Costs External costs drive social efficiency. Imagine you're in the market for a motorcycle. In trying to figure out which model to buy, you take the price of the bike into consideration as well as its style and performance. The motorcycle's manufacturer chooses what type of bike to engineer based on profit maximization, as it seeks to make as much money as possible. As a consequence, the company chooses the most efficient, least costly method of production. To that end, it doesn't take into account external costs—neither the pollution it contributes to the environment nor the pollution it could minimize if it takes the place of a car.

For the most part, neither do you. You consider only how the purchase of the motorcycle benefits you. Like the motorcycle company, you ignore the cost and benefits to third parties—the people who are not involved in the transaction yet are impacted by the decisions you (and the manufacturer) make. These benefits and costs are known as **externalities**—effects on people other than producers and consumers directly involved in the transaction. These are also known as spillover effects. They are described in more detail in the next topic.

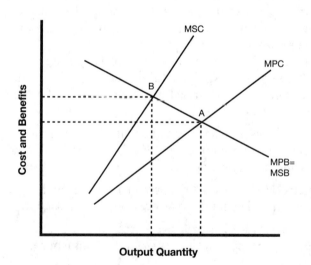

You can graph social efficiency on a supply and demand curve, such as the one below. As you can see, at point B, marginal social cost (MSC) equals marginal social benefit (MSB). A manufacturer who does not take into account externalities will choose to increase its own profits at point A, the spot where marginal private cost (MPC) equals marginal private benefit (MPB), creating a socially inefficient market.

Inefficiencies and Market Failure

Sometimes a socially inefficient allocation of goods is large enough that people perceive the market as failing. Economists have identified several types of inefficiency:

- *Productive Inefficiency* If supplies do not fully utilize resources to produce the most cost-effective product, the system has a **productive inefficiency.** These most often occur when the market has imperfect competition. In such situations, manufacturers will produce less and keep prices high. Productive efficiency is when resources for production are used in the most-cost effective way.

- *Allocative Inefficiency* While productive inefficiency focuses on how suppliers use resources, **allocative efficiency** occurs when resources are not distributed effectively to meet the wants of consumers. It is also most common in cases of imperfect competition. As a consequence, companies can raise prices above their marginal cost of production, which ultimately reduces consumer surplus. Allocative efficiency means that resources are used to produce the most wanted goods for society.

- *Dynamic Inefficiency* In some markets, companies have no incentive to upgrade technology or innovate, a condition called a **dynamic inefficiency.** These are most likely to occur in a monopoly. As a consequence, production and retail costs soar, products are inferior, and there are fewer choices for consumers. Dynamic efficiency is when companies upgrade their production processes to reduce costs.

One solution to inefficiency is trade. For example, imagine you trade an apple to a friend for an orange. You might both feel the trade made you better off. Or maybe you preferred the orange, but your friend had no preference. In either case, the trade increased efficiency. An economy in which every trade that has been conducted makes at least one person better off and no one worse off is described as **Pareto efficient**.

Rational Agents

Economists look through the prism of rationality when it comes to the economic choices that people make. In making rational choices, people weigh all the costs and benefits before making a decision. Economists call these people **rational agents**.

Most people behave as rational agents when they make most economic decisions. Here's an example: It's an hour or two before dinner time and there are no vegetables in the fridge to eat. There are two grocery stores in town. Store A has green beans on sale for $1.68 a pound, while Store B's price is $1.88. Which store do you visit?

The obvious answer, it would seem, would be Store A because the beans are 20 cents cheaper. But Store A is four miles away. Store B is just down the block. You ask yourself: Do I want to drive to Store A and possibly sit in traffic for some undetermined amount of time, or do I walk down the street to Store B? The savings in time and gasoline might offset the price savings.

The decision you make is based on all relevant rational information. You'll do whatever makes you happy. In other words, you're a rational agent.

Adam Smith

Economists used to believe that humans are capable of *always* making rational decisions in the marketplace.

Adam Smith, the 18th century economist and philosopher, called rationality the "invisible hand" in describing the hidden forces that move free markets. He believed that both consumers and producers were motivated primarily by self-interest. Each would make decisions by balancing the benefits and costs of an action for them. The result of all these separate decisions, Smith argued, would be the best possible mix of products to satisfy consumer demands. The concept of rational choice, then, explains what goods and services will be produced and at what quantities.

Government Intervention The actions of rational agents don't always result in socially efficient decisions. It might have been rational for the power companies that created acid rain not to spend money on installing pollution-abating devices. However, installing these devices was socially efficient because they countered the negative externalities of pollution. In this case, government intervention caused them to overcome the decision they had made as rational agents.

A government can force individuals and businesses to act in ways that it hopes will result in socially efficient outcomes. Governments do this in several ways:

- Addressing inefficient allocations that result from market structures such as monopolies, oligopolies, or monopolistic competition

- Responding to negative externalities by trying to allocate costs to the individual or firm that benefits from the action causing the externality

- Providing accurate information to consumers by requiring nutrition labels on food and testing medicines so consumers can make rational choices

- Providing public goods, such as roads and schools, that make economic activity more productive

The Cost of Intervention Government actions cost money. Enforcing rules requires tax dollars to pay regulators. Further, regulations that increase costs for producers are often passed on to consumers. Governments attempt to balance the benefits to the public interest with the costs of implementation. However, government does not have a single measure to guide its actions the way private firms have profit, and people disagree on what truly is in the public good. So, government intervention that attempts to promote the general good is usually controversial. In the United States, the general good is determined by elected officials who respond to people who are involved in the political process by voting, protesting, and making campaign contributions.

The U.S. government has clearly decided that transparency about the content of people's food is in the public interest. Whether that means caloric, fat, or vitamin content, or the presence of common allergens, company's must bear the cost of testing their foods and providing honest labeling.

ANSWER THE TOPIC ESSENTIAL QUESTION

1. In one to three paragraphs, explain how perfectly competitive markets allocate resources efficiently, while imperfect competition often results in market inefficiencies.

KEY TERMS

private cost	marginal social cost	productive inefficiency
market power	marginal private cost	allocative efficiency
social costs	marginal private benefit	dynamic inefficiency
economic efficiency	profit maximization	Pareto efficient
marginal social benefit	externalities	rational agents

MULTIPLE-CHOICE QUESTIONS

1. If it costs a farmer $500 to plant an acre of soybeans, yet the use of fertilizers causes $200 worth of damage to the environment, what is the marginal social cost?

   (A) $200

   (B) $300

   (C) $500

   (D) $700

   (E) $900

2. If it costs a farmer $500 to plant an acre of soybeans, yet the use of fertilizers causes $200 worth of damage to the environment, what is the marginal private cost?

   (A) $200

   (B) $300

   (C) $500

   (D) $700

   (E) $900

3. Which shows a rational agent making a socially efficient decision?

   (A) a carpenter using substandard wood to build a house

   (B) a car company installing better braking systems on all its models

   (C) an airline ignoring federal safety guidelines

   (D) a grocery store using uncalibrated produce scales

   (E) a housing developer who refuses to cooperate with zoning laws

FREE-RESPONSE QUESTION

1. A local chemical factory sells products all over the globe that help with cleaning floors. The factory is situated on a river that borders several small towns in the area. It has been found through governmental studies that the byproducts of the chemical plant are harming the river.

    (a) Give an example of one possible spillover effect (external cost) of the chemical factory.

    (b) Which rational actor can force the factory to stop polluting?

    (c) Does the chemical company have to take into account the collective well-being of society? Explain your answer.

    (d) Identify the type of economic inefficiency illustrated in this problem.

    (e) Identify one governmental action that would likely decrease the amount of pollution produced by the chemical factory.

THINK AS AN ECONOMIST: *USE ECONOMIC PRINCIPLES TO EXPLAIN HOW A SPECIFIC OUTCOME OCCURS*

Economists use economic principles to explain why economic actors make the decisions that they make. One of those principles is that economic actors are rational actors.

Apply the Skill

Biggs Pharma owns the exclusive rights to a new prescription medication that provides quicker and longer-lasting relief to asthma sufferers than other asthma drugs on the market. More than 25 million Americans suffer from asthma. Biggs charges $100 a dose for a biweekly dose of the medication. That price gives Biggs a $50 profit from the medication but precludes 15 percent of the market from being able to afford it.

What principle explains Biggs' pricing decision? How would you describe this situation in terms of market efficiency and social efficiency?

Externalities

"If you're in a system where you must make profit in order to survive, you're compelled to ignore negative externalities, effects on others."
—Noam Chomsky, U.S. linguist, historian, cognitive scientist (b. 1928)

Essential Question: What are externalities, how do they impact markets, and what actions might be taken to correct for externalities?

A firm that makes automated phone calls, or robocalls, is a particular type of supplier. Its customers are other firms, ones that want to advertise a good or service. A sign that robocalls are successful for the supplier and the consumer is that in 2018, firms produced almost 60 billion robocalls in the United States. That was almost enough for one call every other day for every adult and every child in the United States.

However, in addition to the primary transaction between the supplier and the customer, all those robocalls in 2018 had important effects on others. In particular, they affected the people receiving the calls. Many found the calls so annoying that they simply stopped answering their phone if they did not recognize the caller's number. Further, they demanded that the government attempt to regulate these calls. People receiving the calls felt they suffered a cost, even though they were not part of the first transaction. Their frustration was not figured into the cost paid by the original consumers for the product.

Negative Externalities

The societal side effects of robocalls are an example of an **externality**, an effect on people other than producers and consumers directly involved in the transaction. Externalities can be either benefits or costs. When analyzing the production side of an economic transaction, economists tend to focus on the **negative externalities**, harmful costs to society paid by a third party. Clear examples of negative externalities, such as air pollution from a factory or from burning coal, result from the decisions by individuals running businesses.

However, individuals also make personal decisions that affect others. Even just taking an antibiotic to treat an illness has negative externalities. The widespread use of modern antibiotics has been one of the most important life-saving revolutions in medical care. Before the development of penicillin and other drugs in the mid-20th century, many serious bacterial infections such as pneumonia and meningitis were difficult to treat and even minor scratches could cause deadly infections. Today, when someone takes an antibiotic, that person benefits by getting healthier more quickly, sometimes by avoiding death. So, a doctor has a strong incentive to prescribe antibiotics, even when their value is unclear. The Centers for Disease Control concluded in 2018 that at least 30 percent of antibiotic prescribed were unnecessary.

Extensive use of antibiotics comes with a cost. It contributes to the development of disease strains that are harder to treat. These strains put everyone at risk. By 2020, the CDC estimated that 35,000 people in the United States died annually from antibiotic-resistant bacteria or fungi. That is about the same number as die from car accidents. Fearing a future with untreatable diseases, the CDC and other medical organizations have issued guidelines to reduce antibiotic use.

Doctors first used penicillin widely during World War II to save the lives of wounded U.S. soldiers. Most of the country's supply of penicillin at that time was grown from mold that first developed on a cantaloupe (similar to the one shown) at a federal government research facility in Peoria, Illinois.

Lack of Property Rights The failure to account for negative externalities when people take antibiotics leads to their overconsumption, a type of a market failure. Another type of market failure occurs when ignoring negative externalities leads to overproduction, as when a factory produces air pollution. Both types of failures are more likely to occur when no one has well-defined property rights that they can defend. For example, who is the owner of the air that a factory pollutes? Who can claim the general health of people in a community or country as a property right? If no one can demonstrate that an action is violating their property rights, then the government often steps in on behalf of the public.

Transaction Costs One reason for negative externalities is high **transaction costs**, the expenses that occur when something is bought or sold. For example, when buying a house, the total costs to the purchaser are usually the price of the house plus 5 percent to 10 percent for fees for real estate agents, lawyers, surveyors, and others, as well as taxes. The higher the transaction costs, the greater the incentive for purchasers to avoid paying for externalities.

Although producers know the economic cost of negative externalities, it's common for them to pass those costs on to third parties not involved in the transaction. As a consequence, these manufacturers maximize profits by having lower marginal costs.

Negative Externalities and Consumers Still, manufacturers are not the only ones in a market that benefit from negative externalities. Most consumers don't take into account the overall impact to society of their decisions. Consumers often act in their own self-interest as long as their marginal cost equals their marginal benefit. Sometimes they consume a good, such as buying a new carbon fiber tennis racquet or using electricity from a coal-fired power plant, which impacts third parties in a negative way.

Negative externalities, like positive externalities, can be graphed. Look at the supply/demand graph below for negative externalities in production. As you can see, in the private market, the marginal private benefits (MPB) equal the marginal private costs (MPC) at an output of Q1. This means that the private market produces an amount of output of Q1. You should also see that the MPB and marginal social benefits (MSB) are the same; this means there are no external benefits. Negative externalities create additional costs, marginal external costs (MEC), which are added to the MPC, resulting in a marginal social cost (MSC) curve that is shifted to the left of MPC. When the external cost is considered, the socially optimal output is Q2. This shows that the private market over-produces the good and over-allocates resources to produce the good. There is also a deadweight loss to society as a result of the negative externality.

NEGATIVE EXTERNALITY IN PRODUCTION

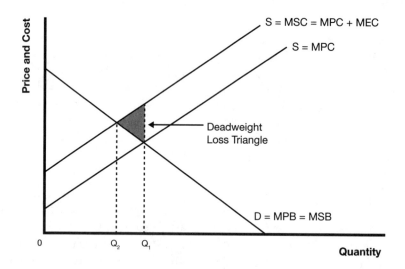

Other Examples Negative externalities come in many forms. Some are less obvious than air pollution.

- *Traffic congestion* Too many drivers on the road can lead to traffic jams, which result in car accidents, wasted time, and health-related costs from stress.
- *Neglected property* Properties that fall into disrepair can have a negative impact on the property values of nearby homes and businesses.

- *Poor health practices* People who are unable to, or choose not to, lead healthy lives or to follow public health guidelines often suffer negative outcomes themselves. However, their actions can also increase health risks for others. Further, they can increase health care costs for everyone who pays insurance premiums or taxes.

Responding to Negative Externalities Federal, state, and local governments often implement policies to counteract negative externalities. Various policies attempt to protect the public by allocating the costs of an economic decision to those who benefit from it:

- *Taxes* Imposing taxes on an action is one way to discourage it. Taxes on cigarettes were effective in reducing smoking.

- *Subsidies* Subsidies to firms that provide substitute goods—for example, by helping them to lower costs and therefore prices—can encourage consumers to switch from one good to another. Subsidies for installing solar energy systems can reduce the cost of using solar energy rather than carbon fuels.

- *Environmental regulations* The government can regulate behavior to prevent actions with high negative externalities. This is the goal of many restrictions on releasing waste products into the air or water.

- *Assignment of property rights* Giving a private individual or organization property rights can help minimize negative influences on or outcomes for the property. For example, if the government turns over wilderness land to a nonprofit organization, that organization can defend it from pollution or misuse, just as any other property owner can.

Positive Externalities

Some economic actions produce **positive externalities**, which provide benefits to people not directly involved in the primary economic transaction. They help society in general. Just as economists focus on the negative externalities of production, they focus on the positive externalities of consumption. For example, to become a doctor, a person first consumes the service of a medical education. The transaction of an individual purchasing a medical education has great **private benefits**, positive outcomes for an individual. Some of these are as a high salary, high prestige, and a rewarding career.

In addition, well-trained doctors generate many positive externalities. The patients a doctor cares for remain healthier. Healthy individuals miss less work, make more money, and pay more taxes. So, employers, merchants, and governments all benefit. Because the positive externalities of medical education are so high, many states run medical schools that train doctors at below the market price. In 2019–2020, the average annual cost of medical school for an in-state student at a state-run school was about $38,000. At a private school, it was about $61,000.

Social Benefits Positive externalities occur when **marginal social benefit** is greater than **marginal private benefit**. Economists define social benefit as the total benefit to society from producing or consuming a good or service. It includes all private benefits + **external benefits**. Education is an example of a private benefit for consumers, while for businesses it is increased profits. Economists define external benefits as benefits to a third party not involved in the transaction.

Positive externalities for both consumers and producers can be graphed on a supply/demand curve. The diagram below is a visual representation of a positive externality based on consumption. As you can see, the marginal social benefit is greater than the private marginal benefit.

POSITIVE EXTERNALITIES IN CONSUMPTION

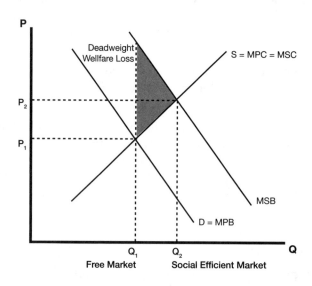

Notice that at Q_1, demand (marginal private benefit) equals supply (marginal private cost), creating a socially inefficient market. Here is why: If a person consumes only at Q_1, **marginal social cost** (MSC) is less than marginal social benefit (MSB). That creates a deadweight loss. But, if you add the external benefit, the socially efficient output increases to Q_2, where marginal social cost equals marginal social benefit.

For producers, positive externalities occur when marginal social cost is less than private marginal cost. When you study the graph that follows, you will see that at Q_1 in a free market, a producer will ignore any benefit to a third party. At Q_2, the firm takes into consideration those third-party benefits. At that point, the market becomes socially efficient because the marginal social cost equals the marginal social benefit. This can be expressed in a formula:

$$MSC = MSB$$

In general, positive externalities create less controversy than do negative externalities. Because they benefit rather than harm others, no one feels hurt by them. However, when people receive benefits from transactions they were not part of, it indicates a limit on the ability of prices to communicate information. The price of the transaction does not fully reflect the value of the transaction to everyone affected by it.

POSITIVE EXTERNALITIES IN PRODUCTION

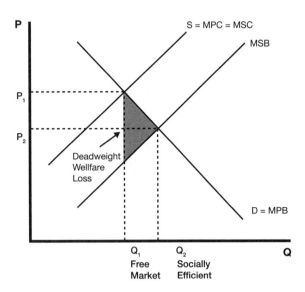

Other Positive Externalities Examples of positive externalities abound. Here are a handful:

1. Getting vaccinated for measles, the flu, or for some other malady benefits other people because you are less likely to contract and then spread disease and they are less likely to get sick.

2. Riding in a subway or bus instead of a car cuts down on pollution, which benefits the health of people and creates less traffic congestion on the roadways because people are driving less.

3. Keeping your home well maintained benefits your neighbors because it increases the market value of their properties.

4. Providing first-aid training as part of a company's benefits to employees can save lives outside the workplace.

Free Riders

In Topic 6.1, you read about rational agents—people who weigh all the costs and benefits associated with a transaction before making a decision. Since most people make decisions based on their own self-interest, a **free rider** problem emerges.

A free rider problem occurs when people use a shared resource but don't pay for it. Workers who commute from their suburban homes into a city are free riders because they don't pay to repair or clean the city's streets or sidewalks. They don't pay for trash pickup or the city's water system, which they use. In other words, the out-of-towners consume a shared resource but pay nothing, or at the very least, less than their fair share. The free rider problem is an example of a market failure because goods and services are inefficiently distributed.

Rational agents are incentivized to become free riders when goods are **non-excludable,** products that are available to others even if they have not paid for them. For example, one of your neighbors is a beekeeper who makes a few dollars producing honey. Beekeeping creates a positive externality because the bees pollinate flower gardens up and down the street at no cost to the neighbors. Pollination is a non-excludable good because the beekeeper cannot produce honey without granting benefits to the rest of the neighborhood.

Free riders and positive externalities walk hand-in-hand in non-excludable situations. Imagine it is the Fourth of July and a local pyrotechnic company is charging a $10 fee to watch fireworks at a local park. The show is a positive externality. Since you don't want to pay the price of admission, you go to your uncle's house down the street to watch the fireworks for free in his backyard even though others are paying for the show. That means you're a free rider.

Government Actions

As you read earlier in Topic 2.8, governments can take actions to address inefficiencies in a market. Governments also intervene to change how businesses and individuals behave.

Correcting Negative Externalities Governments, whether local, state, or federal, often address negative externalities and property rights problems—usually by taxing producers for the social costs. Governments tax both the consumer and producer in an attempt to force them to consider the external costs of their economic actions. You saw that at work in 2017 when Philadelphia imposed its tax on sugary beverages.

Passing laws is another way to combat negative externalities. One example of how this works comes from California, where the state legislature passed a law to regulate greenhouse gas emissions caused by dairy cows.

Cows have a four-chamber stomach including a rumen, where food is digested. As food passes through the rumen, tiny microbes break down and absorb the nutrients contained in the different grasses and feed that cows eat. The microbes do their job, but they produce methane as a waste product, which the cows emit in various ways.

Although the amount of methane in the atmosphere is small compared to carbon dioxide, methane is a more potent greenhouse gas. The U.S. Environmental Protection Agency (EPA) says roughly 33 percent of all methane emissions in the United States are generated on large dairy farms and other livestock operations.

In California, the state's 1.7 million dairy cows are responsible for 19 percent of methane emissions. To cut down on that amount, the state passed a law requiring farmers to reduce emissions from cow manure by building digesters that can turn methane from manure into electricity, which the farmers can then sell to electric companies.

In an effort to comply with legislation in California that regulates heat-trapping gases from livestock operations and landfills, many farmers have installed methane gas digesters to turn the gas, emitted by dairy cows, into useable energy.

Subsidies If a market is failing because MSB does not equal MPB, government intervention can correct for underconsumption of a good. One way is through the use of **subsidies**. Subsidies are government payments that lower the cost of producing a good or service. Subsidies can take many forms. For example, in the midst of the Civil War in the 1860s, the federal government provided private railroad companies more than 12,000 acres and between $16,000 and $48,000 per mile to lay tracks to connect Nebraska and California. Between the 1950s and 1990s, the government spent over $100 billion to build the interstate highway network. Other subsidies have helped build port facilities, canals, and mass transit lines. One goal of these investments in transportation is to promote trade and prosperity.

Encouraging Positive Externalities Like other economic actions, those by government have both positive and negative externalities. When the federal government funded the interstate highway system, towns located near the new roads enjoyed a positive externality. Their hotels, restaurants, and manufacturing plants benefited from being close to new, better roads. However, towns and businesses along older highways suffered a negative externality as travel through them declined. Many of these communities became poorer.

1. In one to three paragraphs, define the two different categories of externalities, how these externalities impact market equilibrium and the allocation of resources, and what actions might reduce externalities.

KEY TERMS

externality	positive externalities	external benefits
negative externalities	private benefits	marginal social cost
transaction costs	marginal social benefit	free rider
deadweight loss	marginal private benefit	subsidies

MULTIPLE-CHOICE QUESTIONS

1. Which of the following is most clearly affected by a good that generates a positive externality?
   (A) Marginal private cost
   (B) Marginal private benefit
   (C) Marginal total benefit
   (D) Productive efficiency
   (E) Social efficiency

2. Which is an example of a negative externality?
   (A) Construction of a sewer plant that cleans wastewater from a new housing development
   (B) The removal of an abandoned building in a neighborhood
   (C) The application of a new medical technique that can detect cancerous cells
   (D) A chemical leak from a factory that poisons local wells
   (E) The sale of electric cars

3. Which statement best describes marginal social benefit?
   (A) Benefits to all stakeholders in society from producing or consuming a good or service
   (B) Benefits received by a third party not involved in the transaction
   (C) Benefits enjoyed by producers when a market under-consumes a positive externality
   (D) Benefits enjoyed by consumers who weigh all the costs associated with a transaction before making a decision
   (E) Benefits enjoyed by producers in socially efficient markets

1. Study the graph and answer the questions that follow.

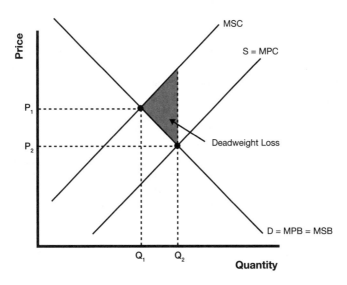

(a) Identify the quantity that would be produced by the market with no government intervention.

(b) Assume that current production is at Q_1. Is this quantity produced socially (allocatively) efficient? Explain.

(c) Would the amount produced at Q_2 produce deadweight loss?

(d) Suppose that the government decides to put a per-unit tax on this industry. Identify the change this effect would have on equilibrium price and quantity.

(e) Instead of a per-unit tax, what other actions could government take to deal with the industry?

Governments can use various strategies to push markets to socially efficient points so that marginal social cost and marginal social benefit meet. It can impose taxes on producers, which means they make up the difference between marginal private cost and marginal social cost. It can put caps on production, driving down marginal social cost. It can also subsidize consumption, which can drive up demand to a level needed for social efficiency.

Apply the Skill

Suppose that the federal government determines that it is in society's interests for homeowners to have energy-efficient windows. Preventing the inflow of hot air in summer and cold air in winter will cut down energy consumption in home cooling and heating systems. Draw a supply and demand curve that shows the original demand for energy-efficient windows and the demand with the subsidy. Show and label market quantity and socially efficient quantity, supply and the area covered by the subsidy.

Public and Private Goods

"Whenever there's something that affects the public good, then there does need to be some form of public oversight."

—Elon Musk (b. 1971), entrepreneur involved in SpaceX, Tesla, and PayPal

Essential Question: Why can markets supply only private goods efficiently?

Murphy's Shoes has a sale every spring in honor of St. Patrick's Day. Knowing this, you might wait until you see its sign "30 percent off on all athletic shoes! This week only!" before you purchase new shoes. However, some goods and services never go on sale. You purchase fire protection from your local government through taxes. The fire department never puts up a sign "30 percent off on all firefighting! This week only!" Shoes and fire protection are very different types of products.

- Shoes are one example of a **private good,** an item or service produced and marketed to individual consumers.
- Fire protection is a **public good,** an item or service available to the general public.

Private Goods and Public Goods

It can be difficult to understand economic news about inflation, stock markets, and recessions. However, when you have a solid understanding of how private goods and public goods differ, you will be better able to comprehend why people and markets act the way they do.

Private Goods Did you buy a snack on the way home from school yesterday? If so, you probably purchased a private good. Private goods are **excludable**, which means that the person or organization providing the good can stop people who do not pay for it. That means that if you go to a convenience store and ask for a banana without paying for it, then the cashier won't give it to you.

Private goods are also **rival** in consumption. In other words, they get used up. If you eat that banana, then there will be one fewer for other customers to purchase and eat. If bananas become more popular, then private suppliers will charge more for them.

Much of the time, private markets do an effective job supplying private goods. Because they are excludable and rival, private goods are relatively easy to track, and it is possible to motivate consumers to purchase them. (You have probably seen signs that say "Exclusive Distributor" and "While Supplies Last.") But economic markets also include public goods, and that makes things a little more complicated.

Public Goods You have probably consumed public goods and services this week. Did you use tap water to shower or brush your teeth? Did you drive on a public road or use a sidewalk? What about breathing clean air?

Many public goods are non-excludable because their providers cannot, or do not, stop people from using them, even if those people didn't pay for them. For example, an adult who pays no taxes can still benefit from streetlights. Municipalities have no practical way to detect who has paid taxes and allow only those people to benefit from well-lit streets. Rival, non-excludable goods are also called common goods.

Public goods also tend to be **non-rival**, meaning that lots of people can use them at the same time without the goods being used up. If your community spends money putting filters on its trash incinerators, then you will benefit from breathing cleaner air. But no matter how much clean air you breathe, there will still be plenty of it left for others in your community. Excludable, non-rival goods are also known as club goods or toll goods.

TYPES OF GOODS AND SERVICES		
	Rival	**Non-rival**
Excludable	• Food • Clothing • Houses and apartments • Tickets to sporting events • Paperback books	• Apps • Software • Streaming services • On-demand TV shows • E-books
Non-excludable	• Firefighters • Police • Clean water • Public libraries • Public parks	• National defense • Clean air • Streetlights • Lighthouses

When Public Goods Become Private Sometimes market forces affect whether a good or service is public or private. For example, wildfires raged in California in 2019. Some wealthy people there paid for private firefighters, even though local communities offered firefighting services to everyone. This issue became controversial. Some people criticized those who hired private firefighters, while others said it was a reasonable measure in an area where wildfires are so frequent and fierce.

Much of Southern California is vulnerable to wildfires, especially during periods of drought.

Free Riders and Public Goods

What happens when a good is public instead of private? Often, people are unwilling to pay anything for it. Although most people know that it costs money to clean up water so that it is drinkable, they are uninterested in paying a local government or donating to a private charity to help with that cleanup. After all, every person's resources are scarce, and there are so many other things to do with that money—such as pay for private goods and services.

Free Riders and Commonly Held Resources As you learned in Topic 6.2, someone who uses a public good or service without contributing to it is a free rider. A historical example of a free rider has to do with common lands. In colonial times, the city of Boston and many other communities had commons where anyone could graze sheep, goats, or cattle. However, if a few community members allowed their entire flocks or herds to graze there, then those animals would eat all the grass. Because of the actions of a few free riders, the land would be useless for its intended purpose. For this reason, in 1646 Boston limited the number of cows allowed on Boston Common to 70 at a time.

Government Production of Public Goods What happens when private individuals and companies refuse to pay for public goods? In many cases, the government steps in. A local, state, or national government may decide to produce private goods and make them available publicly. Instead of people paying for what they use, everyone pays a relatively small amount in taxes or fees. Because of free riders, it is difficult to adequately assess demand for these goods. Therefore private producers likely under-produce these goods.

Why do governments fund public goods and services? In most cases, these publicly funded items contribute to the greater good of society as a whole. After all, it says in the preamble to the U.S. Constitution that one of the reasons for establishing the country's government is to "promote the general welfare." A community of well-educated, healthy, safe people is more likely to be productive and content—continuing to support and maintain the government in its present form.

Comparing Public and Private Services Sometimes public and private services compete in the marketplace. For example, say you are considering what to do after high school. You have done well in your courses and on standardized tests, and you feel ready and able to attend a prestigious four-year university. Would you choose a publicly funded school (such as the University of California at Berkeley) or a privately funded school (such as Stanford University)?

Both schools are expensive, but Berkeley costs much less if you are an in-state student. (Both schools also offer scholarships and financial aid, so in either case you might pay much less than the official price.) Both schools are exclusive, attracting a far higher number of highly qualified applicants than they can admit.

What does this comparison say about microeconomics? It shows that even when publicly funded options are available, some producers may develop private alternatives that are popular and highly desired. Even though tap water is widely available, some people choose to pay for bottled or boxed water because they perceive it as better-tasting, purer, or just more convenient. Both of these examples show that the existence of rival or excludable goods influences the behavior of individuals and groups.

A national park and an amusement park are examples of public and private services that compete in the marketplace.

Government Regulation of Natural Resources

Who decides how many people will be allowed to hike in a park or fish in a stream? In some cases, the land is privately owned, and its owners decide how many people to allow in and how much to charge. In many cases, however, it is the local, state, or federal government that monitors the use—and limits the overuse—of natural resources.

Open Access Resources Some natural resources are inherently non-excludable and rival. Economists refer to these as open access resources. They include national parks and some state and local parks. They are non-excludable because they are so large and rugged that it is not practical to fence them off and guard them, and they are rival because it is possible to use them up.

For instance, Yellowstone National Park is vast, with almost 3,500 square miles of wilderness in Wyoming, Montana, and Idaho—more than 2 million acres. However, the park hosts more than four million recreational visitors most years. If that number increases substantially, then natural resources in the park may be used up, and trash and waste may overwhelm the facilities there.

Private Individuals and Open Access Resources What happens to these non-excludable, rival resources? Some private individuals inefficiently overconsume them—in other words, they use them without regard for whether someone else will be able to regenerate or replace them.

Even though these resources are non-excludable, governments can take steps to control individual overconsumption. For example, governments can charge money for hunting licenses and fishing licenses. They can also limit the amount of hunting or fishing that any one person can do, and they can impose fines or other punishments on people who hunt or fish for endangered species. For example, the Key deer of southern Florida are so endangered that someone who kills one faces a fine up to $100,000 and up to one year in prison.

ANSWER THE TOPIC ESSENTIAL QUESTION

1. In one to three paragraphs, explain why markets supply only private goods efficiently. What types of goods and services do governments often supply instead and why?

KEY TERMS

private goods	excludable	non-excludable
public goods	rival	non-rival

1. Which of these are examples of excludable, rival goods and services?

   (A) Public elementary schools, bus shelters, water fountains

   (B) Video game online subscriptions, national parks, free medical clinics

   (C) Traffic signals, guardrails, crosswalks

   (D) Video game consoles, private ambulances, an indoor climbing wall at a gym

   (E) Online subscriptions to newspapers or magazines, unmetered public parking lots

2. A local government is considering offering free job training in computer coding to local residents. What economic argument would provide the best support to offering the training?

   (A) Coding training is a private good, but it makes sense for local government to produce it and allow free access to it if doing so would provide significant benefits to the community.

   (B) Coding training is a public good, and it is difficult or impossible for private institutions to provide it effectively because it is a non-rival good.

   (C) Creating a program that teaches coding to anyone who wants to learn eliminates the problem of free riders who inefficiently overconsume resources.

   (D) Private institutions lack the incentive to create coding classes, so public institutions such as local governments must do what others cannot for the overall good of the people.

   (E) The intelligence and initiative involved in learning to code are natural resources, so it makes sense for local governments to manage and use those resources effectively.

3. NASA and the United Nations have both expressed concern about space debris, also known as space junk. According to NASA, more than half a million pieces of space debris currently orbit Earth, threatening satellites and the International Space Station. How would an economist classify outer space in this example?

   (A) As an excludable resource

   (B) As a public service

   (C) As an open access resource

   (D) As a public good that has become private

   (E) As a private good that has become public

1. In an effort to boost revenue, a local school is considering a proposal from community members that would fence in the current running track and put in place membership fees for community members to use it.

   (a) Does the track feature shared or rival consumption? Explain.

   (b) What type of good is the current, unfenced track? Explain.

   (c) If the proposal is accepted, the fence is installed, and membership fees are collected, what type of good is the track now?

   (d) Identify one possible negative externality the track might generate if the proposal is rejected.

   (e) Identify one possible positive externality the track might generate if the proposal is accepted.

THINK AS AN ECONOMIST: *IDENTIFY AN ECONOMIC CONCEPT ILLUSTRATED BY AN EXAMPLE*

Economists say that private goods tend to be excludable and rival whereas public goods tend to be non-excludable and non-rival. These distinctions affect consumption patterns—and how many individuals can benefit from the good.

Apply the Skill

The city of Springfield has a number of swim clubs with limited membership and membership fees. It also has a public beach open to all residents for free, though visitors from other communities have to pay a tag fee to enter the beach. Explain how these examples illustrate the differences between public and private goods in terms of excludability and rival suppliers.

The Effects of Government Intervention in Different Market Structures

"Monopolies are inconsistent with our form of government. . . . If we will not endure a king as a political power, we should not endure a king over the production, transportation, and sale of any of the necessaries of life."

—John Sherman, Ohio senator, c. 1880

Essential Question: How can well-designed government policies reduce waste in imperfect markets?

Imagine you go to a grocery store to buy a three-pound bag of apples. Like most consumers, you will probably make your choice based on factors such as price and quality. You probably won't think about whether the scale at the store is accurate, whether the apples are safe to eat, whether the store purchased apples from the supplier legally, or if the store will even accept your cash. These are issues that the government takes care of. Using the taxes you pay, the government sets the framework for competition. However, the government does not set the price for apples nor require that stores even sell apples. It leaves those decisions to market forces.

Government intervention occurs even in the freest of markets, but how a government intervenes varies greatly depending on the market structure. In a highly competitive market, such as the one for apples, it might intervene lightly, setting only very basic rules. In a market that is nearly a monopoly or a monopsony, though, it might intervene heavily. The choices about government intervention can have a large influence on how efficiently a market operates.

Reasons for Government Intervention in Imperfect Markets

Why would a government intervene in a market? In general, the market will approach an equilibrium without extensive direct intervention. Buyers and sellers will decide what prices they can each accept. In some situations, though, governments often intervene in **imperfect markets**, ones with neither perfect competition nor pure monopoly.

Equity Markets tend to be efficient: Sellers use the fewest resources possible to make a product or service that someone else will want. However, most people and governments believe that equity is important. In other words, people should be treated fairly.

For example, the most efficient way for a contractor to build bathrooms would be to make them small, using the fewest materials possible to make the most bathrooms possible. But a person who uses a wheelchair, walker, or scooter needs a bigger bathroom to maneuver in. Most people agree that public bathrooms should be available to all. Even if you do not use a wheelchair, you may be concerned about people who do, or you may realize that you could need a wheelchair someday. So the government passes laws such as the Americans with Disabilities Act to ensure that a certain number of wheelchair-accessible bathrooms, sinks, showers, and water fountains are available in workplaces, restaurants, hotels, and other locations. The government interferes in the market to achieve a certain basic level of equity.

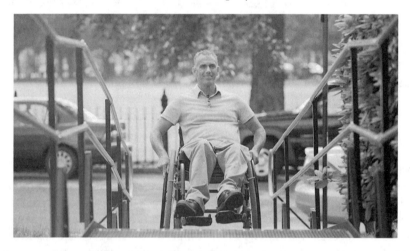

Mandatory construction of ramps for people who have physical difficulty using stairs is another example of a government intervention in the name of equity.

Breaking Up Monopolies Sometimes a single person or company achieves a monopoly or near-monopoly on a product or service. Customers for that good or service must either pay high prices or do without, which makes that market inefficient and wasteful. In these cases, a government may decide to intervene to bring about lower prices for consumers.

One of the most famous examples of this in U.S. history was the **Sherman Antitrust Act**. In 1890, the U.S. government passed this law, which makes most monopolies illegal. The law also forbids businesses from working together to keep prices artificially high, limit outputs, or exclude competition. Businesses and labor unions have faced punishments and fines because of this law. Whether a business or labor practice violates the act is up to the courts and the U.S. Federal Trade Commission (FTC) to decide.

This law from 1890 is still in force. Over the decades, the federal government has used the law to increase competition by challenging one company's domination of an industry. Major enforcements have affected the oil, camera, phone, and credit card industries. Sometimes the lack of competition affects only one specific part of an industry. For example, in the early 2000s, Microsoft's internet browser controlled about 95 percent of the market, in part because it was bundled with Microsoft's popular operating system. The government ruled that bundling the browser with the operating system illegally prevented other companies from selling competing browsers. It ordered Microsoft to sell its operating system and browser separately. This made it easier for other companies, such as Google, Apple, and Mozilla to enter the browser market.

Different Methods of Government Intervention

If government leaders decide a particular market is inefficient, wasteful, or otherwise harmful to people, what can the leaders do about it? A government can pass a law, and a government agency can file a lawsuit, but other methods are available.

Per-Unit Taxes and Subsidies A per-unit tax (also called an excise tax) is one that a government imposes each time you buy a certain good or service. "Why would the government make me pay more money for something?" you might ask. Sometimes governments see an inefficiency or wastefulness that the market is not accounting for.

For instance, when people buy a lot of cigarettes or alcohol, they may develop long-term health problems that the government may end up partially or fully paying for. So most governments impose a per-unit tax on these items. The more you buy, the more you pay, and the more the government collects. The tax increases the marginal cost for a consumer buying cigarettes. The higher cost should discourage consumption.

Sometimes the government also offers per-unit subsidies, such as a tax break if you buy an electric car or another device that is less polluting than its rivals.

What effects do these per-unit taxes and subsidies have?

- *Total price* These taxes and subsidies affect the total price you and others pay for the item.

- *Net price* They also affect how much the producer receives. The producer may pass all of the cost or benefit on to the buyer, or the producer may absorb some of it.

- *Equilibrium quantity* This is the point at which supply meets demand. If the government imposes a per-unit tax, then the quantity demanded may decrease because the overall price is higher. If the government offers a per-unit subsidy, then quantity demanded may increase.

- *Consumer and producer surpluses* As the equilibrium quantity changes, the excess amounts of goods or services may change too.

- *Deadweight loss* This refers to the cost that society pays because a market is inefficient. For example, consumers may decide not to buy a good or service that has a high per-unit tax on it, which means that producers do not get to produce as much of that good or service as they normally would.

- *Government revenue or cost* Imposing per-unit costs can bring in significant money for governments, and providing subsidies can reduce the amount of money available for a state to spend. For example, every gallon of gas sold includes state and local taxes. In some states, these taxes are dedicated to repairing and building roads. If gas taxes are low, then governments may not have enough to repair roads—but if they are high, then consumers may avoid driving.

How much of a difference will these taxes or subsidies make? That depends in part on elasticity. You learned in Unit 2 that some products and services are elastic (a change in price makes a big difference to the quantity supplied or quantity demanded) and some are inelastic (a change in price makes little difference).

Lump-Sum Taxes and Subsidies A lump-sum tax or subsidy is the same no matter what actions people take. For instance, the government might decide that all pig farmers must pay a lump-sum tax because runoff from feeding lots can contaminate water supplies. Farmers who have only a few dozen pigs would most likely protest a lump-sum tax because they would have to pay the same amount as farmers who have thousands of pigs.

A lump-sum tax or subsidy does not affect marginal costs or marginal benefits because each producer pays the same amount. But it affects fixed costs, and therefore total costs, because it changes the dollar amount required to produce each unit of a good or service, and the producer must decide how much of those costs or savings to pass on to consumers.

Price Ceilings and Price Floors You already know from Topic 2.8 that even in free-market economies, governments sometimes impose price ceilings (the most a producer can charge for a good or service) and price floors (the least a producer can charge for a good or service). In the 1970s, in response to a shutoff of imports by several oil-producing countries, the U.S. government temporarily set limits on how much a company could charge for a gallon of gasoline. And you know about price floors such as a minimum wage—the least an organization can pay a worker.

Imposing limits on rent costs or gas prices might address a short run problem, such as an oil crisis, but price ceilings and price floors make a market inefficient in the long run. The effects these controls have depend on the type of market.

Price Controls and Perfectly Competitive Markets If a city's apartment rental market is almost perfectly competitive, there are lots of buyers and sellers, which means the market (rather than a few buyers or a few sellers) sets the price. What happens if that city's government imposes a price ceiling on the monthly cost of an apartment?

- **Quantity demanded will increase:** More people will decide to, and will be able to afford to, rent their own apartments rather than living with family or friends.

- **Quantity supplied will decrease:** Some apartment owners will decide that the profit they make from renting out units is not sufficient to justify their work as landlords.
- **Quality may decrease:** Renters may be willing to put up with lower quality because of the price, and owners may not have as much money to improve the quality of units.

The following graph shows how this scenario would play out.

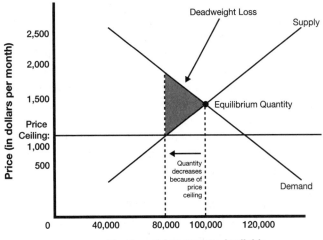

What the Graph Means The dot right in the middle of this graph is the equilibrium quantity—what buyers and sellers settle on when there is no government interference. If the government set the price ceiling at $1,800, it would not matter because the equilibrium would stay where it was. But in this case, the government has set the price ceiling below the equilibrium quantity, which means the ceiling is **binding**. In other words, it changes how buyers and sellers behave. In this case, the quantity exchanged in the market decreases because producers reduce the quantity supplied due to the below equilibrium price set by the ceiling. In addition, because of the below-equilibrium price ceiling, the quantity demanded will increase since the price of the good has been reduced. Adding these together creates a shortage of the good or service.

What would happen if the government sets a price floor on a market price, such as a minimum wage? The quantity exchanged in the market will decrease because the price has been set above the equilibrium price. Thus, the price floor is binding. With a price floor above the equilibrium price, producers react by increasing the quantity supplied, but the amount purchased by consumers declines because of the higher price. This results in a surplus of the good or service.

Government Regulation of Monopolies

While government interference often makes markets less efficient in order to serve another goal for society, sometimes government interferes to make markets more efficient. Monopolies are by nature inefficient because one person or organization, not the market, sets the price for a good or service.

Government Regulation Can Increase or Decrease Efficiency If a government regulates prices on a monopoly, then that market may become more efficient. Consumers will be able to obtain that good or service at a lower price, and producers will still make enough profit to make it worth their while to be in the market. However, to be successful, the price regulation must correctly address the incentives that led to the market failure.

About one-seventh of the people in the United States in 2020 had access to only one internet service provider. Most lived in rural communities, where low population density made providing service more expensive. In these areas, prices are higher than they would be if the provider faced competition. Monopoly makes the market inefficient.

To make the market more competitive and efficient, the government could encourage other providers to enter it by offering a subsidy or tax break. This approach might result in lower internet prices for some people, but it would require raising taxes or cutting expenses on other government programs.

These rules also apply when a government is considering regulation of a monopsony or a type of monopolistic competition. As with monopolies, these situations require careful consideration of consumers' needs and providers' desire to make a profit and the various effects of any action.

Government Regulation of Natural Monopolies Topic 4.2 explained that in a natural monopoly the costs of entry are so high that one supplier can deliver a good or service at a lower cost than could multiple competing firms. That is, a second provider could not make a profit entering the market. Providing water to homes and business is a natural monopoly. The cost of building a system of water tanks, pumps, and pipes is enormous. Once one provider has done it, a second provider would have difficulty competing. Because water is a natural monopoly, most water systems in the country are run by local governments.

However, about one-fourth of local governments contract with private businesses to provide water. This allows governments to regulate the business. Governments want to keep the monopoly performing at an allocatively efficient quantity, which means that the price is at least as much as the marginal cost of production. The price is high enough that the supplier can make what the government considers a fair profit but low enough that customers can afford to purchase the water. To do this, governments often pay a lump-sum subsidy to the provider that has a natural monopoly. A government does not want to spend its scarce resources on a service provider. But if that service provider has a natural monopoly, then it might decide not to produce at all for that community if there is government intervention.

1. In one to three paragraphs, explain how well-designed government policies can reduce waste in imperfect markets. What steps can government leaders take to control inefficient markets, and why do those steps work?

KEY TERMS

imperfect markets   Sherman Antitrust Act   binding

MULTIPLE-CHOICE QUESTIONS

1. The city of Birminghampton is currently providing a yearly lump-sum subsidy to two local electric car manufacturers, which generate several positive externalities. What effect(s) will this subsidy have?
    i. Decrease ATC of the car manufacturers
    ii. Increase market efficiency
    iii. Decrease MC of the car manufacturers
    iv. Increase deadweight loss

   (A) i only
   (B) ii only
   (C) i and ii only
   (D) i, ii, and iii only
   (E) i, ii, iii, and iv

2. The government decides to increase the minimum wage. With the new higher minimum wage, the wage paid to workers will _____, the quantity supplied will likely _____, and the quantity demanded will likely _____.
   (A) increase; increase; increase
   (B) decrease; decrease; decrease
   (C) increase; increase; decrease
   (D) decrease; decrease; increase
   (E) decrease; increase; increase

3. Which of the following government interventions would be most likely to provide increased profit for a company that sells electric cars?

(A) Impose a price floor on the market

(B) Impose a price ceiling on the market

(C) Impose an excise tax on the company

(D) Provide a lump-sum subsidy to the company

(E) Increase regulations on the electric car industry

FREE-RESPONSE QUESTIONS

1. Your state elects a new governor, who is a dairy farmer. To protect her industry, she imposes a price floor on cow's milk throughout the state. The least any store can charge for cow's milk is $5 per gallon. Review the graph below, which shows the impact of the price floor. Then answer the questions.

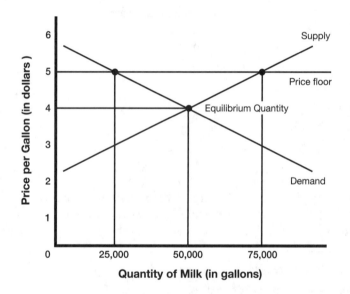

(a) Is this price floor binding? Explain.

(b) Does the price floor on the diagram above create a shortage, a surplus, or neither? Of how many units? Show your work.

(c) As a result of the price floor, are sales of milk likely to increase, decrease, or stay the same? Explain.

(d) Calculate the dollar value of consumer surplus after the imposition of the price floor in the market above. Show your work.

(e) If the government later decides to remove the price floor, will quantity demanded increase, decrease, or stay the same?

Economists can demonstrate the effects of a change by using accurately labeled graphs. Doing so requires them to answer three questions:

- What variable in the situation changed?
- What effect did that change have on economic outcomes?
- How can we illustrate that change and the effect on a visual?

As you have read in this topic, a lump-sum tax or subsidy doesn't affect marginal costs or but does affect fixed costs. In the case of a tax, the tax changes the cost required to produce each unit of a good or service. The producer must decide how much of those costs or savings to pass on to consumers.

Apply the Skill

When there is no tax, a perfectly competitive firm will have a supply curve that looks like the graph below. In this graph ATC is average total cost and MC is marginal cost. Because the market is perfectly competitive, marginal revenue (MR) equals demand (D), which also equals average revenue (AR) and price (P).

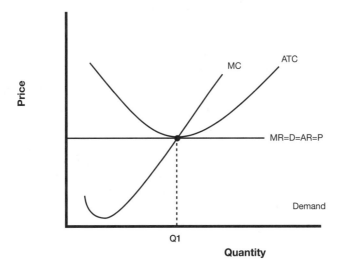

A lump-sum tax will have an effect on a firm's production costs. Graph the changes, if any, to MC and ATC and explain why they occur. Also explain the impact of the tax on the firm's total profit and on demand.

Topic 6.5

Inequality

"I believe that if you want to fight inequality you have to do it starting at infancy."

—Michelle Bachelet (b. 1951), pediatrician and first female president of Chile

Essential Question: How and why do market outcomes result in inequality?

In economics, **inequality** means that some people, groups, regions, and nations have more resources or wealth than others do. Few topics in economics generate such strong debates as those over the role of inequality in an economic system and whether it is an issue that government should address. Economists use various tools to measure inequality, its effects, and how public policies increase or decrease it.

Measuring Economic Inequality

How can people know how economically equal—or unequal—individuals in a neighborhood, city, or country really are? Outward appearance is not reliable. Some people emphasize showing off wealth to others, while others emphasize downplaying one's wealth.

Economists have developed different ways to measure the spread of income. One uses an income level to identify who is poor. Another, commonly shown on a graph, reflects income inequality across different groups, countries, and time periods. The third uses a single number to summarize wealth distribution.

Identifying Poverty In the United States, the primary statistics used by the federal government to measure the number of people considered poor is the federal **poverty level,** or poverty line. It is the annual income that the government determines that an individual, family, or household needs to pay for food, housing, utilities, and other necessities.

In 2019, the federal poverty level for a family of four was $25,750. (It was slightly higher in Alaska and Hawaii because the cost of goods was higher in those states.) According to this measure, the official **poverty rate,** the percentage of people living below the poverty level, was 10.5 percent.

The Lorenz Curve One way to express the amount of inequality in a society is to show it in a graph. In 1905, the American economist Max Lorenz developed the **Lorenz curve** to show what percentage of a population controls what percentage of that society's income or wealth.

Income and wealth aren't the same. **Income inequality** is based on measuring the money people receive in salaries and wages. **Wealth inequality** is based on measuring the value of what people own, such as homes, land, cars, boats, art, stocks, bonds, and savings. Following are examples of Lorenz curves.

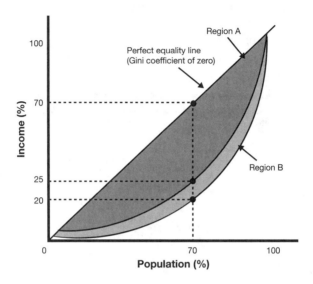

Notice the diagonal line. In an entirely equal society, 60 percent of the population would earn 60 percent of the income, 70 percent of the population would earn 70 percent of the income, and so on.

Comparethe Lorenz curves of two societies, Region A and Region B :

- In region A, 70 percent of the population earns only 25 percent of the income. That means big earners in the remaining 30 percent of the population earn the other 75 percent.

- In region B, the inequality is even more extreme: 70 percent of the population earns only 20 percent of the income. So, the wider the curve is from the diagonal line, the higher the degree of inequality in that society.

Gini Coefficient In 1912, the Italian statistician Corrado Gini developed the **Gini coefficient**—a relatively simple way to represent levels of income inequality in societies. It measures the distribution of wealth (or some other quality or possession) throughout a population. It uses a scale that goes from 0 to 1, with the higher the number, the greater the inequality. At 0, everyone would have the exact same amount of wealth. For example, in a population of 100 people, 1 person would have 1 percent of the wealth, 2 people would have 2 percent, and so on, up to 100 people having 100 percent of the wealth. If some individuals had more or less than 1 percent of the wealth, then the Gini coefficient would be greater than 0. At the most extreme, all wealth would be held by one person. That is, 1 person would have 0 percent of the wealth, 2 people would have 0 percent, and so on, up to 99 people having 0 percent of the wealth, and the 100th person having 100 percent of the wealth. The global average is around 0.39.

Economists often use the Gini coefficient to compare economic inequality between different countries. You could also use it to compare economic inequality in a region of the world, a state, a city, or even a neighborhood. The following table shows the Gini coefficient for several countries, including some of the lowest and highest numbers.

GINI COEFFICIENT FOR SELECTED COUNTRIES	
Gini coefficient	Country (year)
0.27	Norway (2017)
0.33	Switzerland (2017)
0.39	China (2016)
0.48	United States (2019)
0.41	Argentina (2018)
0.45	Mexico (2018)
0.51	Angola (2018)

Source: World Bank

One limit to the Gini coefficient is that it measures only the distribution of wealth, not the overall level of wealth, in a country. A country where everyone is poor and a country where everyone is rich could have the same Gini coefficient. For example, Canada and Vietnam have similar Gini coefficients, but Canada is much wealthier overall.

Gini coefficients change over time. In the United States, the number increased from 0.34 in 1979 to 0.48 by 2019. This indicates that economic inequality rose significantly in those 40 years.

Using the Lorenz Curve and the Gini Coefficient Economists often use Lorenz curves and Gini coefficients to measure differences between countries. However, it's possible to use both tools to measure inequality in other groups:

- The same country or society during different time periods
- Men and women in the same society
- Different racial or ethnic groups or different language speakers in the same society
- Different age groups in the same society
- People with disabilities and people without disabilities
- The same country or society before and after a certain policy (such as the establishment of a minimum wage)

Causes of Inequality

One way to explain inequality is that each factor of production receives the value of its marginal product. The factors of production are the land, labor, and capital that individuals, firms, and the government use to create goods and services. The marginal product is the extra output a person or group gets from one more unit of input.

So, someone who owns land keeps getting marginal products from that land—maybe the owner grows wheat or rents apartments on that land. Someone who owns a factory keeps getting products (or rent) from that factory space. And someone who sells his or her labor keeps getting a paycheck for that labor. Over time, the people who control those factors of production get more income, which increases inequality.

Differences in Tax Structures One government policy that influences inequality is the tax structure. Under a **flat tax**, everyone pays the same percentage on what is being taxed. For example, if a state has a flat income tax of 5 percent, all people pay that amount, whether their income is $40,000 or $80,000 or $800,000.

Under a **regressive tax,** the tax decreases as a percentage of income as income increases. Sales taxes and property taxes are usually regressive. For example, if a sales tax is 5 percent on cars, everyone who buys a car for $30,000 will pay an additional $1,500 in taxes. However, that $1,500 represents twice the percentage of the income of someone who earns $40,000 a year as for someone who earns $80,000.

Under a **progressive tax**, the tax rate increases as a percentage of income as income increases. The table shows an example of a very simple progressive tax system.

PROGRESSIVE INCOME TAX PLAN	
Income	Tax rate
Under $20,000	0%
$20,000 to $50,000	10%
Over $50,000	20%

Note that the higher tax rate only applies to the income over a certain amount; it does not apply to the entire income. So, under this tax system, a person who made $90,000 would pay the following:

- 0 percent on the first $20,000
- 10 percent on the $30,000 they received between $20,000 and $50,000. This would be $3,000.
- 20 percent on the $40,000 they received over $50,000. This would be $8,000.

Total income tax on income of $90,000 would be $11,000, or about 12 percent. In the United States, the federal income tax and many state income tax systems are progressive.

Human Capital Some communities or regions have a highly educated workforce with technical or other specialized skills. These places tend to generate more wealth than those that have a workforce with little education and few skills.

Social Capital This term refers to the value of connections or networks within a group or society. For instance, imagine you find out that the company that one of your parents works for has a scholarship award for college tuition. You write a superb essay, win the scholarship, and pay less for college. Because of your use of social capital, you have lessened your debt in a way that may benefit you, your family, and your community. A community with strong social capital is less likely to face severe inequality than one with weak social capital.

Inheritance If you win the lottery, you have to pay taxes on your prize. But if you win the "lottery" of having wealthy relatives, should you have to pay taxes on any money or property they leave to you after they die? The United States federal government says no, unless the inheritance is very large. In 2019, less than 1 percent of the people who inherited wealth had to pay some federal taxes on it. Some states also tax inheritances so they can reduce pressure to raise other taxes that affect low- and middle-income people.

Effects of Discrimination If a group of people loses access to jobs, education, social networks, and other benefits because of discrimination, then inequality in that society is likely to increase. The 1964 Civil Rights Act banned discrimination in employment on the basis of race, religion, or sex.

In 1972 the U.S. government made a further effort to reduce discrimination against women and girls in education by passing Title IX. This statute required schools that received federal funds to stop discriminating against women when it came to educational and training programs. Most people think of Title IX as being related to women's sports, but this law also made it possible for qualified women to attend and graduate from medical schools, dental schools, veterinary schools, and many other programs that can provide high incomes and high status.

Access to Financial Markets Do you have a bank in your community? The federal government and many states have passed laws against **redlining**, the practice of denying someone a loan, mortgage, insurance, or other financial services based on the neighborhood they live in rather than their own creditworthiness or assets. Redlined neighborhoods tend to be poor and tend to have high percentages of nonwhite residents. When a society allows equal access to financial markets, then inequality tends to decrease.

Mobility In economics, mobility means how likely a person is to end up with a different level of wealth than he or she was born into. Mobility varies widely between countries and within countries. In 2013, the chances of a child born in the poorest 20 percent of the population growing up to become part of the wealthiest 20 percent varied from city to city within the United States. It was a little more than 10 percent for children born in San Francisco but only about 4 percent for children born in Atlanta.

Bargaining Power Within Economic and Social Units Within your own family, your bargaining power may be strong or weak. Your family members may consider giving you what you ask for, or they may decide you have little say in things.

Within companies, people also have varying amounts of bargaining power. Having unique or in-demand skills also gives a person bargaining power. People who can design software to manage complicated business operations are not "a dime a dozen." These skills are both unique and in demand, and as a result, the people who possess them can leverage their skills for greater compensation. Professional athletes are another example. The income and wealth garnered by top professional athletes stem directly from the bargaining power their skills afford them.

Two other factors that influence bargaining power are unionization and willingness to work. Unionized workers can negotiate higher wages, better health insurance, and stronger workplace safety rules. Individuals who spend more time working and sacrifice leisure time are worth more to a company than an individual who chooses to work less and have more leisure time.

ANSWER THE TOPIC ESSENTIAL QUESTION

1. In one to three paragraphs, explain how and why market outcomes result in inequality within a society. What steps can people or governments take to reduce inequality, and why do those steps work?

KEY TERMS

inequality	income inequality	regressive tax
poverty level	wealth inequality	progressive tax
poverty rate	Gini coefficient	
Lorenz curve	flat tax	

MULTIPLE-CHOICE QUESTIONS

1. An economist is studying economic inequality in income and wealth in a city of 8 million people. She is studying different groups within the city, such as women, men, wage earners, retirees, and independently wealthy people. Which of these statements would you expect the economist to confirm at the end of the study?

   (A) Income levels and poverty rates varied across groups but not within groups.

   (B) Income levels varied within groups, but poverty rates did not.

   (C) Poverty rates varied within groups, but income levels did not.

   (D) Income levels and poverty rates varied within groups but not across groups.

   (E) Income levels and poverty rates varied within groups and across groups.

2. You are studying the Gini coefficients of different societies. Based on the information in the table, which of these societies would you expect to have the lowest Gini coefficient?

INEQUALITY LEVELS IN FIVE SOCIETIES		
Society Name	Inheritance Laws	Tax Structure
A	Inheritances taxed lightly	Regressive
B	Inheritances are tax-free	Regressive
C	Inheritances taxed heavily	Regressive
D	Inheritances are tax-free	Progressive
E	Inheritances banned	Progressive

   (A) Society A
   (B) Society B
   (C) Society C
   (D) Society D
   (E) Society E

3. Given the Gini coefficients below, _____would demonstrate the most even distribution of income and _____ would demonstrate the least even distribution of income.

Country A	Country B	Country C	Country D	Country E
0.38	0.67	0.89	0.14	0.75

(A) Country A; Country B
(B) Country C; Country D
(C) Country D; Country C
(D) Country E; Country A
(E) Country A; Country E

FREE-RESPONSE QUESTIONS

1. Two neighboring countries, Slovenia and Italy, have the Gini coefficients listed below.

Country	Gini Coefficient
Italy	0.36
Slovenia	0.24

Source: World Bank

(a) Identify the country that has a more equal distribution of income. Explain.

(b) Would the country with a more even distribution of income be more or less likely to have progressive tax systems?

(c) If Italy wanted to have a more even distribution of income, would it be more likely to institute regressive or progressive taxes?

(d) Assume that Italy's Gini coefficient rises to 0.41. Identify one reason that might explain this change.

(e) Assume that Slovenia's Gini coefficient falls to 0.21. Identify one reason that might explain this change.

Economists use economic models to attempt to describe economic conditions and behavior Some models, such as the production possibilities curve, look at the factors that go into economic decisions. Others, such as the Lorenz curve, attempt to analyze the impact on society of economic decisions so that government decision makers can identify whether any remedial steps are needed and where they should be directed. In explaining how specific models work, economists take these steps:

- Explain the significance of the behaviors or conditions the model applies to.
- Describe how the model illuminates those behaviors or conditions.
- Identify any limitations to the model.

Economists note that in a market with perfect competition, supply and demand push a market toward an equilibrium price and quantity. They also recognize that markets rarely have perfect competition. For example, barriers to entry can prevent competition on the supply side and imperfect information among consumers can limit their ability to act as fully independent actors.

Apply the Skill

In this topic, you learned about the Lorenz curve.

- Explain the significance of the behaviors or conditions the Lorenz curve applies to.
- Describe how the Lorenz curve illuminates those behaviors or conditions.
- Identify any limitations to the utility of the Lorenz curve.

According to Angel Gurría, secretary-general of the Organization for Economic Co-operation and Development (OECD), "We have reached a tipping point. Inequality can no longer be treated as an afterthought. We need to focus the debate on how the benefits of growth are distributed." That was in 2015. In the years that followed, inequality increased in many countries—including the United States.

Reasons for Economic Inequality A number of factors account for economic inequality. Wages are determined by the market price of a person's skills. People with different levels of education usually earn different wages. Technology has eliminated many jobs, particularly those formerly done by less skilled workers. Race and gender still affect wages. Finally, personal factors play a big part. Two people of equal ability may have very different incomes based on their personal preferences. One may be motivated to work hard for long hours, while another may value free time.

Comparing Rates of Inequality In 2017, the first World Inequality Report was published by the World Inequality Lab at the Paris School of Economics. According to the report, the United States and the European Union had similar levels of inequality in 1980. The top 1 percent of adults received about 10 percent of the national income in both regions. Since then, however, the income gap had surged in the United States. The income of the top 1 percent rose slightly in the EU to 12 percent, but doubled in the United States to 20 percent. In the United States, most of the increase was concentrated among the wealthiest sliver of that 1 percent.

Meanwhile, the average annual wage of the bottom 50 percent in the United had stagnated since 1980, falling from 20 to 10 percent of the national income. In contrast, incomes in Europe matched overall economic growth.

Policy Options Some economists think that current government policies do not need to be changed. Among them, some believe that growing inequality is not a problem for the economy. As inequality increases, people have greater incentives to innovate and work hard. Others argue that revising government policies will not be effective. The growth in equality reflects fundamental changes in technology and global competition that increasingly favor highly educated people with specialized skills.

Economists who want to change public policies point to Europe, which has kept the income gap from widening rapidly. They generally support policies to raise the minimum wage, make the tax code more progressive, increase funding for education, and enable workers to organize unions more easily.

LONG FREE-RESPONSE QUESTION

1. Quarkies are a good that generates a negative external cost. Quarkies are a necessity for everyone. In the market for Quarkies, the demand is relatively inelastic and the supply is relatively elastic.

   (a) Using a correctly labelled graph, show each of the following:

       i. The marginal social cost and marginal social benefit labeled as MSC and MSB respectively.

       ii. The marginal private cost labeled as MPC.

       iii. The quantity and price produced by the private market labeled as Qm and Pm respectively.

       iv. The socially optimal quantity and price labeled as Qso and Pso respectively.

       v. Shade in the area of deadweight loss completely.

   (b) In order to increase efficiency in the Quarkies market, should the government increase subsidy payments or increase taxes? Explain.

   (c) What two characteristics would be necessary for Quarkies to be considered a public good?

   (d) If the government decided to tax the Quarkies market, would the suppliers or consumers of Quarkies pay more of the tax? Explain.

   (e) Assume now that the government decides to place a highly regressive tax on consumers of Quarkies. Is this tax likely to increase, decrease, or not affect the country's Gini coefficient?

AP® Microeconomics
Practice Exam

MULTIPLE-CHOICE QUESTIONS

1. What is the fundamental economic problem that exists because of society's seemingly unlimited wants but limited resources?
   (A) Say's Law
   (B) Theory of Utility Maximization
   (C) Scarcity
   (D) Underconsumption
   (E) Overproduction

2. When the price for Good Z increases by 20 percent and the resulting effect on quantity supplied is to increase by 10 percent, the coefficient for elasticity of supply is _____ and supply would be relatively _____.
   (A) 2; elastic
   (B) 1/2; elastic
   (C) 1/2; inelastic
   (D) 2; inelastic
   (E) 20; elastic

Use the following table to answer questions 3 through 5.

Quantity of Workers	Total Output	Marginal Output
0	0	-
1	10	10
2	30	X
3	80	50
4	Z	30
5	115	5

3. What is the marginal output of the 2nd worker?

(A) 10

(B) 20

(C) 30

(D) 40

(E) 50

4. With the addition of which worker does diminishing marginal returns begin?

(A) 1st worker

(B) 2nd worker

(C) 3rd worker

(D) 4th worker

(E) 5th worker

5. What is the total output when 4 workers are hired?

(A) 85

(B) 30

(C) 110

(D) 115

(E) 130

6. The MR = MC profit maximizing rule applies to which of the following market structures?

(A) Monopolistically and perfectly competitive industries only

(B) Oligopoly and monopoly industries only

(C) Monopolistically competitive and oligopoly industries only

(D) All industries

(E) Perfectly competitive and monopoly industries only

7. In a market that generates a positive externality, which of the following could increase efficiency in the market?

(A) Decreased production from higher input prices

(B) Government subsidy payments to firms that produce those goods

(C) Increased regressive taxes on the good

(D) Increased progressive taxes on the good

(E) Increased regulation which limits the production of firms in the market

8. In a market that features a relatively elastic demand curve and relatively inelastic demand curve, which economic actor will be burdened more by a per-unit tax?

(A) Buyers are more burdened by the tax.

(B) Sellers are more burdened by the tax.

(C) Both buyers and sellers would be burdened equally.

(D) Buyers would bear the entire burden of the tax.

(E) Sellers would bear the entire burden of the tax.

9. Steak costs $10 each and fries cost $3. Jaden enjoys both steaks and fries and is currently attempting to maximize the utility of his budget. The last unit of steak he bought gave him a marginal utility of 50 and the last unit of fries he bought gave him a marginal utility of 35. Thinking like an economist, what could you say about Jaden's attempt at utility maximization?

(A) Jaden is currently maximizing utility.

(B) Jaden should be buying more steak and fewer fries.

(C) Jaden should be buying more fries and less steak.

(D) Jaden cannot maximize utility given the information.

(E) Jaden should buy more steak and more fries.

10. An economic system in which the government, or other central authority, makes all of the economic decisions in an economic system would be considered a _____.

(A) Mixed market economy

(B) Pure command economy

(C) Central authority economy

(D) Pure capital economy

(E) Keynesian economy

11. When comparing a perfectly competitive industry to a firm operating inside that industry, the firm's price is _____ the industry price.

(A) Equal to

(B) Greater than

(C) Less than

(D) Unrelated to

(E) Never

12. A perfectly competitive firm is currently maximizing profits while producing 10 units at a price of $5, an ATC of $8, an AVC of $6, and an AFC of $2. In what situation does the firm find itself?

   (A) Earning positive economic profits of $3 per unit

   (B) Earning economic losses of $3 per unit

   (C) Earning economic losses and shutting down

   (D) Earning economic losses of $1 per unit

   (E) Earning positive economic profits of $5 per unit

13. Which of the following is correct when comparing perfectly competitive and imperfectly competitive firms?

Answer	Perfect Competition	Imperfect Competition
(A)	P = MC = MR	P > MC = MR
(B)	P > MC = MR	P > MC = MR
(C)	P = MC = MR	P = MC = MR
(D)	P = MC = MR	P < MC = MR
(E)	P < MC = MR	P < MC = MR

14. Which of the following is not a barrier to entry for firms wishing to enter an industry?

   (A) High start-up costs

   (B) Patent

   (C) Governmental contract

   (D) Exclusive ownership of a key resource

   (E) Increasing marginal revenue

15. There has been a sharp increase in the demand for new home construction across the country. Which combination best describes the likely effects on the lumber market, an input needed for new home construction, and new home construction carpenters?

Answer	Market for Lumber	Market for Carpenters
(A)	Demand Increases	Supply Decreases
(B)	Demand Decreases	Supply Decreases
(C)	Supply Decreases	Demand Increases
(D)	Supply Decreases	Supply Decreases
(E)	Demand Increases	Demand Increases

16. Which of the following creates a situation in which the production level of the profit-maximizing firm does not underallocate resources?

(A) A good that generates a positive externality

(B) A good produced in a monopolistic market

(C) Labor hired in a monopsonistic market

(D) A good produced in a monopolistically competitive market in a long-run equilibrium

(E) A good produced in a perfectly competitive market in a short-run equilibrium

17. Which of the following combinations shows the correct impacts of a tariff placed on a good?

Answer	Price	Deadweight loss	Government Revenue
(A)	Increase	No change	Decrease
(B)	Decrease	Decrease	Decrease
(C)	Increase	Decrease	Decrease
(D)	Decrease	Increase	Increase
(E)	Increase	Increase	Increase

18. Assume the market for widgets is competitive and in equilibrium at a price of $10 per unit. If the government decides to place a price floor at $8, what would an economist expect to happen?

(A) A surplus to occur

(B) A shortage to occur

(C) Neither a shortage nor a surplus to occur

(D) Both a shortage and a surplus to occur simultaneously

(E) The government to collect lots of tax revenue

19. Given a typical market with no externalities, how would an increase in the price of wood impact the price and quantity in the housing market, which uses wood as an input?

(A) Increase price; decrease quantity

(B) Increase price; increase quantity

(C) Decrease price; decrease quantity

(D) Decrease price; increase quantity

(E) No change in price or quantity

Use the following chart to answer questions 20 and 21.

Carter's Bakery produces both cookies and cakes according to the production possibilities below.

Cookies	Cakes
50	0
45	1
35	2
20	3
0	4

20. If Carter's Bakery is currently producing 40 cookies and 1 cake, how can we categorize this production level?

(A) Efficient production

(B) Inefficient production

(C) Economic growth

(D) Unattainable production

(E) Beneficial production

21. If Carter's Bakery is currently producing 45 cookies and 1 cake and wants to increase cake production to 2 cakes, what would the opportunity cost be if Carter's Bakery continues efficient production?

(A) 2 cakes

(B) 1 cake

(C) 35 cookies

(D) 10 cookies

(E) 10 cakes

22. If consumers start increasing their preferences for electric vehicles, how would that impact the market for nonelectric vehicles?

(A) Increase demand

(B) Decrease demand

(C) Increase supply

(D) Decrease supply

(E) Increase both supply and demand

23. If the price of a pack of gum increases from $0.25 to $0.50, what will the impact be on the market for gum?

(A) Increase in demand

(B) Decrease in demand

(C) Increase in supply

(D) Decrease in quantity demanded

(E) Decrease in quantity supplied

24. Which of the following are considered fixed cost for a typical company?

    i. Wages of workers

    ii. Costs of inputs for the product

    iii. Monthly lease payment

    iv. Yearly insurance payment

(A) i. only

(B) i. and ii. only

(C) ii. and iv. only

(D) iii. and iv. only

(E) i., ii., and iii. only

25. As quantity increases, what would an economist expect to happen to each of the following?

Answer	Fixed Costs	Average Fixed Costs	Total Variable Costs
(A)	Increase	Increase	Decrease
(B)	Decrease	Decrease	Decrease
(C)	Not change	Decrease	Increase
(D)	Not change	Increase	Not change
(E)	Increase	Decrease	Not change

26. Which of the following correctly explains demand curves in the given market structure?

(A) Monopolistically competitive firms' demand is perfectly elastic.

(B) Monopolies feature a perfectly elastic demand curve.

(C) A monopolistically competitive firm's demand curve is more elastic than a monopoly's demand curve.

(D) Perfectly competitive firms face a downward sloping demand curve.

(E) Both perfectly competitive and monopolistically competitive firms face a perfectly elastic demand curve.

27. Which of the following is false regarding a monopolist engaging in perfect price discrimination (sometimes called first-degree price discrimination)?

(A) There is no consumer surplus.

(B) There is no deadweight loss.

(C) The firm is allocatively efficient.

(D) The firm faces a perfectly elastic demand curve.

(E) The firm charges different prices to different consumers.

Use the following chart and scenario to answer questions 28 and 29.

		Rashaun's Movie Screens	
		High Price	Low Price
Evans' Movie Emporium	High Price	$11, $14	$7, $15
	Low Price	$13, $9	$10, $8

Rashaun's Movie Screens and Evans' Movie Emporium are the only two movie theaters in town. They both have the choice to set either a low price or a high price for movie tickets. These movie tickets are published in local newspapers weekly on Sunday. Both companies know all of the information in the payoff matrix. The first number in each box represents the hourly profits of Rashaun's Movie Screens and the second number indicates Evans' Movie Emporium's hourly profits.

28. Which of the following statements is true regarding dominant strategies of the two firms?

(A) Evans' Movie Emporium has a dominant strategy to set a high price while Rashaun's Movie Screens has no dominant strategy.

(B) Both Evans' Movie Emporium and Rashaun's Movie Screens have a dominant strategy to set a high price.

(C) Evans' Movie Emporium has no dominant strategy while Rashaun's Movie Screens has a dominant strategy to set a high price.

(D) Both Evans' Movie Emporium and Rashaun's Movie Screens have a dominant strategy to set a low price.

(E) Evans' Movie Emporium has no dominant strategy while Rashaun's Movie Screens has a dominant strategy to set a low price.

29. Which of the following best represents the hourly profits of each firm in the Nash Equilibrium of this payoff matrix?

(A) Evans' Movie Emporium $14; Rashaun's Movie Screens $11

(B) Evans' Movie Emporium $15; Rashaun's Movie Screens $7

(C) Evans' Movie Emporium $9; Rashaun's Movie Screens $13

(D) Evans' Movie Emporium $8; Rashaun's Movie Screens $10

(E) There is no Nash Equilibrium for this problem

30. Public goods feature which combination of characteristics?

(A) Rival and excludable

(B) Non-rival and excludable

(C) Non-rival and non-excludable

(D) Rival and non-excludable

(E) Shared consumption and excludable

31. If the government is considering how to ensure the most efficient outcome in the electricity market for a city that is controlled by a natural monopolist, what would be the best course of action for the government to use?

(A) Increase taxes on consumers of electricity to help boost production and profits of the natural monopolist

(B) Increase taxes on the natural monopolist to help raise prices enough to increase profits of the natural monopolist

(C) Regulate so that the natural monopolist is forced to produce at the fair return pricing which ensures a positive economic profit for the natural monopolist

(D) Institute a binding price floor which will ensure a higher price for the natural monopolist which will increase the supply of electricity available

(E) Regulate so that the natural monopolist is forced to produce at the socially optimal pricing while providing a lump-sum subsidy equal to the economic losses at this level of production

32. Which measure helps an economist determine the level of economic inequality in a region?

(A) The Herfindahl-Hirschman Index

(B) Gross Domestic Product

(C) Gini Coefficient

(D) The Coase Theorem

(E) Game Theory

33. In an unregulated market that generates a large positive externality, which of the following is true?

(A) Marginal Private Cost > Marginal Private Benefit

(B) Marginal Private Benefit > Marginal Private Cost

(C) Marginal Social Benefit > Marginal Private Benefit

(D) Marginal Private Benefit > Marginal Social Benefit

(E) Marginal Social Benefit < Marginal Private Cost

Use the following scenario and chart to answer questions 34 and 35.

Brian's Cleaning Service has the following output structure based on hiring a varying number of workers. The firm hires workers in a perfectly competitive labor market and sells its services in a perfectly competitive product market. The price of the services is $10.

Number of Workers	Wage Paid ($)	Total Output
1	100	15
2	100	35
3	100	50
4	100	60
5	100	62

34. What is the profit maximizing number of workers that Brian's Cleaning Service should hire?

(A) 1 worker

(B) 2 workers

(C) 3 workers

(D) 4 workers

(E) 5 workers

35. What is the total profit of hiring 5 workers in this scenario?

(A) $100

(B) $120

(C) $520

(D) $620

(E) $20

36. Which is correct when comparing perfectly competitive and monopolistically competitive firms?

(A) They both create excess capacity.

(B) They both earn zero economic profits in the long run.

(C) They both use advertising as a non-price determinant.

(D) They both reduce consumer surplus to zero.

(E) They both feature a downward sloping demand curve.

37. Neha's Farm is a perfectly competitive firm in long-run equilibrium. Which of the following is true for Neha's Farm?

(A) It is allocatively efficient only.

(B) It is both allocatively and productively efficient.

(C) It is productively efficient only.

(D) It is not efficient.

(E) It is operating in diseconomies of scale.

38. Which of the following are characteristics of a perfectly competitive firm?

    i.   No barriers to entry

    ii. Downward sloping demand curve

    iii. Perfectly elastic demand curve

    iv. Price takers

(A) i. only

(B) i., ii., and iv. only

(C) i., iii., and iv. only

(D) iii. and iv. only

(E) iii. only

39. If the supply and demand for jelly beans both increase by the same amount, what would the impact be on equilibrium price and quantity?

(A) Price increases; quantity increases

(B) Price increases; no change in quantity

(C) No change in price; quantity increases

(D) No change in price; quantity decreases

(E) Price decreases; no change in quantity

40. If the price of a box of pens increases from $2 to $3, what will the impact be on the market for pens?

(A) Increase in supply

(B) Decrease in supply

(C) Increase in demand

(D) Decrease in quantity supplied

(E) Increase in quantity supplied

41. Za'Niya currently works as a Medical Doctor earning $200,000 per year working for a local hospital. She is considering starting her own hospital, which she expects will earn her $500,000 in revenue but cost her $150,000 in expenses. If Za'Niya decides to open her own hospital, she would incur _____ in explicit costs and _____ in implicit costs.

(A) $150,000; $200,000

(B) $500,000; $200,000

(C) $200,000; $500,000

(D) $150,000; $500,000

(E) $350,000; $200,000

42. Good A and Good C are related. Economists notice that when the price of Good A increases, the quantity demanded for Good C rises. How are these goods related?

(A) They are both normal goods.

(B) They are both inferior goods.

(C) They both feature a perfectly elastic supply curve.

(D) They are complements.

(E) They are substitutes.

43. If a firm's current marginal costs exceed the firm's current marginal revenue, what advice would an economist give to this firm?

(A) Shut down.

(B) Exit the industry.

(C) Enter the industry.

(D) Produce less.

(E) Produce more.

44. What is the major difference between firms operating under perfectly competitive conditions and firms operating in monopolistically competitive conditions?

(A) Monopolistically competitive firms tend to be more efficient than perfectly competitive firms.

(B) Perfectly competitive firms charge a higher price overall than monopolistically competitive firms.

(C) Monopolistically competitive firms are price takers, while perfectly competitive firms are price makers.

(D) Monopolistically competitive firms sell slightly differentiated products, and perfectly competitive firms sell identical products.

(E) Monopolistically competitive firms sell to only one buyer, while perfectly competitive firms sell to many buyers.

45. Which of the following would not help to correct a negative externality created from the production of electricity by burning coal?

(A) Increased subsidy payments for coal burning power plants

(B) Increased taxes on coal

(C) Increased regulation around pollution from coal burning

(D) Increased research and development into solar panel construction and design

(E) An effective price floor set on the price of coal burning electricity

46. Over a range of quantities when marginal cost is increasing as the quantity of output is increasing, what must also be true over that entire range?

    i. Marginal product of labor is rising

    ii. Marginal product of labor is falling

    iii. Average variable cost is rising

    iv. Average total cost is rising

(A) i. only

(B) ii., iii., and iv. only

(C) iii. only

(D) i., iii., and iv. only

(E) ii. only

47. Which of the following are reasons for a downward sloping market demand curve?

  i.   Wealth effect
  ii. Substitution effect
  iii. Income effect
  iv. Diminishing marginal returns

(A) i. only
(B) ii. and iii. only
(C) ii., iii., and iv. only
(D) i. and iv. only
(E) i., ii., iii., and iv.

48. Which of the following would be considered as the productive resource of land?

  i.   Forest
  ii. Factory
  iii. Machinery
  iv. River

(A) i. only
(B) iii. only
(C) i. and ii. only
(D) i. and iv. only
(E) i., ii., iii., and iv.

49. When the price for Good X increases by 20 percent and the resulting effect on quantity demanded is to decrease by 60 percent, the coefficient for elasticity of demand is _____ and demand would be relatively_____.

(A) 3; elastic
(B) 1/3; inelastic
(C) 1/3; elastic
(D) 3; inelastic
(E) $3; elastic

50. Assume the market for popcorn is currently in equilibrium. When the price of popcorn increases, economists would expect the quantity demanded to _____, the quantity supplied to _____, and a _____ to exist as a result.

(A) Increase; decrease; surplus

(B) Decrease; increase; surplus

(C) Decrease; decrease; shortage

(D) Increase; increase; shortage

(E) Increase; increase; surplus

51. In the long run, suppose a firm increases total inputs by 20 percent and, as a result, total output increases by 100 percent. This firm is

(A) producing at the efficient scale

(B) experiencing increasing returns to scale

(C) facing diseconomies of scale

(D) experiencing decreasing returns to scale

(E) facing diminishing marginal returns

52. Which of the following best describes the efficient production level of a profit-maximizing perfectly competitive firm operating with short-run economic losses?

(A) $P = ATC$

(B) $P = AVC$

(C) $AVC = MC$

(D) $ATC = MC$

(E) $P = MC$

53. When a monopolistically competitive firm is in a long-run equilibrium, which of the following is not true?

(A) The firms still create excess capacity.

(B) The production level created deadweight loss.

(C) The firms must be earning negative accounting profit.

(D) The firms must be earning zero economic profit.

(E) The firms charge a price that is higher than marginal cost.

54. Which of the following is a reason for an upward sloping supply curve?

(A) Wealth effect

(B) Substitution effect

(C) Diminishing marginal utility

(D) Increasing marginal cost

(E) Income effect

55. Good H and Good J are complementary goods. If income levels rise, causing an increase in demand for Good H, economists can classify Good H as a/an _____ and would expect the demand for Good J to _____.

(A) Normal good; increase

(B) Normal good; decrease

(C) Inferior good; decrease

(D) Inferior good; increase

(E) Normal good; remain the same

56. Juan works as an accountant currently earning $100,000 per year. Juan is considering opening a new business and figures that his total revenue of the new venture would be $250,000, while total costs would equal $120,000. What would Juan's economic profits be if he opened his new business at those numbers?

(A) +$100,000

(B) +$130,000

(C) +$30,000

(D) −$100,000

(E) −$30,000

57. Nisrin's Gardens produces plants for sale and operates in a constant-cost, perfectly competitive industry while currently earning positive economic profits. Which combination below best describes what will occur as the industry adjusts to a new long-run equilibrium?

Answer	Market Supply	Equilibrium Price	Nisrin's Profits
(A)	Increase	Decrease	Decrease
(B)	Decrease	Decrease	Decrease
(C)	Increase	Increase	Increase
(D)	Decrease	Increase	Decrease
(E)	Increase	Decrease	Increase

Use the following chart for a single-price monopolist to answer questions 58 and 59.

Price ($)	Quantity	Marginal Cost ($)
15	1	3
14	2	4
13	3	5
12	4	6
11	5	7
10	6	8

58. What is the marginal revenue of producing the third unit of output?

(A) $11

(B) $13

(C) $5

(D) $8

(E) $3

59. At what unit of output would the firm maximize profits?

(A) 2 units

(B) 3 units

(C) 4 units

(D) 5 units

(E) 6 units

60. How would a rise in income affect the market for an inferior good?

(A) Demand increase

(B) Demand decrease

(C) Supply increase

(D) Supply decrease

(E) Both demand and supply increase

1. Assume that Carl's Gas Company is a single-price monopolist currently earning short-run economic profits.

   (a) Draw a correctly labeled diagram and show each of the following.

      i. The profit-maximizing price and quantity labeled as P* and Q*, respectively.

      ii. Shade in completely the area of profits.

   (b) If Carl's Gas Company is currently maximizing profits, what will happen to its total revenue if price is increased? Explain.

   (c) Is the profit-maximizing quantity allocatively efficient? Explain.

   (d) Now assume that the government wishes to regulate the firm's production to institute socially optimal pricing. Either in your graph in part (a) or on a new graph, label the socially optimal price for Carl's Gas Company as P_{so}.

   (e) Now assume instead that Carl's Gas Company is allowed to practice perfect price discrimination (also called first-degree price discrimination).

      i. What is the dollar value of consumer surplus at the profit-maximizing quantity?

      ii. Draw a correctly labeled diagram showing the ability of the firm to now price discriminate showing the firm's marginal cost, marginal revenue, and demand curves.

      iii. On your graph in part (e) (ii.), label the profit-maximizing quantity as Q_{pd}.

      iv. Is the quantity labeled in part (e) (iii.) allocatively efficient? Explain.

2. Below is the production function for Kyla's Delivery Service (KDS), which operates in a perfectly competitive output market and hires workers in a perfectly competitive labor market.

Quantity of Workers	Number of Deliveries/Day
1	30
2	70
3	95
4	115
5	130
6	135

(a) Assume KDS charges $8/delivery and pays a wage of $150/day for each worker.

   i. What is the Marginal Product (MP) of the 4th worker? Show your work.

   ii. Which number of workers illustrates the diminishing marginal returns stage of the production function?

   iii. How many drivers will KDS hire in order to maximize profits? Explain using numbers.

(b) Assume the demand for deliveries increases so now the firm can charge $10/delivery.

   i. Does the Marginal Product (MP) of the 4th worker increase, decrease, or remain the same?

   ii. Will KDS hire more workers? Explain.

3. Umbrellas are produced in a perfectly competitive, constant-cost industry. In the short run, the equilibrium price is $7 per umbrella and the typical firm is operating with a loss. The typical firm has the total cost function shown in the table below.

Daily Output	Total Cost Per Day
0	$10
1	$13
2	$18
3	$24
4	$32
5	$45
6	$60

(a) Using a correctly labeled graph, draw the demand curve for a typical firm in this industry.

(b) Using the data above, determine each of the following for the typical firm.

   i. Total fixed cost.

   ii. The loss-minimizing level of output.

   iii. The value of losses at the output level you found in part (b)(ii.). Show your work.

(c) If the total cost per day remains unchanged in the long run, what is the long-run equilibrium price for umbrellas?

Index

Note: Page numbers followed by an "f" refer to figures.

North American Free Trade Agreement
(NAFTA), 146, 146*f*

O

Oil, nonrenewable natural resource, 7*f*
Oligopoly(ies), 225, 254*f. See also* Monopoly
    cartels, 255–256
    collusion, 255
    defined, 254
    high barriers to entry, 254
    in United States, 261
    working of, 255
One size fits all approach, 14
Open access resources, 324–325
Opportunity cost, 5. *See also* Production
    possibilities curve (PPC)
    calculation of, 27–28
    and choices, 41
    constant, 28
    decreasing, 29
    defined, 25, 27, 41
    explicit, 43–44
    implicit, 43
    increasing, 28
    of producing rope and wire, 35–36
Optimal choice, 45
Optimal quantity, 56
Organization for Economic Co-operation and
    Development (OECD), 8, 347
Output(s), 161
    positive, 201
    price, 267
    zero, 201
Own-price, 68, 79, 88

P

Pareto efficient, 305
Paulson, Henry, 135
Perfect competition, 117, 210*f,* 224. *See also*
    Imperfect competition
    cost curves, 213*f*
        with cost and profit, 213*f*
    defined, 210
    efficiencies, forms of
        allocative, 215
        productive, 215
    equilibrium price, 211
    firms activities in, 211
    marginal costs and benefits
        private marginal benefit, 216
        private marginal cost (or marginal
            cost of production), 216

movement of price by market and firm,
    211, 212*f*
Perfectly competitive factor market
    defined, 283
    labor vs output markets, 285
    many buyers and sellers, 283–284
    marginal costs and products, 285
    similar skills and abilities, 284
    VMPL, calculation of, 286
Perfectly elastic, 92
Perfectly inelastic, 92
Perfect price discrimination, 240–242
Personal protective equipment (PPE), 72
Positive income elasticity, 108
Positive output, 201
    level, 202–203
Poverty level, 338
Poverty rate, 338
Price ceiling (PC)
    defined, 137
    and market disequilibrium, 138*f*
    reduce incentive for producers, 137
    use for rent, 137
Price discrimination
    consumer surplus, 240
    defined, 238
    elimination of deadweight loss, 242
    features of, 238
    firms can charge different prices for
        products, 239
    graphing, 240
    perfect (*see* Perfect price discrimination)
    principles of, 239
Price effect, 93
Price elasticity of demand, 92*f,* 239
    applying, 90, 93–94
    calculation of, 89–90
    categories of
        elastic, 91
        inelastic, 91
        perfectly elastic, 92
        perfectly inelastic, 92
        unit elastic, 92
    curve, 95*f*
    defined, 89
    factors influence, 91
Price elasticity of supply
    applying, 99–100
    calculation of, 99
    categories of
        elastic, 100, 100*f*
        inelastic, 100, 100*f*
        perfectly elastic, 101, 101*f*
        perfectly inelastic, 101, 101*f*

T

Tariff(s), 83, 146
   effect on quantities supplied, 149,
      150, 150*f*
   form of protectionism, 149
   government revenues, increase in, 150
   impact on surplus
      consumer, 150–151
      producer, 150–151
      total, 150–151
   market with, 156*f*
   raise domestic prices, 149
   trade war between US and China, 149,
      151*f*
   on US baseball caps, 155*f*
Tariff-rate quotas, 151
Tax
   flat, 341
   progressive, 341
   regressive, 341
Thaler, Richard H., 14
The Economist magazine, 9
Total benefits, defined, 45
Total costs (TC), 45, 170–171, 204
Total economic surplus (or total surplus),
   121*f*, 122
Total fixed costs, 170–171
Total net benefits, maximization of, 44–48
Total output (TO), 170
Total price, 331
Total product, 164
Total revenue (TR), 93, 172, 204
   calculation of, 194
   defined, 194
Total variable cost (TVC), 169–171
Trade-offs (economic), 25
   defined, 4
   reason for rise of, 7
Traditional economy, defined, 16–17
Trump, Donald, 149, 151*f*

U

Underutilized, 27
Unfair trade practices, 149
Unitary income elasticity, 109
Unit elastic, 92
User fees, 138
U.S. Federal Trade Commission (FTC), 330
Utility maximization rule
   defined, 56
   formula for calculation, 57

V

Value of the marginal product of labor
   (VMPL), 264, 286
Variable, 89
   costs, 169–171
Voluntary restraints (VER) quotas, 151

W

Wage rate, impact of
   on employment, 267
   labor supply, 267
Wallerstein, Immanuel, 192
Wealth inequality, 339
World War II, 138

X

Xiaoping, Deng, 20*f*

Z

Zero economic profit, 215
Zero income elasticity, 109
Zero output, 201